FOURTH EDITION

THE
ECONOMICS
AND FINANCING
OF EDUCATION

ROE L. JOHNS
University of Florida,
Gainesville

EDGAR L. MORPHET
University of California,
Berkeley

KERN ALEXANDER
University of Florida,
Gainesville

Prentice-Hall, Inc., Englewood Cliffs, New Jersey 07632

Library of Congress Cataloging in Publication Data

JOHNS, ROE LYELL, (date)
  The economics and financing of education.

  Includes bibliographies and index.
  1. Education—United States—Finance. I. Morphet,
Edgar Leroy, (date) II. Alexander, Kern.
III. Title.
LB2825.J57 1983   379.1'21'0973   82-9802
ISBN 0-13-225128-0   AACR2

to our wives

Gladys, Camilla, and Ruth

©1983, 1975, 1969, 1960 by Prentice-Hall, Inc., Englewood Cliffs, N.J. 07632

Printed in the United States of America

10 9 8 7 6 5 4 3 2 1

Editorial/production supervision: Jeanne Hoeting
Manufacturing buyer: Ron Chapman
Cover Design: Ray Lundgren

ISBN 0-13-225128-0

PRENTICE-HALL INTERNATIONAL, INC., *London*
PRENTICE-HALL OF AUSTRALIA PTY. LIMITED, *Sydney*
PRENTICE-HALL CANADA INC., *Toronto*
PRENTICE-HALL OF INDIA PRIVATE LIMITED, *New Delhi*
PRENTICE-HALL OF JAPAN, INC., *Tokyo*
PRENTICE-HALL OF SOUTHEAST ASIA PTE. LTD., *Singapore*
WHITEHALL BOOKS LIMITED, *Wellington, New Zealand*

CONTENTS

CHAPTER THIRTEEN
FINANCING CAPITAL OUTLAY   274

CHAPTER FOURTEEN
PERSONNEL POLICIES AND SALARIES   293

CHAPTER FIFTEEN
THE FEDERAL ROLE
IN FINANCING EDUCATION   322

CHAPTER SIXTEEN
MANAGEMENT OF RESOURCES   346

INDEX   363

PREFACE

This fourth revision of *The Economics and Financing of Education* is practically a new book on the financing of education. Four chapters have been added and all of the old chapters have been completely revised, combined, or eliminated.

The four new chapters deal with the following topics: the social and individual benefits of education, the legal basis of school financing, the politics of school financing, the inequalities of educational opportunity, and the redistributional effects of education.

The decade of the 1970s has been called the decade of school finance reform. However, despite the progress that has been made in this area, significant differences in educational opportunity still exist from state to state, from district to district within states, and even from school to school within districts. Furthermore, at this writing the following issues are being debated throughout the nation: the amount of school revenue needed; the percent of the total to provide at each level of government—federal, state, and local; the types of taxes to levy at each level of government; the methods used by the federal and state governments for apportioning school funds; the types and amount of fiscal control to exercise at each level of government; and whether vouchers or tax credits shall be used for the support of private and parochial schools.

The struggle for free, tax-supported public schools available on an equal basis to all children and youth has not yet been won. Taxpayer resistance to school financing is greater now than at any time since the Great Depression in the 1930s. Furthermore, the public schools are being blamed for many problems—increase in crime, use of drugs, illicit sexual activity, breakdown of family life, and increase in one-parent families—which arose from the community and not the schools. Schools are also charged with a decline in achievement, which if true is no doubt at least partly due to problems in the adult community. Variations in achievement among public schools and between public schools and private schools are primarily due to variations in the socioeconomic background of students, but those variations are frequently ignored by critics of the public schools.

A brief history of the development of tax-supported public schools up to 1900 is presented in the introductory chapter of this book. We can get a better appreciation of the problems we are having today in supporting the public schools as we contemplate the antecedents of the common schools and the problems faced by our predecessors in the eighteenth and nineteenth centuries. We all stand on the "shoulders of the giants who have preceded us." Therefore we are confident that we will win the battles of the future for tax-supported, free public education because of the firm foundations laid by our courageous predecessors and our commitment to the belief that equality of opportunity preserves and extends "life, liberty and the pursuit of happiness" to everyone.

Finally, we wish to express our appreciation for the many helpful suggestions for this revision given us by our colleagues: Patricia Anthony, Nelda H. Cambron, T. Wayne Keene, Julia Underwood O'Hara, Richard A. Rossmiller, Richard G. Salmon, Martin W. Schoppmeyer, Stephen B. Thomas, Lee Shiver, Dewey H. Stollar, and L. Dean Webb.

R.L.J.
E.L.M.
K.A.

CHAPTER ONE
INTRODUCTION

This book is devoted primarily to a study of the financing of the public schools of the United States. Although major emphasis is given to the financing of the tax-supported public schools, many of the concepts in this book are applicable to higher education, both public and private, and to private elementary and secondary schools. The evolution of tax-supported public education in the United States has reflected the needs, values, goals, and aspirations of the American people. As Johns stated in a Horace Mann lecture: "A treatise on the social, economic, political, and religious history of the United States could be centered around the history of the financing of United States public schools."[1] Therefore, the study of the financing of education should not be considered an exercise in statistical analysis or a problem of data storage. The school financing policies of a nation reflect the value choices of the people, the order of priorities they establish in the allocation of their resources, and their political philosophy.

This chapter presents a brief discussion of the antecedents of the common schools and the evolution of tax support for the public schools.

ANTECEDENTS OF COMMON SCHOOLS

State concern for public education and tax support for the public schools can be traced to actions of the colonial legislature of Massachusetts. The Massachusetts

1

law of 1642 directed "certain chosen men of each town to ascertain from time to time, if parents and masters were attending to their educational duties; if the children were being trained in learning and labor and other employments . . . profitable to the state; and if children were being taught to read and understand the principles of religion and the capital laws of the country and empowered them to impose fines on those who refuse to render such accounts to them when required."[2] Cubberley observed that this was the first time in the English-speaking world that a legislative body enacted legislation requiring that children be taught to read.[3]

The 1642 law was tried for five years and found to be unsatisfactory. Therefore in 1647 the General Court (the legislative body of the colony) enacted the famous "ye old deluder law." The preamble of the law stated that one of the chief projects of "ye old deluder Satan" was to keep people in ignorance of the Scriptures. The obvious way to defeat Satan was to teach the people to read and write. Therefore the court, under the provisions of the 1647 law, ordered:

1. That every town having fifty householders shall at once appoint a teacher of reading and writing, and provide for his wages in such manner as the town might determine; and
2. That every town having one hundred householders must provide a grammar school to fit youths for the university, under a penalty of 5 pounds (afterward increased to 20 pounds) for failure to do so.[4]

This act is remarkable for the following reasons:

1. It set the precedent for the authority of the state to establish educational requirements.
2. It gave local governmental bodies authority to levy taxes to assist in financing both elementary and secondary schools.
3. It demonstrated that if the state requires an educational program to be provided, it must also provide a means for financing that program if it is to become available.

The Massachusetts laws of 1642 and 1647 had great influence on other New England colonies. Connecticut, Maine, New Hampshire, and Vermont all enacted legislation establishing public schools by 1720. The acts passed by those colonies closely resembled the Massachusetts laws of 1642 and 1647.

In the central colonies of New York, Pennsylvania, and New Jersey, various church denominations established parochial schools. These were financed by the respective churches and from fees or rate bills. A rate bill is a special tax levied on parents, assessed in proportion to the number of children sent to school. The teaching of religion, in addition to reading, writing, and arithmetic, was a central purpose of both the New England and the central colonies.

It is interesting to note that the New England colonies did not establish a school system similar to that of England. The early settlers of New England were almost all religious dissenters and they came to America to establish a society different from that in England.

The early settlers of Virginia and the other southern colonies were not church dissenters. They came to America primarily in order to improve their fortunes and they supported the Church of England. Therefore the southern colonies provided for education by much the same system as that used in England at the time. Under that system the schools were under either church or private control. Private schools were financed by tuition charges and were patronized primarily by the well-to-do. The southern colonies did provide a limited amount of schooling for orphans and the children of paupers. Cubberley, in commenting on education in colonial Virginia, stated the following: "The tutor in the home, education in small private pay schools, or education in the mother country were the prevailing methods adopted among well-to-do planters, while the poorer classes were left with only such advantages as apprenticeship training or charity schools might provide."[5]

In summarizing the colonial period of American educational history, it should be noted that public education was available in only a few New England colonies, and even in those it was not entirely free because it was partly financed by tuition or rate bills. In the remainder of the thirteen colonies, education was provided by parochial or private schools financed primarily by parents of the children attending them. Under that system educational opportunity was basically a function of the wealth of a child's parents.

EVOLUTION OF TAX SUPPORT
FOR PUBLIC SCHOOLS

Let us next take a look at the beginnings of public education in the early national period. The general public attitude toward education in the beginning of our history as an independent nation is perhaps best expressed in the prefix of the Ordinance of 1787, enacted by the Congress of the Confederation for the organization of the Northwest Territory. It reads as follows: "Religion, morality, and knowledge being necessary to good government and the happiness of mankind, schools, and the means of education shall forever be encouraged." This ordinance, which applied only to the states carved from the Northwest Territory, implied that education was a state responsibility.

This section on the evolution of tax support for the public schools, emphasizes the statements and contributions of leaders in the advocacy of public education which reflect their political and educational philosophies. The beliefs of frontier thinkers of any age have a profound influence on subsequent events, even though the policies advocated may not be accepted at the time. Current problems of school financing can be understood better by contemplating the contributions of leaders of public education who have preceded us.

Public education developed slowly in the early national period. However, public education had some vigorous advocates in our early developmental period. The most well known of these early advocates was Thomas Jefferson. In 1787 he wrote in a letter to James Madison: "Above all things I hope the education of the common people will be attended to; convinced that on this good sense we may rely with the most security for the preservation of a due sense of liberty." In 1816, after his retirement from the presidency, he wrote to Colonel Yancy: "If a nation expects to be ignorant and free in a state of civilization it expects what never was and never will be. . . . There is no safe deposit (for the foundations of government) but with the people themselves; nor can they be safe with them without information."[6]

Despite the advocacy of Jefferson and many others, tax-supported public education did not generally become available in the middle Atlantic and midwestern states until after 1830 and in the southern states until the last quarter of the nineteenth century. Although some progress had been made, free public education was not generally available in the United States by the middle of the nineteenth century. According to the Seventh Census of the United States, in 1850 only about half of the children of New England were provided free education, one sixth in the West and one seventh in the Middle states.[7] Even in 1870 only 57 percent of the population 5–17 years of age was enrolled in the public schools and the average length of the school term was only 78 days.[8] Following are some comments concerning the statements and contributions of the leading advocates of the public schools during the nineteenth century.

The most influential advocates of tax-supported public schools in the United States were lay people and lay organizations. Professionally trained educators offered very little leadership in the nineteenth century for the establishment of free public education. Actually very little professional training was provided for educational leadership prior to 1900. Horace Mann, who became secretary of the State Board of Education of Massachusetts in 1837, and his contemporary, Henry Barnard, who served as chief state school officer of both Rhode Island and Connecticut, both had powerful influence on the establishment of tax-supported public schools, but both of these men were trained to be lawyers.[9]

Horace Mann is particularly worthy of special mention because he not only revitalized public schools in Massachusetts, but also had a powerful influence throughout the nation. Many states called upon him for advice and counsel and his twelve annual reports to the State Board of Education will always remain memorable documents.[10] Mann was particularly effective in educating public opinion in support of tax-supported public schools.

Organized labor has historically supported free public schools financed by taxes. Organized labor had gained some strength in the United States by the end of the first quarter of the nineteenth century and had begun to advocate tax-supported public schools. For example, an association of working men in Philadelphia expressed their support for public education as follows in a report adopted in 1830:

> When the committees contemplate their own condition, and that of the great mass of their fellow laborers; when they look around on the glaring inequality of society, they are constrained to believe, that, until the means of equal instruction

shall be equally secured to all, liberty is but an unmeaning word, and equality
an empty shadow, whose substance to be realized must first be planted by an
equal education and proper training in the minds, in the habits and in the feelings
of the community.[11]

The legislator, Thaddeus Stevens, in an eloquent plea to the Pennsylvania
House of Representatives in 1835 for the continuance of tax supported public
schools, stated the following:

If an elective republic is to endure for any great length of time, *every* elector
must have sufficient information, not only to accumulate wealth, and take care
of his pecuniary concerns, but to direct wisely the legislatures, the ambassadors,
and the executive of the nation—for *some* part of all these things, *some* agency
in approving or disapproving of them, falls to every freeman. If then, the per-
manency of our government depends upon such knowledge, it is the duty of
government to see that the means of information be diffused to every citizen.
This is a sufficient answer to those who deem education a private and not a public
duty—who argue that they are willing to educate their *own* children, but not
their *neighbor's* children.[12]

Tax support for the public schools was largely confined to the elementary
grades until the latter part of the nineteenth century. Cubberley reported that
up to 1840 not many more than a dozen high schools had been established in
Massachusetts and not more than an equal number in all the other states.[13]
Private academies and parochial schools provided most of the secondary education available. Legislation providing for the establishment of high schools was
attacked in the courts of many states. Great emphasis was given to the establishment of tax-supported high schools by the famous Kalamazoo case in Michigan in 1875. The Supreme Court of the State of Michigan rendered an opinion
so favorable and so positive in support of tax support for high schools that it
greatly influenced the development of high schools in many other states. It
should not be assumed that a high-school education was universally available
by the close of the nineteenth century. As a matter of fact, only 8 percent of
the population 14–17 years of age was enrolled in grades 9 through 12 in public
high schools in 1900.[14] In fact, public high schools did not become available in
many of the rural areas of the United States until after World War I. In 1979–
80, approximately 86 percent of the population 14–17 years of age was enrolled
in public high schools.

Free public education developed very slowly in the United States during
the first quarter of the nineteenth century. However, between 1830 and 1960
constitutional and statutory authorization for tax-supported public schools was
general in the middle Atlantic and midwestern states.[15] All of the New England
states had authorized tax support of the public schools prior to 1830. Legal
authorization for tax support of the public schools in the South was not generally
authorized until the last quarter of the nineteenth century. But even after tax
levies for public schools were authorized, supporters of public schools, not only

in the South but also in other states, frequently faced bitter opposition to those levies. The colonial belief that church and parents were responsible for the education of children died slowly.

Even though taxes for the public schools were generally authorized during the nineteenth century, they were frequently supplemented by tuition charges and/or rate bills. Rate bills were abolished in most of the northern and midwestern states between 1834 and 1871.[16] However the practice of charging tuition, especially for public high schools, continued well into the twentieth century. Frequently, tuition was disguised by calling it "an incidental fee."

The difficulties faced by those advocating tax-supported public schools in the South was well described by Walter Hines Page in his famous lecture "The Forgotten Man," delivered at the State Normal and Industrial School for Women at Greensboro, North Carolina, in June 1897. In that address he stated the following concerning educational conditions in North Carolina, his native state:

> In 1890, twenty-six percent of the white persons of the State were unable even to read and write. One in every four was wholly forgotten. But illiteracy was not the worst of it; the worst of it was that the stationary social condition indicated by generations of illiteracy had long been the general condition. The Forgotten Man was content to be forgotten. He became not only a dead weight, but a definite opponent of social progress. He faithfully heard the politicians on the stump praise him for virtues that he did not have. The politicians told him that he had lived in the best state in the Union, told him that the other politician had some harebrained plan to increase his taxes, . . . told him to distrust anybody who wished to change anything. What was good enough for his fathers was good enough for him. Thus the Forgotten Man became a dupe, became thankful for being neglected.[17]

Page, through his writings and lectures, had a significant influence on the development of public education in the United States. He stated his creed as follows:

> I believe in the free public training of both the hands and the mind of every child born of woman.
> I believe that by the right training of men we add to the wealth of the world. All wealth is the creation of man, and he creates it only in proportion to the trained uses of the community; and, the more men we train, the more wealth everyone may create.
> I believe in the perpetual regeneration of society, in the immortality of democracy, and in growth everlasting.[18]

Those words express very well the philosophy of the advocates of public education today.

In concluding this chapter, it should be noted that, although great progress has been made, we have not yet developed satisfactory systems of tax support for the public schools in many states and that the struggle for a satisfactory level of financial support continues in all states. As will be shown later in this book, the public schools are still involved in Huxley's "struggle for existence," and the battle for tax-supported public schools is a continuing struggle for survival and growth beyond survival. In a rapidly changing world, there must be change and improvement in the public schools or their survival will be threatened. This in turn will threaten liberty, equality of opportunity, and democratic government "of the people, by the people, and for the people."

NOTES

1. Roe L. Johns, *Full State Funding of Education: Evolution and Implications* (Horace Mann Lecture) (Pittsburgh: University of Pittsburgh Press, 1973), p. 5.

2. Ellwood P. Cubberley, *The History of Education* (Boston: Houghton Mifflin Company, 1920), p. 364.

3. *Ibid.*, p. 364.

4. *Ibid.*, p. 365.

5. *Ibid.*, p. 372.

6. *Ibid.*, p. 526.

7. Newton Edwards and Herman G. Richey, *The School in the American Social Order* (Boston: Houghton Mifflin Company, 1963), p. 292.

8. U.S. Department of Commerce, Bureau of the Census, *Historical Statistics of the United States: Colonial Times to 1957* (Washington, D.C.: U.S. Government Printing Office, 1960), p. 207.

9. Johns, *op. cit.*, p. 9.

10. Cubberley, *op. cit.*, p. 689.

11. Edwards and Richey, *op. cit.*, p. 281.

12. Hazards Register of Pennsylvania, Vol. 15, No. 18, May 2, 1835.

13. Cubberley, *op. cit.*, p. 700.

14. Computed from U.S. Department of Commerce, Bureau of the Census, *Statistical Abstracts of the United States: 1900 and 1980*.

15. Johns, *op. cit.*, p. 4.

16. Cubberley, *op. cit.*, p. 686.

17. Walter Hines Page, *The School That Built a Town* (New York: Harper & Row, Publishers, 1952), p. 31. This series of lectures by Page was delivered in the latter part of the nineteenth century and the first part of the twentieth century.

18. *Ibid.*, p. 3.

SELECTED REFERENCES

BEARD, CHARLES A., and MARY R. BEARD. *The Rise of American Civilization*. New York: Macmillan, Inc., 1933.

COUNTS, GEORGE S. *Education and American Civilization*. New York: Bureau of Publications, Teachers College, Columbia University, 1952.

CUBBERLEY, ELLWOOD P. *The History of Education*. Boston: Houghton Mifflin Company, 1920.

EDWARDS, NEWTON, and HERMAN G. RICHEY. *The School in the American Social Order.* Boston: Houghton Mifflin Company, 1963.

GROSS, CARL H., and CHARLES C. CHANDLER. *The History of American Education Through Readings*. Boston: D.C. Heath & Company, 1964.

JOHNS, ROE L. *Full State Funding of Education: Evolution and Implications*. Horace Mann Lecture. Pittsburgh: University of Pittsburgh Press, 1973.

PAGE, WALTER HINES. *The School That Built a Town*. New York: Harper & Row, Publishers, 1952.

U.S. DEPARTMENT OF COMMERCE, BUREAU OF THE CENSUS. *Historical Statistics of the United States: Colonial Times to 1970*. Washington, D.C.: U.S. Government Printing Office, 1975.

CHAPTER TWO
ECONOMICS
OF SCHOOL FINANCE
Education
and the
National Economy

The financing of education cannot be adequately studied without giving full consideration to its effect on the national economy. The production and consumption of education is vital to the survival and progress of any modern nation. People throughout the world aspire to the better life. The American people have many aspirations. One of the more important of these is that the economy provide a rising standard of living. Therefore, a major purpose of the economy is to maximize the production and consumption of goods and services which satisfy human wants.

In this chapter, the relationship of some of the basic concepts of economics to the financing of education will be explored. In Chapters 3, 4, and 5, those concepts will be applied directly to the problems and issues of school financing.

SIZE OF THE EDUCATION ECONOMY
IN RELATION TO THE TOTAL ECONOMY

The education economy is comprised of both publicly supported and privately supported institutions. In 1979, 7.65 percent of all gainfully employed workers in the United States were employed in public and private education. There were 96,945,000 full- and part-time employees in the United States in 1979.[1] Of that number, 5,368,000 were employed in the public and private elementary and secondary schools and 2,048,000 in the public and private colleges and universities, making a total education work force of 7,416,000. Education is indeed a labor-intensive industry. About two-thirds of the education work force is comprised of professional employees.

In fact, the education industry produces employment for many more than 7,416,000 workers. That number does not include many workers in the private sector of the economy who provide goods and services needed by the education industry. Examples are workers employed in producing books, instructional supplies, and equipment; workers employed in constructing educational buildings; workers employed in producing energy consumed by the education industry; workers employed in providing contracted transportation and school food service; and workers employed by the private sector to supply many other goods and services. In order to comprehend the total impact of the education industry on employment, it would be necessary to compute how many people would be unemployed if all public and private elementary and secondary schools, colleges, and universities were permanently closed and no other institutions, agencies, or services were instituted to take their place.

Employment in education tends to stabilize employment and the economy. There is little or no reduction in employment in the education industry in times of recession as compared with the automobile industry. Furthermore, education expenditures are slow to increase in times of prosperity and slow to decrease in times of recession. Although total employment in the education industry may decline slowly between 1979 and 1985, due to an anticipated decline in enrollment arising from a reduction in school-age students, employment in the education industry should start increasing again in 1985, when it is anticipated that enrollment will also start increasing. The effect of educational expenditures on inflation and deflation is discussed more fully later in this chapter.

The education industry makes an important contribution to the national economy. The National Center for Education Statistics estimated that the expenditures for public and private elementary, secondary, and higher education totaled $166.2 billion in 1979–80.[2] The Department of Commerce estimated that the gross national product of the United States was $2.369 billion in 1979.[3] Therefore expenditures for education constituted 7.0 percent of the gross national product at that time. However, education offers many benefits besides its contribution to the GNP, as will be shown in Chapter 3.

SOME FUNDAMENTAL CONCEPTS
OF ECONOMICS

The central topic of economics is the allocation of resources and the central concept is scarcity.[4] Economics has been defined in many ways. One of the simplest definitions is that economics is the study of human wants and their satisfaction. The economic system arranges for the production, exchange, and consumption of whatever is needed to satisfy human wants. Cohn states: "In essence, then, economics is the study of the production and distribution of all scarce resources—whether physical goods or intangible services—that individuals desire."[5]

The classical economists have given great emphasis to the study of the behavior of individuals and firms and to price formation but have given very little attention to aggregates such as level of employment and national income. The emphasis of economists upon the small aspects, or the particle, is called microeconomics. During the past few decades, much stress has been laid upon the study of aggregates, or macroeconomics. This recent emphasis sometimes is called Keynesian Economics after its famous advocate, John Maynard Keynes. Both microeconomics and macroeconomics have provided many useful concepts, and the macroeconomic approach has been particularly useful in studying certain educational problems. Therefore, primarily that approach will be used in applying some economic concepts to education.

In order to understand the economics of education, it is necessary to study some of the basic concepts of economics. Some concepts essential to an understanding of the economy are presented, with necessary brevity, in the following paragraphs.

Goods

Anything that satisfies or is capable of satisfying a human want is *a good*. Goods can be classified as free goods or economic goods. If a good is so abundant, such as air, that it need not be economized, it is called a free good. If a good is scarce and capable of being apportioned or economized, it is called an economic good. Economics is concerned only with economic goods. Education is an economic good.

Material and Nonmaterial Goods.   Economic goods are either material or nonmaterial. A *material good* is physical and tangible. A *nonmaterial good* is a service rendered by a free person which satisfies a want. Economists generally consider slaves themselves as goods, so their services cannot be counted as goods. Education is one of the most important of the nonmaterial goods produced by the economy.

Single-Use, Multiple-Use, Durable, and Nondurable Goods.   Economists classify material goods such as food, which can be used only once for their original purpose, as single-use goods. Those goods such as typewriters, which can be used many times, are classified as multiple-use goods. A closely related classification of material goods is durable and nondurable. A durable good is one which can be kept or stored for an extended period of time before use.

Economists do not usually classify education under these categories because it is a nonmaterial good. However, the educated person has acquired a nonmaterial, multiple-use, durable good of great importance, both to himself and to society. Education has the peculiar characteristic that, unlike material goods, it appreciates rather than depreciates with use. On the other hand, education loses its durability with storage or nonuse. For example, if one acquires a knowledge of the German language and does not speak, read, or write that language for ten years, most of the knowledge of the language is forgotten and the "good" is found to have a limited durability. Furthermore, many kinds of education, like machinery, rapidly become obsolete. For example, teachers, physicians, engineers, farmers—in fact, practically all educated persons—find that certain aspects of an education acquired at any one time soon become obsolete because of the continuous discovery of new knowledge. This is particularly true in a rapidly advancing culture.

The phenomenon of the accelerated rate of obsolescence of education in a dynamic culture with a growing economy has great significance for the financing of education. If education is to satisfy the wants of society and the individuals in that society, it is necessary to extend the time spent in schooling the young and to continue providing throughout life inservice and education facilities for adults. Progressive nations will undoubtedly find it necessary in future years to spend increasing amounts of their income to satisfy urgent wants for education.

Consumers' and Producers' Goods.   The distinction between consumers' goods and producers' goods is of fundamental importance to an understanding of the economy. Economists commonly classify both material and nonmaterial goods under these categories. A good used by a consumer to satisfy his wants is a consumer's good and a good used in the process of producing other goods is a producer's good. Education is both a producer's good and a consumer's good. When knowledge (in the broad sense that includes all things learned) is acquired to become an engineer, a teacher, a physician, a mechanic, or for any vocational objective which has as its major purpose the production of material or nonmaterial goods that satisfy human wants, education is a producer's good. When knowledge is acquired to use, enjoy, or appreciate any material or nonmaterial good, it is a consumer's good. Education can be used to enjoy both free goods, such as the beauties and mysteries of nature, and economic goods. It would be futile to produce such economic goods as art, music, and literature if individuals in the society did not possess the consumer knowledge necessary to enjoy them. It would be equally futile to produce such economic goods as bathrooms and healing medicines if the population were too ignorant or superstitious to utilize them.

For these reasons, the arguments between those who insist that education should be for economic and vocational efficiency and those who insist that knowledge should be acquired for its own sake are futile. It seems that both functions are important. There is every reason to believe that in future years human wants for education both as a producer's good and a consumer's good will greatly increase.

Public and Private Goods.   Economic goods can be classified as public and private. When the use of a good such as a public school or a highway is free to an individual, but obtained at a cost to the community, it is a public good. When an individual or a corporation acquires a good for private use, it is a private good. A tax-supported school is a public good and is commonly called a public school. Goods which cannot be produced at all, or as efficiently, by the private economy as by the public economy are usually produced as public goods.

Value and Price

The *usefulness of a good* for satisfying human wants is called its use value. As pointed out above, education is a nonmaterial, multiple-use, durable, consumer's and producer's economic good produced in both the public and private economy. It is also one of the most useful goods produced by human society.

The *exchange value of a good* is the purchasing power of a good over other goods possessed by its owner when he exchanges it. A person may not directly sell or exchange his education for another economic good. However, education can be used to produce both material and nonmaterial goods which have an exchange value; therefore, education might be considered as having an exchange value.

The *price of a good* is its exchange value expressed in money. Therefore, whether education is considered to have a price depends upon whether one accepts the concept that education has an exchange value.

Wealth

Wealth is usually defined by economists as the accumulated stock of material goods which satisfy our wants. Since services are consumed as they are produced, they are not considered wealth by economists. This seems to be an unnecessarily limited concept of wealth. For example, the services rendered by a teacher at a particular moment are consumed at that time and cannot be accumulated (although it might be argued that a teacher's services are accumulated by the pupils). But the learning possessed by the teacher represents an accumulated stock of knowledge. Therefore it might well be considered wealth. Certainly a nation with a highly educated population with a vast store of technological knowledge and skill has a type of wealth not possessed in the same amount by such a country as Indonesia. Wealth can be both public and private. Therefore the total wealth of a country is the sum of public and private wealth.

The broad economic concept of wealth must be modified when analyses are made of variations among school districts in per capita wealth. The wealth of a school district consists only of the tangible wealth which it can tax. Federal, state, and locally owned property cannot be taxed. Furthermore, property owned by religious denominations, charitable organizations, and private schools and colleges cannot be taxed. Some states also provide for homestead exemptions from taxes. This untaxed wealth creates both income and needs for government services. The amount of untaxable wealth is so great that the correlation of the per capita income with per capita wealth among school districts is very low in many states. This contributes to the need of school districts for revenue from higher levels of government.

Capital

Most economists generally use the term *capital* to mean the aggregate of man-made goods used in production. Sometimes unconsumed goods in the hands of consumers are called consumers' capital but it is less confusing to consider such goods as consumers' goods.

Capital is generally considered by economists as man-made material wealth used in production. "The process of adding to productive capacity is capital formation; the thing created is real capital."[6] However nonmaterial wealth such as education may be the most important capital used in many kinds of production.

Traditionally, economists have directed most of their efforts to the study of the production, exchange, and consumption of material economic goods. Adam Smith gave major attention to that aspect of the economy in his monumental work *The Wealth of Nations*, written in 1776. His work has had a powerful influence on the thinking of economists. However, many modern economists are focusing much more than their predecessors on the production, exchange, and consumption of nonmaterial economic goods such as education.

Income

Concepts of income are very important to students of school finance. *Income* can be defined as ". . . the sum of economic goods that becomes available to an individual, firm, or community during a given period, e.g., a year. Whereas wealth and capital are stocks of goods or accumulations, income is a flow of goods."[7] Although it is relatively easy to define income, it is much more difficult for the statistician to assign a dollar value to income because everyone receives considerable nonmonetary income. For example, the services rendered within one's own family; the rent income equivalent of one's own house; the income value of government services received, such as public schools, highways, protection, and parks are difficult to estimate in dollars but they represent real income. This is particularly important for low-income families because the proportion of income of a low-income family that is nonmonetary is probably greater than for a high-income family. Since much nonmonetary income is not included in published data on income, the actual inequalities in income are probably not quite as great as reported.[8] However, the United States Department of Commerce in recent years has made a greater effort than previously to report nonmonetary income.

All taxes for schools and other purposes are paid from income received at one time or another. The ability to pay taxes, the effect of taxes on income, the effect of education on income, and the financial effort made to support schools are all important to the study of school finance.

Measures of Income. Different measures of the national economy are frequently confused. The United States Department of Commerce regularly publishes five measures of income: (1) gross national product; (2) net national product; (3) national income; (4) personal income; and (5) disposable personal income. It is difficult to define precisely the differences in these five measures, but following are brief definitions.

1. Gross national product (GNP) is the total national output of goods and services valued at market prices.
2. Net national product is the GNP less an allowance for capital consumption.
3. National income is the aggregate of labor and property earnings which arise in the current production of goods and services by the nation's economy.
4. Personal income is the current income received by persons from all sources minus contributions for social insurance.
5. Disposable personal income is personal income less personal tax and nontax payments to government.[9]

The periodical *Survey of Current Business*, published monthly by the United States Department of Commerce, presents data on these measures of the nation's economy and demonstrates the method of computation. Table 2–1 gives the data for the national income accounts for 1980. This table shows that the amount for national income differs very little from the amount for personal income.

TABLE 2–1   National Income Accounts for 1980 (in billions of dollars)

INCOME ACCOUNT	AMOUNT 1979
Gross National Product	2,626.1
Net National Product	2,338.9
National Income	2,121.4
Personal Income	2,160.2
Disposable Personal Income	1,821.7

Source: U.S. Department of Commerce, *Survey of Current Business* (Washington, D.C.: U.S. Government Printing Office, May 1981).

The measures—gross national product, net national product, national income, and personal income—are most useful in studying the ability of the nation to finance education. Only one of these measures, personal income, is regularly available to individual states.

Investment and Saving

The economic concepts of investment and saving are very important to the study of educational financing. *Investment* is defined as the incurring of costs for the purpose of adding to capital. Therefore expenditures for education are an investment for the purpose of adding to the educational capital of the people.

When people are *saving*, they refrain from consuming that part of current income which is added to capital. When consumers save, they reduce proportionately the income stream from the circular flow of production and consumption. If much of the amount saved is not invested, the economy stagnates because both production and consumption decline. Investments increase the income stream and add to both production and consumption. Investments must approximately equal saving in order to keep the economy in equilibrium. Uninvested saving results in a decline in the economy. Unused goods and services do not add to the level of living. They must be consumed or invested, because the amount saved by the community cannot be more than the amount invested, no matter how much the people collectively intend to save.

Those charged with the responsibility for securing funds for financing the schools have frequently encountered the old New England theory of "do without and make it do." The refusal to invest funds in education has frequently been justified on the grounds of thrift and economy. Murad's comment on thrift is interesting at this point:

> When people want to save more, they consume less. A decline in consumption discourages investment. And since the volume of investment determines the amounts actually saved by the community as a whole, saving declines as investment declines. Therefore, the net result of the people's efforts to save *more* is that they save *less*. This is known as the *paradox of thrift*.[10]

Marginal Utility

As will be recalled, the central topic of economics is the allocation of resources, and the central concept is scarcity. This means that we have alternative choices as to what we shall do with our resources. We may consume all of our current production, or we may consume part of it and save part of it. What we save we must invest, or we shall reduce the current stream of income and cause a decline in the economy. But we have alternative choices with respect to what investments we shall make. For example, shall we invest all our savings in physical capital, or shall we invest some of it in people, and if in the latter, how much? These are not easy questions to answer.

The individual or householder allocates resources in the private sector of the economy by "voting" with his dollar expenditures, and in the public economy by voting with his ballot. Consumer spending, even in the private economy, is a perplexing problem to economists. Consumer spending in the public economy is even more perplexing.

One approach to explaining consumer choices among economic goods is to use the concept of utility. A good does not need to be useful, but it must be wanted. But there is a change in the utility of a good as the householder obtains more units of it, especially during a relatively short period of time. The marginal utility of a good may be defined as the extent of desire for one more unit of it. The theoretical explanation of the amount of money we spend on education goes somewhat as follows: The increments of satisfaction from the last dollar spent on schooling equal the additional satisfaction received from spending that dollar for clothes, automobiles, television sets, and other economic goods. That is, if the household wants to maximize the satisfaction to be derived from the use of its income, no transfer of purchase from one good to another can increase satisfaction. This theory may explain, in part, consumer spending in the private economy, but it is doubtful that it adequately explains householder spending for education in the public economy. For example, if a householder wants a good produced in the private economy, he alone uses it and he alone pays for it. But if he wants a good produced in the public economy, it must be paid for by taxes. However, controversies over what taxes are to be levied may obscure the utility of a public good.

Many other theories have been advanced to explain householder choices of alternative spending patterns. For example, Veblen advanced the theory that rich householders, in order to demonstrate their eminence, engage in conspicuous consumption and that other householders ape the rich as far as their means allow.[11] James S. Duesenberry has presented the more charitable theory that there is in people the basic drive for self-esteem. With increased income comes the desire to buy goods of better quality. Each contact with a good of better quality tends to demonstrate to the householder its superiority. In order to maintain his self-esteem, the householder decides that the better good must always be obtained.[12]

The householder ranks some goods as superior and others as inferior, but how he does so is unknown. Galbraith has suggested that the householder follows the mores of our society by considering publicly financed goods and services, as a class, to be inferior to privately financed goods. Galbraith also puts great emphasis upon the manufactured demand for privately financed goods through advertising. Since most education is financed through the public economy, these factors may be of some significance in determining householder choices.[13]

In analyzing the allocation of resources, we have applied the standard economic concept of the scarcity of economic goods. This concept, when applied to production, seems to lead to the conclusion that if we choose to produce or consume more of one good, we must also choose to produce or consume less of some other good.[14] Our hypothesis is that this conclusion is fully valid only in an economy of full employment with a shortage of physical capital and undergirded by a stagnant technology. During the past 50 years, we have not had full employment except during war years or the years immediately before and after wars. We have had critical, overall shortages of physical capital only during those same years.

Our technology certainly has not been stagnant. However, we have had a shortage of capital goods in the form of trained people during this entire period of time. But those of us who have been engaged in efforts to increase the investment in education constantly have encountered the economic argument that if we invest more in education, we must invest less in the private economy and this will injure the total economy. Our hypothesis, stated in another way, is that in an economy such as exists in the United States—which may seem to be characterized by chronic unemployment, surpluses of material goods, and a rapidly advancing technology—*we are not compelled to have less of one good in order to have more of another.*[15] This may appear illogical to a given individual, because it may seem that if more is spent for one good, there must be less of other goods. But the individual usually takes a microeconomic view of the economy.

Actually there should be no competition in the American economy between investment in people and investment in the private economy. That fact seems evident when we study the investment in physical capital in the private economy. When we expanded our plants for the manufacture of automobiles, we did not reduce our potential for investing in the physical capital needed for the production of steel, building materials, household furniture, farm machinery, and all the other goods needed for a growing private economy. Actually, as we have invested in the physical capital needed to produce one type of material good, we have increased our potential for investing in other types of capital goods. In our growing economy, we do not have a fixed supply of money, goods, or people that must be carefully apportioned, as no doubt is necessary in a subsistence economy. The only real shortages we have in our economy are a shortage of trained people and a shortage of energy, which can be alleviated only by increased investments in education, research, and development.

Price Elasticity of Demand

Price elasticity is the degree of fluctuation in the quantity of demand for an economic good, accompanied by a change in its price. If an increase in the price of a good causes a reduction in the demand for it, the demand is elastic. However, if an increase in the price causes no reduction in demand, the demand is said to be inelastic. The amount of the price increase is important in determining the degree of demand elasticity. For example, if an increase of 1 percent in price causes more than a 1 percent decrease in demand for a good, then the demand is quite elastic. On the other hand, if it takes a price increase of 10 percent to cause a reduction in demand, the demand is not nearly as elastic as in the case of the 1 percent increase causing more than a 1 percent decrease in demand. Economists measure elasticity by comparing the relative percentage change in quantity demanded with the relative percentage change in price.

The demand for such goods as salt is inelastic. A change in the price of salt will have little effect on the quantity demanded by the household. But the demand for sirloin steak may be quite elastic in times such as the late 1970s and early 1980s, when the average household income did not increase as much as the consumer price index. However, the demand for steak may be inelastic for a very affluent household, which will continue to buy steak regardless of price changes. The possibility of substitution also affects the elasticity of demand for a particular good. For example, lower priced chicken and pork can be substituted for steak.

The price elasticity of demand has a significant relationship to the financing of education. For example, if an increase in the cost to the student of attending a private institution of higher learning causes students to attend less expensive publicly financed institutions, resulting in a reduction in the enrollment of private institutions, then the demand for private education is elastic. If students with limited financial resources elect to attend local community colleges rather than state universities, because of the difference in price, the demand for university education is elastic. School principals have frequently found that an increase in the price of school lunch will cause a reduction in the number and percent of pupils who pay for their lunches.

What effect will changes in the price of higher education to the student have on the demand for higher education? Public institutions and private institutions are both increasing the price of education at this writing primarily because of inflation. If this trend continues, will only the students of affluent parents have access to quality higher education? During the 1970s, the federal government provided a substantial amount of student aid through grants and loans. Was this sound public policy? At this writing, federal student aid is being reduced.

Income Elasticity of Demand

Income elasticity of demand refers to the relative change in quantity of demand accompanied by the relative change in household income, assuming no change in price. For example, changes over a period of years in per pupil expenditures for education can be compared with changes in per capita income. Income elasticity takes on both positive and negative signs. If increases in per capita income are accompanied by decreases in the per capita consumption of a good, the sign is negative and that good is classified as an inferior good. However, if an increase in per capita income is accompanied by an increase in the demand for a good, then the sign is positive and the good can be classified as a superior good. For example, an increase in household income may be accompanied by a decrease in the consumption of potatoes but an increase in the demand for meat. The income elasticity of demand for potatoes then is negative and the demand for meat is positive.

The income elasticity of demand for education is discussed more extensively in Chapter 4.

GOVERNMENT EXPENDITURES
AND THE NATIONAL ECONOMY

No economic system is purely private enterprise, socialist, or communist. The governments of all civilized nations supply certain human wants because private enterprise cannot meet them or can provide for them only inadequately. Furthermore, the private-enterprise system cannot function successfully unless government performs certain services. Every civilized nation needs a system of laws, methods of enforcing those laws, a police force for protecting life and property, a plan for educating the young, health protection, highways, national defense, and many other services and facilities.

We have a mixed economy—partly private and partly public. What criterion can be used to determine whether a particular good or service can be better produced in the private or the public economy? Economists suggest that the exclusion principle is one criterion to use in order to determine the sector of the economy in which a good[16] should be produced.[17] Under this concept, when a person has paid for a service or commodity and that person has exclusive control over it, the benefit is said to be excludable and can therefore be produced efficiently in the private economy. For example, if a person buys a television set, that individual has exclusive control over its use and it can be efficiently produced and distributed in the private economy. On the other hand, the benefits of such goods as national defense, police protection, administration of justice, a system of highways, and many others are not excludable and therefore can be more efficiently produced in the public economy.

It might be argued that the benefits of education are excludable to the person receiving the service, but in chapter 3 it is shown that the social benefits of education are as significant or more significant than individual benefits. In the United States, education is produced in both the public and the private economies. However, most of it is produced in the public economy. The Center for Education Statistics estimated that expenditures for public elementary, secondary and higher education totaled $135.3 billion in 1979–80 and that expenditures for private elementary, secondary and higher education amounted to $30.9 billion in that year. Actually, private education in the United States is not financed exclusively by private funds. For example, many private institutions of higher learning receive substantial amounts of funds from public sources. All private institutions are exempt from taxes, and private contributions for institutional support are exempt from federal income taxes. The same tax benefits are given to all public educational institutions.

Another reason for public financing of education is the social importance of an individual's receiving an education. It is of no concern to the general public whether a person purchases or does not purchase a television set or a sandwich. But it does concern the public whether the person becomes literate and receives sufficient education to function efficiently in the society.

Despite the necessity of satisfying many of our wants and needs through the public economy, there are some who argue that the government produces nothing and that it is a burden on the economy. In the view of economists, if the government satisfies a human want or need, it is producing something the economy needs and it is an essential part of the total economy. In the following paragraphs, the relationship of the government economy to the total economy is explored.

Wagner's Law

The more advanced the civilization, the greater the number and proportion of human wants that must be supplied by government. Adolph Wagner, a famous German economist of the nineteenth century, stated the law of increased state functions as follows:

> Comprehensive comparisons of different countries and different times show that, among progressive peoples, with which alone we are concerned, an increase regularly takes place in the activity of both the central and the local governments. This increase is both extensive and intensive: the central and local governments constantly undertake new functions, while they perform both old and new functions more efficiently and completely. In this way the economic needs of the people, to an increasing extent and in a more satisfactory fashion, are satisfied by the central and local governments.[18]

Wagner derived his law from a study of the economics of a number of progressive countries of western Europe over a long period of time. It will be noted that Wagner's law does not imply that the government economy in progressive nations ever will supplant the private economy. That is, the private economy will continue to satisfy human wants that can best be supplied by private enterprise. However, as civilization advances, the proportion of human wants that are nonmaterial in nature increases. Many of these nonmaterial wants cannot be supplied as well, if at all, by private enterprise.

The Economy of Prehistoric People. In order to understand the operation of Wagner's law, let us first consider the wants of prehistoric human beings. They had little culture, so their wants at that stage of development were biological, or primary, wants. Such wants had to be satisfied in order to survive in the struggle for existence. They had to have air, water, food, and shelter in order to survive and reproduce. Air and water were free economic goods. However, they had to contrive somehow to secure food and shelter by individual efforts.

Their economic system was a purely private-enterprise system. They paid no taxes, and government supplied them no services. The standard of living was low, and the span of life was short. They found it difficult, indeed, to compete with other animals for survival.

Anthropologists have observed that human beings were probably the poorest equipped physically of any of the animals that avoided extinction in the struggle for survival. They could not swim instinctively, they could not fly, they could not run as fast as many other animals, they were not very strong, and their physical equipment in tooth and claw for either offense or defense was very poor.

The Development of Culture. The only thing that saved human beings from extinction was a brain that enabled them to think and reason and predict the consequences of their acts and the acts of other persons and animals.

However, the purely private-enterprise system under which they lived produced such a low standard of living that humans existed precariously for hundreds of thousands of years before they started to develop a culture. When they discovered that the chances of survival would be better if they cooperated with other human beings instead of relying exclusively upon a purely individualistic private-enterprise system, the tribe was created. By banding themselves together, human beings found that they could defend themselves better from predatory animals and also obtain better food and shelter.

As the standard of living of primitive people improved, they began to develop a culture. Wants other than the primary wants for food and shelter developed. Anthropologists have found that even in prehistoric times people attempted to satisfy such nonmaterial wants as art and music, the beginnings of literature, the education of the young, and healing.

We have no authentic record of the economics of prehistoric people, but we have learned a great deal from artifacts. We know that civilization progressed rapidly after the development of oral, and especially written, languages. Communication made it possible to exchange the goods and cultures of different human societies. This greatly accelerated human progress.

The Development of Government.   People soon found that they could not live in a civilized society without government. Systems of laws were developed, and government began to assume a variety of functions that were not recognized as necessary in a primitive society. Therefore, when humans discovered the art of government they really unlocked the potentialities of free enterprise. It is true that when one studies history, many examples are found in which government has not supplied the human wants it should have supplied. Furthermore, as Adam Smith pointed out, government at times has handicapped the free enterprise of human beings. Nevertheless, government that satisfies human wants is necessary to the survival of the culture of any nation. Despite this fact, which is well known to all students of anthropology, there are people who believe that the smaller the role played by government, the better the society.

Wagner's Law and the American Economy

Let us now consider the application of Wagner's Law to the economy of the United States. Table 2–2 presents certain pertinent information for selected years beginning with 1930. In studying economic trends over a period of time, it usually is desirable to avoid peak war-expenditure years and very low depression years. The years 1930, 1940, 1950, 1960, and 1970 are good years, because they were neither low depression years nor peak war-expenditure years. The year 1980 was selected because it was the latest for which all needed data were available at this writing. However, the year 1980 is not a very good year to include in a trend study of government expenditures because the rate of inflation was extremely high in that year, as shown in Table 2–3. The gross national product reflects inflation immediately, while government expenditures usually do not increase as rapidly as the rate of inflation.

TABLE 2–2   Total Government Expenditures Compared with GNP (in current dollars)

YEAR	GROSS NATIONAL PRODUCT (in millions)	TOTAL DIRECT EXPENDITURES OF ALL GOVERNMENTS* (in millions)	PERCENTAGE SPENT ON ALL GOVERNMENTS
1930	90,700	12,094	13.3
1940	100,000	20,367	20.4
1950	286,200	70,334	24.6
1960	506,000	151,300	29.9
1970	982,400	333,000	33.9
1980	2,626,100	569,100	33.1

*Includes all direct expenditures but intergovernmental transfers of federal, state, and local governments.

Source: U.S. Bureau of the Census, *Statistical Abstract of the United States*, for 1930 to 1970 and *Survey of Current Business*, May 1981 for 1980.

Table 2–2 shows that the gross national product increased from 13.3 percent in 1930 to 33.1 percent in 1980. Many people have viewed this trend with great alarm. The proportion of gross national product allocated to government declined slightly from 33.9 percent in 1970 to 33.1 percent in 1980. As pointed out above, this decline was probably due to the extremely high rate of inflation in 1980. Also, that decline may have been partly due to increased resistance to taxes by taxpayers suffering from inflation. Will the proportion of the GNP allocated to government continue to decline or will it increase? It has increased only slightly since 1960 and seems to have stabilized around one-third of the GNP. However, social and economic conditions in the future may create a demand for more governmental service. In that event, the proportion of the GNP allocated to government may increase.

What significance does this have for those concerned with the financing of education? As pointed out in Chapter 7, governmental decisions are made by political processes. Education must compete with other governmental services for the tax dollar. If government expands its role in providing both old and new governmental services, education must compete with those services for the resources taxpayers are willing to allocate to government.

Effect of Increased Government Expenditures on the Private Economy

What is the real effect on the private economy of this trend toward increasing the proportion of the gross national product spent on government? In order to answer this question it is necessary to convert current dollars for the different years into dollars of the same purchasing power and also to convert data on the GNP and government expenditures into per capita measures. Table 2–3 sets forth the data necessary to make these conversions. It will be noted that the price index for the years shown, based on 1967 equal to 100, ranges

TABLE 2–3   Changes in Price Index and Population

YEAR	CONSUMER PRICE INDEX (1967 = 100)	TOTAL RESIDENT POPULATION (July–in thousands)
1930	50.0	123,100
1940	42.0	132,500
1950	72.1	151,900
1960	88.7	180,000
1970	116.3	203,800
1980	247.0	227,000*

*Estimated

Source: U.S. Department of Labor and U.S. Bureau of the Census, *Monthly Labor Review.*

from a low of 42.0 in 1940 to 247.0 in 1980. Furthermore, the most rapid increase in the price index over the past fifty years occurred between 1970 and 1980. The price index of 247.0 for 1980, divided by 116.3, the price index for 1970, equals 2.12. This means that it required $2.12 in 1980 to purchase what $1.00 purchased in 1970. Also, it required approximately $2.47 in 1980 to purchase what could have been obtained for $1.00 in 1967. Rapid inflation greatly complicates the problems of school financing. The householder can do little to control inflation in the private economy, but he can at least have some control over inflation in the public economy when he votes for or against taxes. It is true that the householder votes with his dollars in the private sector when he buys chicken instead of steak because it is cheaper; however, the price of chicken may be inflated as much as the price of steak.

Table 2–4 shows the GNP and expenditures for government in terms of the purchasing power of 1980 dollars for selected years beginning with 1930. The data are expressed in both total amounts and per capita amounts, in order to show the effect of increases in population. Total GNP expressed in 1980 dollars increased 486 percent between 1930 and 1980, and per capita GNP increased 218 percent. Table 2–4 shows that the per capita expenditures for government increased from $485 in 1930 to $3,608 in 1980. This was an increase of 644 percent. The per capita expenditures in the private economy increased from $3,155 in 1930 to $7,961 in 1980. This was an increase of 152 percent. Therefore the enormous increase in expenditures for government during the past 50 years has not destroyed the private economy.

The difference between the rate of increase in the government economy and the private economy has declined during the past 20 years. Per capita government expenditures increased 29 percent between 1960 and 1980, whereas expenditures in the private economy increased 45 percent during that period.

Will increased government expenditures increase or decrease the ability of the economy to satisfy human wants and needs? Economists differ on that point. The conservative point of view is that the great expansion of public economy was made possible by the great expansion of the private economy,

TABLE 2–4   GNP and Government Expenditures in Terms of Purchasing Power of 1980 Dollars

YEAR	GROSS NATIONAL PRODUCT (in millions)	TOTAL DIRECT EXPENDITURES OF ALL GOVERNMENTS (in millions)	PER CAPITA GROSS NATIONAL PRODUCT	PER CAPITA EXPENDITURES FOR GOVERNMENT	PER CAPITA EXPENDITURES IN THE PRIVATE ECONOMY*
1930	448,058	59,744	3,640	485	3,155
1940	588,000	119,764	4,438	904	3,534
1950	981,666	241,245	6,462	1,588	4,874
1960	1,406,680	504,014	7,815	2,337	5,478
1970	2,082,688	705,960	10,219	3,464	6,755
1980	2,626,100	869,100	11,569	3,608	7,961

*Includes savings and investments.
Source: Computed from data in tables 2-2 and 2-3.

and that unlimited expansion of the government economy will reduce the capability of the total economy to meet human needs. The liberal point of view is that the great expansion of the private economy was made possible in part by expansion of the public economy in education, research, social security, and in meeting other needs not met adequately by the private economy. There is undoubtedly validity in both points of view. Actually there should be no competition between the private and the public economies. Each is necessary for meeting human wants.

Two of the most important functions of government in the United States are to provide an environment in which private enterprise can function with maximum efficiency and to provide the services that cannot be supplied by private enterprise or that can be supplied better by government. Government that performs these functions not only assures a high standard of living, but also gives the greatest possible chance for enjoying individual liberties.

The authors do not intend to imply that government spending per se will cause a rise in the level of living. Some unproductive government spending no doubt is due in part to the tendency of government bureaus to proliferate and expand more than the service requires. This tendency is made explicit in what is now known as Parkinson's Law.[19] But the tendency of officials to expand their own departments operates in business and industry as well as in government. The purpose of government service is to satisfy the wants of the people served—not to create meaningless jobs. Inefficiency in either the public or the private economy has an unfavorable effect upon the standard of living of the people.

It is not the function of students of school finance to defend all governmental expenditures, but rather to examine the effect of governmental expenditures upon the economy and to relate the general effect of all governmental expenditures to the effect of educational expenditures.

Effect of Expenditures for Public Elementary and Secondary Education on the National Economy

As noted before, some people believe that taxes levied by any level of government for any government function result in a subtraction from the private economy. Let us first examine the effect upon the economic activity or the standard of living of the people that is created by a government expenditure that does not satisfy a human want. A good example would be the expenditure by the federal government of $5,000,000 for a small ballistic missile that is launched at Cape Canaveral and lands in the Atlantic Ocean seven minutes afterwards. The missile satisfies no human want.[20] The federal government must collect $5,000,000 in taxes to pay for the missile. These taxes might be collected before the missile is purchased, while it is being constructed, or even after it is used. In any event, the taxes collected would reduce private spending by an equal amount. But the missile would be constructed in the private economy, and the government would pay $5,000,000 to a private enterprise for the missile. This money would pay for labor and materials used in the construction and would provide profits for the owners of the enterprise. The government would return to the private economy all that it had subtracted from it by taxes. Therefore, the net effect upon the economy of this government expenditure should be zero, because no human want would have been satisfied by the missile.

But what effect does this kind of activity have upon the standard of living? If the construction of the missile required the use of labor and materials that were necessary to supply food, clothing, shelter, and other valid human wants, then it would reduce the standard of living. This might be the result in an underdeveloped country such as Pakistan. But in a highly industrialized country such as the United States, it probably would have no such measurable effect.

Let us now consider the effect upon the economy of constructing a high-school building costing $5,000,000. The board of education constructing the building would have to take $5,000,000 in taxes from the private economy, but it would return a like amount to the private economy when it paid the contractor, the architect, the suppliers of equipment, and others involved in constructing and equipping the building. However, assuming that a plant of this size is needed to house the student population, it satisfies a human want, and it will last for fifty years instead of seven minutes. This building, if wisely planned, will contribute to the improvement of the educational program for half a century. Therefore, during its life it will increase the producing and consuming capacity of thousands of persons and thus will have a favorable effect upon the people's standard of living.

Next let us consider the effect upon the economy of current expenditures for education. Let us assume that it would cost $1,250,000 annually to pay the current expenses of operating this school. This would include the salaries of teachers and of other employees and all other expenses of maintaining and operating the school. The board would have to take $1,250,000 annually from the private economy by taxes, but the employees of the board would provide purchasing power for the private economy and spend this income in the private economy in the same proportion as employees in the private-enterprise system. Furthermore, the board would purchase many supplies, materials, and equipment replacements from the private economy. For example, its purchase of a typewriter has exactly the same effect upon the private economy as has the purchase of a typewriter by a merchant. Finally, the education of the pupils will increase their capacity to produce, to consume, and to pay taxes.

Effect of Non-Tax-Supported Elementary and Secondary Schools on the National Economy

In the private-enterprise system of the United States, as was discussed earlier, votes are cast by dollars. This has proved to be an extraordinarily efficient system for producing and distributing material economic goods such as automobiles, washing machines, food, and clothing. Mankind has not yet discovered a better system for supplying such goods. Even the material economic goods used by the government economy are almost all produced by the private economy. No other system is so sensitive to material human wants. The competitive, profit-incentive elements of the free-enterprise system continually force private enterprise to supply those wants efficiently. Furthermore, numerous nonmaterial human wants also are well satisfied by the private economy.

A small minority of persons in the United States believes that the nonmaterial economic good called education can best be supplied by the private economy. It has been charged that the public schools constitute a monopoly and that if the public school system should be broken up, private schools could then be established that would compete with one another, and dollars would vote in the same manner as in the private-enterprise system. This argument is readily answered by directing attention to the fact that it has been found necessary to establish government-approved monopolies in the private economy in order to satisfy certain kinds of human wants. Examples are telephone, telegraph, and electric power services. An atomized school system directed by numerous independent groups and individuals would create the same type of chaos as a public utility system similarly administered. A monopoly would have to be granted to some private group to administer the schools. Just what church or corporation should be trusted with the monopoly for supplying education? The overwhelming majority of the people of the United States apparently want to trust only themselves to control their schools. They do this when they cast their votes.

Let us next consider the effect upon the economy of a private high school operating on the same budget as the public high school described above. Let us assume that the educational programs of the two schools are of comparable quality. Both schools would provide equivalent markets for the private economy. Both schools would make equivalent contributions to the producing and consuming capacities of pupils. The only real difference would be the impact upon the economy and upon individuals of the methods used to procure the funds necessary to operate the school. In the case of the public school, the funds would be obtained by taxation, and the school would be open to all. The private schools would have to obtain its funds by levying fees on the parents of pupils or by soliciting donations or by using a combination of the two methods. If fees are the chief basis of financial support, either some parents must pay out of proportion to their ability, or the school will be patronized only by people of wealth. If people pay beyond their financial ability, their standard of living is lowered. If the school is patronized only by the wealthy, it strengthens the barriers of caste and class and injures the economy. Therefore, an equitable taxing system is a more efficient method of financing a school than is dependence upon fees and donations, because it has a more favorable effect upon the economy.

Some supporters of private elementary and secondary schools advocate the issuance of vouchers financed by taxes to parents desiring to send their children to private schools. Others advocate the giving of tax credits to such persons. In either case the so-called private school becomes a tax-supported school governed by special interests rather than by the general public through the ballot.

Effect of Public School Expenditures on Inflation and Deflation

Economists and the people generally have been concerned for many years about business cycles. Periodically throughout our history, the nation has passed through booms and depressions that have caused much suffering and economic dislocation. Some have thought that these cycles are an inevitable part of a free-enterprise economy. Others have thought that it is possible even in a free economy to minimize the severity of business cycles. The federal government has made many attempts to regulate these cycles by both long-range and emergency measures. Some of the long-range measures have been the establishment of the Federal Reserve System, federal insurance of bank deposits, various types of social security provisions, the regulation of securities exchanges, and similar moves. Emergency measures have included increasing or decreasing government expenditure for public works, extension or contraction of credit, emergency relief expenditures, increasing or decreasing taxes, and many other devices.

This is only a brief description of the activities of government to regulate the economy. But it is evident that the policy of the federal government through many different administrations has been to reduce the severity of business cycles and at the same time facilitate an expanding economy. It is in this context that the effect of school expenditures upon business cycles is discussed.

The public school enterprise is one of the most stable factors in our economy. The demand for education is affected very little by business cycles. Pupils report to the public schools regardless of booms or depressions. Therefore, there is little or no unemployment in the schools during periods of economic depression and general unemployment. On the other hand, there is little or no increase in employment in the public schools during business booms. The number of persons employed by the schools is governed much more by the number of pupils to be served than by business cycles. School budgets rise slowly in inflationary periods and decline slowly in periods of depression. Changes that are made in school budgets during business cycles are due much more to changes in the wage and price structure than to changes in the number of persons employed or of material goods consumed. Therefore, public school expenditures generally constitute an important stabilizing influence in the economy.

Should public school expenditures be reduced or increased in deflationary times, and should public school expenditures be reduced or increased during times of inflation? There are those who argue that school expenditures should be reduced in depression times in order to provide more money for the private economy and there are others who argue that expenditures should be reduced during inflationary times in order to reduce inflationary pressures. A number of state legislators with a considerable number of years of service have used these same arguments at different points in business cycles. Obviously, such legislators could not be correct in their reasoning at both points.

It seems that it would be unwise, as a general policy, to increase or decrease school expenditures as an emergency measure to regulate inflation or deflation. An exception might be a stepping up of school building construction during periods of unemployment as part of a general public works program. Certainly if the federal government inaugurated such a program during depression times, the public schools should be included. But such a program would be of little benefit to the people unless the buildings were actually needed.

Educational expenditures affect the economy most favorably when they are determined by human wants for education. Such a policy makes educational expenditures a stabilizing factor in the economy and also satisfies human wants. Increases in educational expenditures can be justified in either deflationary or inflationary times if such expenditures are necessary to maintain or increase the quantity and quality of educational services desired by the people.

Competition and Educational Productivity

Private educational institutions compete with each other for students, and to some extent with public educational institutions. Some have charged that public educational institutions constitute a monopoly and that there is no competition among them. However, there is no doubt that public institutions of higher learning within the same state compete with each other for students. There is also some evidence that school districts compete with each other. In the private sectors of our economy, competition among firms undoubtedly promotes efficiency of production and a continuous search for "the better mouse trap." The profit motive is the basis of competition in the private sector of our economy. But no public educational institutions and very few private educational institutions are operated for profit. Therefore it is not a valid assumption that competition among educational institutions would have the same desirable results as competition among firms in the private sector. It is probable that cooperation among educational institutions, both public and private, would result in more efficient production and quality of service than would competition. For example, cooperation could eliminate or reduce unnecessary duplication of services and result in a more efficient use of resources. This is particularly true of institutions of higher learning.

Finally, educational productivity and efficiency are much more likely to be increased by research and development designed to improve educational resources management than by competition. Most of the useful research and development will have to be accomplished in the public sector of the economy. The productivity and efficiency of American agriculture largely resulted from the public-supported research and development in our experimental farms administered by the land grant colleges. The public schools have been criticized for failure to develop and adopt innovations that increase the productivity and efficiency of education. However, less than one-half of 1 percent of public school expenditures has traditionally been expended for research and development. Substantially increased expenditures for well-planned research and development are much more likely to increase the economic efficiency of the public schools than a system of vouchers.

NOTES

1. U.S. Department of Commerce, Bureau of the Census, *Statistical Abstract, 1980*, 101st ed. (Washington, D.C.: U.S. Government Printing Office, 1980), p. 406.

2. W. Vance Grant and Leo J. Eiden, *Digest of Education Statistics, 1980* (Washington, D.C.: U.S. Department of Health, Education and Welfare, Education Division, National Center for Education Statistics, 1980), p. 23.

3. U.S. Department of Commerce, Bureau of Economic Analysis, *Survey of Current Business* (May 1980) (Washington, D.C.: U.S. Government Printing Office, 1980), p. 6.

4. Charles S. Benson, *The Economics of Public Education*, 3rd ed. (Boston: Houghton Mifflin Company, 1978), p. 5.

5. Elchanan Cohn, *The Economics of Education*, rev. ed. (Cambridge, Mass.: Ballinger Publishing Company, 1979), p. 1.

6. C. Lowell Harris, *The American Economy*, rev. ed. (New York: Holt, Rinehart and Winston, 1946), p. 40.

7. Anatol Murad, *Economic Principles and Problems*, rev. ed. (Ames, Iowa: Littlefield, Adams & Company, 1954), p. 13.

8. Harris, *op. cit.*, p. 385.

9. Adapted from U.S. Department of Commerce, Bureau of the Census, *Statistical Abstract, 1979*, 100th ed. (Washington, D.C.: U.S. Government Printing Office, 1979), pp. 433–34.

10. Murad, *op. cit.*, p. 180.

11. Thorstein Veblen, *The Theory of the Leisure Class* (New York: Augustine M. Kelley Publisher, 1899).

12. James S. Duesenberry, *Income, Savings, and Theory of Consumer Behavior* (Cambridge, Mass.: Harvard University Press, 1949).

13. John Kenneth Galbraith, *The Affluent Society* (Boston: Houghton Mifflin Company, 1958).

14. This concept is related to the concept of Pareto-optimality. Under that concept, the lot of no one can be improved without making the lot of someone else worse. See Paul A. Samuelson, *Economics*, 10th ed. (New York: McGraw-Hill Book Company, 1976), p. 462.

15. The present energy shortage may seem to invalidate this conclusion. However, we have the technology to solve that problem. With wise investment in both physical and human capital, it and other shortages that may develop will be solved.

16. The term "good" as used in this book includes both tangible, physical goods and services.

17. See for example Richard A. Musgrave and Peggy B. Musgrave, *Public Finance in Theory and Practice*. 2nd ed. (New York: McGraw-Hill Book Company, 1973), Chap. 3.

18. Adolph Wagner, *Grundlegung der politischen Oekonomie*, [Principles of political economy], 3rd ed. (1893), Bk. VI, Chap. e., translated and quoted in C.J. Bullock, *Selected Readings in Public Finance*, 3rd ed. (Boston: Ginn and Company, 1924), p. 32.

19. C. Northcote Parkinson, *Parkinson's Law* (Boston: Houghton Mifflin Company, 1957), pp. 2–13.

20. Unless the want is to possess the capability of destroying other human beings on the assumption that this would prevent aggression against the possessor of the missile. Also, some information might be obtained that would be useful for other purposes.

SELECTED REFERENCES

ALEXANDER, KERN, and K. FORBIS JORDAN, eds. *Educational Need and the Public Economy*. Gainesville, Fla.: University Presses of Florida, 1976.

BENSON, CHARLES S. *The Economics of Public Education*, 3rd ed. Boston: Houghton Mifflin Company, 1978.

BLAUG, MARK. *An Introduction to the Economics of Education*. New York: Penguin Books, 1970.

COHN, ELCHANAN. *The Economics of Education*, rev. ed. Cambridge, Mass.: Ballinger Publishing Company, 1979.

GINZBERG, ELI. *The Human Economy*. New York: McGraw-Hill Book Company, 1976.

HEILBRONER, R.L., and LESTER THUROW. *The Economic Problem*, 6th ed. Englewood Cliffs, N.J.: Prentice-Hall, Inc., 1981.

JOHNS, ROE L., and others, eds. *Economic Factors Affecting the Financing of Education*. Gainesville, Fla.: National Educational Finance Project, 1970.

ROGERS, DANIEL C., and HIRSCH S. RACHLIN. *Economics and Education: Principles and Applications*. New York: Free Press, 1971.

SILK, LEONARD. *Economics in Plain English*. New York: Simon & Schuster, Inc., 1978.

CHAPTER THREE
HUMAN CAPITAL
AND THE
ECONOMIC BENEFITS
OF EDUCATION

The value of the human being to a nation is evidenced historically by the physical strength of conquering armies, both ancient and modern. In its crudest form, human value was recognized by the treatment of human beings as property in slave trade throughout the centuries. Value of the human being was largely determined by physical rather than mental capability. Human valuation and the labor of individuals have shaped markets, whether provided by freemen, serfs, or slaves.[1] The market value of the human changes dramatically with fluctuations in the supply of workers; as Tuchman observes, a decline in population caused by the bubonic plague of the fourteenth century placed such a premium on the laborer that the value of the individual was reflected in wage reforms which swept western Europe and affected commerce for centuries.[2]

Throughout these earlier eras, valuation was based on people's physical productivity as "hewers of wood and drawers of water," not as philosophers, scientists, teachers, or physicians. According to this method of valuing the individual, the nation with the greatest population had the greatest human capital value. The fallacy in this approach became apparent in the nineteenth and twentieth centuries, as the world's work force became less "labor intensive" and more "brain intensive." The country with the greatest population was not necessarily the most productive or influential. If sheer numbers had been the measure of human value then England would have been a dependency of India rather than vice versa.

It was not until the 1960s that an awakening to the real value of human capital actually occurred. Guided by Theodore W. Schultz, later to win the Nobel Prize for Economic Science, economists and educators began to recognize the economic importance of the human being in the production process and to begin to seek ways to measure the magnitude of human capital.[3] This is not to say that human knowledge and skill were never observed before, but it is certainly true that no attempts were made in an economic sense to quantify the value of human capital. The economist Petty had earlier observed "that the value of mankind is worth twenty times the present annual earning of labor,"[4] but Petty's estimates were without empirical base. Though he recognized the value of human capital his imprecision of measurement tended to create problems of academic credability.

CLASSICAL ECONOMIC VIEWPOINT

The insight of the various early economists into this issue was reflected in whether they recognized the human being in their overall definition of wealth or capital. John Stuart Mill, for example, did not define wealth as including human capital. He said: "In propriety of classification, however, the people of a country are not to be counted in its wealth. . . . They are not wealth themselves, though they are means of acquiring it."[5] On the other hand, Adam Smith in 1776 did include human capital in his definition of fixed capital, saying it consisted "of the acquired and useful abilities of all the inhabitants or members of society. The acquisition of such talents by the maintenance of the acquirer during his education, study or apprenticeship, always costs a real expense, which is a capital fixed and realized, as it were, in his person."[6] Yet Smith never really related the educational function of government to the development of human potential nor did he attempt to measure it. Basically, Smith was unable to perceive of man in any terms other than that of an "expensive machine," a position fundamentally adhered to by the Cambridge economist Alfred Marshall.[7] Marshall, an economist of great prestige, maintained that while human beings were certainly capital from an abstract point of view, it was impractical to include them as an element to analyze national investment and development.[8]

Interestingly, some antecedents in both education and economics do exist which provide precedents for the work of Schultz and others of the 1960s beyond the political economy of Smith and Marshall. Smith and Marshall both recognized that more training and experience increased the productivity of the worker, but neither apparently realized that overall increases in human knowledge, aside from skills directly related to production, could have a profound effect on a nation's economy.

The limitations of this narrow view were recognized by a few educators and economists over 100 years ago at a time when the public schools of this country were yet in infancy. In fact, Horace Mann in his 1848 education report said that

> . . . our means of education are the grand machinery by which "raw material" of human nature can be worked into inventors and discoverers, into skilled artisans and scientific farmers, into scholars and jurists, into the founders of benevolent institutions, and the great expounders of ethical and theological science. By means of early education, these embryos of talent may be quickened, which will solve the difficult problems of political and economical law.[9]

Mann attacked the philosophy of Smith and others whose views of political economy failed to recognize the condition of the poor uneducated workers of the Industrial Revolution and admonished that the true wealth of a nation lay largely in the intelligence of the people. In this regard Mann said,

> For creation of wealth, then—for the existence of a wealthy people and a wealthy nation—intelligence is the grand condition. The number of improvers will increase, as the intellectual constituency, if I may so call it, increases. In former times, and in most parts of the world even at the present day, not one man in a million has ever had such a development of mind, as made it possible for him to become a contributor to art or science. Let this development proceed, and contributions, numberless, and of inestimable value, will be sure to follow. That Political Economy, therefore, which busies itself about capital and labor, supply and demand, interest and rents, favorable and unfavorable balances of trade; but leaves out of account the element of a wide-spread mental development, is nought but stupendous folly. The greatest of all the arts in political economy is to change a consumer into a producer—an end to be directly attained, by increasing his intelligence.[10]

With few exceptions, Mann's perception of the thinking of political economists of the nineteenth century was accurate for their efforts were spent almost entirely on matters of relating to physical capital and little if any concern was directed toward human capital. The balance sheet of political economy did not include entries for the store of human potential or lack of it.

An exception to the general trend of economic thought was reflected by the economist Von Thunen, who, a decade after Mann's report, pointed out the importance of counting human beings as part of a nation's capital. He said:

> There is no doubt about the answer to the very controversial question of whether the immaterial goods (services) of mankind form a part of national wealth or not. Since a more highly schooled nation, equipped with the same material goods, creates a much larger income than an uneducated people, and since this higher schooling can only be obtained through an educational process which requires a larger consumption of material goods, the more educated nation also possesses a larger capital, the returns of which are expressed in the larger product of its labor.[11]

In spite of Mann and Von Thunen, only sporadic recognition was given in the literature until Schultz measured the value of human capital in 1961.[12]

HUMAN CAPITAL APPROACH

Schultz observed that the classical economists had "put us on the wrong road" of economic thought. Adam Smith, David Ricardo, and others viewed economic growth in light of land and labor, with land fixed by nature and labor homogeneous. That is, Smith, in spite of his acknowledgment of the importance of labor skills, basically assumed labor to be of a given quality regardless of technological change. His equations did not allow for an expanded view of capital which would account for increasing knowledge and advancement of technology.[13] What Schultz observed was the heterogeneity of capital and he saw that the human being was a form of capital which could be developed. Schultz's important contribution was the assertion that skills and knowledge are a form of capital. He observed,

> Although it is obvious that people acquire useful skills and knowledge, it is not obvious that these skills and knowledge are a form of capital, that this capital is in substantial part a product of deliberate investment that has grown in Western societies at a much faster rate than conventional (nonhuman) capital, and that its growth may well be the most distinctive feature of the economic system.[14]

Schultz and others noted that the income of the United States and other countries had been increasing at a vastly higher rate than could be accounted for by combining the amount of land, hours worked, and stock of reproducible goods used to produce this income. As the discrepancy between the two amounts became larger, economists, without knowing its nature, called the difference "resource productivity." Schultz said that to call this discrepancy "a measure of 'resource productivity' gives a name to our ignorance but does not dispel it."[15]

With Schultz's work as impetus, a rejuvenation of thinking occurred in the 1960s, with many economists suddenly becoming very busy in an attempt to measure the effects of human capital on the economy. Educators eagerly sought evidence to support their assertions that greater investment in the public schools would yield higher economic returns. Within a few years, the volume of research was so great that the question of the value of human capital became an important subspecialty of both economic and social science. The ultimate acknowledgment of the importance of human capital research was given in 1978 when the Nobel Prize for Economic Science was awarded to Theodore W. Schultz and Sir W. Arthur Lewis for their efforts in this area.

HUMAN RESOURCES AND
ECONOMIC DEVELOPMENT

The importance of human resources to economic development is richly illustrated in a book by Frederick H. Harbison, where he maintained "that human resources—not capital, nor income, nor material resources—constitute the ultimate basis for the wealth of nations."[16] As this quotation indicates, Harbison takes to task those economists of the Adam Smith school who largely ignored human resources in their theories of political economy. Harbison points out that capital and material resources are passive factors of production which can only be activated by the catalyst of human resources. He says that

> Human beings are the active agents who accumulate capital, exploit natural re-
> sources, build social, economic, and political organizations, and carry forward
> national development. Clearly, a country which is unable to develop the skills
> and knowledge of its people and to utilize them effectively in the national economy
> will be unable to develop anything else.[17]

Accordingly, Harbison maintains that the wealth of nations should not only be measured in terms of gross national product, national income, and gross domestic product, but also reflect what should be the primary objective of national economic policy, the stock and condition of human capital. The strength of national economies would, therefore, be more accurately judged by whether human resources were, first, adequately developed, and secondly, appropriately used. Education, he noted, is a primary instrument for resolving economic problems related to both underdevelopment and underutilization of human resources.

Research and writing in the area ranged from the broad sociological aspects to precise mathematical measurement of the contribution of human capital enhancement on economic development. Much work was conducted internationally to analyze the importance of education and new knowledge acquisition in underdeveloped countries. W. Arthur Lewis, working extensively in non-industrialized countries, observed that the level of literacy and the type of social conditions combined to either enhance or retard technological development. Societies with rigid class systems tended to withhold education from the masses, thereby retarding economic growth.[18] Too, it was observed that a certain "absorption effect" was at work wherein the masses had to have a minimum level of education in order for them to become intelligent consumers.[19] An illiterate populace could not appreciate or take advantage of technological advances. Education is, thus, important not alone as a direct investment in output but also as a consumer good, to enable people to enjoy and to understand things better.[20]

Beyond the absorption or consumption aspect, a nation's economic output "is a function of the infrastructure it has developed and the skill of its people."[21] Skills and competence in the work force are acquired primarily through formal educational systems designed to transmit acquired knowledge, skills, and techniques. Ginsberg observes that formal education is the primary source of the skill acquisition necessary for economic development.

> [M]any years of exposure to didactic instruction in the classroom, supplemented
> by reading assignments on the outside, result in young people's acquiring a con-
> siderable stock of knowledge that helps inform their judgments about private and
> public issues on which they must act. The schools are not solely responsible for
> these horizon-stretching, comprehension-deepening efforts, for the media play

important complementary roles. But the contribution of the formal education system is primary.[22]

Of course, it would not be accurate to attribute all acquisition of knowledge and skill to formal school processes. Knowledge and skill formation actually comes about through three modes: first, general formal schooling; second, formal vocational education which extends from early high school through graduate professional schools; and third, learning opportunities provided by employers through on-the-job training or in special industry-financed programs, which usually take the form of short intensive seminars and institutes for management and white-collar workers. All of these combine to constitute the sum total of a nation's educational investment.

More broadly, investment in human resources should not be viewed as limited to knowledge and skill acquisition, but must also include the health of the nation. It goes without saying that a nation of people suffering from hunger and poor health will not be economically productive. Politics and, indeed, political economy of any society is first of all "bread politics," a set of measures founded on a nutritional determinant.[23] When basic nutritional needs are met the individual can then turn thoughts and actions to higher levels of economic considerations which ultimately enhance overall productivity. Advancements in health generally extend the productivity of one individual and make any investment in education longer lived and more rewarding.[24]

MEASURING THE BENEFITS OF EDUCATION

The benefits of education may be broadly defined as including anything which (a) increases production through enhancement of the capacity of the labor force; (b) increases efficiency by reducing costs, thus reserving or releasing resources for other productive pursuits; and (c) increases the social consciousness of the community so that the standard of living is enhanced.[25] Beyond these generalizations, though, the actual measurement of benefits of education becomes more difficult. Since the early 1960s, literally hundreds of research projects have been undertaken which have sought to quantify the benefits of education, all supplying pieces to a complex puzzle but none really giving the precision of measurement which is desirable. Most of the analyses can be categorized into four basic approaches: (1) simple relationship analyses, (2) the residual approach, (3) cash value or direct monetary return, and (4) cost-benefit or rate-of-return method.[26]

Relationship Analysis Approach

Probably the least satisfactory approach to measuring benefits of education is simply comparing levels of educational attainment with other socioeconomic indicators. For example, the number of years of schooling for persons in certain age groups can be compared to their annual income.[27] One may also compare the relationship between earnings of certain wage earners and education level, retail sales and years of schooling, economic attitudes and education level, or high-school dropouts and annual loss in dollars.[28]

On a macroeconomic scale, such studies may relate an index of educational attainment to the GNP per capita, national income per capita, or any other broad economic measure. For example, enrollment ratios have been found to have a positive correlation with GNP per capita.[29]

While helpful, these studies are far from definitive, because they are unable to show cause-and-effect relationships between education and economic growth. Other important factors which relate to both may be present, influencing the positive relationships.

Residual Approach

Recognition that the classical inputs of land, labor, and capital were not the sole determinants of a nation's economic advance is the basis for other macroeconomic analyses which have sought to ferret out the various contributors to economic growth. Economists found that even after all physical inputs were considered, a persistent and unidentified residual remained. Kendrick examined this phenomenon in 1961 and estimated that for the period between 1889 and 1957 a combined index of inputs increased 1.9 percent annually while the nation's output index increased 3.5 percent annually, leaving an unexplained discrepancy of 1.6 percent annually.[30] He found that about 80 percent of the increased output per unit of labor input was attributable to a residual, something other than land, labor, and capital. Massell employed different procedures, but also found a residual to equal roughly 90 percent of the increase in output per man-hour in the United States economy from 1915 to 1955.[31] Fabricant found that only 1.0 percent of the annual increse in GNP of 3.1 percent could be attributed to land, labor, and capital. He suggested, but did not substantiate, that the residual may be largely explained by investments in education, research, and development and other intangible capital.[32]

The residual—that portion of economic growth as measured by increase in national income which cannot be explained by increased production of land, labor, and capital—is arrived at by a method whereby each of the three major input categories is estimated to make up a particular constant part of an aggregate production function which constitutes all output.[33] If then a period of time is taken, for example from 1929 through 1957, and the growth rate per year is found to be x percent for land, y for quality changes in labor, and z for changes in capital, then the constant percentage from the production function times the growth rates x, y and z, should account for the entire increase in national income over that period. But, in fact, when each of these was multiplied, for 1929 through 1957, by its respective percentage Denison found that the average annual rate of growth in material income was 2.93 percent, but the total of land, labor, and capital was only 2.0 percent, leaving a .93 percent discrepancy. Thus, national income had increased 2.93 percent annually, and the traditional inputs of land, labor, and capital could not account for all the increase. This unexplained difference is referred to as the residual, an inquiry into which sparked the research on the value of education and knowledge.

Schultz and Denison set out to explain this residual and to determine what portion of it was attributable to education. Schultz's was the first serious attempt, and his approach was to determine how much the increase in the labor income was attributable to an increase in human capital. To do this, he estimated the total school years completed by the labor force from 1900 to 1957. Then he placed a value on this total schooling for 1929 and for 1957. He found that the value of the education stock during this period had increased by $286 billion, adjusted to 1956 dollars. During this same period, he found that labor income had increased by $71 billion beyond the level of earnings necessary to maintain the same earning potential per person through these years. The next step was to determine what portion of the $286 billion increase in value of education stock could be counted as productive investment return that would increase national income. Here Schultz used three alternative rates-of-return to investment in education (to be fully explained later in this chapter) which he had calculated earlier. The middle rate was 11 percent, which he multiplied times $286 billion, giving $31.5 billion. This is the value of additional education which could be assumed to be productive investment. He then divided $31.5 billion by $71 billion (increase in labor earnings) and multiplied the quotient by 100, to get the final percentage of 44. This 44 percent constituted that portion of the increase in earnings of labor which could be attributed to additional education during the period 1929 through 1957.

This figure, of course, varies substantially, depending on the rate-of-return used.* Using other rates-of-return of 9 and 17 percents, Schultz showed that the percentage of labor earnings could also be estimated at 36 and 70 percents respectively.[34]

Schultz's methodology, although giving quite a range of results depending on the rate-of-return used, nevertheless was a major contribution because it constituted the first attempt to treat education as a separate production factor in a nation's economic growth.

Shortly following the publication of Schultz's study, Denison produced a more complete analysis of sources of economic growth and in 1974 he conducted a follow-up study.[35] His methodology was basically this: First he calculated a weighting index by composing the relative average earnings of men and women at seven different levels of education, beginning with a base of an eighth-grade education, which he designated at an index of 100. He then proceeded upward with, for example, four years of high school having 124, four years of college 189, and five or more years of college 219. Second, he calculated the proportion

---

*More will be said about rates-of-return later in this chapter.

of workers falling within each educational level for each year under examination. Third, he multiplied the education indexes by the employment distribution at each educational level. The indexes take into account unemployment and are further adjusted for school years with fewer than 180 days.

By proceeding thus, Denison was able to construct a level of education index for each year, depending on the overall educational level of the labor force. For example, for 1970 he found that 10.82 percent of full-time-equivalent males in the labor force had only an eighth-grade education, at which level he had assigned an index of 100. He found that 36.77 percent of the FTE males in the labor force had four years of high school, to which applied a 124 earning index. At the college level (four years) he found 7.27 percent of the FTE males at a 189 earning index and at the graduate level (five or more years) he found 4.62 percent of FTE males at a 219 earning index. He then multiplied each of the percentages by grade level by the earning index and obtained a total. When he combined data for males and females, he found that the total for 1929 was 83.71, increasing to 106.71 by 1969 (see Table 3–1).

These data indicate that the educational level of the labor force was responsible for increasing input per day by 27.5 percent between 1929 and 1969. Since labor accounts for about 75 percent of national income, the increase in national income attributable to increased education would be 27.5 percent times 75 percent, equaling 20.6 percent over the period. If the annual growth rate of per capita national income were 1.89 between 1929 and 1969, the contribution of education would be 0.39 percentage points.[37] This shorthand estimate is quite close to Denison's actual figures as shown in Table 3–2. Table 3–2 gives Denison's estimates of the contribution of education to growth in real national income for selected time intervals.

In Table 3–2, notice that part I of the data refers to the growth rate of total real national income, while part II gives the growth rate of real national income per person employed. The amount of growth rate is the same for the total and per person. This amount refers to the numerical portion of the growth rate which is attributed to education. Notice that the percentage of growth rate ascribed to education varies markedly because of the lower denominator. Also, observe that there has been some decline in more recent years, as indicated by the 1948–69 data when compared with the 1929–48 data.

TABLE 3–1   Denison's Indexes for Effect of Quantity of Education on Labor Input

Year	Males 1	Females 2	Combined 3
1929	83.18	86.79	83.71
1948	93.40	96.33	93.85
1969	107.08	105.01	106.71

Source: Edward F. Denison, *Accounting for United States Economic Growth, 1929–1969,* (Washington D.C.: Brookings Institution, 1974), Table 1–21, p. 259.

TABLE 3–2 Estimates of the Contribution of Education to Growth of Real National Income

	1929–1948	1948–1969	1929–1969
I. Growth Rate of Total Real National Income	2.75	3.85	3.33
Amount of Growth Rate Ascribed to Education	0.40	0.41	0.41
Percent of Growth Rate Ascribed to Education	14.5	10.6	12.3
II. Growth Rate of Real National Income Per Person Employed	1.47	2.27	1.89
Amount of Growth Rate Ascribed to Education	0.40	0.41	0.41
Percent of Growth Rate Ascribed to Education	27.2	18.1	21.7

Source: Elchanan Cohn, *The Economics of Education* (Cambridge, Mass: Ballinger Publishing Company, 1979), Table 7-10; as taken from Edward F. Denison, "Measuring the Contribution of Education (and the Residual) to Economic Growth" (Paris: OECD, 1964) Table 8, p. 35; and Edward F. Denison, *Accounting for United States Economic Growth, 1929–1969* (Washington, D.C.: Brookings Institution, 1974), Tables 9-4 and 9-7.

The residual approach continues to be a useful tool in the measurement of education's contribution to real national income growth. Studies using similar methodology have been conducted for other countries, with widely varying results. In a study of South American countries, Correa found the contribution of education as a percentage of growth in national income ranged from a high of 16 percent in Argentina to a low of 1 percent in Mexico.[38] Denison himself in 1967 studied nine European countries for the period 1950–62, finding no country in which education contributed as high a percentage of growth as in the United States. His results varied widely, showing a range in percentage of growth in national income per employed person of 18 percent in the United Kingdom to a low of 2 percent in Germany, with the United States showing 23 percent.[39]

Economic analysis fails to explain why the contributions of education vary so greatly among countries. Two countries may have a relatively high growth of national income but yet make much different educational contributions to this growth. Several explanations have been advanced. First, it has been pointed out that the aggregate education of the labor force increases as the labor force itself expands, even though the level of each worker does not increase. Thus, variations in the increase of numbers in the labor force can make estimates vary among countries. Second, the type and level of education in the labor force can have an influence on productivity. Third, little is known about the combinations of education, labor, and capital which produce the greatest economic benefits. Overall, the research has failed to produce definitive findings regarding the optimal levels of each of the components of economic growth. Further study will be required before one can proceed much beyond conjecture in this area.

Cash Value Approach

Educational benefits can also be measured by relating earnings to the educational level of individuals. On the average, individuals with a high-school education will have higher earnings than those with only a tenth-grade education, and college graduates will earn more than high-school graduates. This pattern has held for many years. In 1939, the average annual earnings of a high-school graduate was 64 percent of the college graduate; in 1949 the figure was 61 percent; in 1957, 60 percent; and in 1968, 69 percent. Today, the earnings of high-school graduates remain about two-thirds those of college graduates. Table 3–3 shows how the differential broadens when a graduate-school education of five or more years is compared with a high-school education.

Figure 3–1 shows age-income profiles by levels of education without costs taken into account. In other words, this figure shows the cash value of education over the working life of an individual, by elementary, high-school, and college level. The line ABC shows the average pattern of income for the elementary-school graduate. DEF gives the pattern for the high-school graduate, and GHI shows that of the college graduate.

The continuity of the relationship between more education and higher earnings rebuts earlier warnings by such economists as Seymour Harris of Harvard, who in 1949 warned that a persistent increase in college graduates would flood the employment market and make relative earning power fall. He had erroneously concluded that "college students within the next twenty years are doomed to disappointment after graduation, as the number of coveted openings will be substantially less than the numbers seeking them."[40]

Such conclusions overlook the expansive influence of education on the economy; a better-educated work force will create economic demand for products which can only be produced by a better-educated employee. "The demand for highly trained workers has kept pace with the supply, so that they are, by and large, fully employed."[41] Thus, the monetary benefits to education are well documented and a person progressing ever upward through the educational system can be comforted by the knowledge that he or she, on the average, stands a better chance of having a higher income throughout a lifetime. This does not, of course, assure that every individual will earn more than if he or she had only completed, say, the tenth grade. Our history is replete with examples of "self-made" persons, who without formal education became economically independent. Actuarially, though, the odds are much better for one to become economically successful if he or she has more education than less.

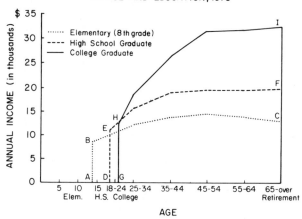

MEAN YEAR-ROUND FULL-TIME WORKERS' INCOME,
BY AGE AND EDUCATION, 1978

FIGURE 3-1

Costs. At different school levels, the direct-monetary-returns approach to measuring the economic desirability of obtaining an education does not give the entire picture, for although it is accurate as far as it goes, it does not take into account the important element of costs. It only looks at the benefits. To take costs into account requires a more complex analysis of the value of education.

The benefit-cost approach is schematically represented in Figure 3–2. Notice how this differs from Figure 3–1 in that costs are a negative feature, which must be overcome by income in order for there to be a positive return

TABLE 3–3 1978 Mean Income by Educational Level

Educational Level	Mean Annual Income		
	25-34	25 years and over	18+
Elementary School			
dropout (less than 8 years)	$ 8,174	$ 7,149	$11,297
graduate	9,553	9,367	13,561
High School			
dropout (1–3 years)	10,699	11,784	14,194
graduate	13,505	15,152	16,385
College			
dropout (1–3 years)	14,328	16,708	18,273
graduate (4 years or more)	17,471	23,724	25,974
graduate (5 years or more)	18,424	25,687	28,509

Source: U.S. Bureau of the Census, Current Population Reports, *Consumer Income: Money Income of Families and Persons in the United States: 1978*, Series P–60, No. 123, (June 1980), Table 50, pp. 212–15. Data refer to males of all races by age groups.

at retirement age. This schematic is, of course, not to scale. If it were, the costs would possibly show an even more dramatic difference because of foregone income. If we assume that the profile represents individual or private returns on educational investment, and we further assume that the education is taking place in a public school, then the costs to the individual at the elementary level ABC are quite small. Foregone income is very little, since the value of annual earnings of an illiterate or semiliterate person amounts to very little. Additionally, the individual does not incur direct costs in attending a public school, since the state pays for the education in its entirety. Thus, benefit-costs of elementary education to the individual can be expected to be quite impressive, since the costs are so low. On the other hand, if one is considering social benefits, then the direct costs of schooling must be taken into account, thereby reducing the benefit-cost ratio (see Figure 3–2).

With a public high-school education, the costs, FGH, are expected to be greater for the individual because of foregone income. The benefit-cost ratio will therefore be reduced somewhat even though income, HIJ, of the high-school graduate is greater.

The individual costs to a college graduate are relatively greater than to either the elementary- or high-school graduate, since the state does not pay the full cost of a higher education and the student must pay out of pocket for tuition, books, room and board, in addition to greater foregone earnings. In the schematic, then, KLM is of greater magnitude and the income, MNO, must be correspondingly higher to offset costs and potential interest thereon over the working life of the individual.

MEAN YEAR-ROUND FULL-TIME WORKERS' INCOME & COSTS
BY AGE AND EDUCATION, 1978

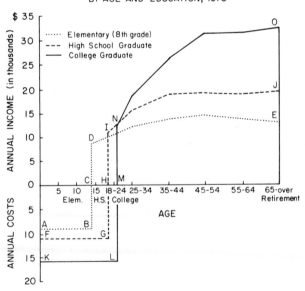

FIGURE 3-2

Cost-Benefit Approach

An alternative method of showing the value of education is to relate costs of education to the benefit to be derived, and from this calculate rates-of-return or cost-benefit ratios. This is a method of net valuing education wherein the costs of obtaining an education are deducted from monetary gains over the working life of the individual.

Costs. Education has both private and social costs, which may be both direct and indirect. If the student is attending a private school, direct private costs are incurred for tuition, fees, books, room and board. In a public school, the majority of these costs are subsumed by the public treasury, and, thus become social costs. Indirect costs of education are embodied in the earnings which are foregone by all persons of working age, but foregone earnings are also a cost to society, a reduction in the total productivity of the nation. This may be viewed in macroeconomic terms, but can also be measured in the amount of tax funds which a state foregoes when an individual is not employed. Of course, the state here assumes, as does the individual, that earnings foregone for the sake of education at some early point in the person's career will yield greater returns later. This is the essence of the idea of investment in education. Table 3–4 shows the major types and categories of costs.

It is within the realm of costs that much of the disenchantment with rate-of-return studies has been generated. Schultz maintained that only about half of the total social cost for education should be considered as an investment. It must be acknowledged that all education is not undertaken as an investment. Much of the educational experience of most persons is simply consumed and enjoyed with no thought to what the expenses for the education will earn them

TABLE 3–4   Types and Categories of Social and Private Educational Costs

TYPES OF COSTS	CATEGORIES OF COSTS	
	SOCIAL	PRIVATE
Direct Costs	1. Salaries of teachers, administrators, and nonprofessional personnel	Tuition and fees
	2. Books, supplies and equipment (total)	Books, supplies, and equipment (out-of-pocket expenditures)
	3. Transportation (total)	Extra travel
	4. Room and board (total)	Room and board
	5. Scholarship and other subsidies to students	
	6. Capital expenditures	
Indirect Costs	7. Earnings foregone	Earnings foregone

in the future. Does the student make an economically rational choice to invest in education, as he or she would in stocks and bonds?

Shaffer has maintained that the entire notion of rate-of-return analysis of education has no place in economic theory because there is no way to appropriately apportion costs between consumption and benefit. He says that:

> Any attempt to show that rational individuals tend to undertake expenditure on education up to the point where the marginal productivity of the human capital produced by the process of education equals the rate of interest—a point at which the marginal expenditure on education yields a return equal to the return on marginal expenditure for any other factor of production—would be a mockery of economic theory. [42]

Shaffer admittedly represents a rather extreme viewpoint, which rejects the idea of education being treated as a pecuniary benefit, but even an advocate of investment must admit that there is much imprecision of measurement introduced by the intractable problems of delineating consumption from investment. If, for example, only one-half the costs of education were attributable to consumption, then the benefits derived, compared to actual investment, would be doubled. As Bowen observes, for those who say that the college years were the "best years of his life," the consumption portion may even be more than one-half. [43] Too, the study of humanities, art, and music may well have a much higher consumption purpose than the study of business, education, or law. Certainly, there would appear to be less consumption in vocational training, which is designed specifically for a particular job.

This issue has not been satisfactorily resolved and is not likely to be. Yet, education advocates may be secure in knowing that in most studies few or none of the costs are attributable to consumption and most or all costs are assumed to be investment; thus rates of return to education are generally understated.

Benefits.   Benefits from education may be either monetary or nonmonetary and either private (individual) or social. Monetary returns are measurable and are therefore most commonly used in cost-benefit studies. The social externalities of education are difficult to quantify and are, therefore, seldom relied on in estimating returns to education. A discussion of social nonmonetary benefits is presented later in this chapter. Table 3–5 presents a categorization of both private and social benefits of education.

Direct benefits to the individual are typically measured by increases in earning power after completion of the educational program. Natural ability of the individual, ambition, family connections, family social and economic status, inherited wealth, race, sex, and education of parents may all have a bearing on future earning potential, but cannot be accurately quantified. For example, it has been estimated that anywhere from 5 to 35 percent of income differentials are attributable to differences in ability, [44] while Griliches and Mason have calculated the bias attributable to ability at only about 10 percent. [45] While estimates of the influence of native ability on economic returns vary widely, the overstatement does not appear to be a serious source of bias to determination of returns to investment in education.[46]

The most widely used method of calculating the cost-benefit of education is through rate-of-return analysis. This approach takes into account the costs of education to both the individual and society and relates them to the benefits to each. Benefits are measured only in terms of higher earnings throughout the working life of those who acquire the education. Rate-of-return analysis represents a major alternative to manpower studies for educational planning. The manpower method seeks to estimate the supply and demand of the work force by various educational levels and types, while the rate-of-return approach determines the economic benefits of acquiring higher levels and different types

TABLE 3–5 Private and Social Benefits of Education

PRIVATE (INDIVIDUAL) BENEFITS	SOCIAL BENEFITS
Direct Benefits	

Monetary
  Net increase in earnings after taxes
 	
  Additional fringe benefits
	Increase in taxes paid by the educated as a result of education

Nonmonetary Increased satisfaction derived from exposure to new knowledge and cultural opportunities for both students and parents	
Indirect Benefits	

Monetary
  Work options available at each educational level
 	
  Increased consumption of goods and services due to extra income
	Increases in other income
	a) due to increasing productivity of future generations as children become better educated (intergeneration effect)

Nonmonetary
  Intergenerational effect between parent and child
 	
  Job satisfaction
	b) due to previously unemployed workers taking jobs vacated by program participants (vacuum effect)—indirect income effect
	
	c) due to reduced tax burden (tax effects)
	
	d) due to incremental productivity and earnings of workers (indirect income effect)

	Availability to employer of well-trained and skilled labor force
	Improved living conditions of neighbors

Source: Adapted from table by Asefa Gabregiorgis, "Rate of Return on Secondary Education in the Bahamas." (Ph.D. dissertation, University of Alberta), p. 75.

of education. For example, one may calculate the rates-of-return to various vocational training programs or to investment in teacher or legal education in universities.[47] Rate-of-return analysis measures the demand for a certain type of training among various types of occupational groups.

Rates-of-return are the interaction between several supply-and-demand effects. These groups will probably operate differently over time in various age groups. An oversupply of lawyers will likely drive down legal fees, reducing the return to investment in legal education. Although the freedom of the marketplace does not operate as fully for public school teachers as for lawyers because of the state's control of salaries, nevertheless, a scarcity of teachers in a certain geographical area or in a particular field of study would likely be reflected in higher wages to attract competent teachers and a resultingly higher rate of return.

Two methods are used for the measurement of costs and benefits, the net-present-value approach and the internal rate-of-return. The net present value is the sum of the benefits minus the sum of costs, both discounted at an appropriate rate. The result is the net value today of payments in the future.[48] The net present value requires that benefits minus costs be larger than zero.[49] To explain more fully, the value of both benefits and costs may be determined at any point in time. If one is looking into the future, it must be assumed that money invested today in education could have also been invested in alternative sources of income. It is, therefore, necessary to take into account the interest (or discount rate) that could have been earned by this alternative investment. Studies of this type will usually include two or three alternative discount rates of possibly 5, 8, and 12 percent. The net-present-value approach includes the discount rate in the formula and it is modified until the present value of benefits equates to the present value of costs.

Another model is the internal rate-of-return (IROR), which does not use the discount rate internal to the formula. Instead, the IROR is concerned only with the relationship of costs to benefits, not the total value of each. In this calculation the rate-of-return is derived and then compared to a chosen discount rate. For example, if it is found that a high-school education produces a rate-of-return of 16 percent and if a realistic alternative investment would produce a 10 percent rate, then the investment in education is more favorable by 6 percent. Those who want to delve more deeply into rate-of-return analysis may wish to refer to formulas given by Psacharopoulos, Cohn, and Alexander and Melcher.[50]

The IROR may be graphically represented as the interest rate which equates the present value of benefits with the present value of costs. The discount rate (or interest rate), r, at which the curve for benefits intersects the curve for costs, is the internal rate-of-return (see Figure 3–3).

A third model is the benefit-cost ratio, which compares benefits where a ratio is produced, which, if exceeding unity, denotes a positive payoff. Where

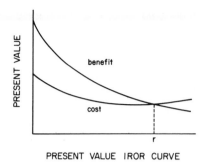

PRESENT VALUE IROR CURVE

FIGURE 3-3

the present value of benefits divided by the present value of costs exceeds one, then the project is worthwhile. For example, if the present value of benefits is $3,000 and the present value of costs is $1,000, then the benefit-cost ratio would be $3000/1000 = 3$. Since 3 is greater than unity, the investment would be a good investment.

RETURNS ON EDUCATIONAL INVESTMENT

The internal rate-of-return is the most commonly used approach in educational investment studies. Many such studies have been conducted since 1961, the results of which vary somewhat, depending on the particular statistical technique employed by the researcher, but by and large they show that education is a good investment for both the individual and the state. This holds true on the international level as well as within the United States. Psacharopoulos, in synthesizing the findings of 53 studies in 32 countries, found that both private and social rates-of-return for education were generally higher than returns to investment in physical capital.[51] Psacharopoulos concluded that per capita income differences among countries "can be better explained by differences in the endowments of human rather than physical capital."[52] Averaging rates-of-return for the 53 studies, he found that private rates-of-return for primary school were 23.7 percent per year, while for high school and college they were 16.3 and 17.5 percent, respectively. For social rates-of-return, he found primary to be 25.1 percent; secondary, 13.5 percent; and college, 11.3 percent.[53] When averages for developed and underdeveloped countries were considered, it was found that overall the returns to investment in human capital were greater in underdeveloped countries.

So many rate-of-return studies have been conducted for various phases of education in the United States that it is virtually impossible to identify them all, much less synthesize their results. Findings of several notable major studies, though, may be singled out. Hansen, in one of the earlier analyses, found that the private IROR for elementary schooling was probably infinite because the elementary-school child has no cost of schooling.[54] Children at such a young age cannot work; therefore, there are no foregone earnings and those who are enrolled in public school obtain their education free. Hanoch made similar observations, and Hines, Tweeten, and Redfern found that the private IROR for elementary-school children was 155 percent.[55]

Social returns for elementary schooling are substantially less, primarily because the state does have costs in conducting the public educational system and the social benefits under the IROR method only include direct returns to the state obtained through taxation. Hansen found the social IROR for elementary school to be 15 percent, and Hines, Tweeten, and Redfern discovered it to be 17.8 percent. Carnoy and Marenbach, in a 1975 study, found the social IROR for elementary schooling for white males to range from a low of 7.2 percent to a high of 13.2 percent, depending upon which year they used.[56]

Internal rates-of-return for the individual have been found to be as low as 13 percent per year[57] and as high as 49.1 percent, but studies have generally revealed rates in the 16 to 25 percent range. Social rates-of-return for secondary education are generally found to be between 10 and 19 percent per year.[58] Secondary education is therefore an attractive investment for both the individual and the state (see Figure 3-4).

Many studies have been conducted at the bachelor's degree level, with results usually indicating that a college education is a slightly less attractive investment than either secondary or elementary education. In 1975, Raymond and Sesnowitz, using data for 1970, reported a private IROR for college graduates to be 17.9 percent per year[59] and Carnoy and Marenbach found the IROR for the same year to be 15.4 percent.[60] Several other studies have found lower returns for various years from 1950 to 1973. In another major study, Eckaus found private rates-of-return for college graduates to be around 12 percent.[61] Such a general figure for all graduates is not of great value because of variations in income to be expected by graduates in different fields. For example, Eckaus shows that depending on certain assumptions regarding base income, the private internal rate-of-return for accountants is in the 12.5 to 16.5 percent range, while the private IROR for chemists may range from 13 to 21 percent.[62] Social rates-of-return for the bachelor's degree level usually appear to fall into the 10 to 13 percent range.

Graduate education reveals lower rates-of-return than any other level of education. Hanoch found that 17 plus years of education had an IROR for the individual of 7.0 percent. Tomaske found it to be 10 percent; Mincer, 7.3 percent; and Bailey and Schotta, interestingly, −1.0 percent.[63] If one proceeds to the doctorate, the returns seem to be improved over completion of a master's degree. The IROR for the Ph.D. has in most studies been found to range between 10.5 and 23.6 percent.[64] Different areas of training, of course, give various rates-of-return; the professor of natural science, for instance, has an IROR of 10.5 percent, if one assumes that without the advanced graduate

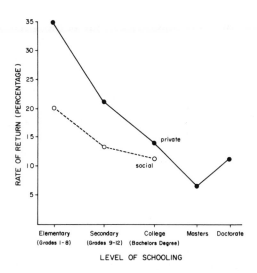

FIGURE 3-4 **Private and social rates-of-return to investment in education by level of education. Averages of several major studies conducted for the United States.**

Note that no good empirical data exist by which to estimate social rates-of-return for graduate education.

education the alternative employment would have been secondary-school teaching.[65] Dentists are shown by Eckaus to have an IROR of from 18.5 to 37 percent. Some studies have produced negative private rates-of-return for some graduate fields of study. Thomas, for example, found that graduate training for teachers produced a negative return,[66] and Siegfried in 1971 found a negative private IROR for the Ph.D. in economics.[67] Other disciplines also suffer from declining returns to educational investment, particularly at the graduate level, as documented by Freeman in his book *The Overeducated American*.[68] Generally, though, the graduate, if he or she uses some economic rationality in selecting a career, can receive a rate-of-return which makes the investment in college education pay a highly positive return. Today, though, it appears that use of careful selectivity in choosing a career is necessary; no longer is it possible for those with a liberal education, with no particular career goal in mind, to gain significant economic returns. This, of course, says nothing of the great and rewarding consumption benefits derived from a liberal college education.

Social rates-of-return to graduate study may be lower than private rates-of-return for the same level, especially where students attended public institutions. Graduate education is quite expensive to the state because of the lower student-teacher ratio and the higher salaries generally paid to graduate professors. Of course, both social and private rates-of-return are substantially diminished by the higher foregone earnings expected from people of high educational levels who attend schools for a period of time in lieu of working. Of course, one should bear in mind that the benefits side of the social rates-of-return is calculated using only increased taxes paid by the educated individual. Researchers have not been able to quantify the effects on the economy of new inventions which have come about as a result of graduate research or the many other social externalities which may benefit society from graduate education. Certainly, as far as school teachers are concerned, economists have not derived methods of measuring the social value of having trained teachers return to the classroom and spend their lives in the direct production of human capital. Actually, if this were taken into account, it could well be shown that the social rate-of-return to investment in teacher education is one of the most productive investments a state can make.

Studies of vocational education programs have generally shown rates-of-return to be quite high for both the individual and the state. Problems related to partitioning benefits between vocational and academic programs have created data difficulties for benefit-cost studies in secondary programs, while postsecondary vocational programs are much easier to analyze. At the secondary level, a study by Hu, Lee, Stromsdorfer, and Kaufman compared a vocational education program to the academic programs in three large cities. The private rates-of-return were found to be extremely high, with an estimated IROR of 56.8 percent.[69] Lower rates were subsequently found in other studies by Corazzini and Taussig.[70] Alexander and Melcher found substantial rates-of-return to certain postsecondary education courses in licensed practical nursing and heating and air conditioning, but found negative private and social returns to cosmetology.[71] As with both undergraduate and graduate programs, the rates-of-return vary substantially among the courses and programs in vocational education. While on the whole vocational education appears to be quite productive, studies which disaggregate both the costs and benefits should be conducted to provide more definitive information.

EXTERNAL BENEFITS TO INVESTMENT IN EDUCATION

To this point we have considered only a portion of the benefits to investment in education. The entire value of education must also be viewed in light of its social possibilities and consequences. The monetary benefits considered in rates-of-return include only the value of increased earnings of the individual and the value of additional taxes collected by the state. Actually, the direct monetary returns are not inclusive of all the economic returns accruable from investment in education. In the broader economic context, benefits include:

> (1) anything which increases production; (2) anything which reduces the need to incur costs such as for law enforcement, thereby releasing resources for alternative uses; and (3) anything which increases welfare possibilities directly, such as development of public-spiritedness or social consciousness of one's neighbor.[72]

Increased Labor Productivity. The first of these refers to the overall strengthening of the economic system through increased worker productivity. This is not a direct monetary return to education, but a broader economic externality of education. Of course, as Denison documents, human capital does not alone determine the optimum productivity of a country, but it is a major contributor. In recent years, the United States has experienced a relative decline in worker productivity which cannot be attributed to a decrease in educational level but rather to inadequacy of capital formation and obsolescence of physical assets of many of the major industrial firms in the United States. Further, in some cases, the relative decline may also be attributed to poor planning and questionable management practices.

By and large, though, education can improve the general environment in which production takes place, having a positive effect beyond that to those who are actually receiving the education. The educated may be better prepared to pass on or receive training than the uneducated or may more adequately enhance productive psychological and motivational factors.

Even though the value of education as it relates to work has been drawn into the question and an all-out attack on credentialism has been launched in recent years,[73] the value of education for employment is readily apparent. The more educated person in the job market receives preferential treatment from the employer. Whether this is justified is largely irrelevant if the marketplace responds in this manner. Employers appear to recognize that the educated worker has favorable external effects on other workers and on the firm in general. An interdependence exists whereby both the worker and the firm have a financial interest in the education of fellow workers.[74]

Employers believe that education of the employee improves the financial potential of the firm. There is a definite positive relationship between the amount of formal education and on-the-job training received.[75] Firms apparently have found that greater productivity can be achieved with less cost of investing in the more educated employees. Greater benefits can be obtained by grafting job training on to the knowledge already acquired from formal schooling.[76] It may also be that the employer responds in part to the worker's own willingness to invest in himself, since employer investment in the worker appears to increase in about the same proportion as the worker's self-investment in schooling.

The less-educated experience a greater amount of unemployment. On the average, "job losers" have almost a year and a half less education than "job keepers."[77] Labor turnover and unemployment are related to consumer demand for goods and services. Even though the correlation is rather weak, the more educated, being more generally employed in service jobs, have greater employment stability.[78] Some evidence also shows that in certain areas of the economy, physical capital is more likely to be substituted for unskilled than for skilled labor. Consequently, the less-educated labor force is more susceptible to layoffs due to advances in technology and fluctuations in types of goods produced and methods of production.[79] Thus, education may be viewed as a type of private (and social) hedge against technological displacement. Weisbrod called this the "hedging option," the value of which is difficult to quantify.[80] Further, inexperienced and uneducated workers who earn less than minimum wage have higher unemployment. Better-educated workers may well have the edge in communication, discipline of the mind, flexibility, and adaptability. Also, the more educated the worker, the more likely he or she is to be receptive to new ideas and knowledge.[81]

The production process may be regarded as the transformation of resources into goods and services. Transformation is generally more efficient if the process utilizes educated workers, even though the precise nature of the interaction between education and economic productivity is not known. Bowen lists six ways that worker productivity is increased by education:

(1) *Quantity of product*—workers with higher levels of education produce more goods and services in a given time period because of their greater skill, dexterity, and knowledge.

(2) *Quality of product*—the more educated produce better goods and render services with greater skill and/or sensitivity to human conditions.

(3) *Product mix*—educated workers may be able to produce goods and services which are more highly prized by society than those produced by workers with less education.

(4) *Participation in the labor force*—educated workers are less susceptible to lost time from unemployment and illness, and are usually characterized by higher aspirations.

(5) *Allocative ability*—workers, through education, may be better able to assess their own talents; to achieve greater skills; and to be more receptive to new technologies, new products, and new ideas.

(6) *Job satisfaction*—the educated may have greater job satisfaction because they tend to acquire jobs with greater psychic rewards.[82]

Machlup has summarized the effects of education on increased productivity as follows:

It is with regard to . . . improvements in the quality of labor, that education can play a really significant role. Positive effects may be expected on five scores: (a) better working habits and discipline, increased labor efforts, and greater reliability; (b) better health through more wholesome and sanitary ways of living: (c) improved skills, better comprehension of working requirements, and increased efficiency; (d) prompter adaptability to momentary changes, especially in jobs which require quick evaluation of new information, and, in general, fast reactions; and (e) increased capability to move into more productive occupations when opportunities arise. All levels of education may contribute to improving the quality of labor.[83]

Education differs in a basic way from most other major social or public services in that it constitutes an investment in knowledge and skills which can yield economic and social benefits in the future. It differs materially from governmental welfare or health expenditures, which may be characterized as maintenance of human capital rather than development. While it is true that payment of health bills for the needy may help heal and return them to the work force or that welfare payments for food or shelter preserve human capital, it is nevertheless important to note that neither of these public programs actually increases the worth of human capital. The same human raw material is maintained but not necessarily enhanced. More nonproductive yet is public expenditure for police protection and prison systems. While every society expends large sums on these public functions, the benefits cannot be classified as investments in the development of human capital except in a limited sense where rehabilitation of prisoners actually works and the individual is returned to the labor force as a positive factor in the production process. Largely, though, penal expenditures must be viewed as nonproductive in the economic sense. While it is true that benefits from these public services cannot be completely self-contained, it is obvious that provision of public education is quite different from those services characterized as social services, and education should not be treated in the same light by legislators. There is a fundamental difference between the mere maintenance of human capital and the development of human capital.

Reduced Need for Other Services. This is not to say, of course, that public expenditures for health and welfare are not desirable and necessary on humanitarian grounds, nor is it to say public expenditures for law enforcement should or can be reduced; but it is important to note that education must be considered in a different context—as a remedy to the problems and not as a problem itself. Increased investment in education will tend to reduce the necessity of placing more public revenue into health, welfare, and the penal system. An increment of education reduces government expenditures on crime prevention, fire protection, public health, and medical care.[84] It may be argued that education reduces crime primarily because education reduces unemployment, and the employed commit fewer crimes.[85] Some portion of criminal behavior can be attributed to a lack of education.[86] With a rise in family income, a corresponding decrease in delinquency may be found; since more education and greater income are related, a similar relationship exists between education and crime.[87]

Ehrlich found that inequalities in the distribution of schooling may have an effect on the amount of crime, suggesting that equalization of educational opportunity may be a proper governmental goal in crime reduction. Whether more education will serve as a deterrent to crime may depend, according to Ehrlich, on the extent to which the economic returns to crime are reduced. Whether crime pays or not will thus depend on education coupled with alternative methods of impairing the economic success of criminals.[88]

Certain studies have shown that prisoners have lower educational attainment than the average person[89] and that illiteracy among criminals is much higher than for the population as a whole.[90] Low educational attainment seems to increase the likelihood of one's "turning to illegal means to fulfill his social and economic desires."[91] One national commission found in a survey of riot participants that inadequate education and underemployment were among the top four causes of disorder.[92]

Levin estimated the cost of crime against persons and property in the United States to be $1.1 billion per year; the cost of law enforcement and the criminal judiciary to be $4.2 billion; private costs, $1.9 billion; and income foregone by inmates to be $1 billion;—a total of $8.2 billion. If one-half the costs, an upper limit, are attributable to lack of education, we find that an astonishing $4.1 billion could have been saved by further education. Even with the lower limit of Levin's estimate, 25 percent attributable to inadequate education, over $2 billion in costs of crime could have been prevented by more education.[93]

Some contrary assertions have suggested that student riots of the late 1960s were evidence that education does not inculcate a respect for the law,[94] and that compulsory attendance beyond a certain grade level may lead to antagonism and juvenile delinquency. Such assertions are, though, outweighed by the positive relationship between education and crime reduction.

Recipients of welfare generally have lower educational attainment than the average person. Studies by the U.S. Department of Health, Education and Welfare have shown that incapacitated and unemployed AFDC fathers have median levels of education far below the average. About 76 percent of the incapacitated fathers and 61.2 percent of the unemployed fathers did not have a high-school education. Since this high percentage did not reflect the 15.9 percent of incapacitated and 22.8 percent of unemployed for whom no educational data were available, the percentages of inadquate education may be even higher.[95] Other data show that 84 percent of all AFDC unemployed fathers had less than a high-school education.[96] Over 82 percent of the AFDC mothers lacked a high-school education.[97] AFDC recipients who did become self-supporting generally had more education than those who did not.[98]

In attempting to quantify the impact of welfare costs on the taxpayer, Levin, in another part of the aforementioned study, found that AFDC, medical assistance, and general welfare assistance cost $5.9 billion in 1970, and unemployment compensation amounted to $4.3 billion. Levin estimated that an upper limit of 50 percent and a lower limit of 25 percent of public assistance, $2.96 billion and $1.48 billion respectively, could be attributed to low levels of education. With an upper limit of 25 percent and a lower limit of 15 percent, he determined the costs of unemployment compensation due to inadequate education to be $1.08 billion and $648 million, respectively.[99] Whether these costs are precisely accurate is probably of little consequence; the importance of the data rests on the establishment of an apparently strong relationship between level of education and public expenditure on welfare. Theoretically, the efficiency of the use of public resources may be enhanced by increasing educational levels, with a corresponding decline in the necessity for welfare.[100]

Social Consciousness and Intergenerational Transfers. Education benefits many people other than the student, including the student's children, who receive positive intergenerational transfers of knowledge, and neighbors who are affected by favorable social values developed by schooling.

Certain nonmonetary returns to education are well known and taken largely for granted. Ignorant people can be more easily misled and propagandized than the educated. As discussed more fully in Chapter 1, the freedom implicit in a democratic society is premised on an educated citizenry (see Table 3–5).

If one can assume that the household is a small economic enterprise or multiproduct firm which produces many desirables from which members of the family derive satisfaction—such as good health, physical exercise, and nutrition, which are the result of such production activities as convalescing, jogging, and eating—then it is possible to measure the impact of education on the efficiency of the enterprise. In devising this model, Michael theorized that the introduction of additional education into the household's production process would be analogous to applying new technology to a firm.[101] He concluded that the level of schooling systematically influences consumer behavior independent of the effect of income. His data further suggest that education increases the efficiency of the household's production process.

The general well-being of the family may also be affected by education's role in increasing the individual's capacity to utilize and capitalize on situations which will increase both his or her consumption and economic benefits. Presumably a more highly educated individual will possess a certain economic serendipity which affects his or her economic choices. Solmon examined the influence of education on saving behavior over and above the ability to earn more on the job, to consume more efficiently, and to generally enjoy life more fully.[102] From reviewing existing saving and consumption-function theories, Solmon concluded that saving propensities tend to rise with schooling level of the family head. It may be presumed that such tendencies toward frugality will contribute to ordered growth of the income and wealth of society and provide for general economic stability. He further found, in studying attitudes, that one could infer that additional private benefits of schooling may be found in greater efficiency of portfolio management.

Today's problems created by worldwide overpopulation will certainly have an important impact not only on the socioeconomic systems of the world, but also on the ecological system of the planet. In recent years, great controversies have surrounded the desirable goal of zero population growth. Population growth usually starts at home, and its economic aspects can be reduced to the micro level of the household. Familial benefits can be maximized by the proper balance of "child services" passed on to the offspring. It may be theorized that the quality of the child is higher if the time and goods devoted to him are greater. For example, family resources may permit the parent to both purchase a musical instrument and provide music instruction for the child. There is little doubt that positive intergenerational transfers are enhanced by limiting the number of children and increasing the parental time devoted to each child. It has been found that the correlation between education and family size is negative. This may be the result of the impact of schooling on the husband's and wife's preferences, or it may be the result of a realistic economic assessment of the household, reflecting an increase in the price of children as the educational level of the couple increases.

The level of education has been found to have a consistently high relationship to the use of contraceptives.[103] In 1965 the percentage of women who had used oral contraceptives was over three times as high among the highest educated group as among the lowest. The educated are more aware of, more receptive to, and more effective in their use and selection of contraceptive techniques.[104] Michael found that the relationship between education of the wife and fertility was negative and statistically significant, indicating that the price of the wife's time accruing from increased education may be an important deterrent against overpopulation.[105]

The influence of the education of women on the economy of the family and the nation has not gone unnoticed. Although the rates-of-return for investment in women's schooling are less than for men's, for reasons including job discrimination and home care options,[106] the benefits of education are nevertheless substantial. Women's participation in the labor force is accompanied by a striking relationship with the level of education. Better-educated women are more likely to be in the labor force.[107] The economic explanation for this is that education raises women's productivity in the labor market more than productivity at home, making it more costly for highly educated women to remain at home.

The positive impact of education on women is not lost, though, by the time they expend at home. As women become more educated and spend a greater amount of time in the labor force, one might assume that they spend a smaller proportion of their time in home production and that a decrease in home production time indicates a corresponding decrease in child care activities. The data do not bear out such assumptions. To the contrary, better-educated working mothers generally spend more time with their children in effective and positive intergenerational transfer. The better-educated mothers spend more time in "physical care" and in activities related to social and educational development of children, including reading to them, helping with lessons, and taking them to social and educational functions.[108]

Intergenerational transfer of knowledge is therefore much more pronounced among educated households. Educational investments in one generation undoubtedly have an important impact on succeeding generations.

NOTES

1. For an excellent discussion of the history of human capital see Elchanan Cohn, *The Economics of Education*, rev. ed. (Cambridge, Mass.: Ballinger Publishing Company, 1979), pp. 13–26.

2. Barbara W. Tuchman, *A Distant Mirror: The Calamitous 14th Century* (New York: Alfred A. Knopf, 1978), pp. 119–20.

3. Theodore W. Schultz, "Investment in Human Capital," *American Economic Review*, 51 (March 1961), 1–17.

4. Sir William Petty, *Political Arithmetick, or A Discourse Concerning the Extent and Value of Lands, Buildings, etc.* (London: 1666).

5. John Stuart Mill, *Principles of Political Economy*, Vol. I, rev. ed. (London: Colonial Press, 1900), p. 9.

6. Adam Smith, *The Wealth of Nations*, rev. ed. (New York: Modern Library, 1937), p. 265.

7. R. Blandy, "Marshall on Human Capital: R Note," *Journal of Political Economy*, 75 (December 1967), 874–75

8. Alfred Marshall, *Principles of Economics*, 8th ed. (London: Macmillan & Company, 1930), pp. 787–88.

9. Horace Mann, From the 12th Report (1848), One of twelve *Annual Reports*, made by Mann to the State Board of Education, Massachusetts.

10. *Ibid.*

11. H. Von Thunen, "Costs of Education as Formation of Productive Capital," in *Readings in the Economics of Education*, eds. M. J. Bowman and others (Paris: UNESCO, 1968).

12. See E.A. Caswell, *The Money Value of Education* (Washington D.C.: Government Printing Office, 1917).

13. Theodore W. Schultz, *Investment in Human Capital* (New York: Free Press, 1971), p. 22.

14. *Ibid.*

15. Schultz, *op. cit.* in f. 3, pp. 1–17.

16. Frederick H. Harbison, *Human Resources as the Wealth of Nations* (New York: Oxford University Press, 1973), p. 3.

17. *Ibid.*

18. W. Arthur Lewis, *The Theory of Economic Growth* (London: George Allen & Unwin Ltd., 1977), pp. 183–84.

19. Mark Blaug, (ed.) *Economics of Education* (New York: Penguin Books, 1972).

20. Lewis, *op. cit.*, p. 183.

21. Eli Ginsberg, *The Human Economy* (New York: McGraw-Hill Book Company, 1976), p. 47.

22. *Ibid.*, pp. 70–71.

23. Pitirim A. Sorokin, *Hunger as a Factor in Human Affairs* (Gainesville, Fla.: University Presses of Florida, 1975), pp. 156–57.

24. Burton A. Weisbrod, "Education and Investment in Human Capital," *Journal of Political Economy*, 70, No. 5 (Pt. 2, 1962 Suppl.), 106–23.

25. *Ibid.*

26. W.G. Bowen, "Assessing the Economic Contribution of Education: An Appraisal of Alternative Approaches," *Higher Education. Report of the Committee under the Chairmanship of Lord Robbins, Report: 961–63* (London: H.M.S.O., 1963), 73–96.

27. Education Department, Chamber of Commerce of the United States, *Education: An Investment in People* (Washington D.C.: 1961), pp. 2–3.

28. *Ibid.*, pp. 4–23.

29. "Targets for Education in Europe" (paper delivered at Washington Conference of O.E.C.D., 1961), p. 75.

30. John W. Kendrick, *Productivity Trends in the United States* (Princeton, N.J.: Princeton University Press, 1961), p. 79.

31. B.F. Massell, "Capital Formation and Technological Change in United States Manufacturing," *Review of Economics and Statistics* (May 1960), pp. 182–88.

32. Solomon Fabricant, *Prerequisites for Economic Growth* (New York: National Conference Board, 1959).

33. For an excellent explanation of the aggregate production function, see Cohn, *op. cit.*, pp. 142–45.

34. Theodore W. Schultz, "Education and Economic Growth," in *Social Forces Influencing American Education*, ed N. B. Henry (Chicago: University of Chicago Press, 1961), pp. 46–88.

35. Edward F. Denison, *The Sources of Economic Growth in the United States*, (New York: Committee for Economic Development).

36. Edward F. Denison, *Accounting for United States Economic Growth, 1929–1969* (Washington, D.C.: Brookings Institution, 1974).

37. See explanation of Denison's methodology in Cohn, *op. cit.*, p. 155.

38. Hector Correa, "Sources of Economic Growth in Latin America," *Southern Economic Journal* 37 (July 1970), pp. 17–31.

39. Edward F. Denison, *Why Growth Rates Differ?* (Washington, D.C.: Brookings Institution, 1967).

40. Seymour E. Harris, *The Market for College Graduates and Related Aspects of Education and Income* (Cambridge, Mass: Harvard University Press, 1949), p. 64.

41. Herman P. Miller, *Rich Man, Poor Man* (New York: Thomas Y. Crowell Company, Inc., 1971), p. 168.

42. H.G. Shaffer, "Investment in Human Capital: Comment," *American Economic Review* 52, No. 4 (1961), 1026–35.

43. W. G. Bowen, *op. cit.*, pp. 73–96.

44. P. Taubman and Terence Wales, "Education as an Investment and a Screening Device," in *Education, Income and Human Behavior*, ed. F. Thomas, Juster (New York: McGraw-Hill Book Company 1975), pp. 95–121; and P. Taubman "Personal Characteristics and the Distribution of Earnings," in *The Personal Distribution of Incomes*, ed. A. B. Atkinson (London: George Allen and Unwin, 1976), pp. 193–226.

45. Zwi Griliches and William M. Mason, "Education, Income and Ability," in *Investment in Education*, ed. T. W. Schultz (Chicago: University of Chicago Press, 1971), p. 87.

46. John C. Hause, "Earnings Profile: Ability and Schooling," in ed., T. W. Schultz, *op cit.* in f. 45, p. 131.

47. Richard S. Eckaus, *Estimating the Returns to Education: A Disaggregated Approach* (Berkeley, Calif.: Carnegie Commission on Higher Education, 1973).

48. Asefa Gabregiorgis, *Rate of Return on Secondary Education in the Bahamas*, (Ph.D. dissertation, University of Alberta), p. 117.

49. See formulas in Appendix.

50. George Psacharopoulos, *Returns to Education* (San Francisco: Jossey-Bass, Inc., Publishers, 1973). Cohn, *op. cit.*; Kern Alexander and Thomas Melcher, *A Computerized System for Benefit-Cost Analysis in Vocational Education* (Gainesville, Fla.: Institute for Educational Finance, University of Florida, 1980).

51. Psacharopoulos, *op. cit.*

52. *Ibid.*, p. 17.

53. *Ibid.*, p. 65.

54. W. Lee Hansen, "Total and Private Rates of Return to Investment in Schooling," *Journal of Political Economy* 71 (April 1963), 128–40.

55. G. Hanoch, "An Economic Analysis of Earnings and Schooling," *Journal of Human Resources* 2 (Summer 1967), 310–29; F. Hines, L. Tweeten, and M. Redfern, "Social and Private Rates of Return to Investment in Schooling, by Race-Sex Groups and Regions," *Journal of Human Resources*, 5 (Summer 1970), 318–40.

56. M. Carnoy and D. Marenbach, "The Return to Schooling in the United States, 1939–69," *Journal of Human Resources*, 10 (Summer 1975), 312–31.

57. Jacob Mincer, *Schooling, Experience and Earnings* (New York: Columbia University Press, 1974).

58. Carnoy and Marenbach, *op. cit.*

59. R. D. Raymond and M. L. Sesnowitz, "The Returns to Investments in Higher Education: Some New Evidence," *Journal of Human Resources* 10 (Spring 1975), 139–54.

60. Carnoy and Marenbach, *op. cit.*

61. Eckaus, *op. cit.*, p. 5.

62. *Ibid.*, p. 22.

63. Hanoch, *op. cit.;* J.A. Tomaske, "Private and Social Rates of Return to Education of Academicians: Note," *American Economic Review*, 64 (March 1974), 220–24; Mincer, *op. cit.;* D. Bailey and C. Schotta, "Private and Social Rates of Return to Education of Academicians," *American Economic Review*, 62 (March 1972), 19–31.

64. See: O. Ashenfelter and J.D. Mooney, "Graduate Education, Ability, and Earnings," *Review of Economics and Statistics*, 50 (February 1968), 78–86; Y. Weiss, "Investment in Graduate Education," *American Economic Review* 61 (December 1971), 833–52.

65. Eckaus, *op. cit.*, p. 24

66. S. Thomas, *Development of a Prototype Teacher Salary Schedule for the State of Florida Based on Rates of Return Analysis* (Ph.D. dissertation, University of Florida, 1974).

67. J.J. Siegfried, "Rate of Return to the Ph.D. in Economics," *Industrial and Labor Relations Review*, 24 (April 1971), 420–31.

68. Richard B. Freeman, *The Overeducated American* (New York: Academic Press, Inc., 1976).

69. T.W. Hu and others, *A Cost-Effectiveness Study of Vocational Education* (University Park, Pa.: Institute for Research on Human Resources, The Pennsylvania State University, 1969).

70. A.J. Corazzini, "The Decision to Invest in Vocational Education: An Analysis of Costs and Benefits," *Journal of Human Resources* 3 (Supp.), 88–120; M.K. Taussig, "An Economic Analysis of Vocational Education in the New York City High Schools," *Journal of Human Resources* 3 (Supp.), 59–87.

71. Alexander and Melcher, *op. cit.*

72. Burton A. Weisbrod, *External Benefits of Public Education* (Princeton, N.J.: Princeton University Industrial Relations Section, Department of Economics, 1964), p. 17.

73. *Work in America*, Report of a Special Task Force to the Secretary of Health, Education and Welfare (Cambridge, Mass.: MIT Press, 1973), pp. 134–52.

74. Burton A. Weisbrod, "Investing in Human Capital," in *Education and the Economics of Human Capital*, ed. Ronald A. Wykstra (New York: Free Press, 1971), pp. 79–81.

75. Jacob Mincer, "On-the-Job Training: Costs, Returns, and Some Implications," *Journal of Political Economy* 70 (October 1962 Supp.).

76. Richard Perlman, *The Economics of Education* (New York: McGraw-Hill Book Company, 1973), p. 32.

77. John D. Owen, *School Inequality and the Welfare State* (Baltimore: Johns Hopkins University Press, 1974), p. 91.

78. *Ibid.*

79. *Ibid.*

80. Weisbrod, *op. cit.* in f. 72.

81. J. Ronnie Davis, "The Social and Economic Externalities of Education," in *Economic Factors Affecting the Financing of Education*, Vol. 2, eds. R.L. Johns and others (Gainesville, Fla.:

National Educational Finance Project, 1970), p. 66.

82. H.R. Bowen, *Investment in Learning* (San Francisco: Jossey-Bass, Inc., Publishers, 1977), pp. 159-60.

83. Fritz Machlup, *Education and Economic Growth* (Lincoln, Nebr.: University of Nebraska Press, 1970), pp. 7–8.

84. Carl S. Shoup, *Public Finance* (Chicago: Aldine Publishing Co., 1969), p. 97.

85. Weisbrod, *op. cit.*, p. 31.

86. Werner Hirsch, Elbert W. Segalhorst, and Morton J. Marcus, *Spillover of Public Education Costs and Benefits* (Berkeley: University of California Press, 1964), p. 342.

87. Belton Fleisher, "The Effect of Income on Delinquency," *American Economic Review* 56, No. 1 (March 1966), 118–37.

88. Isaac Ehrlich, "On the Relation between Education and Crime" in ed. F. Thomas Juster *op. cit.*, pp. 313–37.

89. Joseph D. Lohman, Llyod E. Ohlin, and Dietrich C. Reitzer, *Description of Convicted Felons as Manpower Resources in a National Emergency*, p. 24, cited by Edwin H. Sutherland and Donald R. Cressey, *Principles of Criminology*, 7th ed. (New York: J.B. Lippincott Company, 1968), p. 251.

90. Price Chenault, "Education," in *Contemporary Corrections*, ed. Paul W. Tappan (New York: McGraw-Hill Book Company, 1951), p. 224.

91. Lillian Dean Webb, *The Development of a Model to Measure Selected Economic Externalities of Education* (Ph.D. dissertation, University of Florida, 1975).

92. National Commission on the Causes and Prevention of Violence, *Crimes of Violence*, Vol. 11 (Washington, D.C.: Government Printing Office, 1968), p. 394.

93. Henry M. Levin, *The Effects of Dropping Out: A Report to the Select Committee on Equal Opportunity of the United States Senate* (Washington, D.C.: Government Printing Office, 1972).

94. Machlup, *op. cit.*, pp. 55–56.

95. David B. Epply, "The AFDC Family in the 1960's," *Welfare in Review* 8, No. 5 (September–October 1970), 11–13.

96. Edward Prescott, William Tash, and William Usdane, "Training and Employability: The Effect of MDTA on AFDC Recipients," *Welfare in Review* 9, No. 1 (Janaury–February 1971), 2.

97. Perry Levinson, "How Employable Are AFDC Women?" *Welfare in Review* 8, No. 4 (July–August 1970), 12–13.

98. Webb, *op. cit.*, p. 58.

99. Levin, *op. cit.*

100. See Kern Alexander, "The Value of an Education," *Journal of Education Finance* Vol. 1, No. 4 (Spring, 1976), 447–50.

101. Robert T. Michael, "Education and Consumption," in ed. F. Thomas Juster, *op. cit.*, pp. 235–52.

102. Lewis C. Solmon, "The Relation between Schooling and Savings Behavior: An Example of Indirect Effects of Education," in ed. F. Thomas Juster, *op. cit.*, pp. 253–93.

103. Norman B. Ryder and Charles F. Westoff, *Reproduction in the United States, 1965* (Princeton, N.J.: Princeton University Press, 1971).

104. *Ibid.*

105. Robert T. Michael, "Education and Fertility," in ed. F. Thomas Juster, *op. cit.*, pp. 339–64.

106. F.U. Edgeworth, "Equal Pay to Men and Women for Equal Work," *Economic Journal* 32 (December 1922), 431–57; See also Gary S. Becker, *The Economics of Discrimination* (Chicago: University of Chicago Press, 1971).

107. Arleen Leibowitz, "Education and the Allocation of Women's Time," in ed. F. Thomas Juster, *op. cit.*, pp. 171–72.

108. *Ibid.*, p. 174.

SELECTED REFERENCES

BLAUG, MARK. *An Introduction to the Economics of Education*. New York: Penquin Books, 1970.

BOWEN, HOWARD R. *Investment in Learning*. San Francisco: Jossey-Bass, Inc., Publishers, 1977.

COHN, ELCHANAN. *The Economics of Education*. Cambridge, Mass.: Ballinger Publishing Company, 1979.

ECKAUS, RICHARD S. *Estimating the Returns to Education: A Disaggregated Approach*. Berkeley, Calif.: Carnegie Commission on Higher Education, 1973.

GINSBERG, ELI. *The Human Economy*. New York: McGraw-Hill Book Company, 1976.

HARBISON, FREDERICK H. *Human Resources as the Wealth of Nations*. New York: Oxford University Press, 1973.

MACHLUP, FRITZ. *Education and Economic Growth*. Lincoln, Nebr: University of Nebraska Press, 1970.

MILLER, HERMAN P. *Rich Man Poor Man*. New York: Thomas Y. Crowell Company, Inc., 1971.

PSACHAROPOULOS, GEORGE. *Returns to Education*. San Francisco: Jossey-Bass, Inc. Publishers, 1973.

JOHNS, ROE L., and others, eds. *Economic Factors Affecting the Financing of Education*. Gainesville, Fla: National Educational Finance Project, Vol. 2, 1970.

ROGERS, DANIEL C., and HIRSCH S. RUCHLIN. *Economics and Education: Principles and Applications*. New York: Free Press, 1971.

SCHULTZ, THEODORE W., ed. *Investment in Education: The Equity-Efficiency Quandry*. Chicago: University of Chicago Press, 1972.

SCHULTZ, THEODORE W. *Investment in Human Capital*. New York: Free Press, 1971.

SCHULTZ, THEODORE W. *Investing in People: The Economics of Population Quality*. Berkeley: University of California Press, 1981.

VAIZEY, JOHN. *The Economics of Education*. London: Faber & Faber, 1962.

CHAPTER FOUR
ECONOMICS
OF SCHOOL FINANCE
*Trends in Demand
and Support
for the Public Schools*

In the private economy of a free-enterprise nation, the individual votes with dollars for the economic goods he or she chooses to purchase. This economic system stimulates the private economy to produce quickly many types of goods to satisfy consumer wants. But as was pointed out in Chapter 2, some consumer wants cannot be supplied by the private economy as well as they can be by the public economy. Public education is one of the principal goods provided by the public economy.

The machinery for determining what economic goods should be produced and what the quantity and quality of those goods should be differs considerably in the two economies. The machinery of the private economy moves quickly to supply a human want very soon after the want emerges, provided the enterprise can earn a profit. For example, the private economy is so responsive to public demand that it has the power to supply within a few months great quantities of such trivial economic goods as the latest children's toy fads.

It has been apparent to informed observers for many years that the survival of individuals and even of the welfare of the nation requires a greatly expanded and considerably improved educational program. It has been extremely difficult to translate this obvious need into public demand for more adequate investment in education.

At this point it is important to note the difference between the concept of need and the concept of demand. What is needed for the welfare of the individual and of society may not always be wanted. For example, people need physical exercise in order to preserve health, but some may not want to make the effort to obtain the exercise needed. A state may need to improve the quality of its school system, but the legislature may not want to levy the additional taxes necessary to meet that need. On the other hand, a demand for a good is always wanted, but it may not be needed. A corpulent individual may want a second piece of cheesecake, and therefore there is a demand for it although it is not needed. At this writing there seems to be a popular demand for major increases in defense expenditures, but there are some people who question the need for them. In a free society the people individually and collectively make the decisions which result in the demands for the goods and services wanted, regardless of need.[1]

In the private sector, the policy of some progressive business organizations is to "make needers wanters, make wanters buyers and make buyers satisfied users." This seems to be a reasonable policy for educational leaders to follow. But the public economy moves slowly to meet educational needs, because political consensus must be obtained before the decision can be made to provide for a need through the public economy. At this writing, such political decisions must be made by some sixteen thousand local school districts, fifty states, and the federal government.

There is another important difference between the two economies. In the private economy, the individual purchases only the economic goods he wants. But in the public economy, once a political decision has been made to provide an economic good, all individuals subject to the taxes levied must purchase the good whether they want it or not. For example, if a decision to provide public kindergartens is made, each taxpayer must participate in the financing of kindergartens regardless of whether he or she wants them. The political decision may be made by popular vote of the electorate concerned or by representatives of the electorate in such bodies as boards of education and legislatures. Usually decisions of this kind are made by majority vote, but in some cases more than a majority is required. The process of obtaining a political decision frequently involves much controversy. For these reasons, the time required to supply a human want usually is much greater in the public economy than in the private economy.

Expenditures for different economic goods in the private economy represent fairly accurately current consumer choices, assuming that the supply of goods is equal to the demand. But the same thing is not true in the public economy, because consumer wants may go unsatisfied for a long period of time. Also, demands for goods produced in the private economy are stimulated by clever advertising and high-pressure selling. Public funds cannot be expended directly for these purposes by most governments. Therefore, it is not entirely accurate to assume that expenditures for public education for a given year represent consumer demand for public education during that year.

The purpose of this chapter is to explore trends in expenditures for the public schools since 1930 and to appraise the social and economic forces that will affect demand and expenditures for public education in future years. Trends in expenditures for higher education are not presented here because of the difficulty of obtaining comparable data for this fifty-year period.

It is not a simple matter to appraise trends in school expenditures. Comparison of total current dollar expenditures for one year with those of another reveals only that more such dollars were expended during one year than during another. Such a comparison becomes more misleading as the time span increases. This is especially true during times of rapid changes in prices, population, and economic growth. Certain years have been selected in order to point up long-range trends during this period. Depression and war years have been avoided in order to eliminate unusual conditions. The year 1929–30 was selected because it was a predepression year; 1939–40, because it was a late depression, prewar year; the years 1949–50 and 1959–60, because they were fairly normal postwar years; and the years 1969–70, 1975–76, and 1979–80, to show the effect of inflation on educational expenditures during the most recent decade.

Conclusions regarding the amount of change are vitally affected by the base year or years selected for making comparisons. For example, in order to maximize the percentage of increase in expenditures, a biased person attacking an increase in school expenditures may select a low depression year with which to compare expenditures for the current year. Also, a biased person advocating an increase in educational expenditures may select for comparison the base year that will minimize the percentage of increase. The objective student of school finance will avoid, insofar as possible, either extremely high or extremely low years when appraising long-range trends.

Educational expenditures are affected by many factors including number of pupils educated, purchasing power of the dollar, gross national product, quantity and quality of educational services, and demand for education. Therefore, trends in educational expenditures will be appraised in this chapter in terms of these factors.

TRENDS IN POPULATION, PUBLIC SCHOOL ENROLLMENT, AND AVERAGE DAILY ATTENDANCE

Data presented in Table 4–1 show that total population, school enrollment, and average daily attendance have had different rates of increase or decrease over the fifty-year period 1930–80. Total population has increased in each decade since 1930, but both public school enrollment and attendance have decreased substantially since 1970. There was very little change in school enrollment and attendance between 1930 and 1950, but large increases occurred between 1950 and 1970.

The wide fluctuations in school enrollment create problems in school financing. Rapid increases in school enrollment, such as occurred between 1950 and 1970, created school plant shortages which required major increases in capital outlay and current expenditures. Taxpayers resist rapid increases in school taxes. School enrollment declined substantially in the 1970s and it is anticipated that this decline will continue until the middle of the 1980s, when it will probably start increasing again. This decline in school enrollment has created a school building surplus and a surplus of teachers in many school districts. This has caused many boards of education to close schools and to reduce the number of teachers employed. These actions frequently involve boards of education in political controversies, which do not enhance their chances of obtaining needed school revenue.

It is interesting to note from Table 4–1 that average daily attendance has increased much more rapidly since 1930 than has school enrollment. This shows that pupils attended school more regularly in 1980 than in 1930. It is evident that the consumer demand for education is increasing because parents are insisting that their children attend school more regularly. Undoubtedly, both improved health of children and improved transportation have contributed to better school attendance. But the greater valuation placed on education by the parents of 1980 than by the parents of 1930 probably has accounted for most of the improvement in attendance.

TABLE 4–1   Trends in Public School Enrollment, Attendance, and Population (in thousands)

YEAR	ENROLL-MENT	PERCENT CHANGE OVER PREVIOUS PERIOD	AVERAGE DAILY ATTEN-DANCE	PERCENT CHANGE OVER PREVIOUS PERIOD	TOTAL RESIDENT POPULA-TION (July)	PERCENT CHANGE OVER PREVIOUS PERIOD
1929–30	25,678	—	21,265	—	123,100	—
1939–40	25,434	− 1.0	22,042	3.7	132,500	7.6
1949–50	25,111	− 1.3	22,284	1.1	151,900	14.6
1959–60	36,087	43.7	32,477	45.7	180,000	18.5
1969–70	45,619	26.4	41,934	29.1	203,800	13.2
1975–76	44,791	− 1.8	41,525	− 1.0	215,150	5.6
1979–80	41,823	− 6.6	38,419	− 7.5	227,000	5.5
Percent Increase 1929–30 to 1979–80	62.5		80.7		84.4	

Sources: Enrollment and attendance data from the U.S. Office of Education, except for 1979–80, which was estimated by the National Education Association; population data from U.S. Department of Commerce, Bureau of the Census.

TRENDS IN TOTAL PUBLIC
SCHOOL EXPENDITURES

The term *total school expenditures* as used in this book includes expenditures for current expenses, capital outlay, and interest on school indebtedness but excludes payments to retire the principal of indebtedness. This is the definition used by the United States Office of Education and by the National Education Association. Payments on the principal of indebtedness should be excluded from total expenditures in order to eliminate a meaningless inflation of expenditures. For example, assume that the expenditures of a school system for a twenty-year period are being studied and that a $5 million bond issue for buildings, maturing over a twenty-year period, has been floated during the first year of the period. To include principal payments in total expenditures for each of the twenty years would be double reporting—once for capital outlay and once for payments on principal of indebtedness. The inflation would total $5 million over a twenty-year period.

Many studies of school finance use the term *total expenditures* to include all items of current expense, plus capital outlay and debt service, even though it includes an unexplained inflation. It would be better to define this type of total as gross expenditures. Therefore, in this book the term *gross expenditures* will include all expenditures of boards of education for day school, and *total expenditures* will include all expenditures except payments on the principal of indebtedness. Due to the current lack of uniformity in the use of terms, the student of school finance should examine carefully the composition of any total of school expenditures before it is compared with a total reported from another source.

Some very significant trends in school expenditures are presented in Table 4–2.[2] Data for each decade from 1929–30 to 1979–80 are presented in order to show long-range trends, and data for 1975–76 are compared with data for 1979–80 in order to show the effect of inflation and the recent decline in school enrollment on school expenditures. Total school expenditures increased 3,928 percent between 1929–30 and 1979–80. But the consumer price index increased 355 percent during that same period, and therefore total school expenditures increased only 785 percent in dollars of the same purchasing power. But school attendance increased about 81 percent between 1929–30 and 1979–80, and therefore expenditures per pupil increased only 390 percent over that period of time. However, a 390 percent increase in expenditures per pupil between 1930 and 1980 is a remarkable increase. It is noted from Table 4–3 that the per capita GNP increased 214 percent between 1929–30 and 1979–80 in dollars of the same purchasing power. Therefore, since expenditures per pupil increased more than the increase in per capita GNP, it is evident that there was a greater demand for public education in 1979–80 than in 1929–30. Table 4–2 shows that the percent of the GNP expended for public elementary and secondary schools increased 54 percent between 1929–30 and 1979–80. This is further evidence of the growing demand for education.

The changes in educational expenditures between 1975–76 and 1979–80 are highly significant, because the consumer price index increased 39.8 percent, total expenditures decreased 6.5 percent in constant dollars, per pupil expenditures increased 1 percent in constant dollars, and the percent of the GNP expended for education decreased 15.9 percent. Table 4–1 shows that school attendance decreased 7.5 percent between 1975–76 and 1979–80. What do these data mean? It seems that expenditures per pupil increase very slowly in periods of inflation. Taxpayers are no doubt frustrated by rapidly rising prices in inflationary times and are probably not in the mood for increasing taxes for schools or other governmental functions.

Table 4–2 indicates how expenditures for public education increase rapidly in times of prosperity but very slowly in times of depression and inflation. The years 1930 to 1940 were depression years, the years 1950 to 1960 and 1960 to 1970 were years of relative prosperity, and the years 1970 to 1980 were years of rapid inflation. It can be computed from the data in Table 4–2 that expenditures per pupil in constant dollars increased only 15 percent between 1930 and 1940, 50 percent between 1950 and 1960, 57 percent between 1960 and 1970, and 21 percent between 1970 and 1980.

Trends in Salaries of Instructional Staff

The data presented in Table 4–3 reveal some interesting trends in instructional staff salaries. In dollars of the same purchasing power, the average salary of the instructional staff increased 160.3 percent between 1929–30 and 1979–80, but it decreased 8.1 percent between 1975–76 and 1979–80. Data in table 4–2 show that total expenditures per pupil in average daily attendance increased 390 percent between 1929–30 and 1978–80 and 1 percent between 1975–76. Why have expenditures per pupil increased relatively much more than instructional staff salaries? Table 4–3 shows that the number of pupils enrolled per instructional staff member decreased from 29 in 1929–30 to 17 in 1979–80. Some critics of public education charge that the productivity of teachers has declined since 1930 because the enrollment per teacher has declined. Supporters of public education argue that the quality of education has been greatly improved since 1930. They point to the great expansion of educational opportunity for vocational students and the handicapped, the increased provisions for education in remote areas, and the necessity of reducing the pupil-teacher ratio in order to provide more assistance to individual students. These factors have all no doubt contributed to the reduction in pupil-teacher ratios. However, the recent decline in school enrollment has also contributed to the decline in pupil-teacher ratios. Many boards of education with declining enrollment have accumulated a surplus of teachers. Boards of education have found it difficult to reduce staff to the number needed because of humanitarian reasons and opposition of teachers' organizations and parents. Large reductions in the teaching staff sometimes require the closing of schools, which is usually bitterly opposed by patrons of the school being closed.

TABLE 4–2 Trends in Total Expenditures for Public K–12 Schools

YEAR	TOTAL EXPENDITURES IN CURRENT DOLLARS (millions)	CONSUMER PRICE INDEX (average for two calendar years)	TOTAL EXPENDITURES IN 1979–80 DOLLARS (in millions)	EXPENDITURES PER PUPIL IN ADA IN 1979–80 DOLLARS	GNP IN CURRENT DOLLARS (average for two calendar years in billions)	PERCENT OF GNP EXPENDED FOR PUBLIC SCHOOLS
1929–30	$ 2,307	51	$10,495	494	$ 97	2.4
1939–40	2,344	42	12,948	567	96	2.4
1949–50	5,838	72	18,811	844	272	2.1
1959–60	15,616	88	41,170	1,268	494	3.2
1969–70	40,683	113	83,526	1,992	959	4.2
1975–76	71,100	166	99,369	2,393	1,616	4.4
1979–80	92,924	232	92,924	2,419	2,505	3.7
Percent Increase 1929–30 to 1979–80	3,927.0	354.9	785.4	389.7	2,482.5	54.2
Percent Increase 1975–76 to 1979–80	30.7	39.8	−6.5	1.0	55.0	−15.9

Sources: Data on expenditures and attendance from the U.S. Office of Education, except for 1979–80, which was estimated by the National Education Association; data on consumer price index from the Bureau of Labor Statistics, U.S. Department of Labor; and data on GNP from *Survey of Current Business,* U.S. Department of Commerce.

TABLE 4–3 Trends in Salary of Instructional Staff, Pupil Enrollment per Instructional Staff Member, and Per Capita GNP

YEAR	NUMBER OF INSTRUCTIONAL STAFF (in thousands)	AVERAGE SALARY OF INSTRUCTIONAL STAFF (in current dollars)	AVERAGE SALARY OF INSTRUCTIONAL STAFF (in 1979–80 dollars)	PUPIL ENROLLMENT PER INSTRUCTIONAL STAFF MEMBER	PER CAPITA GNP (in 1979–80 dollars)
1929–30	892	$ 1,420	$ 6,460	29	$ 3,582
1939–40	912	1,441	7,960	28	4,000
1949–50	962	3,010	9,678	26	5,767
1959–60	1,464	5,174	13,641	25	7,233
1969–70	2,253	8,840	18,149	20	9,661
1975–76	2,470	13,094	18,300	18	10,523
1979–80	2,485	16,813	16,813	17	11,035
Percent Increase 1929–30 to 1979–80	178.6	1084.0	160.3	−41.8	208.1
Percent Increase 1975–76 to 1979–80	.6	28.4	−8.1	−5.6	5.1

Source: U.S. Department of Commerce, Bureau of the Census, *Historical Statistics of the United States. Colonial Times to 1970* for data up to 1970 on instructional staff; U.S. Office of Education for 1975–76 and National Education Association for 1979–80.

The instructional staff of the public schools has not shared equally with the public in the great increase in the standard of living of the people since 1929–30. Table 4–3 shows instructional staff salaries in dollars of the same purchasing power increasing only 160.3 percent between 1929–30 and 1979–80, whereas the per capita GNP in constant dollars increased 208.8 percent. During the five-year inflationary period between 1975–76 and 1979–80, instructional staff salaries decreased 8.1 percent, while the per capita GNP increased 5.1 percent.

TRENDS IN CURRENT EXPENDITURES
AND REVENUE RECEIPTS

Trends in current expenditures and revenue receipts reported in Table 4–4 correspond in general to trends in total expenditures reported in Table 4–2. Total expenditures in dollars of the same purchasing power increased 785.4 percent between 1929–30 and 1979–80; total current expenditures, 881.1 percent; and total revenue receipts, 886.1 percent. Total expenditures in dollars of the same purchasing power increased 389.7 percent per pupil in average daily attendance between 1929–30 and 1979–80; current expenditures, 443.7 percent; and revenue receipts, 445.6 percent. Total expenditures per pupil in average daily attendance in dollars of the same purchasing power increased 1 percent between 1975–76 and 1979–80; current expenditures, 5.6 percent; and revenue receipts, 6.8 percent. Although expenditures per pupil and revenue receipts per pupil in dollars of the same purchasing power increased during all periods studied, total school expenditures in dollars of the same purchasing power declined 6.5 percent between 1975–76 and 1979–80; total current expenses declined 2.3 percent; and total revenue receipts declined 5.3 percent.

The data presented in Tables 4–2 and 4–4 show that the same general trends are revealed regardless of whether total expenditures, current expenditures, or revenue receipts are selected as the measure of trends. However, each of these measures must be studied in terms of amount per pupil in dollars of the same purchasing power to reach valid conclusions from the study.

RETURNS FROM INCREASED
EDUCATIONAL EXPENDITURES

What has the public received from the major increases in educational expenditures during the fifty-year period 1930 to 1980? There is indisputable evidence that both the quantity and the quality of public education have been greatly increased during that time. Our goal has been to provide suitable educational opportunities for all pupils, regardless of sex, race, physical or mental characteristics, and place of residence. The percentage of the enrollment in the public schools in grades 9–12 has increased from 17 in 1930 to 34 in 1980. Most

TABLE 4–4 Trends in Current Expenditures and Revenue Receipts, Grades K–12

YEAR	CURRENT EXPENDITURES (in millions of current dollars)	CURRENT EXPENDITURES (in millions of 1979–80 dollars)	CURRENT EXPENDITURES PER PUPIL IN ADA IN 1979–80 DOLLARS	REVENUE RECEIPTS (in millions of current dollars)	REVENUE RECEIPTS (in millions of 1979–80 dollars)	REVENUE RECEIPTS PER PUPIL IN ADA IN 1979–80 DOLLARS
1929–30	$ 1,844	$ 8,388	$ 394	$ 2,089	$ 9,503	$ 447
1939–40	1,942	10,727	487	2,261	12,489	567
1949–50	4,687	15,101	678	5,437	17,518	786
1959–60	12,329	32,504	1,001	14,747	38,879	1,197
1969–70	34,218	70,253	1,675	40,267	82,672	1,971
1975–76	60,259	84,218	2,028	70,803	98,954	2,283
1979–80	82,297	82,297	2,142	93,707	93,707	2,439
Percent Increase 1929–30 to 1979–80	4363.0	881.1	443.7	4385.7	886.1	445.6
Percent Increase 1975–76 to 1979–80	36.6	−2.3	5.6	32.4	−5.3	6.8

Source: National Center for Education Statistics, U.S. Office of Education, except for 1979–80, which was estimated by the National Education Association.

senior-high-school students today have access to extensive programs of vocational education, which was not the case fifty years ago. Vocational education is more expensive than academic education. Extensive programs of special education for the physically and mentally handicapped are now required by law. In many school systems as much as 10 percent of the elementary pupils are enrolled in special education classes. These special education programs may cost as much as two to five times the cost for a nonhandicapped pupil. In 1930 very few school systems had such programs. Major expenditures are now being made to meet the educational needs of the culturally handicapped. In some school systems, this may amount to as much as 4 percent of current expenditures. Practically nothing was expended for programs of that type in 1930. The average number of school days attended increased from 143 in 1930 to 162 in 1980. This increase resulted largely from increasing the average length of the school term from 173 days in 1930 to approximately 180 days in 1980 and increasing the percent of the enrollment transported from 7 percent in 1930 to 56 percent in 1980.

All fifty states now make at least some effort to equalize educational opportunity within the state by allocating state funds through such approaches as the foundation program, the guaranteed tax base, complete state support, or by providing most of the school revenue by flat grants from state sources. In 1930 only a few states made any attempt to equalize educational opportunity. The equalization of educational opportunity in general has been achieved by a policy of increasing the revenue of districts with limited financial resources without decreasing the financial support of the more fortunate districts. A considerable amount of the increase in school expenditures since 1970 has been used to equalize educational opportunity.

Perhaps the greatest single improvement that has been made in public education between 1930 and 1980 has been the abolishment of legal segregation by race in the public schools. Prior to the famous *Brown* v. *Topeka Board of Education* case in 1954, seventeen states legally permitted segregation by race in the public schools. In many of those states, the educational provisions for black pupils were quite inferior to those provided for white pupils. In fact, in some of the southern states in 1930 the average expenditure for white pupils was more than double the average expenditure for black pupils and the average white teacher was paid about twice the average salary of a black teacher.[3] When the schools were desegregated, school costs were greatly increased in the states that had been maintaining segregated schools, because the expenditures for black pupils had to be increased to the level provided for white pupils.

The median number of school years completed by those 25 years of age and over has increased from 8.6 in 1940 to 12.2 in 1970. Perhaps the most significant single piece of evidence of school improvement during the past fifty years is the fact that only 30 percent of the pupils who entered school in the fifth grade in 1924 graduated from high school eight years later, whereas more than 75 percent of the pupils who entered the fifth grade in 1962 graduated from high school in 1970. Some critics of the public schools at this writing complain about a decline in the standardized test scores of high-school graduates. Fifty years ago most high-school graduates came from the intellectually elite.[4] Today more than 75 percent of all pupils graduate from high school; therefore, they constitute a wide range of intellectual ability and it is to be expected that average test scores would decline. However, there is no evidence that pupils of high intellectual ability achieve at a lower level than their peers in prior years. As a matter of fact, gifted students in high school today have far more opportunities in modern high schools to have that ability challenged than did their predecessors. The goal of the public-school system of the United States has been to educate all of the children of all of the people. No other nation in the history of the world has come as near to achieving that goal as the United States of America: The attainment of that goal costs money. However, the evidence presented in Chapter 3 shows that education has contributed substantially to the economic growth of the nation, which has made it possible to increase educational resources without depriving other sectors of the economy of needed resources.

INCOME ELASTICITY OF DEMAND FOR EDUCATION

The per capita gross national product has rapidly increased since 1929, except for depression years. Has public school support increased in proportion to the increased economic productivity of the nation? One way of looking at this problem is to compare the relative change in household income. Economists call this measure the "income elasticity of demand." For education it usually has been determined by comparing changes in expenditures per pupil for education with changes in per capita personal income. A coefficient of 1 means that a 1 percent change in per capita income has been accompanied by a 1 percent change in per-pupil expenditures. When the coefficient is more than 1, the demand is said to have been elastic; and when less than 1, inelastic. Eugene P. McLoone found that the coefficient of elasticity was 0.96 between 1929–30 and 1957–58, 1.45 between 1943–44 and 1957–58, and 1.34 between 1947–48 and 1957–58.[5] Werner Z. Hirsch found that a 1 percent increase in per capita personal income between 1900 and 1958 was associated with only a 1.09 percent increase in per-pupil expenditures.[6] Both researchers found that the coefficient of elasticity of income demand for education in the early part of this century was 1 or below. However, each noted that the demand for education has been more elastic since 1950 than in the first half of the twentieth century.

What has been the elasticity of demand for education since 1950? In order to compute the coefficient of elasticity accurately, data for each year of the period being studied should be available, and refined statistical techniques involving the computation of the slope of a regression line should be utilized. However, it is possible to make a crude estimate of the coefficient of elasticity since 1950 by comparing the real annual growth rate of the economy with real annual increase in school expenditures. The average annual per capita growth rate of the GNP in constant dollars between 1949–50 and 1979–80 was 1.90 percent. The average annual increase in total expenditures per pupil in average daily attendance in constant dollars was 3.73 percent between 1949–50 and 1979–80. Considering this thirty-year period as one period, it is evident that the income elasticity of demand for education has been quite elastic. However, the per capita GNP increased an average of 1.63 percent per year between 1975–76 and 1979–80, whereas total expenditure for the public schools increased an average of only one-quarter of 1 percent per year during that period. Therefore the income elasticity of demand for education was not elastic during the highly inflationary period between 1975–76 and 1979–80. There is some evidence that indicates that the demand for education may be elastic in prosperous times but inelastic in times of inflation or depression. The following section discusses other factors affecting the demand for education.

SOCIAL AND ECONOMIC FACTORS
THAT MAY AFFECT FUTURE DEMANDS
FOR EDUCATION

It would require an entire book to give an adequate presentation of this topic. Only a brief discussion of a few of the more important factors can be undertaken here. Some of them are growth in national income and productivity, change in pattern of skills and abilities, changing role of government, changes in the class and caste structure, and social mobility.

Effect of a Rising Gross National Product.   Both the total and the per capita gross national product have been increasing. A growing national product makes possible a rise in the level of living, which creates a consumer demand for more and better goods and services of all kinds, both public and private. As the productivity of our economy increases, consumers will inevitably demand a greater quantity and a better quality of education than now available.

At this writing, which is in a period of inflation and recession, there has been a slight reduction in the rate of economic growth. Will this reduction in the rate of economic growth continue until there is no economic growth in the United States? The economist Rohatyn was asked the following question in 1980: "Can we get by on limited or no growth in times ahead?" His reply was: "No. The idea of a zero-sum society is baloney. We cannot function as a zero-sum society, because we are not equipped to handle the taking away from some to give to others that a zero-sum society involves."[7] Zero-sum is a term used by economists in game theory in which the amount one player wins in an economic game is exactly equal to the amount that the other player loses. It is somewhat similar to the Pareto-optimal concept under which no one can be made better off without making someone else worse off.[8] A fixed quantity of goods and services is implied by both concepts. As pointed out in chapter 2, the people of the United States have always sought the better life. In order to have economic growth, we cannot consume all that we produce. We have saved some of our production and invested it in both physical and human capital. There is no reason to believe that we will abandon that policy.

Effect of Changes in Pattern of Skills and Abilities. The pattern of skills and abilities of the working population is changing rapidly. The proportion of the total national income derived from primary production (farming, fishing, and forestry) is decreasing, and the proportion derived from manufacturing and services is increasing. For instance, the proportion of the total national income derived from agriculture in 1979 was less than half the proportion in 1929. There has been a long-range trend of migration from farms to cities. We have changed from a predominantly agrarian economy in 1800 to a predominantly urban industrial economy in 1980. The early waves of migration from the farm to the city and from Europe to our cities were largely absorbed at first by the needs of the nation for a large supply of common labor. But as machines began to replace hand labor in the nineteenth century and as automation developed in the twentieth century, the need for untrained common labor decreased, and the need for highly skilled and semiskilled workers increased. The nation no longer needs a large supply of unskilled workers. Furthermore, with the development of machines, child labor was no longer needed for production, and this increased the demand for education. The change in the pattern of skills, from emphasis on common labor to emphasis on types of skills and abilities requiring more education, added to this demand for more education.

These trends evidently will continue in the future. Increased automation of industry will increase production and decrease need for the labor of youth. The school term probably will be extended and the number of years of schooling increased. It is quite probable that within twenty years, most young people will remain in school through junior college years. The percentage of women obtaining postsecondary education is rapidly increasing. The knowledge, skills and abilities required to earn a living will require more education in future years than in the past. The increased leisure provided by the shorter work week and the changing pattern of skills will increase the demand for adult education.

Effect of the Changing Role of Government. The changing role of government in our lives requires a constantly rising level of education of the citizenry. Many decisions that formerly were made in the marketplace now are made by political action. Governmental services consumed 13.3 percent of the gross national product in 1930 and 33.1 percent in 1980. In the free market, each individual may purchase, or not purchase, a good or service. But in the government economy, all must purchase or not purchase a service, because the relevant decisions must be made collectively by the ballot, either directly or indirectly. In a democratic form of government, the wisdom of decisions made by government is determined largely by the level of education of the people and their values. Therefore, as government assumes greater importance in our lives, the welfare of the nation is vitally involved in the education of the people.

Effect of the Struggle to Remove Class and Caste Barriers.   The twentieth century has been called the age of the common man. Underprivileged nations throughout the world and underprivileged groups within all nations have been struggling for growth beyond mere survival. Class always has been present in all societies, and caste in most societies, but today as never before, their validity is being challenged. The denial of equal educational opportunities always has been one of the principal means of perpetuating the barriers between caste and class. Therefore, underprivileged groups in the United States, as well as throughout the world, are demanding equality in educational opportunity. The barriers have hindered social mobility and prevented society from attaining its maximum potential in production. Increased investment in education may well be the most productive investment the nation can make.

NOTES

1. An exception might be a small child who wants to eat only sweets but needs to eat some vegetables in order to stay healthy, but whose mother will allow dessert only after the vegetables have been eaten. However, it might be argued that the child does not live in a free society at home.

2. Expenditures for a given school year are made over two calendar years. In order to study the relationship of consumer prices and the gross national product to school expenditures, it is desirable that these two items also be considered for the two calendar years that correspond to the school year. This is accomplished in Table 4–2 by averaging data for the consumer price index and the GNP for the two calendar years corresponding to the school year.

3. The statistics presented in this discussion were taken largely from U.S. Department of Commerce, Bureau of the Census, *Historical Statistics of the United States: Colonial Times to 1970* (Washington, D.C.: U.S. Government Printing Office, 1975) and National Center for Education Statistics, *Digest of Education Statistics, 1979* (Washington, D.C.: U.S. Office of Education, U.S. Government Printing Office, 1979).

4. Roe L. Johns, "Historical Changes: Recurring Themes in the New South" (Paper delivered at the Southern Regional Council of Educational Administration, November 7, 1977 in Atlanta, Ga.)

5. Eugene P. McLoone, "Effects of Tax Elasticities on the Financial Support of Education" (Ph.D. dissertation, University of Illinois, 1961).

6. Werner Z. Hirsch, "Analysis of the Rising Costs of Education," Joint Economic Committee, Eighty-sixth Congress of the United States, Study Paper No. 4 (Washington, D.C.: U.S. Government Printing Office, 1959).

7. Felix G. Rohatyn, "Bitter Medicine for Ailing U.S. Economy," *U.S. News and World Report,* September 1, 1980, p. 31.

8. See Edwin Mansfield, *Micro-Economics; Theory and Applications,* 3rd ed. (New York: W. W. Norton and Company, 1979), p. 342, and p. 444.

SELECTED REFERENCES

DORNSBUSCH, RUDIGER, and STANLEY FISCHER.   *Macro-Economics*. New York: McGraw Hill Book Company, 1978.

LIND, C. GEORGE.   *Digest of Education Statistics, 1979*. Washington, D.C.: U.S. Government Printing Office, 1979.

MANSFIELD, EDWIN.   *Micro-Economics: Theory and Application*. 3rd ed. New York: W. W. Norton and Company, 1979.

U.S. OFFICE OF EDUCATION, NATIONAL CENTER FOR EDUCATION STATISTICS.   *The Condition of Education*. 1980 edition. Washington, D.C.: U.S. Government Printing Office, 1980.

U.S. DEPARTMENT OF COMMERCE, BUREAU OF THE CENSUS.   *Historical Statistics of the United States: Colonial Times to 1970*. Washington, D.C.: U.S. Government Printing Office, 1975.

U.S. DEPARTMENT OF COMMERCE.   *Statistical Abstract of the United States*. Washington, D.C.: Published annually by the Bureau of the Census.

U.S. DEPARTMENT OF COMMERCE.   *"Survey of Current Business."* Washington, D.C.: Published monthly by the Bureau of Economic Analysis.

U.S. DEPARTMENT OF LABOR.   *Monthly Labor Review*. Washington, D.C.: Published monthly by the Bureau of Labor Statistics.

CHAPTER FIVE
TAXATION
FOR PUBLIC SCHOOLS

The power to tax is inherent in the sovereignty of an independent state. In the United States taxing power is vested in the state and federal governments. State government has the inherent power to tax as an attribute of sovereignty. This power of the state to tax can be delegated to the local level for school and other governmental purposes. The federal government derives its power to tax from the Constitution, which provides in Section 8 of Article I, "The Congress shall have power to lay and collect taxes, duties, imposts and excises, to pay the debts and provide for the common defense and general welfare of the United States . . . ." Taxing powers of state government are prescribed and limited by state and federal constitution, while the federal power to tax is constrained only by the federal Constitution. Since "the power to tax involves the power to destroy,"[1] constitutional limitations are essential to preservation of the rights and liberties of the American people.

DEFINITION OF A TAX

* A tax is the compulsory payment by a person to government for the purpose of providing for the general well-being of society. Ricardo, in 1817, defined taxes as "a portion of the produce of the land and labour of a country placed at the disposal of the government."[2] In one of the most commonly quoted definitions, Seligman defined a tax as "a compulsory contribution from the person to the government to defray the expenses incurred in the common interest of all without reference to special benefits conferred."[3] Compulsion is a general characteristic of taxation. Certainly taxes cannot be termed voluntary for if they were they would be by nature a gift.

As with a gift, though, a tax is not paid with the idea that a specific benefit will be received back. Taxes are presumed to be used for the common interest or the public good, hence the latter portion of Seligman's definition. But this definition, which says "without reference to special benefits conferred," may be too prescriptive, for, as Taylor observes, it would be difficult to argue that tax deductions from workers' weekly paychecks for old-age annuity purposes are entirely "without reference to special benefits conferred."[4]

On the other hand the "common interest" is certainly served by providing security to the aged of a nation. It would be hard to identify a tax of the state or federal governments which did not have as its goal the basic intent to aid the "common interest." Usually in state constitutions there is a requirement to tax and expend monies only for a "public purpose," that is, for the common interest. Even earmarking of particular taxes for specified purposes, such as gasoline taxes for highway construction, while it short-circuits normal budget procedure does not change the definition of a tax as a general contribution in the common interest.[5]

A tax is not a fee charged directly for benefit received. There is no relationship between the tax paid and the direct benefit received, as would be the case with a price or fee. Taxes are distinguishable from less compulsory and more contractual revenue devices. Seligman points out that "The essential characteristic of a fee is the existence of a measurable special benefit, together with a predominant public purpose: the absence of the public purpose makes the payment a price; the absence of a special benefit makes it a tax."[6]

A knowledge of taxation as well as human nature makes one aware that taxpayers will attempt to push taxes away from themselves onto others. David Hume pointed this out in 1725 when he wrote,

> Every man, to be sure, is desirous of pushing off from himself the burthen of any tax, which is impos'd, and laying it upon others. But as every man has the same inclination, and is upon the defensive; no set of men can be suppos'd to prevail altogether in this contest.[7]

Tax Shifting

The process by which a tax is passed on to someone else is called tax *shifting*. Such shifting is accomplished through transactions between the person who pays the tax and the person to whom the actual burden of the tax is shifted. The shifting is accomplished by either changes in the price or alterations by the seller in the quality of the item sold. If such shifting takes place the *incidence* of the tax is borne by a person other than the party toward whom the tax is directed. The incidence of a tax falls on the person who in effect pays the tax through higher prices or reduced quality. The point of incidence is the final resting place of the tax.

Good examples of this process can be found in the sale of gasoline, cigarettes, or whiskey. When one purchases a gallon of gas he or she pays one price which can be broken down into two components—the price of the gasoline and the federal, state, and, maybe, local taxes. The price paid at the pump does not separate these payments. The person filling a gasoline tank at the pump does not pay the tax directly to government; instead, either the processor or the distributor actually pays the tax, depending on how it is levied. Therefore, the impact of the tax is upon one of them.[8]

The *effect* of a tax is quite another matter. Effect is the result or consequences derived from the interaction of the impact, the incidence, and the shifting process. To measure effect, one must look to the broad basic economic behavior which takes place; such as saving, variations in work patterns, and fluctuations in consumption, investment, and production.

The essential variable in this entire process is *how* the shifting takes place. Forward shifts may result in one kind of behavior, while backward shifts may produce others. Here the concern is for the method by which the original taxpayer, or subject of the tax, can reimburse himself by removing the amount paid to others. He may only partially reimburse himself, whereby the tax will be divided. Commonly the payer will shift the tax *forward* by raising the price. Occasionally, however, backward shifting takes place where the manufacturer, for example, may if possible, buy raw materials for less or be able to pay less in labor costs. Another type of backward shifting is called *tax capitalization*. In the case of long-term durable goods, capitalization results when the present owner is unable to pass along the taxes to a buyer. This may also be known as buying tax free. What actually takes place is that the buyer, of say a piece of farmland or a home, calculates what the future anticipated taxes will be and then subtracts the discounted present value from the price of the property.

Thus, the ability to shift the incidence of a tax is largely contingent on whether there is a price vehicle available by which to shift the tax, whether the demand to buy is great enough to allow the seller to increase the price, or whether the demand is such that the seller can reduce the quality of the item purchased. Concerning the availability of a vehicle to shift the tax, some taxes such as an income tax are not normally shifted, because it must be assumed that the wages, salaries, rent, interest, or profit are at the maximum allowed by productivity and there is no mechanism for raising before tax incomes to offset the taxes to be paid later.[9] The key to easy shifting is that the payer have the ability to sell or transact business with another party where the elasticity of demand is such that the price can be raised without reducing consumption.

Shifting the Geographical Incidence of a Tax

Certain states collect a substantial percentage of all their tax revenue from severance taxes on such mineral products as petroleum and from taxes on tourists. These taxes are largely paid by nonresidents. Such states are able to shift a substantial portion of their tax burden to the people of other states.

The ability to shift taxes from one state to another varies widely. Manufacturing states can pass on much of the incidence of both their state and local taxes through pricing of their products. This is especially true for petroleum products, tourist industries, and such substantial monopolies as the automobile industry. Because of the absence of monopoly, states that are predominantly agricultural can shift few of their taxes to other states. In general, the wealthiest states shift more of their taxes to other states. It is the opposite of equalization because the wealthy states, through their taxing systems actually are receiving more tax benefits from the states of least wealth than the reverse.

Effect of Tax Shifting on Local Effort

Much has been said about local effort to support schools. The people are quite properly encouraged to make great local effort. Relative local effort to support schools usually is determined by dividing the amount of local school taxes collected by the equalized assessed valuation of the district. But in many school districts, half or more of the assessed valuation is composed of railroad assessments and other public utilities. In such cases, half or more of local school taxes are paid by nonresidents of the district. The residents have effectively shifted to the people of other districts the incidence of most of their school taxes. The same thing is true in districts that contain concentrations of business and manufacturing corporations.

OBJECTIVES OF TAXATION

The purposes for which taxes should be levied have been a matter of much controversy almost from our nation's beginning, as they were a bitter issue in other nations much earlier. Should taxes be levied solely to yield revenue for the support of necessary government services, or should they also be levied for other purposes? The founding fathers debated this issue in relation to the wisdom of levying tariffs on imports to protect infant industries.

The trend of the times is to use taxes for a number of purposes besides furnishing revenue to support government. At the present, taxation in the United States has three major objectives:

   1. to raise revenue to support government
   2. to redistribute wealth and income
   3. to regulate and protect the general well-being

Revenues from taxation are needed to finance expenditures for the public schools. Whether the tax is levied at the federal, state, or local level, it is an involuntary payment which government requires from each person, to provide for the salaries, supplies, land, and capital outlay necessary for the state education system. In deciding how and to what extent to tax themselves, the people are actually determining the quantity and quality of educational programs the state will supply. To gain revenues, though, is a rather obvious objective of taxation; the other two objectives are less so.

One of the major purposes of taxation in this country is to redistribute wealth and income, and thus to effect change in the economic structure. To take funds into the governmental treasury and then to redistribute them through various public social programs tends to raise more money from the rich and give it to the needy.

The German economist Wagner, referred to in Chapter 2, was one of the first to advance the radical idea that the tax system should have not only a fiscal purpose of providng revenues for government, but should also have a "socio-political" purpose of altering the distribution of wealth. Wagner maintained,

> In the first place, the state should so order its expenditures, tax system, and loans as to remove certain economic and social evils which have attended them in the past. And in the second place, the state, by adopting appropriate policies, should remedy evils which are not due to its previous action in financial or other matters. From this second demand it follows that, in the domain of public finance, expenditures should increase in order to enable the state to assume new functions; and that taxation, in addition to serving the purely financial purpose of providing sufficient revenue, should be employed for the purpose of bringing about a different distribution of wealth from that which would result from the working of free competition upon the basis of the present social order.[10]

In this statement, Wagner rejects the arguments of those who maintain that free competition from private initiative is all that is required to meet the needs of society. Accordingly, Wagner's philosophy calls for a role of government in taxation which can reject the existing economic order and seek to change it through redistribution of wealth and income. Wagner's position has long since been adopted by most modern nations. In the United States, redistribution through the federal income tax continues to be a major objective of governmental taxation.

Some taxes, such as income and inheritance, tend to redistribute more readily than others, because they impact to a greater degree on the more able. The redistributional effects of taxation for the public schools are sizable, since the poor pay less taxes and derive the same or greater educational benefits than the wealthy. They are usually greater because poor families tend to have more children than the more affluent and thus benefit more from public education. More will be said about this in Chapter 9.

The third objective of taxation is to regulate, control, and protect the general well-being of the citizenry. At least two subpurposes lie within this overall objective: (1) protection of domestic productivity, health, and welfare; and (2) overall economic stabilization.

The first subobjective includes the well-established use of tariffs and levies to protect domestic producers. America had experience with tariffs as early as

July 4, 1789, when the first tariff act laid duties ranging from 5 to 15 percent on over 80 manufactured articles imported into the United States. In his *Report on Manufactures* in 1791, Hamilton defended the tariff as not only providing a source of revenue, but also encouraging American enterprise by "protecting" it against European competition. The protective tariff remains a weapon in the American trade arsenal.

Higher taxes may also be used to discourage consumption or to reduce the size of corporations. Several states today levy higher taxes on tobacco and liquor, not only to gain revenues but also to reduce harmful usage. Other examples of such taxes are numerous, including higher taxes on gasoline to reduce America's oil consumption and the "windfall profits" tax on oil companies to reduce an unfavorable flow of capital toward extraordinarily powerful corporations.

The second subobjective of taxation is to bring about economic stability. Whether or not taxes were needed to gain revenues for governmental services, the government would still need to levy taxes to stimulate or restrain private demand. Higher taxes combined with lower government expenditures help to fight inflation by restraining private demand in the marketplace; lower taxes and higher expenditures help fight recession by stimulating private demand. The federal income tax is the leading economic stabilizer among all taxes. When incomes fall, under the federal personal income tax system, individuals who were formerly taxable fall below the taxable level and others are pushed down into lower tax brackets. Correspondingly, when incomes rise, individuals who were not before taxed are then taxed and others are pushed into higher tax brackets. The effect of the system is to use taxes to reduce economic fluctuations and increase stability.[11]

Thus, the objectives of taxation greatly exceed the mere raising of revenues to support expenditures for governmental services. Taxation is a comprehensive way to promote the general welfare and the broad sociopolitical interests of the government. Refer to Def. on Pages 80, 81.

DESIRABLE CHARACTERISTICS OF TAXATION

Refer To Notes of 21 June 1983

Desirable characteristics of taxation have been developed over the years by various scholars. While none of these actually amounts to laws, canons, rules, or principles, most, nevertheless, have the ring of importance and universality which may justify them as basic precepts. Such authorities as Hicks and Fagan and Macy use the term "ideals" of taxation to describe the desirable characteristics of a good tax system.[12] Reference to such ideals may be appropriate, since ideals might not be ultimately attained and many of the maxims of good taxation are never wholly accomplished either. The restraints on attainment of an ideal tax system were best described by Alfred Marshall when he wrote of the desirability of nourishing ideals in one's heart, but added that one's thought and action must be occupied mainly with the actual.[13] A visionary approach may not result in objective measures of ideals, or whatever one calls the desirable characteristics, but perhaps it is good to recognize that all desirable outcomes are not always measurable anyway and the fact that they are not should not detract from their pursuit.

Any type of tax can be either praised or condemned on the basis of one or more characteristics of taxation. Sometimes taxation is called a "class struggle" (for example, labor versus capital, with various subgroups of each involved) in which each economic group strives to minimize the taxes levied on itself and thereby indirectly maximize the proportion of taxes paid by other groups. Self-interested economic groups have no difficulty in finding one or more principles of taxation by which they can imply that practically any suggested tax is bad. On the other hand, those advocating the extension or continuation of government services find support in one or more principles of taxation for practically any type of tax proposed.

Since those responsible for financing the public schools inevitably become involved, directly or indirectly, in tax struggles, it is advisable that they know something about the properties of taxes being considered. Therefore, the most commonly accepted desirable characteristics of taxation are discussed briefly in this section. Some of these deal primarily with apportioning the tax burden and others with administrative considerations governing the selection of tax sources.

When first considering characteristics or principles of taxation, one usually begins with Adam Smith's *Wealth of Nations,* published in 1776, wherein he enunciated his four celebrated maxims; *equity, certainty, convenience,* and *economy.* Stated in full these were,

1. The subjects of every state ought to contribute towards the support of the government, as nearly as possible in proportion to their respective abilities . . .

2. The tax which each individual is bound to pay ought to be certain, and not arbitrary.

3. Every tax ought to be levied at the time or in the manner in which it is most likely to be convenient for the contributor to pay it.

4. Every tax ought to be so contrived as both to take out and to keep out of the pockets of the people as little as possible, over and above what it brings into the public treasury of the state.

Under the first of these maxims, Smith noted that the tax system should be comprehensive and not fall exclusively on a single tax base; to do so would create obvious inequality. For, as he pointed out, all persons do not have the same capacity to pay taxes in the first place, and, additionally, if they did, the types of capacity they possessed would not be identical. Therefore, to tax wages and not to tax profits would press unequally on one class of taxpayer.

About the second maxim, popularly known as the *certainty* maxim, Smith observed that the "time of payment, the manner of payment, the quantity to be paid, ought to be clear and plain to the contributor, and to every other person." Third, convenience of payment was recognized by Smith as being a desirable attribute of a tax and largely relates to the time and wherewithal to pay. Consumer taxes such as sales taxes, which are paid little by little as people buy goods, are more convenient than the property tax, which may be collected only once a year in one large sum.

Last, Smith suggests that the government should leave as much of the money as possible in the hands of the people and not withdraw into the public treasury amounts in excess of those needed to conduct essential affairs of government. Here Smith views the role of taxation in the more simplistic light of collection of revenues for governmental operation, and less as a tool to regulate or stabilize the economy. Regardless, though, overcollection may ultimately lead to abuses of the tax system by either the government, which expends the resources, or the taxpayers, who may resort to various types of evasion and thus subvert the law.

Smith's maxims have been lauded by some as prophetic and as applicable to today's economies as to yesterday's. Other commentators, though, have maintained that Smith's maxims were of no great moment, being merely a collection of simple considerations of common sense.[14]

Buchanan advances the idea that the desirable characteristics, principles, or guidelines for taxation are not useful in the democratic system in which we live. In the democratic process, taxation decisions are made by individuals acting in their own interests and making choices which result in a collective decision. Buchanan has said that "Once the *individualistic* basis for collective decisions is recognized, it becomes clear that there is no "scientific' or "expert' answer to the question as to the 'needs' for public educational spending or for anything else." Thus, to him the primary criterion which governs taxation in our society is "rationality." This "rationality" criterion merely maintains that fiscal decisions be made within the parameters of national choice. Here the political structure becomes most important and the "quest for any single 'best' distribution is abandoned, and attention is concentrated on the rationality of the decision-making process itself. . . . [15]

Buchanan argues further for the criterion of certainty, as did Adam Smith. He maintains that the citizen should be as fully informed as possible about the real burden of taxation. The concept requires that the taxpayer be aware of the actual incidence of the tax, or where the burden of the tax finally rests.

Equity

Regardless of source or rationale for taxation, all theories center on the concept of equity. Not equity in the narrow sense mentioned by Adam Smith, but equity in the broader context which includes justice and fairness. Equity not only extends to considerations of fiscal ability of the individual, but further to natural justice and fairness of government's treatment of the individual. In this light, it is expected that a desirable tax should encompass each of Adam Smith's maxims by not inappropriately classifying individuals or introducing some irrefutable bias against the taxpayer. In a legal sense, this means that the tax should affect individuals uniformly in nondiscriminating classifications and should provide for the fairness which is incumbent under due process.

An important aspect of equity is the quality of tax administration. Equity requires objective and effective tax administration. Protection against arbitrariness and favoritism is essential to both objectivity and effectiveness.[16]

In a purely economic sense, the broad requirements of fairness and justice are held to encompass the dual concepts of horizontal and vertical equity. Horizontal equity means equal treatment of equals; persons in the same economic position should be taxed equally. The corollary, vertical equity, requires that persons with unequal ability should be taxed unequally. The key to these standards is (1) the nature of the classification, and (2) the definition of economic position or ability. If a group of individuals is very narrowly or discriminatorily classified, then equity may be offended even though everyone in the class is taxed equally. For example, if a tax classification included only blond, blue-eyed, unmarried females, then the classification could be literally viewed as equitable but yet violate the intent of the principle. "To be acceptable, a tax must be applied to rather broad groupings; in other words, 'equals' for fiscal purposes must be defined in some reasonable and not wholly arbitrary manner."[17]

The definition of economic position requires that ability of the taxpayer be accurately assessed. Presumably, with an income tax the person's ability can be properly assessed; however, with various deductions and exemptions the true impact may be hard to determine. Similarly with other taxes, the true base to which the tax rate is applied may be rather illusive, creating potential inequity.

How equity will be interpreted depends largely on the relative emphasis given to the various principles of taxation stated above or to some combination of these or other principles. Concepts of equity, though, are largely subjective.[18] Despite this fact, the United States Supreme Court has given a definition of justice or equity with respect to classification for taxation purposes. In an opinion rendered in 1890, the Court declared that "clear and hostile discriminations against particular persons or classes" is a violation of the Fourteenth Amendment to the Constitution.[19] The Court has held in later opinions that any classification that has a reasonable relation to the permitted ends of government is constitutional.[20] Although these opinions of the Supreme Court have afforded some guidance in formulating tax policy, they necessarily leave to subjective determination most of the major decisions that must be made in constructing tax systems.

Thus, equity taken in its broadest sense covers most tax considerations of fairness, justice, efficiency, effectiveness, uniformity, objectivity, and ability to pay.

Benefit and Sacrifice

That all citizens should pay for education on an equal basis regardless of whether they have children in the public schools is a fundamental of public education. Whether the old and childless should pay even though they receive no direct benefits is not merely a question of educational philosophy but one of taxation theory as well. The two major rationales for taxation are the *benefit theory* and the *sacrifice theory*. Each has profoundly different results for education.

Benefit Theory. The benefit school of thought assumes taxes should be paid on the basis of the value of governmental services received. This *quid pro quo* principle is well entrenched in our economic thought, as evidenced by the issues which surrounded the establishment of public schools in this country. As discussed earlier, the vestiges of the English system of education adopted in some of the American colonies resulted in the levy of "rate bills," which called for parents of children participating in the public schools to pay a tax based on the number of their children receiving education. Rather than having all people paying a uniform tax, the rates were varied according to the benefits received. The "benefit" theory was rejected by the common-school movement, which eventually became the predominant view in this country.

The benefit theory has serious limitations when applied to education, because of the impossibility of partitioning educational benefits into neat categories. The social benefits of education, extending beyond mere individual benefits, are so broad that accurate quantification is impossible. John Stuart Mill rejected the benefit theory, saying,

> There is in this (benefit notion) a false air of nice adaption, very acceptable to some minds. But in the first place, it is not admissible that the protection of persons and that of property are the sole purposes of government. The ends of government are as comprehensive as those of the social union. They consist of all the good, and all the immunity from evil, which the existence of government can be made either directly or indirectly to bestow.[21]

The nature of education itself prevents estimation of the degrees of benefit, both direct and indirect, which various persons may be expected to receive from an education. Carried to its logical conclusion, the benefit theory supports the proposition that persons who send their children to public schools should pay school taxes while those who send their children to private schools should pay no school taxes. To adopt the benefit theory of taxation for the public schools is contrary to the premise on which the public schools were founded. The social benefits to education are so great, with benefits flowing to every segment of society, that a system of taxation for public schools based on the benefit theory is undesirable.

Despite its limitations when applied to the public schools, the benefit principle has found some application in our taxing system. Motor fuel taxes and motor vehicle license taxes have been levied in accordance with the theory that highways should be paid for by users. But highways benefit far more people than the actual operators of motor vehicles. Highways are essential for national defense and the transportation of civilian goods and persons. Our entire economy would collapse if all highways should be closed. Therefore, it is impossible to apportion accurately even the benefits of motor vehicle fuel and license taxes.

Sacrifice Theory.   The sacrifice theory requires that government establish a desirable pattern of sacrifice on the part of each individual.[22] It means that the contribution of each person toward the expenses of government should be so apportioned that one individual will feel neither more nor less convenience than any other.[23] This is an input theory which assumes that government expenditures are for the general public good and social welfare and as such should be contributed to in accordance with some measure of ability to pay. *Ability to pay* is the essence of the sacrifice theory. In order to determine accurately ability to pay, two essentials must be determined: (1) a tax base capable of measuring ability to carry burdens and (2) schedules of rates which truly equalize those burdens.[24] Ability to pay refers to the relative real sacrifice put forth by an individual in payment of a tax. "That individual who can with least personal sacrifice give up a dollar from his income is the individual among all individuals who has the greatest ability to pay the next dollar in taxes."[25] The principle, simply stated, is that each should contribute to the support of government according to his ability. But how is ability to be measured? Some would accept that the possession of property and other wealth is the best test of ability, others consider volume of spending, and still others point to income as the most valid test. If one accepts the first test as best, the property tax is the best tax. If one accepts the second test, it is assumed that the sales tax is the best tax. If the third test, the corporate or the individual income tax would be advocated. Therefore, one can justify any one of the four principal taxes used in the United States by the ability-to-pay principle, even though these taxes are quite different in nature.

The progressive income tax is considered by experts in public finance to be the best expression of the ability-to-pay principle. It is the sacrifice theory which supports the philosophy of progressive taxation. As indicated in Figure 5–1, a proportional tax is one in which the rate of taxation remains the same while the tax base changes; with a progressive tax, the tax rates increase as the tax base increases; and, a regressive tax provides for a decrease in tax rates as the tax base increases. The amount of tax to be paid is the result of multiplying the rate times the base. As can be readily seen, with progressive taxation the multiplier increases as the multiplicand increases, taxing those with greater ability at a higher rate.

Progressive income taxes leave proportionately more of earned income in the hands of the lower income groups. A progressive income tax makes possible some saving by all income levels, resulting in some accumulation of wealth at all levels. Income is in effect redistributed, because the person with

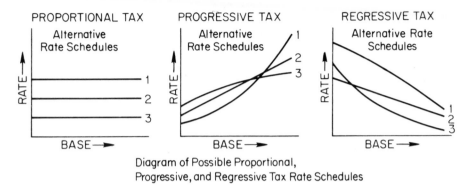

Diagram of Possible Proportional,
Progressive, and Regressive Tax Rate Schedules

FIGURE 5–1   Source: Philip E. Taylor, *The Economics of Public Finance* (New York: Macmillan, Inc., 1961), p. 293.

low income receives more benefits than he pays for in taxes, whereas the reverse is true of the person with high income.

It has been suggested that there are at least three schemes with which to determine the amount of sacrifice for each taxpayer: equal sacrifice, proportional sacrifice, and minimum or least sacrifice.[26] Equal sacrifice means that the burden of governmental services should be borne by all taxpayers equally. Proportional sacrifice is based on the utilitarian view that assumes that the utilities of different persons added together form a composite social utility. This means for taxation purposes that if each extra dollar results in less and less satisfaction to a person, and if the rich and poor have the same capacity to enjoy satisfaction, then a dollar taxed away from a rich person and given to a poor person increases the total utility of society.[27]

Adam Smith, long before the development of the theory of marginal utility, reasoned that "the subjects of every state ought to contribute towards the support of the government, as nearly as possible, according to their respective abilities, that is to say, in *proportion* to the revenue, which they respectively enjoy under the protection of the state."[28]

Minimum sacrifice posits that when taxes are imposed with the least sacrifice possible and when the revenue is expended to confer maximum advantage, then the state has maximized its social obligation.[29] To fully pursue the minimum sacrifice approach leads the government into consideration of ability to pay. Certainly, minimum sacrifice of the rich person is far different from that of the poor person, and both may be quite different from minimum sacrifice of the total population.

Directness and Certainty

According to this theory, hidden taxes should be avoided insofar as possible, and the incentive for tax evasion should be minimized. Hidden taxes are a violation of the broader concept of equity. Persons and corporations should know which tax they are subject to and what the amount will be. This is necessary for planning on the part of the individual, the corporation, and the government. Tax evasion is unfair to persons who pay their just obligations, because it gives an unfair advantage to their competitors who avoid payment of taxes. From an ethical standpoint, because of the protection given to those who comply with the tax laws, government can be justified in spending a substantial amount in order to require compliance.

Neutrality

The supporters of this principle argue that a tax should be as neutral in its effects as possible. That is, the tax should leave a person, a firm, or a corporation in the same relative economic position after the tax is collected as before. Taxes should not reallocate resources. Nor should they affect choices or actions made by the taxpayer. This point of view places major emphasis upon "tax consequences" and has many supporters, especially in the business community. Like most other principles of taxation, it has some validity, but consequences cannot really be determined without at the same time assessing benefits received, and this brings into play the need for redistribution. Neutrality alone does not accomplish this.

Adequacy of Yield

Governments must be financially sound or the nation and the economy will fall. Deficit financing may be used as a temporary, emergency measure, but the costs of government must eventually be paid. State and local governments, particularly must "balance their budgets" because of statutory and constitutional provisions and because they are not permitted to print money. Continued deficits of the federal government that contribute to inflation actually utilize inflation as a hidden tax. No reputable authority on taxation advocates inflation as a tax measure, because it cannot be defended by any valid principle of taxation. Thus, taxes for each level of government should be adequate to provide for essential public services.

Stability of Yield

To supporters of this theory, tax yields should be sufficiently stable to supply needed services without the use of deficit financing. The stability principle must be coupled with the flexibility principle discussed next, because it asserts that there should be an element of stability in the tax yield regardless of fluctuations in the economy. For instance, when bonds are issued, the yield of the taxes pledged must be sufficiently stable to pay the necessary debt service on the bonds, or they cannot be sold. Stability of revenues is particularly important to local governments that have limited flexibility in obtaining revenues. The property tax has been defended because of its stability of yield. Yet, during a major depression extending over a period of years even the property tax will tend to lose its stability. Stability in revenues of local government can be appraised only after giving consideration to the policies of the state and federal governments with respect to grants-in-aid to local governments.

Flexibility of Yield

The needs for government services change, and the necessary dollar amounts are modified as the purchasing power of the dollar changes. Therefore, the revenue system should be sufficiently flexible to provide for the government services needed during prosperous times and in times of population increases. In other words, when the costs of government rise rapidly, the revenues should rise rapidly. Income taxes and sales taxes have considerable flexibility, because they increase or decrease with the economy and with population growth. Flexibility can be provided either by taxes whose yield automatically increases proportionately to a rise in the economy or by rates that can be changed in times of need. Even property taxes can be given a degree of flexibility by establishing flexible rates. But income taxes and sales taxes are inherently more flexible than the property tax, because the yield of these taxes with no increase in rate automatically rises in prosperous times and because the rates of these taxes still can be changed if additional flexibility is needed.

Nonrigidity

This usually is called the adaptability principle. It is similar to flexibility but not the same. A tax system is rigid if constitutional or other restrictions on the rates or types of taxes levied prevent local governments from adapting their revenue systems to their needs. State governments, by constitutional provision, sometimes have prevented legislatures from developing appropriate revenue systems. Rigidity usually is built into a constitution to protect special interests. Constitutional and statutory restrictions have greatly handicapped many boards of education in their efforts to produce local school revenues. State-imposed exemptions from the property tax also greatly handicap local governments in some states, as will be explained later in this chapter.

Economy of Administration

The cost of collecting the tax should not be excessive. It may cost 2 percent of the yield to collect one type of tax and 10 percent to collect another. Other things being equal, the tax that can be collected at a low cost is better than the one that is expensive to collect.

When different levels of government are using the same tax, economy of administration can be improved by providing for a coordinated administration of the tax. For example, county, city, and school governments within the same county can reduce the cost of administering the property tax by using the same assessing and collecting authorities.

Ease of Payment

Payment of taxes should be as convenient to the taxpayer as possible, say those who advocate this theory. For example, the retail sales tax is very convenient for the taxpayer to pay. The ease of payment of the income tax was greatly improved when payroll withholding deductions were instituted. The property tax seems inconvenient to pay, because in many states the entire year's tax is due at one time. However, since the property tax cannot be collected by payroll deductions, its ease of payment can be greatly improved by instituting monthly or quarterly payments.[30] Ease of payment greatly affects public acceptance of a tax or resistance to it. This is important for public school financing, since so high a percentage of the cost of the public schools is derived from the property tax.

The Eclectic Principle

This is sometimes called the *social expediency theory* of taxation. It combines all principles, theories, and criteria of taxation. There is no one satisfactory "field theory" of taxation. It is the eclectic theory that ordinarily is used by tax-levying bodies. The eclectic principle is applied with varying degrees of equity. Some tax-levying bodies interpret this principle as "pluck the goose that squawks the least." Others levy taxes after giving due consideration to recognized principles and criteria of just and equitable taxation. Most tax-levying bodies probably operate somewhere between these two extremes.

Economic efficiency sometimes is referred to as a principle, or criterion, of taxation. It is related to the eclectic principle. Lawler and Thomson summarize the concept of economic efficiency as follows:

> Other things being the same, a high rate of economic progress is more advantageous and desirable than a low rate; in a materialistic society, economic welfare is directly proportional to the size of the national income which the community produces and consumes. The relation between taxation and economic progress is shrouded in conjecture; nevertheless there exists an optimum tax structure under given social and economic conditions which offers maximum assistance or minimum handicaps to the attainment of a high level of national product. The major policy problem in designing such a structure is the choice between generous exemptions and low rates on small incomes in order not to discourage the incentive to work, and low rates on the higher brackets in order not to discourage the incentive to invest. . . . Unfortunately the optimum amount of tax and the optimum rate structure from the point of view of economic efficiency may not correspond to the social consensus on tax equity.[31]

MAJOR TYPES OF TAXES TO SUPPORT PUBLIC SCHOOLS

Taxes may be categorized into two groups: (1) those on the *flow* of production of current output derived from purchases and sales, and (2) those on a *stock* or wealth. Taxes on the monetary flow in the production process include the major ones: individual income, corporate income, and retail sales taxes. Property taxes, which are so familiar to the public schools, are considered taxes on stocks or a portion of the wealth. Taxes within the cycle of monetary flow are those derived from individual or corporate income coming from market activity producing wages, dividends, payrolls, and profits. Household consumption or expenditures of the firm may be taxed through a sales tax on the purchase of consumer or market goods.[32] The second broad type of tax, on wealth, is typified by the property tax but also includes those taxes which are imposed on the transfer of wealth by inheritance or gift.

Another classification of taxes, *in rem* and *in personam*, is commonly used. Taxes *in rem* are levied on "things"; taxes *in personam*, on the person. Property taxes are classified as *in rem* rather than *in personam* because as a "thing" the property has a distinct location, can be assessed, and can be held as security for payment of taxes. The *in rem* tax makes no provision for taxing the equity in the property, only the value of the property itself. It makes no difference that the owner's equity is only a small percentage of the full value and a mortgagee holds the major value. On the other hand, *in personam* taxes assume the location of the individual being taxed, rather than his possessions, as is the case with income or poll taxes.[33]

Property Taxes

The property tax has always been the mainstay of public school financing in this country. Although general usage of the term property tax may refer to tangible personal, intangible personal, or real property, the primary source of revenue for public schools derives from the tax on real property. This tax is sometimes called an *ad valorem* tax, meaning a tax levied on a percentage of the value of the property. *Ad valorem* taxes are different from taxes levied earlier in Western states and called "specific acreage taxes"—constituting a set amount per acre regardless of the value of the land.[34]

The tax levied on property may be expressed in terms of *mills* or as a percent of the value. A *mill* is a unit of monetary value amounting to .001 of a dollar or one-tenth of a cent. Thus, a tax rate of 5 mills would be equal to 0.5 percent. The formula for determining the exact rate would be:

$$\frac{\text{Amount of tax revenue to be raised}}{\text{Tax base (value of property)}} = \text{Rate}$$

$$\frac{\$125,000}{\$25,000,000} = 0.5 \text{ percent or 5 mills}$$

The property tax has been roundly criticized for many years and improvements have not come easily. Comments about the inequity of the property tax today are not unlike that of Adam Smith in the *Wealth of Nations*,

A land tax . . . necessarily becomes unequal in process of time according to the unequal degrees of improvement or neglect in the cultivation of the different parts of the country. In England the valuation according to which the different countries and parishes were assessed to the land-tax by the 4th William and Mary was very unequal, even at its first establishment.

More recent expression of the unpopularity of the property tax is given by Shannon:

No other major tax in our public finance system bears down so harshly on low-income households, or is so capriciously related to the flow of cash into the household.

When compared to the preferential treatment accorded outlays for shelter under both the income and sales taxes, the property tax, stands out clearly as an anti-housing levy. Moreover, as the tax increases steadily, it is viewed by a growing number of families as a threat to homeownership.

Unlike income and sales taxes, the property tax imposes a levy on unrealized capital gains. . . . (Homeowners unlike economists are inclined to view such gains as mere "paper profit" and beyond the purview of taxation until converted to income.)

The administration of the property tax is far more difficult than in the case of either the income or sales tax. At best, the property tax assessment is based on an informed estimate of the market value of property. . . .

The dramatic increase in taxes (and resultant taxpayer shock) that often follows in the wake of an infrequent mass reappraisal has no parallel in the administration of the income or sales tax. As inflation pushes property values up, the assessment hikes become more pronounced and the taxpayer shocks become more severe.

The property tax is more painful to pay than the 'pay as you go' income and sales taxes. This is especially true for those property taxpayers who are not in a position to pay the tax on a monthly installment basis.[35]

Although all of these criticisms of the property tax are valid, some contribute more to taxpayer resentment than others. Two of them, harshness on low-income households and general administrative problems, bear further consideration.

Regressive or Progressive Taxes.   It is often said that the property tax is a regressive tax, and therefore government should be encouraged to move toward more progressive or proportional revenue sources. There are, though, differing schools of thought on this issue, each based on a different theory of property-tax incidence. One school, the traditional, maintains that the property tax is regressive, particularly in the case of owner-occupied homes where the owner is unable to shift the burden. It is assumed that renters bear the burden of the tax through higher rent payments. Under this theory, the property tax is assumed to be an excise tax on users of commodities and services produced by the taxable real property.[36] Several studies have shown that the lower the income class, the higher the percentage of property taxes which must be paid. For example, the Advisory Commission on Intergovernmental Relations found in 1970 that property taxes on owner-occupied, single-family houses were 16.6 percent of family income for the $2,000 and under category and 2.9 percent for the $25,000 and over category.[37]

The opposing view maintains that the property tax is primarily levied on capital and is shared by all owners of capital in proportion to their holdings.[38] Where the owner's effective tax rate is above the national average, it is assumed that the excess burden is distributed among landowners, workers, or consumers in the particular community. This theory asserts that property-tax incidence is split between an average national property-tax rate of between 1.50 and 2 percent and a second component of incidence, which is the amount that a particular jurisdiction varies from the average. This "new view" argues that owners of capital cannot avoid the average or uniform tax, since the tax is uniform on all capital. If the property is in a school district with higher than average tax, then the owner must bear the excess burden. This theory assumes that reactions of taxpayers will have differing effects in the long run, since in the short run taxpayers may not be able to shift the incidence of a higher than average tax.

If this theory is correct, the property tax should be classified as a progressive tax or at least a proportional one. If one assumes that assessment procedures are relatively uniform and capital market conditions are perfect, then a 2 percent tax levied on the valuation of property may be translated into an income tax on the income derived from that piece of property. If, for example, the asset is worth $10,000 and yields an annual income of $1,000, this amount of income is reasonable, since one could expect to earn 10 percent at a market rate of interest on property or other investments. If a 2 percent property tax is levied against the value of the asset, then the tax yield would be $200. If this is expressed as a percentage of income, it equals a 20 percent income tax rate. The 2 percent property tax is the equivalent of a 20 percent tax on the property income (income tax). It follows then, it is argued, that in a market where capital yields a 10 percent return, the incidence of a 20 percent tax on income would be the equivalent of a 2 percent tax on capital assets (property). This being the case, the net return on capital or income becomes a share of the total income and may be assumed to be absorbed by the recipients of capital income. And as the recipients' income increases, the total share of income moves up the income scale and the incidence of the tax is progressive.[39] Therefore, if all these assumptions are valid, then a tax on property may well have the attributes of a progressive tax.

Whether the property tax can be classified as either regressive or progressive must hinge on assumptions regarding the nature of the market, uniformity of property tax assessments, and, most important, on whether tax burdens are distributed among all owners of capital. All in all, the prevailing view still appears to be that the property tax is regressive and at best proportional, but with the "new view" becoming more acceptable among public finance theoriticians the property tax's reputation may be enchanced in the future.

The second major issue regarding the property tax has to do with its general administration. It is probably the most difficult of all the important taxes to administer equitably and has less justification for use as a major tax on the basis of many of the accepted principles of taxation than any other important tax. Nevertheless, it continues to be a major source of revenue for the local support of schools (and other local governmental agencies) in most states.

There still are many inequities and injustices in most states in the procedures utilized to assess property and collect property taxes, even though significant improvements have been made in many states during the past few decades.

Property-Tax Administration. *   The concept of tying an expenditure for any single governmental service (especially a service as extensive as education) to a single source of taxation has been challenged by political scientists and authorities in public administration. A strong case can be made, however, for revenue sources such as gasoline and similar taxes being levied and used primarily for the benefit of those who operate automobiles and utilize the highways. Such a distinction does not exist in relation to education and the property tax. Many persons who benefit from schools do not pay property taxes in the community, and many who pay property taxes receive little direct or easily identifiable benefit from existing public school systems. Moreover, the mobility of the population has given rise to another inequity with reference to the use of the property tax as a major base for the support of education. Many youths educated in one locality may become taxpaying citizens in a locality far removed from the one that contributed to their economic status.

Within the "system" of property tax administration—determining fair property values, carrying out equitable assessment procedures, establishing rates of taxation, and collecting taxes—there are many variations and anomalies throughout the nation. For some years authorities have been concerned about the defects in existing policies and practices relating to property taxation.

In both theory and law in most states, property is to be assessed at a uniform percentage of full market value. In many localities, local assessors (who in most states are elected officials) determine the value of property. In many states, these officials have no required training or background for arriving at fair and just property values. Another significant disparity often results from the time span between reappraisals or reassessments of property in many areas. An extended period between reassessment years means that property values may increase or decrease significantly.

Property tax assessment in the cities creates special complexities and difficulties. The property evaluators or assessors within a city may be called upon to place a fair value on multimillion dollar industrial complexes, slum rental buildings, and commercial establishments that range in value from a few thousand dollars to many millions of dollars—all within the radius of a few

---

*This section was prepared with the collaboration of Harry L. Phillips, Office of Legislation, U.S. Department of Education, and formerly Executive Director, Maryland Commission on the Structure and Governance of Education.

blocks. A study prepared for the U.S. Department of Housing and Urban Development includes considerable information on assessment practices within cities. It details the long-term effects of the property tax in central city areas in relation to the distribution of the tax burden among different socioeconomic classifications of citizens and the effect of property taxes on improvements and rehabilitation. The summary of this study spotlights some important factors relating to the property tax and its long-range effects on cities:

> Equalization of tax rates could create an immediate increase in the market value of blighted properties in many cities. On the average these properties are currently paying some 16% of gross income for taxes. This could very well be reduced to 10% or less if these properties were taxed at effective rates based on market value, similar to those found in other neighborhoods in the same cities. Lowering property values in blighted areas would allow long-term owners to sell out at a somewhat higher price by permitting these owners to "bail out" without the excessive capital losses they want to avoid. . . . Such a transfer of properties to a new class of owners whose ability to manage blighted properties is greater, would be a positive and helpful trend.[40]

The fragmentation of governmental units impairs the equity of the property tax. Many local governmental units are too small to employ full-time, well-trained assessors or to utilize modern assessing techniques. Moreover, dividing the state into a large number of school units results in great disparities in taxable wealth and extreme variations among different units in terms of the tax burdens they bear.

To illustrate the variation among the 50 states and some 16,000 school districts in terms of assessed valuation per pupil and the influence on educational expenditure levels, Walker analyzed the information for The President's Commission on School Finance and reached the conclusion that: "The states with the largest number of districts generally have a much greater range in assessed valuation and expenditures per pupil than those with the smallest number of districts." This indicates the school financing problems created by the existence of many school districts in many states. The difficulties of equalizing educational revenue across wide-ranging variations in local wealth as measured by assessed valuation per pupil is therefore clear.

In the process of establishing property-tax rates, the usual procedure is that officials of the local governmental body (authorized by state law to establish the rate of taxation) obtain the records giving the aggregate assessed value of properties and the level or amount of expenditures required to meet the anticipated budget for the service needed, then calculate the tax rates to meet the budget requests. This kind of public action gives rise to a very uneven and nonuniform practice of establishing property tax rates from locality to locality, and from year to year, within the same locality. Although this brief explanation is an oversimplification of the fiscal operations of local units of government, it should serve to indicate how major disparities and inequities creep into property tax administration procedure.

Problems arise in equal application of the property tax to all classifications of property and commensurate classifications of families according to age and income. The fact that taxes on residential property (with the exception of farms) are usually passed along to the consumer or renter creates added burdens. The question arises: Given these and other difficulties, should the local property tax be replaced with other forms of local taxation, or should we turn to policies that seek to cope with the major difficulties and bring about reforms in property tax administration? The answer to this question appears to be overwhelmingly the latter course of action. This is partly due to the fact that the property tax plays such a key role in financing the services of local governments, among which public education is of the greatest order of magnitude by far. Approximately 99 percent of all tax revenue raised in fiscally independent school districts comes from property taxes.

Consumption Taxes

Consumption taxes are all levies upon commodities and transactions the incidence of which falls upon the consumer through prices paid for goods and services.[41] Consumption taxes are levied upon expenditures for consumption and may be classified into six major categories: (1) customs, (2) excise, (3) sales, (4) use, (5) transfer, and (6) gasoline. Of these, the most familiar, as a major revenue producer for general state funds, is the sales tax.

Consumption taxes are justified on the basis that they (1) provide an adequate and immediate flow of revenue, (2) are easily controlled, (3) provide a relatively stable source of revenue, (4) promote tax consciousness, and (5) are economical to collect and convenient to pay.[42] The most glaring deficiency of consumption taxes is their regressive nature.

During the past few decades, the use of sales taxes has increased dramatically as states have sought new revenue sources to offset rising costs of government and to substitute for the property tax. Sales taxes used by the states are both selective and general. Selective sales taxes on motor fuel are justified on the grounds of the benefit theory. It is a *quid pro quo* for use of public highways, to which the taxes are usually devoted. If the tax were not levied, the cost of the public highway would be borne not by the user but by the community through general taxes. The selective sales tax may also be a sumptuary tax levied to reduce consumption of certain items. For example, selective sales taxes are levied on liquor, tobacco, and pari-mutuels. Such taxes, though, traditionally have not been high enough to significantly diminish consumption.

State adoption of the general retail sales tax was retarded somewhat by the success of selective sales taxes and by the earlier fear that the levy of such a tax would violate U.S. Supreme Court prohibitions against taxing interstate commerce. This legal interpretation was relaxed in the depression years, which saw the dismal response of income taxes and the collapse of property taxes in many jurisdictions. Also, Congress in 1931–32 indicated that a sales tax at the federal level was unacceptable.[43] Mississippi adopted a general sales tax in 1932, followed by thirteen other states in 1933, and by the end of 1938 nine more states had followed suit. By 1944 the general retail sales tax had become the most important state revenue producer and has been so ever since.

The retail sales tax is a single-stage tax which excludes sales to industrial customers either through the ingredient test or the client-use test. The ingredient test removes from the tax base property which is an ingredient in the product to be sold. The direct-use test excludes from the tax base sale of property which is used directly in the production of goods.[44]

In most instances, the services are excluded from the retail sales tax. The Tax Foundation has estimated that "discretionary exemptions (i.e., goods and services considered suitable for taxation but exempt in most states) amount to one-half the volume of total taxable sales."[45]

Regressive Nature. The most important objection to the sales tax is its inequity. As a tax on consumption, the sales tax absorbs a higher percentage of the income of the poor than of the wealthy. If equity is measured in terms of income, then the sales tax is regressive, since the sales tax paid by the poor man is a higher percentage of his income than that paid by the rich man. Peckman and Okner have shown that "sales and excise taxes are clearly regressive throughout the entire income scale."[46] In their most favorable light, sales taxes consume 9.2 percent of the family income at the $3,000 level and only 1.0 to 1.4 percent at the $100,000 level, with a steady graduation in between. This means that sales taxes generally violate the principle of vertical equity. As for horizontal equity, or equal treatment of equals, the tax may be even more inequitable. Here one must determine if the tax effects families in the same income class similarly. In the absence of definitive studies of this question, one may conclude that horizontal inequity is substantial, since the tax does not account for family characteristics and needs.

Galbraith, in his classic work *The Affluent Society*, minimized the importance of conventional wisdom which opposed extension of the sales tax. He maintained that in the affluent society the spending of most persons is so far above the subsistence level that the regressive nature of the sales tax is of little importance.[47]

Seligman probably best characterized the use of the sales tax, after a survey of the tax systems of several countries, when he said: ·

> The conclusion to be drawn from this historical survey is that the general sales tax constitutes the last resort of countries which find themselves in such fiscal difficulties that they must subordinate all other principles of taxation to that of adequacy.[48]

A state sales tax may be made less regressive by relieving low-income persons of the excessive burden of the tax. John Due recommends that this be accomplished by providing a credit against the state income tax representing sales tax paid on a minimum necessary level of expenditures, with a cash refund to those having no income tax liability.[49] A number of states have attempted to reduce the regressivity of the sales tax by exempting food and medicine. This policy does not reduce the regressivity of the sales tax nearly as much as the policy recommended by Due.

3. Individual Income Taxes

State individual income taxes find their precedence in the faculty taxes of the colonial days. The faculty taxes were a crude form of taxation which combined specific property taxes with income taxes. In the financial panic of 1836 several states adopted state income taxes, but only Virginia was able to administer the tax efficiently enough to produce a significant amount of revenue. Again, the Civil War brought on additional income taxes imposed on salaries and specific kinds of personal incomes. These taxes were generally undesirable because they were levied at a flat rate and were based on "estimated" income as measured by a person's "trade" or "calling" rather than actual income. Administration continued to be weak, and eventually all states except Virginia, Louisiana, and North Carolina abandoned such taxes.[50]

A great advance for state income taxes came in 1911, when Wisconsin first imposed an entirely new type of income tax. It introduced a tax on net income at progressive rates which was placed under the control of a powerful state tax commission. Actual administration was carried on by trained civil service employees assigned to districts in the state. The revenues from this tax were so substantial that other states began to follow in Wisconsin's footsteps. Today all states except four have individual income taxes.

The federal experience with the income tax had its origins with the financial exigency of the Civil War. From 1789 to 1909 the federal government relied almost exclusively on excise and customs taxes for its revenues. The Civil War income tax was in effect from 1862 through 1871, at which time it lapsed. At its peak, in 1866, it accounted for almost 25 percent of federal internal revenues.[51]

After its expiration, the income tax was not revived until 1894, during the wave of enthusiasm for trust and monopoly reform. The tax applied to both personal and corporate income and levied a low flat 2 percent. This tax was almost immediately challenged under the constitutional restraint that no "direct tax" shall be levied except in proportion to population.[52] In a five-to-four decision, the U.S. Supreme Court held that the income came "from property" and that the tax was tantamount to a direct tax on property itself, and was thus unconstitutional.[53] The effect of this ruling was that no federal income tax could be levied until the Constitution was amended. This was not accomplished until 1913, when the Sixteenth Amendment removed the constitutional barrier. The Amendment provided:

The Congress shall have power to lay and collect taxes on incomes, from whatever source derived, without apportionment among the several states, and without regard to any census of enumeration.

Only seven months after this amendment was adopted a new income tax was imposed on both personal and corporate incomes. This rather low but modestly graduated income tax was upheld as constitutional by the Supreme Court in 1916.[54]

Today the federal income tax is graduated to much higher levels and is the major federal revenue producer, supplying about 44 percent of the federal budget receipts in recent years. The federal individual income tax is, according to Peckman, the "fairest and most productive source of revenue" among the nation's federal and state taxes.[55]

Despite the apparent virtual preemption of the individual income tax by the federal government, states have found the income tax to be a lucrative source of revenue. Most states have adopted the federal tax base, with some modifications, a move which helps both the state and the taxpayers in determining the tax liability.

Peckman has found that the burden of state and federal individual income taxes combined is progressive over virtually the entire income scale, but becomes regressive at the very top. This pattern shows that slippage only comes at the highest income levels, where advantage may be taken of various exemptions.[56]

State individual income taxes are graduated, but to a more modest level than the federal income tax. Delaware has the highest graduation, 18 percent at the top income level. The graduation includes five to seven brackets in one-half the states. At lower levels, the brackets are quite narrow (often only at $1,000 intervals) and the effective rates of progression are at first rather steep, but level out and turn down at about $15,000.[57] In recent years states have begun to index personal income tax brackets to deter higher tax burdens on individuals occurring from inflation rather than from a real increase in income. The index prevents "budget creep" by adjusting the tax brackets in proportion to the rise in inflation. California and Colorado indexed in 1978, and in 1979 Arizona, Minnesota, Iowa, and Wisconsin did likewise.

4. Corporation Income Taxes

The corporation income tax has been in use at the federal level since 1909 when, to avoid a constitutional confrontation, Congress levied the tax as an excise on the privilege of doing business as a corporation.[58] Before 1941 this tax was the most effective revenue producer at the federal level, yielding the most revenue in 17 of the 28 years immediately prior to World War II. After 1941 it was the second major revenue producer until it was overtaken by payroll taxes in 1968.[59] The corporation income tax at the state level found its origins, as did the individual income tax, in the Wisconsin tax of 1911. Today, only 4 states do not have the tax. Thirty-three states use flat rate and 13 use graduated rates.

The basic method for determining taxable income under this tax is to ascertain the net income by subtracting the costs of doing business from the gross income. One of the major criticisms of the corporation income tax is that it may tend toward "double taxation" of distributed corporate profits. Profits are taxed as a corporation tax and then, when distributed, are taxed again as an individual income tax. Some maintain this is appropriate, since the corporation is an independent legal entity with a taxable capacity quite separate from the individual shareholder and, thus, should be taxed as an independent being. Regardless of views, the governments of the various states have found the tax to be an important source of revenue which should be continued. A strong mark in favor of the corporation income tax is its high progressivity. Peckman has estimated that this tax imposes a burden of only about 2 percent at the lowest income levels and nearly 26 percent at the top.[60] This is a result which is to be expected, since shareholders in corporations are generally not poor. If it is assumed, though, that corporations are able to shift the burden of taxation to consumers, then the progressivity disappears.

Another major issue surrounding the state corporation income tax is its apportionment among states so as not to impede interstate commerce. Presently, states use different methods for division of the net income base for tax purposes. This assumes that business activities can be split into separate pieces based on geography, when in fact most are unitary.[61] Congress has only acted to prohibit state taxation if the corporation only solicits business in the state and does not operate therein.[62] The basic issues of taxation of interstate commerce have not been resolved and the result has been discrimination against certain businesses and excessive costs of administration.

Other Taxes

Aside from the major taxes discussed above, the state and federal governments levy a wide variety of taxes including estate, death, gift, and use taxes. Of particular importance, though, to this discussion are the payroll taxes which were first introduced at the federal level in 1935 by the Social Security Act.

In 1935 the original programs provided for two social insurance programs: federal old-age benefits, more commonly known as "social security," and a federal-state system of unemployment compensation. The original programs have undergone substantial change, including the addition in 1966 of hospital and medical benefits for persons over 65. The federal unemployment compensation tax rate began at 1 percent and reached 3.4 percent by 1977. As the benefits rise, the rates of this earmarked tax rise, producing revenues which are a higher percentage of the gross national product each year.

Forms of estate, death, and gift taxes are among the oldest forms of taxation. In fact, the trust as we know it today was developed as a device to subvert the state's efforts in England to tax or take property by death transfer as early as the thirteenth century.[63] Taxes at death were also avoided by making direct transfers of property by gift *inter vivos* (between living persons). The federal and some state governments have, thus, tied estate, inheritance, death, and gift taxes together to prevent avoidance by various means. State governments impose inheritance taxes on the privilege of receiving property from the dead, while the federal government imposes an estate tax on the privilege of transfer on the one who dies. Bequests and gifts increase the recipients' ability to pay and could conceivably be taxed as income; however, it would be somewhat unfair to tax a possibly one-time transfer at the fully graduated rates of the personal income tax. The rates of gift taxes are, therefore, set at lower levels.

Before 1977, at the federal level estate and gift taxes were separate taxes, but were unified in that year. The tax base for the estate tax consists of the gross value of all property at the time of death, including stocks, bonds, real estate, mortgages, and any other quantifiable property. The gross estate encompasses gifts made within three years before death, insurance, and the value of any revocable trust. The gift tax is determined by the additional property acquired during the taxable year.

Estate and gift taxes are levied on only a small portion of the privately owned wealth in the United States.[64] Generous exemptions, especially since 1976, when larger exemptions were authorized, prevent encroachment of the tax on the estates of most middle-income taxpayers.

Possible New Taxes

Three new major taxes have been proposed by various sources in recent years: wealth tax, value-added tax, and expenditure tax.

Wealth Tax. The wealth tax is a tax on assessed wealth. Wealth is synonymous with capital or "net worth." Its base is determined by the value of the stock of all physical and financial assets, less those liabilities held at a particular time.[65] It differs from the "real property tax," which is a tax on the gross value of only one type of property. The wealth tax is used principally in Europe—Denmark, West Germany, The Netherlands, Norway, and Sweden for instance. Tax rates are usually about 1 percent of the annual net worth of an individual: Denmark has a progressive rate of .09 to 1.0 percent; West Germany, proportional at 2.7 percent; Netherlands, proportional at 0.8 percent; Norway, progressive at 0.4 to 1.0 percent; Sweden, progressive at 1.0 to 2.5 percent.

Advocates of the wealth tax maintain that it increases horizontal equity because it captures the entire ability to pay of each family, whereas an income tax only identifies one element. This view has been illustrated by the comparable positions of the beggar who has neither income nor property and the Maharajah who has no income but keeps the whole of his wealth in jewels and gold. They both would pay the same income tax, but a much different wealth tax.[66] Another advantage observed by Due is that a wealth tax, "while not taxing increases in capital values as such, does reach the higher values as they accrue,"[67] where a capital gains tax only reaches those values when they are realized. A third argument for the wealth tax is that it is very effective in redistribution of wealth. Finally, it is argued that such a tax is direct and cannot be readily shifted to the consumer or to lower economic groups.

Those opposing the wealth tax maintain that it poses very difficult administrative problems and that it can have adverse overall economic consequences. Concerning the latter, it almost certainly would reduce the incentive to save which has been the bulwark of personal economic objectives since the founding of this country. Importantly, some maintain the wealth tax is not needed because the diverse system of taxation of both state and federal governments in this country covers those bases—real, personal, and intangible personal property—and is nearly as pervasive as the wealth tax anyway.

Although this tax is not under serious consideration in the United States, it has been widely discussed in Great Britain. If such a tax were imposed at the state level in this country, the yield would be sufficient to make all residential property tax exempt, with a very substantial surplus.[68]

Value-added Tax.   The value-added tax (VAT) has, unlike the wealth tax, been seriously advocated in this country at the federal level. The value-added tax base is the value that a business firm adds in the course of its operations to the goods and services it has previously purchased from other firms.[69] That amount added at each level of production can be measured as the difference between the dollar amounts of the firm's purchases and its sales. The amount of purchases would include costs for merchandise and supplies, advertising, freight, utilities, and so on.

Proponents of the VAT observe that it is economically neutral; it would not distort economic decisions among "products and methods of production or between present and future consumption" and it would not favor labor-intensive industries over those that are capital intensive.[70] On the other hand, it is a consumption tax and as such is regressive in nature. The tendency would be for business to forward shift the tax to the consumer who is least likely to have the ability to pay.[71] The regressivity could, to some extent, be ameliorated by exemptions or tax credits, but the burden is likely to remain on the poorer segment of society. Further, other critics of a federal VAT say that it would upset the uneasy balance in fiscal federalism by allowing the federal government to encroach on the consumption revenues now largely dominated by the state sales tax. It is, though, maintained by some that the tax would be particularly desirable as a state tax. At the federal level, the ACIR has concluded that the tax has two intergovernmental strikes against it: (1) it is viewed as an intrusion on the state-level use of the sales tax, and (2) it cannot be readily coordinated with the retail sales tax of states and localities.[72] This, coupled with its lack of equity, greatly diminishes its attractiveness as a major new tax.

Expenditure Tax. A tax which has gained considerable attention of late is the personal expenditure tax. Some experts now believe that this tax is a better alternative than trying to reform the federal individual income tax.[73] Proponents of progressive taxation advance this tax as superior to the value-added tax. The expenditure tax has the theoretical attractiveness of being neither a *personal* tax, like the income tax, or an *in rem* tax, like consumption taxes, but constitutes a combination of the two.[74] Unlike the other taxes now in use, this one would use consumption as an index of taxpaying ability. The taxpayer would determine his or her consumption for the year, subtract out exemptions and deductions, and apply a progressive tax rate to the residual amount. The Musgraves suggest that the most feasible approach to determining taxable expenditure would be to (1) determine bank balance at the beginning of the year, (2) include all receipts, (3) add net borrowing (borrowing minus debt repayment or lending), (4) subtract net investment (costs of assets purchased minus proceeds from assets sold), (5) minus bank balance at the end of the year, (6) end up with the year's consumption.[75]

Proponents of the expenditure tax maintain that it is superior to the income tax because it encourages saving and offers incentive for capital formation. Those who oppose the tax claim that it would not be as progressive as the present federal income tax and that it would lead to excessive accumulations of wealth. The opposition further points out that it would be much more difficult to administer than the present federal income tax. On the other hand, advocates of the expenditure tax say the federal income tax has now become so unwieldy that a completely new tax is the only answer. On balance, the expenditure tax appears to be well worth extensive examination, particularly in an era when the nation's economy is in need of policy to encourage the formation of capital.

The Tax Burden

Various studies over the years have analyzed the tax structure to determine where the tax burden ultimately falls. Peckman estimated the vertical equity of the tax burden by using differing assumptions.[76] As discussed earlier in this chapter, he illustrates the impreciseness of determining burdens by showing that if property taxes are paid by the owners of property, then state and local taxes combined are much more progressive than if it is assumed that property taxes are borne by consumers. Under the former assumption, state-local taxes are progressive, ranging from 9.8 percent on families with incomes of $3,000 or less up to 13.8 percent for families with incomes of over $1 million. On the other hand, if it is assumed that property taxes are borne by the consumer, then state-local effective rates are regressive, ranging from 14.0 percent for the family with an income of $3,000 to less than 4.2 percent for the family with over $1 million.

More recently, Lile estimated the family tax burden for typical families living in the largest city of each of the 48 contiguous states.[77] He is able to provide a good assessment of both vertical and horizontal equity. His estimates were made for major taxes including state and local income, state and local sales, residential property, motor vehicle, gasoline, excise and other types, and cigarette excise. From his analysis he determined the effective tax rate by income class of family by state and the regressivity of the state-local tax burden. Table 5–1 shows his estimates.

Using this table, Lile then observes that an index of regressivity can be constructed by merely dividing the effective tax rate for the family of $50,000 income. A quotient of 1.0 indicates a proportional distribution of tax burden, a number less than 1.0 indicates progression and one of more than 1.0 indicates a regressive tax system. With this methodology the most progressive taxes were found in Minneapolis, Minnesota, and Portland, Oregon, an index of 0.55, while the most regressive was found to be 2.89 in Seattle, Washington. Other cities with very regressive taxes (over 2.0) were found in Connecticut, Florida, Nevada, New Hampshire, South Dakota, Tennessee, Texas, and Wyoming.

TAX REFORM LIMITATIONS AND EXEMPTIONS

State tax reform measures are generally attempts to make the various taxes more equitable, but in recent years a wave of public sentiment has demanded tax reductions. Inflation and a relative decline in the American standard of living since 1974 have caused taxpayers to seek shelter from taxation, restricting sources for school districts.

As part of this trend, in 1978 New York and Minnesota lowered their individual income tax rates in the highest brackets and Maine lowered rates for middle incomes. Idaho, New Mexico, Rhode Island, and Minnesota increased various income tax credits, while Indiana and Maine increased personal exemptions. During the same year, New Mexico lowered its general sales tax rates and Minnesota, Mississippi, and Texas exempted residential heating fuels from sales taxes. Corporation income taxes were lowered in Maine.

In 1979 the movement to limit local spending intensified and three states passed revenue and expenditure limitations, while two other states placed tax restraint initiatives on the ballot. Oregon, Washington, and Louisiana enacted laws to restrict state appropriations to the annual increase in the states' personal income. Utah passed a state and local appropriations limit which takes effect

TABLE 5–1   Major State-Local Tax Burdens as Percentage of Family Income; Comparisons for Largest City of 48 States, 1976

STATE	ADJUSTED GROSS INCOME, FAMILY OF FOUR			
	$7,500	$15,000	$25,000	$50,000
All states	9.8	7.9	7.6	7.5
Alabama	9.3	7.0	6.7	6.0
Arizona	10.6	7.7	7.4	7.1
Arkansas	8.4	6.6	6.6	7.1
California	10.5	8.7	8.6	10.3
Colorado	9.6	7.2	7.3	7.1
Connecticut	15.2	10.5	8.3	6.3
Delaware	10.1	8.8	9.8	11.3
Florida	6.4	4.4	3.4	2.5
Georgia	9.5	7.5	7.5	7.6
Idaho	7.6	7.1	7.8	8.3
Illinois	10.7	8.4	7.2	6.1
Indiana	11.5	8.8	7.4	6.2
Iowa	11.6	9.0	8.8	8.6
Kansas	9.3	7.1	6.6	6.5
Kentucky	11.5	9.5	9.2	8.5
Louisiana	5.1	4.4	3.7	3.4
Maine	11.8	8.9	8.6	9.7
Maryland	12.8	10.8	10.7	10.4
Massachusetts	17.5	14.2	12.7	11.4
Michigan	11.5	9.6	9.3	9.6
Minnesota	6.3	8.5	10.1	11.4
Mississippi	9.4	6.4	.6.6	6.2
Missouri	10.9	8.6	8.2	7.6
Montana	8.4	6.4	6.9	6.9
Nebraska	10.2	8.8	7.9	8.1
Nevada	7.3	5.0	3.9	2.9
New Hampshire	11.3	8.0	6.5	5.1
New Jersey	14.8	11.6	10.0	8.7
New Mexico	6.1	5.5	5.7	6.8
New York	13.0	11.2	12.1	15.8
North Carolina	9.6	7.9	8.2	8.3
North Dakota	8.0	6.4	7.3	7.5
Ohio	9.4	7.7	7.2	7.0
Oklahoma	7.2	5.3	5.4	6.0
Oregon	5.5	7.0	9.0	10.0
Pennsylvania	14.8	12.3	11.1	9.9
Rhode Island	14.9	11.9	10.2	9.7
South Carolina	9.0	7.0	7.4	7.8

(cont. on p. 110)

TABLE 5–1   Major State-Local Tax Burdens as Percentage of Family Income; Comparisons for Largest City of 48 States, 1976

STATE	ADJUSTED GROSS INCOME, FAMILY OF FOUR			
	$7,500	$15,000	$25,000	$50,000
South Dakota	10.4	7.4	5.9	4.5
Tennessee	7.8	5.4	4.2	3.1
Texas	7.2	4.9	3.7	2.7
Utah	9.0	7.1	7.2	6.7
Vermont	7.7	9.5	9.9	10.6
Virginia	9.3	7.4	7.1	7.0
Washington	8.1	5.3	4.0	2.8
West Virginia	6.5	4.6	4.3	4.6
Wisconsin	12.6	12.8	13.2	13.3
Wyoming	7.4	5.0	3.8	2.8

Source: Stephen E. Lile, "Family Tax Burdens and Taxpayer Unrest," *State Government* (Lexington, Ky.: Council of State Governments, 1978), p. 202.

in 1982. Florida, Massachusetts, and New Mexico placed new limits on local property taxes.[78]

These, and numerous reforms in other states, were largely directed toward limitation of government expenditure through more restrictive tax policy. Tax limitation legislation in 1979 went as follows: 5 states enacted property-tax-limitation laws, 3 enacted circuit breakers, 19 enacted homestead exemptions, and 10 enacted various credits and rebates. In addition to these changes, 13 states reduced sales taxes, 22 reduced income taxes, and 6 reduced inheritance and gift taxes. In sum, there were 80 acts which in some form reduced taxes in 32 states.[79]

Much of the tax legislation has involved measures to reduce property taxation. Historically, the United States has gone through periods when property taxes were subject to greater taxpayer resentment, as during the Panic of 1870, when many property/tax limits were initiated in an effort to stem the proliferation of local government. Another great push for property-tax limits came during the depression of the 1930s, when property values dropped, resulting in a significant decrease in local school revenues. Indiana, Michigan, Washington, and West Virginia in 1932 and New Mexico, Ohio, and Oklahoma in 1933 responded by revising their tax rate limits.[80] This phenomenon continues today, but nowhere is it more dramatized than in the great Proposition 13 struggle in California in 1977.

Proposition 13

The California taxpayer revolt had a resounding effect on public opinion in all states and set in motion what was to become a highly publicized antitax and anti-big-government crusade. Proposition 13, approved by the California voters on June 6, 1978, was an amendment to the state constitution limiting local property-tax rates and making it difficult for local government to increase other taxes. Specifically, the amendment provided for (1) property taxes to be limited to 1 percent of full cash value plus the rate needed to service bonded indebtedness, approved by the voters before 1978–79; (2) assessed values to be rolled back to 1975–76 levels, with increases of only 2 percent annually, to reflect inflation (newly-sold property could be assessed at market value exceeding the 1975–76 level); (3) statutes to increase state taxes to be approved by two-thirds of each of the two houses of the legislature and no new *ad valorem*, sales, or transaction taxes on real property to be levied; (4) special local taxes, taxes on real property, to be approved by two-thirds of the jurisdiction's voters.

Proposition 13 reduced local governmental revenues by 23 percent, with the greatest portion falling on local school districts, where the loss was estimated to amount to $3.5 billion or 29.2 percent of total revenues.[81] Of the total of $7 billion to be saved taxpayers, about one-third accrued to homeowners, 17 percent to owners of rental units, and 41 percent to commercial, industrial, and agricultural property owners. The remainder represented savings to state governments to be paid to local governments to replace local revenues lost because of various homeowners' and business exemptions.

To offset the effects of Proposition 13, the state increased appropriations from a state general fund surplus. A total of $4.12 billion was distributed, $2.26 billion of which went to local school districts, reducing the net revenue loss for schools to 10.5 percent.

In estimating the impact of Proposition 13, the U.S. Congressional Budget Office concluded that very little impact would be felt on the national economy from this one state action, but it was noted that a series of such actions in several states could initially depress the economy. The action in California did increase unemployment in the labor-intensive public sector by about 60,000 jobs, causing some depressive effect on California's economy.[82] The spillover of the California revolt has been felt in other states, the most dramatic being in Massachusetts, where in 1980 school revenues were drastically reduced as a result of a constitutional tax limitation amendment, popularly known as Proposition 2 1/2.

Property-Tax Control Points

State policy makers can control property taxes and local school expenditures by imposing restrictions on rates, levies, assessments, and revenues of expenditures. A common method is to limit the local school property-tax rate. Maximum rates, expressed in dollars or mills, may be set for governmental policy boards and levied without vote of the people. Maximum rates may also be established beyond which the local electorate cannot go. This method of control does not limit school-tax revenue if assessed valuation of property continues to rise, as inflation, property improvements, economic growth, or reassessment of property will cause it to do.[83]

Controls may also be placed on the rate of increase in assessments, as was done in California under Proposition 13. Assessment-ratio controls may also be used to limit the taxable value to a small percentage of the full market value of the property.

A revenue freeze can also be used to control increases in property taxes. Here the amount of revenue may be restricted to the level of the previous year or may be allowed to increase at a given percentage per year, say 6 percent. Since property values will increase as a result of economic growth or inflation, this type of control will probably result in local school districts having to reduce property-tax rates.

Another device used to control local use of the property tax is the *full disclosure law*, by which the existing political processes are brought more directly into play. Under this method, if a local school board wants to increase its tax rate, or possibly revenues, from the previous year, it must advertise, hold public hearings, and only then can the rate be set. This, it is theorized, will bring about greater public accountability on the part of school boards to more fully justify expenditures.

Homestead Exemptions and Circuit Breakers.   The regressivity features of the property tax have been corrected in two major ways. The first of these is homestead exemptions. Exemptions are provisions enacted by the state that exclude a portion of the assessed value of a single-family home from its total assessed value before applying the existing tax rate. Such action helps taxpayers whose income is modest and/or who live in low-valued residences. For example, in Florida, Georgia, Louisiana, and Mississippi, the first $5,000, or some other set amount, of assessed valuation on properties is not considered in determining the tax for the resident owner. In a number of states, additional amounts of assessed value are allowed for senior citizens and veterans.

The second reform, which constitutes a more complex way of achieving some relief from regressivity difficulties, is called a "circuit breaker." This relief is based on the assumption that an excessive tax burden is borne by householders at the low end of the income scale, particularly the elderly. An effort is therefore made to ensure that the property tax bears a reasonable relationship to the flow of cash income into a household. The circuit breaker (which requires the collection of considerably more information than administration of the homestead exemption) may be efficiently administered by a state agency, which rebates to the taxpayer the calculated relief in accordance with provisions of the program. The taxpayer's individual income-tax returns and information from property-tax administration can usually be used to determine the amount of rebate the state will pay to individuals who qualify.

Two types of circuit breakers are most common: a threshold type and a percentage-of-tax-liability type.[84] The threshold circuit breaker establishes an acceptable amount of tax which a homeowner or a renter in a certain income category should pay. The state will rebate to the taxpayer the amount of money paid for property taxes above that limit. The threshold rate may be held constant (fixed) over the various income groups or it may vary, increasing as income increases. The fixed-threshold approach is used in Connecticut, Nevada, North Dakota, and Oklahoma, while the variable approach is used in Arkansas, the District of Columbia, Illinois, Maryland, Michigan, Missouri, Vermont, and Wisconsin.[85]

The percentage-of-tax-liability formula rebates a part of the actual tax liability, returning higher percentages as the amount of income declines. This approach is demonstrated by the Indiana law which provides that 75 percent of property tax paid be rebated for the $0 to $500 household income category; 70 percent for the $500 to $1,000 category; 50 percent for the $1,000 to $1,500 category; and so on down to 10 percent for the $4,000 to $5,000 household income category.[86]

Assessment Reform. One of the more serious problems in the property-tax program is that of ensuring fairness and equality in the process of assessing properties. To some extent this may be overcome by requiring property assessors to be professionally trained and to maintain and update their competencies to value properties accurately. It also may mean that assessors should become civil-service employees of the state government rather than partisan elected officials. Uniform and standardized procedures for guaranteeing fairness in the assessment process are more easily achieved by state regulation than by attempting to ensure uniform action across many entities of local government. Some states are beginning to effect such measures. In 1973 Maryland enacted a law that requires assessors to exhibit competency and skill in valuing property before they can be appointed. Also, the Maryland reform plan specifies rigid control by the state in updating and reassessing property values. Competently staffed state boards of equalization also tend to level off discrepancies in property-tax assessment procedures and the rate at which properties are taxed.

Nearly all states now have some form of property-tax equalization strategy at the state level, including state assessment of utilities and major corporations. The efficiency and effectiveness of these strategies vary considerably from state to state. The ultimate outcome of property-tax reform measures targeted at assessment and commensurate administrative difficulties is to make the property tax a state-administered tax. Some states have made considerable progress toward achieving this end. For example, the 1973 Maine legislature enacted a law that actually makes the school property tax a state tax.

Property-Tax Classification. Through the utilization of state-mandated programs of property classification, it is possible to deliberately shift the property-tax burden from one class of property to another. For example, if state policy makers believe that residential homeowners are overburdened, through a particular classification scheme, they could shift a major portion of the property-tax burden from residential homeowners to business properties. Six states have now enacted programs that comprehensively classify property for purposes of property-tax administration: Montana, West Virginia, Minnesota, Alabama, Arizona, and Tennessee. Some of the classification schemes are rather complicated. The Minnesota plan, for example, enumerates twenty-five separate classifications of property. The usual plan, however, is a much simpler one in which property is divided into roughly four classes: transportation and communication property, utility property, commercial and industrial property, and residential and farm property. A state may also simply distinguish between purely residential and farm properties.

Site-Value Taxation.   One of the newest forms of property-tax improvements suggested by theorists is site-value taxation. The concept of site-value taxation is old; the possibility of using it is much more modern. Essentially, site-value taxation provides for a tax on land; it varies in accordance with the value of land and excludes improvements in existence on such land. Those who advocate this reform point out that site-value taxation would remove the financial deterrent to rehabilitation, especially of slum properties in the major cities. Opponents of site-value taxation point out that the existing property-tax program takes into account the actual value as the tax base, and if fairly administered would bring about abrupt and dramatic changes in the incidence of the property-tax burden. Though this theory is particularly appealing to many who seek to overcome economic difficulties confronting large cities, the likelihood of its adoption seems to be somewhat remote.

Tax Exemptions

Tax exemptions substantially affect the amount of both state and local revenue available for support of the public schools, as well as other governmental services. The four principal types of tax exemptions are:

1. Exemptions granted for the purpose of adjusting tax liability to taxpaying ability
2. Exemptions granted to attract business and industry
3. Exemptions granted to give preference to certain groups in the population
4. Exemptions granted to governmental, religious, charitable, educational, and other nonprofit institutions

Income Tax Exemptions.   The exemption for dependents allowed by the federal income tax law is a good example of exemptions granted for the purpose of adjusting tax liability to taxpaying ability. This exemption is actually a part of the progressive rate structure, and therefore is fully justified, if one accepts that the progressive income tax is an equitable tax.

Sales Tax Exemptions.   The general sales tax laws enacted by the states vary considerably in the number of items exempted. Some states exempt a great many items, usually on the theory that those items are "necessities."

However, what may be necessities for one person may not be for another. The purpose behind this type of exemption is laudable if it is to make tax liability contingent on ability to pay. However, it is an awkward method of accomplishing the purpose. The regressivity of the sales tax can much more readily be reduced by the methods recommended by Due, already discussed in this chapter. Exemptions from the sales tax also contribute to tax avoidance. It is much easier for a retail establishment to conceal its tax liability when it sells both exempted and nonexempted articles than when all its sales are subject to the tax.

Exemptions to Attract Industry. Exemptions granted to attract industry have been particularly troublesome. Conditions for maximizing the economic progress of the nation are unfavorably affected when artificial barriers or subsidies cause industry to locate at points other than those most favorable for efficient production and distribution.

Despite this fact, states and political subdivisions within states frequently give industry (especially new industry) favored tax treatment. States can do this simply by not having a state corporation income tax or by having very low rates. States also have exempted new industries from property taxes for a given number of years.

The competition for new industries is particularly keen among the political subdivisions of a state. Tax favors usually are granted to industries by entirely exempting them from property taxes for a given number of years or by assessing their properties at a very low rate. Some units of local government have given permanent property-tax exemption to certain industries by actually constructing industrial plants and leasing them to private corporations. Ownership of the property is retained by the local government, and it is completely tax exempt. These types of property-tax exemptions seriously affect school financing in many school districts. New industries often bring many additional pupils, but the tax base remains the same. Thus the school district has less taxable wealth per pupil for school support after the new industry is brought to the district than before. Experts on public finance and economics generally agree that if an industry cannot operate in a particular locality without a tax subsidy, the community is better off without it. Furthermore, it is also believed that the influence of tax exemptions or of low tax rates on the location of industries is greatly exaggerated in public thinking. Such factors as access to necessary raw materials; access to markets; and availability of labor, water, power, and community services far more powerfully affect the location of industry than do tax exemptions or low tax rates.

Exemptions for Favored Groups. As discussed earlier in this chapter, tax exemptions are sometimes given to certain groups, such as veterans or homeowners. Exemptions to veterans seem to have little or no justification. This practice certainly cannot be defended by any generally accepted principle or theory of taxation. Its purpose seems to be to establish a group with special privileges, but that practice finds no defense in the principles of American democracy.

The practice of granting exemptions to homeowners emerged during the depression in the thirties. It had great emotional appeal during those times, because many financially distressed persons were in danger of losing their homes. While homestead exemption has a laudable purpose, it is difficult to defend from the standpoint of fiscal policy. The circuit breaker approach discussed before is a far more preferable policy for increasing the equity of the property tax.

Exemptions for Nonprofit Institutions.   It is practically universal practice in the United States to exempt from property taxes all property used for governmental, religious, charitable, educational, and philanthropic purposes. Some have questioned the wisdom of this policy, but it has become so firmly established that it is not likely to be changed.

Property taxes are levied principally on the enterprises where people work and on the homes in which they live. If the principal enterprises at which people work in a school district are exempted from taxes, then the tax base is greatly reduced. Tax-exempt enterprises bring pupils to a community just as do other enterprises, and this adds not only to school costs, but also to the costs of other local governments. The federal government has ameliorated this condition in communities receiving a heavy impact from federal activities by providing special grants-in-aid for schools. The federal government also makes payments in lieu of taxes where large areas of national forests are located.

But there are many tax-exempt institutions other than federal properties. For example, state institutions and private colleges may be concentrated at certain locations. States that use the equalization method of apportioning state school funds have taken a step toward solving this problem insofar as school financing is concerned.

TAX COLLECTIONS
OF DIFFERENT LEVELS
OF GOVERNMENT

A study of the taxes collected by the different levels of government reveals to some extent the tax-levying capability of each level. Taxes collected by a governmental unit are determined by the types of tax that are legal or practicable for it to levy as well as by its ability to pay. It has been argued that the federal government has no financial ability other than that possessed by the states and that a state has no financial ability other than that possessed by its units of local government. This reasoning is based upon the assumption that the financial ability of the nation is the aggregate ability of the states and that the financial ability of a state is the aggregate ability of its subdivisions. This assumption may appear to be true theoretically, but it does not follow that the states taken together have the same capability to levy and collect taxes as the federal government. Nor does it follow that the subdivisions of a state together have the same capability to levy and collect taxes as the state.

The amount of taxes collected by the various levels of government in 1971 is shown in Table 5–2. The federal government collected 60.8 percent of all taxes collected, state governments 23.8 percent, and local governments 15.4 percent. Note that Table 5–2 excludes charges and miscellaneous revenue, utility revenue, liquor store revenue, Social Security, retirement and other insurance trust revenue. If Social Security taxes were included, the taxes collected by the federal government would approach two-thirds of the total.

Grants-in-Aid

The various levels of government collecting taxes do not always spend directly all the taxes they collect. If deficit financing is excluded, the central governments (federal and state) spend less than they collect, and the local governments more. This is due to the various systems of grants-in-aid of central governments to smaller governmental divisions. For example, between 1954 and 1977 federal government grants-in-aid rose from 11 to 33 percent of state and local revenue from their own sources, while state grants-in-aid increased from 42 to 60 percent of local government general revenue from its own sources.[87]

These grants-in-aid are of tremendous importance to government financing in the United States. The various government services needed by the people cannot be neatly allocated to the various levels of government. The direct administration and supervision of many services may be allocated, but the central governments still retain an interest in the services. Therefore, many

TABLE 5–2 Tax Collections of Different Levels of Government, 1978–79[a] (in millions)

TYPE OF TAX	FEDERAL	STATE	LOCAL	TOTAL
Property	$ —	$ 2,490	$72,453	$ 64,944
Individual income	217,841	32,622	4,309	254,773
Corporation income	65,677	12,128	—	77,805
Sale and gross receipts[b]	26,714	63,668	10,579	100,962
Motor vehicle and license	—	5,155	384	5,529
Death and gift	5,411	1,973	—	7,384
All other	2,289	6,871	2,880	13,040
Total	$318,932	$124,907	$80,605	$524,447
Percent of total	60.8	23.8	15.4	100.0

[a]Excludes charges and miscellaneous revenue, utility revenue, liquor store revenue, social security, and retirement and other insurance trust revenue.

[b]Includes general and selective sales and gross receipts taxes and customs duties.

Source: U.S. Bureau of the Census, *Governmental Finances in 1978-79*, Series GF79, No. 5 (Washington, D.C.: U.S. Government Printing Office, 1980), p. 17.

government services are provided through various types of partnerships between different governmental units. This has necessitated the development of arrangements by which different levels of government can participate in financing a service and at the same time provide for efficient administration of it.

Types of Taxes Collected

The amounts of money collected by each level of government—state, federal, and local—from each major tax are shown in table 5–2, and the percentages are shown in Table 5–3. It is to be noted that there are only four major types of tax—individual income, sales and gross receipts, corporation income, and property. These four types provide approximately 95 percent of the tax revenue of all governments combined. Those seeking substantial revenue for the support of the public schools must find it in one or more of these four taxes.

But the different levels of government vary widely in the percentage of tax money derived from different types of taxation. Table 5–3 shows that in fiscal year 1979, the federal government obtained 88.9 percent of its revenue from individual and corporation income taxes, state governments obtained 35.8 percent of their tax revenue from those sources, and local governments obtained only 5.3 percent. State governments obtained 51.0 percent of their revenue from sales and gross receipts taxes, the federal government 8.4 percent, and local governments 13.1 percent. On the other hand, the federal government received no revenue from property taxes and the states only 2.0 percent, but local governments received 77.5 percent of their revenue from property taxes.

It is evident that school districts rely almost exclusively upon the property tax for local taxation and that local governments other than schools also rely largely upon it. The federal government and the state governments have access to many more types of tax than do local governments. School districts have less possibility than any other important division of government of levying and collecting a wide diversity of local taxes.

TABLE 5–3   Percentage of Tax Collections Derived from Different Types of Taxes by Level of Government, 1979

TYPE OF TAX	FEDERAL	STATE	LOCAL	ALL
Property	—	2.0	77.5	12.4
Individual income	68.3	26.1	5.3	48.6
Corporation income	20.6	9.7	—	14.8
Sale and gross receipts	8.4	51.0	13.1	19.3
Motor vehicle and license	—	4.1	.5	1.0
Death and gift	1.7	1.6	—	1.4
All other	1.0	5.5	3.6	2.5
Total	100.0	100.0	100.0	100.0

TABLE 5–4 Percentage of Each Type of Tax Collected by Different Levels of Government, 1979

TYPE OF TAX	FEDERAL	STATE	LOCAL	TOTAL
Property	—	3.8	96.2	100.0
Individual income	85.5	12.8	1.7	100.0
Corporation income	84.4	15.6	—	100.0
Sale and gross receipts	26.4	63.1	10.5	100.0
Motor vehicle and license	—	93.1	6.9	100.0
Death and gift	73.3	26.7	—	100.0
All other	25.2	52.7	22.1	100.0

It also is important to consider the percentage of each major tax collected by different levels of government. Table 5–4 shows that the federal government collects 85.5 percent of all individual income taxes, 84.4 percent of all corporation income taxes, and 26.4 percent of all sales and excise taxes. The states collect 63.1 percent of all sales and gross receipts taxes, 12.8 percent of individual income taxes, and 15.6 percent of corporation income taxes. The local governments collect 96.2 percent of all property taxes. The federal government, then, has largely preempted the income tax field and is dipping heavily into sales and excise taxes. The heavy use by the federal government of three of the four major types of tax is increasing demands by state and local governments that the federal government return more of its revenue to them either directly, by a tax-sharing plan, or by increased grants-in-aid.

Recent Trends in Types of Taxes Collected

Table 5–5 shows the percentage of tax revenue derived from different taxes by the various levels of government in 1957 and 1979. The revenue derived by the federal government from the personal income tax increased from 51.0 percent of the total in 1957 to 68.3 in 1979, and revenue derived from the corporation income tax declined from 30.3 percent of the total in 1957 to 20.6 percent in 1979. The percent of revenue derived from other tax sources changed little.

TABLE 5–5 Trends in Percentage of Revenue Derived from Different Types of Taxes by Level of Government

Type of Tax	1957			1979		
	Federal	State	Local	Federal	State	Local
Property	—	3.3	86.9	—	2.0	77.5
Individual income	51.0	10.7	1.4	68.3	26.1	5.3
Corporation income	30.3	6.8	—	20.6	9.7	—
Sales and gross receipts	15.9	58.1	7.1	8.4	51.0	13.1
Motor vehicle and licenses	—	9.4	1.0	—	4.1	.5
Death and gift	2.0	2.3	.1	1.7	1.6	—
All other	.8	9.4	3.5	1.0	5.5	3.6
Total	100.0	100.0	100.0	100.0	100.0	100.0

The principal change between 1957 and 1979 in the percentage of revenue derived by state governments from different tax sources was the increased reliance by the states upon individual income taxes. The states obtained only 10.7 percent of their tax revenue from individual income taxes in 1957, but by 1979 the percentage had increased to 26.1.

There was some change between 1957 and 1979 in the percentage of revenue derived by local governments from different taxes. The search by local governments for new kinds of nonproperty taxes has resulted in a decrease in percentage of property taxes from 86.9 in 1957 to 77.5 in 1979.

It also is informative to consider changes in the percentage of total tax collections all governments derived from different taxes. Table 5–6 shows that the percentage derived from property taxes declined from 13.3 percent in 1957 to 12.4 percent, in 1979. Prior to 1957, the percentage of total tax revenue derived from property taxes also declined. In 1942, for example, 21.8 percent of all tax revenue was derived from property taxes. Despite the fact that for fifty years the property tax has been condemned by many tax authorities for being a regressive tax, it has shown remarkable ability to survive. Perhaps this has been due to the fact that central governments in general have been relatively insensitive to the needs of local government. Since the needs of local governments have increased rapidly during the past decade, and since the property tax was the only major tax generally available to them that would produce the required revenue, they had no practicable alternative to increasing property taxes.

TABLE 5–6   Trends in Tax Collections for Each Type of Tax for All Governments (in millions of current dollars)

Type of Tax	1957		1979	
	Amount	% of Total	Amount	% of Total
Property	$13,097	13.3	$ 64,944	12.4
Individual income	37,388	37.8	254,773	48.6
Corporation income	22,151	22.4	77,805	14.8
Sale and gross receipt	20,589	20.8	100,962	19.3
Motor vehicle and license	1,462	1.5	5,539	1.0
Death and gift	1,711	1.7	7,384	1.4
All other	2,461	2.5	13,040	2.5
Total	98,859	100.0	524,447	100.0

Recent Trends in Tax Collections by Level of Government

Tax collections for the years 1957 and 1979 are presented in Table 5–7 by level of government. This table shows that state and local taxes increased at a greater rate between 1957 and 1979 than federal taxes did. The federal government collected 70.6 percent of all tax revenue in 1957 and 60.8 percent in 1979. On the other hand, the percentage of all tax revenue collected by state

TABLE 5–7 Trends in Tax Collections by Level of Government
(in millions of current dollars)

Level of Government	1957 Amount	1957 Percent	1979 Amount	1979 Percent
Federal	$69,817	70.6	$318,932	60.8
State	14,530	14.7	124,907	23.8
Local	14,512	14.7	80,605	15.4
Total	98,859	100.0	524,447	100.0

governments increased from 14.7 percent to 23.8 percent and that by local governments increased from 14.7 percent to 15.4 percent. It should not be inferred from this that the activities of the federal government are declining in comparison with the activities of state and local governments. Proportionately more of the activities of the federal government were funded by deficit financing in 1979 than in 1957. If the federal deficit is reduced substantially by increased taxation, the trends shown in this table may be reversed.

STATE AND LOCAL TAX BURDEN

Americans paid an average of $888 in state and local taxes in 1978, an increase of $75 per person over the previous year.[88] Alaska had the highest revenue per capita, $1,871 compared with a low in Arkansas of $553. New York was second to Alaska, with $1,308, while California collected $1,227. Five other states, Wyoming ($1,156), Massachusetts ($1,098), Hawaii ($1,059), Nevada ($1,004), and Minnesota ($1,001) all had state-local tax burdens of over $1,000. Mississippi ($588) and Alabama ($566) were next to Arkansas at the bottom.

Taken alone these figures would appear to indicate that the lower-revenue states are simply not taxing themselves at as high a rate as they possibly should, but this does not take into account the variations among the states in ability to pay taxes. Rich states will raise more money with the same rates than poor states. Therefore, when attempting to raise the same revenue for governmental services from state-local tax sources, a poor state must put forth greater fiscal effort. See chapter 8 for analysis of tax effort.

TRENDS IN SOURCES OF REVENUE
FOR PUBLIC SCHOOLS

The revenue receipts of the public schools for selected years beginning with 1929–30 are presented in Table 5–8. We are interested here in sources of revenue rather than in trends in real income expressed in constant dollars. Therefore, the data in this table are presented in current dollars. The percentage of total revenue provided by the federal government increased from 0.3 in

TABLE 5–8   Trends in Sources of School Revenue by Level of Government (in millions of current dollars)

Year	Federal Amount	Federal Percent	State Amount	State Percent	Local Amount	Local Percent	Total Amount	Total Percent
1929–30	$ 7	0.3	$ 354	17.0	$ 1,728	82.7	$ 2,089	100.0
1939–40	40	1.8	685	30.3	1,536	67.9	2,261	100.0
1949–50	156	2.9	2,166	39.8	3,115	57.3	5,437	100.0
1959–60	649	4.4	5,766	39.1	8,332	56.5	14,747	100.0
1972–73	4,011	7.7	21.277	41.0	26,568	51.3	51,856	100.0
1978–79	6,787	8.1	38,611	46.2	38,257	45.7	83,655	100.0

1929–30 to 8.1 in 1978–79; the percentage provided by state governments increased from 17 to 46.2; and the percentage provided from local resources declined from 82.7 to 45.7. Although the percentage of total school revenue derived from local sources declined during this period, the amount increased. The relative percentage decline in local revenue was due to the fact that both state and federal revenues increased⊙proportionately more than local funds between 1929–30 and 1978–79.

There has been a substantial increase in federal funds for education since 1930. Most of this increase resulted from enactment of the National Defense Education Act of 1965. Trends in federal legislation concerning school financing will be discussed in detail in Chapter 15.

NOTES

1. McCulloch v. Maryland, 4 Wh. 316 (1819).

2. David Ricardo, *The Principles of Political Economy and Taxation* (New York: E. P. Dutton & Co., Inc., Everyman's Library, 1973), p. 94.

3. Edwin R. A. Seligman, *Essays in Taxation*, 10th ed. (New York: Macmillan, Inc., 1925), p. 432.

4. Philip E. Taylor, *The Economics of Public Finance* (New York: Macmillan Inc., 1961), p. 282.

5. *Ibid.*, p. 283.

6. Seligman, *op. cit.*, p. 431.

7. David Hume, *Political Discoveries* (Edinburgh, 1752), Chap. VII.

8. See William H. Anderson, *Taxation and the American Economy* (Englewood Cliffs, N.J.: Prentice-Hall, Inc., 1951), p. 73

9. Taylor, *op. cit.*, p. 312.

10. Adolph Wagner, *Finanzwissenschaft*, Vol. I, sec. 27 (Leipzip: C. F. Winterśche Verlagshandling, 1883), translated and quoted in Charles J. Bullock, *Selected Readings in Public Finance*, 3rd ed. (Boston: Ginn and Company, 1924), pp. 254–55.

11. Joseph A. Peckman, *Federal Tax Policy* (New York: W. W. Norton & Company, Inc., 1971), pp. 11–12.

12. Ursula K. Hicks, *Public Finance* (New York: Cambridge University Press, 1968), p. 116; Elmer D. Fagan and C. Ward Macy, *Public Finance* (New York: Longman, Inc. 1934), p. 191.

13. See *Memorials of Alfred Marshall*, ed., A. C. Pigou (New York: Macmillan Company, 1925), p. 84.

14. Fagan and Macy, *op. cit.*, p. 230.

15. James M. Buchanan, *The Public Finances* (Homewood, Ill.: Richard D. Irwin, Inc., 1965), pp. 193–95.

16. Anderson, *op. cit.*, p. 108.

17. Buchanan, *op. cit.*, p. 148.

18. Eugene S. Lawler and Proctor Thomson, "Taxation and Educational Finance," in *Problems and Issues in Public School Finance*, eds., R. L. Johns and E. L. Morphet (New York: Teachers College Press, Columbia University, 1952), Ch. 4, p. 113.

19. Bell's Gap Railroad Company v. Pennsylvania, 134 U.S. 232 (1890).

20. Heisler v. Thomas Callienz Company, 260 U.S. 245 (1922).

21. *Principles of Political Economy*, Book VI, (New York: D. Appleton 1895), Chap. 2, SS.2–4.

22. Paul A. Samuelson, *Economics*, 8th ed. (New York: McGraw-Hill Book Company, 1970), p. 155.

23. J. S. Mill, *op. cit.*

24. Taylor, *op. cit.*, p. 292.

25. *Ibid.*

26. Fagan and Macy, *op. cit.*, p. 191.

27. Samuelson, *op. cit.*, p. 155.

28. Adam Smith, *The Wealth of Nations* (New York: Modern Library, 1937), p. 777.

29. Fagan and Macy, *op. cit.*, p. 217.

30. An exception is the inclusion of property taxes in the monthly payments made on home mortgages.

31. Lawler and Thomson, *op. cit.*, p. 117.

32. See Richard A. Musgrave and Peggy B. Musgrave, *Public Finance in Theory and Practice*, 2nd ed. (New York: McGraw-Hill Book Company, 1976), pp. 224–25.

33. Anderson, *op. cit.*, p. 120.

34. *Ibid.*, p. 122.

35. John Shannon, "The Property Tax: Reform or Relief?" *Property Tax Reform*, ed. George E. Peterson (Washington D.C.: Urban Institute, 1973), pp. 26–27.

36. Abt Associates, Inc., *Property Tax Relief Programs for the Elderly, Final Report* (Washington, D.C.: U.S. Department of Housing and Urban Development, 1975), p. 38.

37. Advisory Commission on Governmental Relations, *Financing Schools and Property Tax Relief; A State Responsibility* (Washington, D.C.: ACIR, 1973), p. 36.

38. Henry Aaron, *Who Pays the Property Tax? A New View* (Washington, D.C.: Brookings Institution, 1975), p. 59.

39. Musgrave and Musgrave, *op. cit.*, p. 431.

40. *A Study of Property Taxes in Urban Blight* (Prepared by Arthur D. Little, Inc., for the U.S. Department of Housing and Urban Development and printed for use of the Senate Committee on Government Operations, Washington, D.C., April 23, 1973).

41. Anderson, *op. cit.*, p. 394.

42. *Ibid.*, p. 397.

43. James A. Maxwell and Richard Aronson, *Financing State and Local Governments*, 3rd ed. (Washington, D.C.: Brookings Institution, 1977), p. 102.

44. *Ibid.*, p. 104.

45. *State and Local Sales Taxes* (New York: Tax Foundation, 1970), p. 63.

46. Joseph A. Peckman and Benjamin A. Okner, *Who Bears the Tax Burden?* (Washington, D.C.: Brookings Institution, 1974), p. 58.

47. John Kenneth Galbraith, *The Affluent Society* (New York: New American Library, Inc., 1958), p. 246.

48. Edwin R.A. Seligman, *Studies in Public Finance* (New York: MacMillan, Inc., 1925), pp. 131–38.

49. John F. Due, "Alternative Tax Sources for Education,"*Economic Factors Affecting the Financing of Education*, Vol. 2, eds. Roe L. Johns and others, (Gainesville, Fla.: University of Florida, 1970), p. 310.

50. Anderson, *op. cit.*, pp. 177–78.

51. Joseph A. Peckman, *Federal Tax Policy*, 3rd ed. (Washington, D.C.: Brookings Institution, 1977), pp. 288–89.

52. Art. I, Sec. 9, Cl. 4.

53. Pollock v. Farmers' Loan and Trust Co., 157 U.S. 429 and 158 U.S. 601 (1895).

54. Brushhaber v. Union Pacific R.R. Co., 240 U.S. 1 (1916).

55. Peckman, in f., *Federal Tax Policy*, p. 54.

56. Peckman and Okner, *Who Bears the Tax Burden?*, p. 57.

57. Maxwell and Aronson, *op. cit.*, p. 95.

58. Peckman, in f., *Federal Tax Policy*, 3rd ed., p. 123.

59. *Ibid.*

60. Peckman, *Who Bears the Tax Burden?*, *op. cit.*, in f., p. 60.

61. Maxwell and Aronson, *op. cit.*

62. Public Law 86–272, Sept. 14, 1959.

63. Alexander and Erwin S. Solomon, *College and University Law* (Charlottesville, Va.: Michie Company, 1972), p. 266.

64. Peckman, *op. cit.*, *Federal Tax Policy*, in f., p. 225.

65. C.T. Sandford, J.R.M. Willis, and D.J. Ironside, *An Annual Wealth Tax* (New York: Holmes and Meier Publishers, Inc., 1975), p. 3.

66. N. Kaldor, *Indian Tax Reform* (New Delhi: Ministry of Finance, Government of India, 1956), p. 20.

67. John F. Due, "Net Worth Taxation," *Public Finance*, Vol. XV (1960), 316.

68. Kern Alexander, "The Wealth Tax As an Alternative Revenue Source for Public Schools," *Journal of Education Finance*, Vol. 2, No. 4 (Spring 1977), 451–80.

69. Advisory Commission on Intergovernmental Relations, *The Value-Added Tax and Alternative Sources of Federal Revenue* (Washington, D.C.: ACIR, 1973), p. 18.

70. *Ibid.*

71. Alan A. Tait, *Value Added Tax* (Maidenhead, England: McGraw-Hill Book Company (UK) Limited, 1972), pp. 92–93.

72. *Ibid.*, p. 12.

73. See Joseph A. Peckman, ed., *What Should Be Taxed: Income or Expenditure?* (Washington, D.C.: Brookings Institution, 1980), p. 336.

74. Musgrave and Musgrave, *op. cit.*, p. 333.

75. *Ibid.*, p. 334.

76. Peckman and Okner, *op. cit.*, p. 62.

77. Stephen E. Lile, "Family Tax Burdens and Taxpayer Unrest," in *State Government* (Lexington, Ky.: Council of State Governments, 1978), pp. 194–203.

78. Kenneth E. Quindry and Niles Schoening, *State and Local Tax Performance 1978* (Atlanta: Southern Regional Education Board, 1980), pp. 13–16.

79. *State Laws Enacted Pertaining to the Interests of the Elderly* (Washington, D.C.: American Association of Retired Persons, 1979), p. 52.

80. Advisory Commission On Intergovernmental Relations, in *State Limitations on Local Taxes and Expenditures* (Washington, D.C.: U.S. Government Printing Office, 1977), p. 12.

81. California Legislature Conference, *Report on SB 154 Relative to Implementation of Proposition 13 and State Assistance to Local Governments*, June 23, 1978.

82. Congressional Budget Office, *Proposition 13: Its Impact on the Nation's Economy, Federal Revenues, and Federal Expenditures* (Washington, D.C.: U.S. Government Printing Office, 1978), pp. 2–7.

83. Stephen E. Lile, Don Soule, and James Wead, "Limiting State Taxes and Expenditures," *State Government*, (Autumn–1975), (Lexington, Ky.: Council of State Governments), p. 205.

84. See Abt Associates, Inc., *op. cit.*, p. 47.

85. *Ibid.*, p. 132.

86. *Ibid.*, p. 171.

87. Advisory Commission on Intergovernmental Relations; *Significant Features of Fiscal Federalism, 1978–79 Edition* (Washington, D.C.: U.S. Government Printing Office, 1979).

88. "State-Local Tax Burden" (Chicago, Ill.: Commerce Clearing House, April 3, 1980), pp. 1–2.

SELECTED REFERENCES

AARON, HENRY J. *Who Pays the Property Tax? A New View.* Washington, D.C.: Brookings Institution, 1975.

BREAK, GEORGE F. *Financing Government in a Federal System.* Washington, D.C.: Brookings Institution, 1980.

BUCHANAN, JAMES M. *The Public Finances.* Homewood, Ill.: Richard D. Irwin, Inc., 1965.

DUE, JOHN F. "Alternative State and Local Tax Sources for Education." In *Educational Need in the Public Economy*, edited by Kern Alexander and K. Forbis Jordan. Gainesville, Fla.: University of Florida Press, 1976.

DUE, JOHN F., and ANN F. FRIEDLAENDER. *Government Finance: Economics of the Public Sector.* Homewood, Ill.: Richard D. Irwin, Inc., 1977.

MAXWELL, JAMES A., and J. RICHARD ARONSON. *Financing State and Local Governments*, 3rd ed. Washington, D.C.: Brookings Institution, 1977.

MUSGRAVE, RICHARD A., and PEGGY B. MUSGRAVE. *Public Finance in Theory and Practice*, 2nd ed. New York: McGraw-Hill Book Company, 1976.

PECKMAN, JOSEPH A. *Federal Tax Policy*, 3rd ed. Washington, D.C.: Brookings Institution, 1977.

PECKMAN, JOSEPH A., and BENJAMIN A. OKNER. *Who Bears the Tax Burden?* Washington, D.C.: Brookings Institution, 1974.

CHAPTER SIX
LEGAL ASPECTS
OF EDUCATIONAL
FINANCE

INTRODUCTION

When this country was formed, the function of education was not specifically delegated to the federal government, and by its omission was reserved to the states or to the people. At that time education was considered primarily a private responsibility, and where government education did exist it was considered to be an activity of local government supported by local funds. However, the federal government has historically influenced and regulated certain aspects of educational development. The authority for this, which has not yet been fully defined or clarified, is found in the powers delegated to the federal government in one or more clauses of the Constitution. Although most of these clauses state general principles, in some cases the powers have been more clearly defined by decisions of the United States Supreme Court than by the constitutional provisions themselves.

Since education is primarily a function of the respective states, in reality it becomes a responsibility of the people of each state. The beliefs and attitudes of the people about public education usually are incorporated, in general terms, into the constitution and statutes of the state. If constitutional provisions are restrictive, they are likely to handicap at least some school systems or certain aspects of education. Such restrictions cannot be removed by the legislature or in any other manner except by amendment of the constitution or perhaps a decision by the courts.

The legislature of each state has what is commonly called plenary powers; that is, it may pass any laws it considers desirable, and these laws will have to be observed unless they are found later to be inconsistent with provisions of the state constitution or in conflict with federal constitutional provisions. Such a finding, however, must be made by the courts on the basis of a controversy involving some issue presented to it for a legal decision.

Laws constitute an expression of state policy. If, in any state, a serious attempt has been made to agree upon wise long-range policies, and if the policies relating to finance or to other aspects of the educational program have been wisely and carefully developed, the laws are likely to be much more defensible than those in a state in which this has not been done. Ideas for laws come from many sources. If they come from special-interest groups that are primarily concerned with legislation designed to promote their own goals, they are not as likely to be consistent with a sound overall conceptual design as when they have been developed on the basis of careful study and through the cooperative efforts of groups concerned with all aspects of education and with appropriate state policy. Some of the difficulties in many states arise from the fact that much legislation relating to education or finance is of a patchwork nature and is sponsored by groups that have not had an opportunity or been willing to consider proposals in relationship to bona fide statewide needs.

As explained in Chapter 8, there are some major inequities in educational opportunities and in ability and efforts to support schools in most states. Some of these result from differences in local aspirations, leadership, or management, but many of the most significant have been created or perpetuated by indefensible constitutional provisions or laws. Fortunately, some of these relating especially to educational opportunities and financial support have been or are being ameliorated or eliminated by court decisions, as pointed out in the next section, or by changes in state constitutional provisions or laws.

The most significant judicial decisions for education are made by the federal courts, especially by the United States Supreme Court. Decisions rendered by the supreme court of a state, on the other hand, have direct implications only for policies and practices in the state in which they are made, with some indirect implications for other states in which they are cited or used as precedent.

The courts do not undertake on their own initiative to establish policies or to resolve controversies. They accept cases only after some conflict has not otherwise been resolved and a formal request or appeal has been filed for a decision on some important constitutional question or other legal issue. Most of the questions considered relate rather directly to, or require interpretations of, some provision in the federal Constitution or in a state constitution. Court decisions thus become precedents for decisions at a later time, unless or until they are modified or reversed.

The law governing educational finance derives from issues concerning taxation, distribution, or the appropriate management of public funds. Legal questions of taxation bear on equity and justice to taxpayers with regard to the state or school district's discretion to tax, procedures for level of taxes, and nature of the burden which the taxpayer must sustain. Distribution of state funds has historically been of little concern to the courts until the last decade, when litigation emerged from many states challenging state aid formulas under both the state and federal constitutions. This litigation, although abating somewhat lately, will likely continue. As may be expected, issues pertaining to the stewardship of school funds have been a major subject of litigation. Accountability for public funds is always a concern for the watchful public eye.

POWER TO TAX

The power to tax is vested in the state by virtue of its sovereign and inherent responsibility to provide for the welfare of the people.

The Supreme Court of the United States has explained the general taxing authority of the states in the following way:

> In our system of government the states have general dominion, and, saving as restricted by particular provisions of the Federal Constitution, complete dominion over all persons, property, and business transactions within their borders; they assume and perform the duty of preserving and protecting all such persons, property, and business, and in consequence, have the power normally pertaining to governments to resort to all reasonable forms of taxation in order to defray the governmental expenses.[1]

The power of taxation is exercised through legislative acts and is limited only by state and federal constitutions. The Supreme Court of the United States has said that "Unless restrained by provisions of the Federal Constitution, the power of the state as to the mode, form, and extent of taxation is unlimited, where the subjects to which it applies are within her jurisdiction."[2] The federal Constitution restrains state taxation only where it is imposed in such a way as to deny an individual right or freedom.

Taxing authority must be derived from state constitutions or state statutes and is never considered to be inherent in local school districts. State constitutions may be general or quite specific with regard to state taxation, but some constitutions specifically prohibit certain types of taxes, such as Florida's constitutional prohibition of the personal income tax. State constitutions may also severely restrict the authority of state agencies to tax by means such as the

Indiana and Kentucky debt limitations based on a percentage of the assessed valuation of property. Generally, though, the legislative taxing prerogative is quite broad and has been described by some courts as plenary in nature.[3]

Taxation philosophy has become a judicial consideration in those cases where the courts have adopted the sacrifice theory rather than the benefit theory as justification for taxation. As pointed out in the taxation chapter of this book, controversy has existed for centuries over whether a tax should be justified merely on the *quid pro quo* rationale—that the taxpayer should receive a benefit commensurate with the value of the tax. The courts have rejected this benefit theory of taxation, saying,

> It is no defense to the collection of a tax for school or other purposes that the person or property taxed is not actually benefitted by the expenditure of the proceeds of the tax nor as much benefitted as others. Accordingly, a childless, nonresident or corporate owner of property may be taxed for school purposes.[4]

In the same vein, other courts have said that the taxes do not need to bear relationship to the benefits received. One court observed that the benefits may be "intangible and incapable of pecuniary ascertainment,"[5] thus no direct benefits can be determined, especially in the area of public education.

School taxes are state taxes even though they may be levied at the local level, and the decision to levy is vested in local district education authorities.[6] When public schools were first organized, the state legislatures usually authorized localities to tax for education by levying rates on the assessed valuation of property. This led to a presumption on the part of many that school taxes were local taxes. This, however, is not the case and the state legislature may, in the exercise of its legitimate discretion, arrange to support the schools by taxes levied at the state level or local level or by a combination of the two. Legislatures have in nearly all states used a combination of state and local revenues, but regardless of where the tax is levied public school taxes are considered by law to be state taxes.

As a general rule, legislatures cannot delegate their legislative authority; however, with proper authorization spelling out what is to be taxed and how, the legislature can delegate the power to levy a tax to local school districts. Not only can the legislature delegate the power to tax at the local level, but it can also compel local school districts to levy particular rates.[7] Legislation which is vague or permissive will not be upheld by the courts as a proper legislative delegation of taxing authority. The power to tax must be either expressly granted or derived from necessary implication of powers which have been expressly granted.[8] Courts look on the power to tax with particular circumspection and will not easily grant taxing power on mere implication. The power to tax goes to the heart of the governmental process; there the courts are careful not to interpret implied powers too broadly. The Supreme Court of Kansas has said:

The authority to levy taxes is an extraordinary one. It is never left to implication, unless it is a necessary implication. Its warrant must be clearly found in the act of the legislature. Any other rule might lead to great wrong and oppression, and when there is a reasonable doubt as to its existence the right must be denied. Therefore, to say that the right is in doubt is to deny its existence.[9]

Thus, a school district cannot levy a tax unless the power is conferred by statute. The precise limits of implication are not easy to define. In one of the historic cases in education, the *Kalamazoo* decision, the Supreme Court of Michigan drew very broad implications from a statute allowing taxation for secondary grades when the statute only explicitly conferred authority to tax for primary education.[10] The court reasoned that the grades and branches of knowledge should not be limited if the voters consented to raise taxes for an expansion of educational services.

TYPE OF TAXES TO BE LEVIED

Whether a tax may be levied for school purposes depends on the individual state's constitution and statutes. Although states have traditionally relied on local property taxes for the basic support of public schools, there is no reason that a state cannot also provide for the levy of local sales, income, or other taxes. Some states have used poll taxes, bank shares taxes, liquor license taxes, occupational taxes, and business taxes at the local level. Imposition of a tax on the wages of residents and net profits of businesses and professions by school districts in Pennsylvania has been upheld. Pennsylvania, though, has a relatively unique situation by virtue of the legislature's so-called "Tax Anything Act" which, by its nature, allows local taxing prerogatives not typical of most other states.

The importance of the property tax as a local source of school revenue is evidenced by the substantial amount of litigation which has arisen about it over the years. The general rule is that the governmental unit in which the property is located has the prerogative of levying the tax. *Situs* of property is usually determined by the place where it is located or the domicile of the owner. Real estate may be taxed only in the state or school district in which it is located. Thus, where a piece of real property lies in two school districts, each district can tax only that portion within its geographical boundary.

Tangible personal property, because it can be easily moved, creates problems of taxation not present with real estate. Such property may be taxed at either the domicile of the owner or the place of its location, but not at both. The Supreme Court of the United States held in 1905 that if tangible personal property has acquired taxable situs in one state it cannot be taxed at the owner's domicile in another state without violating the due process clause of the Fourteenth Amendment.[11] Within one state, the legislature may establish the taxable situs of personal property, whether tangible or intangible, at either the situs of the property or the domicile of the owner.

Interstate taxation is another matter. The Commerce Clause of the United States Constitution places restrictions on a state's right to levy taxes which would have a detrimental effect on commerce among states.[12] The dilemma of the Supreme Court in this area has been to protect interstate commerce yet not impose rules which unduly restrict the sovereign power of states to tax in our federal system. Justice Frankfurter has said:

> The power of the states to tax and the limitations upon that power imposed by the Commerce Clause have necessitated a long, continuous process of judicial adjustment. The need for such adjustment is inherent in a Federal Government like ours, where the same transaction has aspects that may concern the interests and involve the authority of both the central government and the constituent states. . . . To attempt to harmonize all that has been said in the past would neither clarify what has gone before nor guide the future.[13]

Thus the Supreme Court has decided interstate taxing questions on a case by case basis, without attempting to construct an encompassing and general rule of law.

Sales and use taxes have in recent years come into the forefront of school financing, having been levied at both state and local levels. A Washington state "use" tax of 2 percent, placed on the privilege of using products from sister states, was upheld by the Supreme Court in 1937.[14] The tax was levied generally, except on property which had already been subjected to an equal or greater sale or use tax whether, in Washington or any other state. This exception, the Supreme Court observed, was within the standard of equality required by the interstate Commerce Clause in that the tax did not impose greater burdens on the stranger than on the dweller within the state; therefore, in-state and out-of-state products were treated the same.

Sales of goods brought in from other states are subject to nondiscriminatory exercise of taxing power by the recipient state. Thus, a tax confined to the sale of goods manufactured outside of the state, and not applying to the same products manufactured within the state, was set aside as unconstitutional.[15] According to Justice Reed, "The Commerce Clause forbids discrimination, whether forthright or ingenious."[16]

Besides property, sales, and use taxes the states rely on both personal and corporate income taxes for educational financing. A state has the authority to tax the income from the property owned by a person who is a resident of another state. Similarly, the income from a business conducted or located in a state can be taxed regardless of where the person who owns the business resides. The Supreme Court of the United States has said:

> That the State, from whose laws property and business and industry derive the protection and security without which production and gainful occupation would

be impossible, is debarred from exacting a share of those gains in the form of income taxes for the support of the government, is a proposition so wholly inconsistent with fundamental principles as to be refuted by its mere statement. That it may tax the land but not the crop, the tree but not the fruit, the mine or well but not the product, the business but not the profit derived from it, is wholly inadmissible.[17]

The cardinal rule, though, is that a state cannot impede trade and the normal flow of commerce beyond state boundaries. Overall, when the sovereign power of taxation is viewed in its broadest context, the state has great legal latitude for deriving revenues to support the schools.

FEDERAL FUNDS

Legal controversies have arisen more as the federal government has become increasingly active in the aid and regulation of education. Federal funds are granted through categorical programs which support state efforts to provide specific educational programs such as vocational education, compensatory education, and education for the handicapped. Another major federal program is the provision of funds for areas with concentrations of federal activities—the Impact Aid laws, Public Laws 815 and 874.

One case important to federal-state relations arose out of a conflict between state and federal interests in the implementation of Title I of the Elementary and Secondary Education Act of 1965, the compensatory education legislation. Provisions in the act for programs in private schools comparable to public schools offended the constitution of Missouri's church-state provision, and local education agencies in that state refused to implement the program as desired by the parochial schools.[18] The plaintiffs for the parochial schools sought to compel the state to implement Title I in spite of the Missouri Constitution, maintaining that the federal statute should prevail over the state constitutional prohibition. The Supreme Court held that it was clear that Congress did not intend for Title I to preempt state constitutional spending proscriptions as a condition of accepting federal funds. Thus, Title I should not be interpreted as overriding state constitutional law, and if a conflict exists between the two, then the solution must be sought short of subordinating the state constitution to federal statute. The Court suggested that the state seek ways of implementing the Title I "comparability" requirement which would not offend the state constitution and that the parochial schools agree to alternatives which would define "comparability" in broader terms and not require that the funds be used for on-the-premises instruction in parochial schools.

A most apparent innovation in public school finance in recent years has been the emergence of greatly increased aid for handicapped children from both state and federal levels. The legal impetus came from two federal district court cases, one in Pennsylvania and the other in Washington, D.C.[19] In the Pennsylvania case, the state was enjoined from denying equal educational opportunity to handicapped children, and shortly thereafter the court in the District of Columbia required that handicapped children be provided publicly supported educational programs suitable to their needs. To the argument that such special programs were too expensive and could not be afforded, the court responded:

> If insufficient funds are available to finance all of the services and programs that are needed and desirable in the system, then the available funds must be expended equitably in such a manner that no child is entirely excluded from a publicly supported education. . . .
>
> The inadequacies of the District of Columbia Public School System, whether occasioned by insufficient funding or administrative inefficiency, certainly cannot be permitted to bear more heavily on the "exceptional" or handicapped child than on the normal child.

These cases played a major role in creating a public awareness of problems associated with funding programs for handicapped children and were instrumental in the federal government's ultimate response, the enactment of Public Law 94–142.

Of all the court decisions which have had an impact on school finance, the case of *National League of Cities* v. *Usery* (426 U.S. 833 [1976]) must rank near the top. In 1974 and 1975, a movement developed at the federal level to enact a federal collective bargaining law which would constitute a kind of National Labor Relations Act for teachers. Passage of the bill by Congress appeared imminent until the Supreme Court rendered the decision in *Usery,* which took the constitutional props from under the collective bargaining bill. The premise behind the bill was that Congress could regulate school wages, a state prerogative, through invocation of the Commerce Clause of Article I of the U.S. Constitution. No funds were attached to the law so that it could not be construed as federal aid to education falling within the scope of the General Welfare Clause, the more traditional justification for federal involvement.

The *Usery* case arose as a challenge to 1974 amendments to the Fair Labor Standards Act, which required that local and state governmental agencies pay at least the established minimum wage for employees. This law required that local school districts pay the minimum wage to lunchroom workers, custodians, grounds keepers, bus drivers, and others, greatly increasing the local school district's operating budgets. Many local school districts had to raise local property tax rates to obtain the needed revenues and/or the states were forced to increase state aid. In reviewing the impact of this legislation, the Supreme Court held that the amendments violated the Tenth Amendment to the Constitution of the United States and that the Commerce Clause could not be used to sustain such federal intervention. The Court said:

> Congress has sought to wield its power in a fashion that would impair the state's "ability to function effectively in a federal system," . . . This exercise of congressional authority does not comport with the federal system of government embodied in our Constitution.

This important decision established that the Tenth Amendment limits the use of the Commerce Clause in federal involvement in education. The most notable effects of this principle were the prevention of federal establishment of minimum wages for school employees, but it also served to remove the Commerce Clause as the constitutional justification for enactment of a federal collective bargaining law. According to the Court, the Tenth Amendment "expressly declares the constitutional policy that Congress may not exercise power in a fashion that impairs states' integrity or the ability to function effectively in a federal system."

Federal legislation can have a direct effect on distribution of state funds to local school districts. When a state statute directly conflicts with a federal statute, and no extenuating constitutional questions are involved, the federal statute takes precedence. One such conflict occurred in a Virginia case in 1968 in which the state foundation program law was challenged by a taxpayer because it charged back Public Law 874 funds against the state foundation program allocation.[20] In order to bring about greater fiscal equalization among school districts, the state of Virginia had decided to count P.L. 874 funds as though they were local funds contributing to the local school district's fiscal ability. The effect of the chargeback was to effectively redirect state funds to financially needy school districts. The federal district court ignored the equalization question and ruled that the Supremacy Clause of the federal Constitution requires that when federal law conflicts with state law the federal intent must be upheld. This case resulted in some fifteen states revising their state aid laws to delete provisions which counted P.L. 874, Impact Aid, funds as local fiscal ability.

ESTABLISHMENT OF RELIGION

According to the U.S. Supreme Court, the establishment-of-religion clause of the First Amendment means that "No tax in any amount, large or small, can be levied to support any religious activities or institutions, whatever they may be called, or whatever form they may adopt to teach or practice religion."[21] In spite of this rather clear proscription, state legislatures and the Congress have time and again enacted laws which aid parochial schools. Among the several federal laws which provide aid to parochial schools, Title I of the Elementary and Secondary Education Act of 1965 is the largest and most influential. Also, state legislatures, particularly in New York, Pennsylvania, Ohio, and Rhode Island, have through various schemes sought to aid parochial schools and have in each instance met with judicial disapproval.

Prior to 1970 the Supreme Court applied two constitutional tests to parochial school legislation; (1) the secular legislative purpose test, and (2) the primary effect test. The former required that the legislature have some purpose for the legislation other than aiding religion. Under the second test, the Court sought to determine whether the primary effect of the legislation was to either advance or inhibit religion. These two tests were used in the famous *Everson* case, in which a New Jersey law providing public funds for transportation of schoolchildren to parochial schools was held to be constitutional and in the later *Allen* case, in which the loan of textbooks to parochial schools was also upheld.[22] Neither of these tests proved to be very restrictive, and after *Allen* in 1968 many states moved to enact funding programs which would more directly aid parochial schools.

The first two of these new laws were almost immediately challenged in Pennsylvania and Rhode Island, and a decision by the Supreme Court invalidated them in 1971.[23] Under Pennsylvania law, the state superintendent was authorized to "purchase" specified secular education from parochial schools, and in Rhode Island the state law gave a salary supplement to parochial school teachers. In reaching a decision in these cases, the Supreme Court relied on a new, third test of establishment—excessive entanglement.[24] This test holds invalid legislation which tends to introduce state regulation into church affairs or to allow church encroachment on public policy decisions. In applying all three tests, the Court held that the aid provisions did not evince a legislative purpose to aid religion nor did they have the effect of advancing religion, but both laws violated the excessive entanglement test, because both would have required such a degree of state scrutiny into the parochial school programs as to excessively entangle church and state.

Other methods of distributing state funds to aid parochial schools have been similarly stricken in recent years. A comprehensive law in New York provided for three methods of aiding parochial schools; (1) maintenance and repair of school facilities, (2) a tuition grant program, and (3) a tax benefit provision. The Court held that all three programs had the effect of aiding and advancing religion.[25] The Court observed that the provision to maintain and repair facilities could actually lead to the use of state funds to renovate classrooms in which religion was taught or to maintain a school chapel. The tuition grant, which provided reimbursement to low-income families who sent their children to private schools, had a sectarian orientation and effectively aided religion.[26] The third program, a plan to give tax benefits, was most innovative in seeking to bypass the excessive entanglement test by simply allowing parents with less than $25,000 income to deduct a specified amount from their adjusted gross income for state income tax purposes. The Court held that such tax benefits were little different from tuition grants, both having the effect of advancing religion. It made no difference that the tax benefits were directed to the parents rather than the parochial schools, since the net effect of the legislation was to strengthen the parochial schools by giving parents financial incentive to enroll their children in such schools. This case appears to foreclose the possibility of other states or the federal government fashioning a constitutionally acceptable scheme for tuition tax credits to aid parochial schools.

Loans of instructional materials and equipment have been held unconstitutional by the Supreme Court in another Pennsylvania case, *Meek v. Pit-
tenger* (421 U.S. 350 [1975]). The Court said in this case that one cannot separate
the secular from the sectarian purposes of church-related elementary and secondary schools and that aid to what may seemingly be a secular aspect of such
school programs will undoubtedly result in spillover aid to the sectarian part
of the schools' programs. The Court said,

> The very purpose of many of those schools is to provide an integrated secular and
> religious education; the teaching process is, to a large extent, devoted to the
> inculcation of religious values and belief. . . . Substantial aid to the educational
> function of such schools, accordingly, necessarily results in aid to the sectarian
> school enterprise as a whole . . . "[T]he secular education those schools provide
> goes hand in hand with the religious mission that is the only reason for the schools'
> existence. Within the institution, the two are inextricably intertwined."

Beyond allowing for state aid for transportation and textbooks, the wall
of separation between church and state in elementary and secondary education
has remained rather firm. The *Wolman* case, however, proved an exception
because in it the Supreme Court upheld certain aspects of a complicated Ohio
statute providing parochial school children not only with textbooks, but also
with testing and scoring services, diagnostic services, therapeutic services,
instructional materials and equipment, and field trips.[27] The Court struck down
instructional materials and equipment and field trip provisions as in effect aiding
and enhancing religion and against the excessive entanglement tests. On the
other hand, testing and scoring services designed to measure the progress of
parochial school students in secular subjects were upheld. Aid for diagnostic
services for speech, hearing, and psychological disorders were upheld as constitutional. The Court found that diagnostic services were unlike teaching and
counseling and, thus, more remotely associated with the mission of the nonpublic school. Potential intrusion of sectarian views was believed to be minimal.
The third element, therapeutic services for nonpublic school students was upheld because the services were provided in public facilities, supervised by public
employees. The Court did not seem to think that the state was enhancing
religion by providing therapeutic services, even though the services were exclusively for nonpublic school students and could be held in mobile units used
as annexes to the parochial school.

With the possible exception of *Wolman*, the Supreme Court during the
last decade has adhered to a strict definition of the Establishment Clause,
effectively preventing most state funding schemes which would aid religious
institutions. Each legislative session, though, brings forth new innovations designed by legislatures to circumvent the intent of the First Amendment and
abatement of such measures is not likely to come during the next decade, which
will see inflationary trends placing greater financial burdens on private schools.

APPORTIONMENT OF STATE FUNDS

Methods of apportioning state funds for public schools have been challenged under both federal and state constitutions. These actions have been brought either by those who claim that the tax system used for raising school revenues does not treat taxpayers uniformly and equally, or by children who maintain that they are denied equal educational opportunity because of unequal distribution of tax revenues among school districts. As plaintiffs, taxpayers have couched their claims in the uniformity and equality of taxation provision; in their equivalent, found in all state constitutions; or in the Equal Protection Clause of the Constitution of the United States. Children, on the other hand, have based their contentions on education provisions in state constitutions, which usually require the state to provide a uniform, thorough, efficient, or equal system of education for all children of the state. School children have also unsuccessfully claimed that unequal distribution of state funds violates the Equal Protection Clause of the Fourteenth Amendment. The remainder of this chapter examines the status of the law on each of the three perspectives: taxpayers' equality and uniformity contentions; school children's complaints under state education provisions; and the apportionment decision by the U.S. Supreme Court, which was based on the Equal Protection Clause of the Fourteenth Amendment.

Equality and Uniformity of Taxation

As a general rule, courts will not hold an act of the legislature unconstitutional unless it can be clearly demonstrated that the legislature exercised its authority in an arbitrary or capricious manner. Instances where the courts have overthrown taxing provisions have been relatively rare among the states. For an act to be arbitrary or capricious in the uniformity or equality sense, it must be shown that the state unreasonably classified a particular group of persons or in some way, through the tax system, discriminated against them. If such discrimination did exist, then state as well as federal guaranties against unconstitutional classifications would be violated. The equality question, with regard to taxation, is clearly enunciated by the U.S. Supreme Court in dictum in the *Bell's Gap* Case, where Justice Bradley explained:

> [The Equal Protection Clause] was not intended to prevent a state from adjusting its system of taxation in all proper and reasonable ways. . . . We think we are safe in saying, that the Fourteenth Amendment was not intended to compel the state to adopt an iron rule of equal taxation. If that were its proper construction it would not only supersede all those constitutional provisions and laws of some of the states, whose object is to secure equality of taxation, and which are usually accompanied with qualifications deemed material; but it would render negatory those discriminations which the best interests of society require.[28]

The state legislature may, therefore, utilize the taxing system to equalize between rich and poor, as is done, for instance, through the redistributional effects of a graduated income tax. Too, if it wishes, the state may collect tax funds from wealthy school districts and redistribute them to poorer districts in other parts of the state. In this light, neither state uniformity and equality of taxation provisions nor the Equal Protection Clause require that proceeds from taxes be distributed in any particular manner or method. In *Sawyer* v. *Gilmore*, a 1912 case, the Supreme Court of Maine reasoned that:

> The method of distributing the proceeds of such a tax rests in the wise discretion and sound judgment of the Legislature. If this discretion is unwisely exercised, the remedy is with the people, and not with the court. . . . In order that taxation may be equal and uniform in the constitutional sense, it is not necessary that the benefits arising therefrom should be enjoyed by all the people in equal degree, nor that each one of the people should participate in each particular benefit.[29]

Uniformity and equality of taxation provisions of state constitutions cannot be invoked by the taxpayer to challenge the distribution of state school funds among school districts. While state and local taxation must be uniform and equal, the distribution of the revenues can be unequal in order to achieve a valid state objective. The law may be summarized thus:

> In the absence of constitutional regulation the method of apportioning and distributing a school fund, accruing from taxes or other revenue, rests in the wise discretion of the state legislature, which method, in the absence of abuse of discretion or violation of some constitutional provision, cannot be interfered with by the courts. . . . The fact that the fund is distributed unequally among the different districts or political subdivisions does not render it invalid.[30]

This principle of law is illustrated in *Dean* v. *Coddington*, a South Dakota case, wherein the plaintiff, a taxpayer, asserted that the state foundation program was unconstitutional because state taxes collected from an admittedly uniform levy were distributed back to school districts on a per pupil wealth basis which did not return the tax revenues to the point of origin. In denying the taxpayer's complaint, the court stated the rule as follows:

> It is generally held that the constitutional provisions requiring equality and uniformity relate to the levy of taxes and not to the distribution or application of the revenue derived therefrom; and hence statutes relative to the distribution or application of such money cannot be held invalid on this ground.[31]

These cases, then, make it quite clear that courts are hesitant to interfere with legislative discretion in the realm of taxation and that taxing provisions of state constitutions will not come under judicial regulation of the methods used by legislatures distribute state school districts.[32] Similarly, the federal courts will tend to exercise a high degree of judicial restraint when the Equal Protection Clause of the Fourteenth Amendment is invoked in challenging state systems of taxation.

Educational Opportunity
under State Constitutions

Although apportionment formulas for state school aid are not subject to state constitutional taxing provisions, they are directly affected by protections to education in state constitutions. Most state constitutions have an education section which by various terminology charges the legislature with the responsibility of providing for the education of all children throughout the state. The constitutions usually require a uniform, equal, thorough, and/or efficient educational system. At least one court has commented that even the word "system" denotes a requirement that the legislature provide an "efficient and sufficient system, with competent teachers, necessary general facilities" and long enough school term.[33] In interpreting these state constitutional provisions, though, the state courts have rendered a diversity of opinions, some holding state school apportionment formulas unconstitutional and others upholding distribution schemes which on their face appear to be constitutionally defective.

Several cases serve as useful examples of judicial intervention where state school fund distribution formulas were found to be contrary to state constitutional requirements. Most influential of these cases was *Serrano v. Priest* (96 Cal. Rptr. 601, 487 P.2d 1241 [1971]), in which the Supreme Court of California invalidated the state school finance program because its net effect was to deny equal treatment under the California Constitution. This case gained much publicity nationwide, and even though a major portion of the California Supreme Court's rationale was tied to a misinterpretation of the Equal Protection Clause of the Fourteenth Amendment, the result nevertheless had an important influence on school financing during the entire decade of the 1970s.

Of comparable acclaim was a case out of New Jersey, *Robinson v. Cahill* (62 N.J. 473, 303 A.2d 273 [1973]), in which the Supreme Court of New Jersey struck down the state school finance program. Here the plaintiffs relied on a state constitutional provision requiring that the legislature provide a "thorough and efficient" system of education. It was maintained that the state distribution formula did not provide sufficient fiscal equalization among school districts and did not take into account the varying educational needs of children. In striking down the state school aid formula, the New Jersey court found that the "thorough and efficient" provision of the state constitution required equal educational opportunity throughout the state. If local government fails to so provide, the state must act to either compel local school districts to meet the constitutional mandate or the state must provide the funds from state tax revenues. This court gave a broad definition to "thorough and efficient," saying:

> The Constitution's guarantee must be understood to embrace that educational opportunity which is needed in the contemporary setting to equip a child for his role as a citizen and as a competitor in the labor market.

In 1977 the Supreme Court of Connecticut struck down that state's school finance program, which at the time provided a rather low level of equalization among school districts.[34] The court held that under the Connecticut Constitution education is considered a fundamental right, and where the state system of school financing operates to create wide disparities in educational funds, the court will strictly scrutinize the situation. Further, and most importantly, in finding that education is fundamental the court effectively shifted the burden of proof from the plaintiff to the state, requiring the state to present compelling reasons, rather than mere rationality in defense of state school finance programs. When the state could not do so, the court held the system unconstitutional.

The Connecticut court noted that the source of the revenue disparities among school districts arose from the state's delegation of fiscal responsibility for schools to local municipalities, which have widely disparate financial capabilities. State legislation had not given sufficient attention to equalizing these disparaties, with the result that some localities had a very poor financial base while others were quite affluent.

State school finance schemes have also been stricken under educational provisions of the Washington and West Virginia constitutions. In Washington, a state trial court's decision found that the method used to finance education, as it impacted on Seattle, violated the state's duty to make "ample provision for the education of all children residing within its borders."[35] The court held that the state was required to provide students in Seattle with "a basic program of education" regardless of whether local levies to supplement state funds were approved by the voters. The Supreme Court of Washington affirmed that the state constitutional mandate to provide "a basic program" required the state to fund more than merely the basic skills of reading, writing, and arithmetic!

As in New Jersey, the words "thorough and efficient" have been a major source of interpretative litigation in West Virginia. There the state Supreme Court struck down the method of financing as violative of the state constitution's "thorough and efficient" and equal protection provisions. The case was remanded back to a lower court to establish standards for a "thorough and efficient system of public education."[36]

State supreme courts, however, have been far from uniform in requiring that legislatures revise school finance programs. In fact, the weight of judicial opinion appears to be adverse to courts' intervention into this traditional area of legislative prerogative. The Arizona Supreme Court has held that even though education is a fundamental right under that state's constitution, the state requirement that education be "uniform" merely mandates that the state finance a school system which serves a particular age group, is open a minimal number of days a year, and does not treat individuals unreasonably, discriminatorily, or capriciously.[37]

In the same vein, the Supreme Court of Michigan held in 1973 that the equal protection clause of the Michigan Constitution was not violated by a state school finance program which left substantial revenue variations among school districts.[38] The court took two basic positions. The first was that equality of educational opportunity is such an "ephemeral concept that judicial review on abstract 'equality' standards is bound to be unmanageable," and the second, that the state constitution does not forbid persons residing in one taxing district from taxing themselves at a higher rate than persons in other districts.

The Supreme Court of Ohio has also upheld the state system of financing, maintaining that revenue inequalities among school districts are not offensive to the state constitutional requirement that guarantees the right of children to attend a "thorough and efficient system of common schools."[39]

Courts in other states have also denied relief to plaintiffs who have sought basic changes in state school finance formulas because of alleged denial of a state constitutional right.[40] In spite of these losses, the litigation has opened a new window of inquiry which will undoubtedly be beneficial to education in years to come. This litigation will continue to redefine the state constitutional standards of uniformity, efficiency, equality, and other concepts which are basic to public schools in every state. Such litigation will also likely bring more precision in measurement, gaining on the goal of equal education opportunity.

Federal Equal Protection and Apportionment of State Funds

Antecedents to school finance litigation of the 1970s are found in the expansion of the judicial concept of equal protection and its application to education during the desegregation decade following *Brown* v. *Board of Education* in 1954. The Equal Protection Clause of the Fourteenth Amendment was used in many and diverse ways to challenge arbitrary and discriminatory classification of persons by government. School finance litigation where the state methods of school finance allowed great differences in school revenues to exist were natural targets for invocation of equal protection. Smoldering discontent with legislative inaction in remediating fiscal inequalities among school districts was given legal foundation in a book entitled, *Rich Schools, Poor Schools*, written by Wise in 1968.[41] Wise's thesis was basically that since education was a state responsibility, wide disparities created by state funding schemes unconstitutionally classified children according to the fiscal ability or inability of their respective school districts.

The first case to challenge the constitutionality of a state school finance program, *Burruss* v. *Wilkerson*, was brought in Virginia in 1968.[42] Shortly thereafter, *McInnis* v. *Shapiro*, filed in Illinois, made similar claims, alleging that the method of financing used by the state of Illinois denied equal protection by depriving schoolchildren in poor school districts resources equal to those in more affluent school districts.[43] Plaintiffs in both *Burruss* and *McInnis* claimed that a state school finance program violates equal protection if it does not correct for financial inabilities among local school districts and if it does not take into account the educational needs of the children. In other words, the state must fiscally equalize among school districts to erase revenue disparities and to provide funds on some type of educational need basis whereby social, economic, cultural, physical, or mental deficiencies, which detract from educational opportunity, can be mitigated.

The federal district courts in both cases held against the plaintiffs, and on appeal the U.S. Supreme Court affirmed the lower court's decisions. The position of the courts with regard to equalization of local tax resources is well encapsulated by the federal district court in *McInnis*:

> Unequal educational expenditures per student, based upon the variable property values and tax rates of local school districts, do not amount to an invidious discrimination. Moreover, the statutes which permit these unequal expenditures on a district to district basis are neither arbitrary nor unreasonable.[44]

Thus, plaintiffs were required to show not only that the expenditure disparities existed, but also that they were the result of invidious discrimination against a particular class of persons. According to the court, even though there were substantial differences, there was a rational relationship between the state's funding scheme and the results it was designed to achieve.

With regard to the educational needs aspect of the plaintiff's argument, the *McInnis* court refused to intervene and substitute its judgment for legislative prescription, saying that: "The courts have neither the knowledge, nor the means, nor the power to tailor the public moneys to fit the varying needs of these students throughout the state." Further, the *McInnis* court concluded that there were no "judicially manageable standards" by which it could accurately determine the extent to which educational needs were being met. Both *Burruss* and *McInnis* were affirmed by the U.S. Supreme Court, but without an opinion. It was, therefore, impossible to know exactly what the Court's rationale was for the summary affirmations in either case.

The position of the Supreme Court was not to be known until 1973, when in the now famous case of *San Antonio Independent School District* v. *Rodriguez*, it held in a 5-to-4 decision that the state foundation program in Texas did not violate the Equal Protection Clause.[45] Plaintiffs maintained that education was a fundamental right and that children attending school in poor school districts constituted a suspect classification, and, thus, the Supreme Court must strictly scrutinize the Texas system, forcing the burden of proof on the state to show that it had a "compelling interest" rather than mere "rationality" in maintaining the state school finance program. If invoked, the strict scrutiny test means that the state's system is not entitled to the usual presumption of validity, rather, the state must sustain a heavy burden of justification.

Texas virtually conceded that it could not withstand the strict scrutiny burden but it could show that its system was at least not irrational. The decision, then, rested on which constitutional test the Supreme Court used. Taking the issues one by one, the Court first found that education is not a fundamental right under the Equal Protection Clause, and secondly, it determined that the plaintiffs had not clearly delineated a suspect class of poor at which the alleged state discrimination was directed. In so finding, the Court concluded that the appropriate test to be applied was not "strict scrutiny" but "rational relationship." In summation, the Court concluded that the extent to which

> the Texas system of school financing results in unequal expenditures between children who happen to reside in different districts, we cannot say that such disparities are the product of a system that is so irrational as to be invidiously discriminatory.

The Court went on to say that education presents a myriad of intractable economic, social, and philosophical problems the complexity of which suggests that the legislatures of the states should be given wide discretion within the limits of nationality.

Following the Supreme Court's decision in *Rodriguez*, school finance litigation under the Equal Protection Clause abated and challenges moved back to the state level. As can be seen from previous sections of this chapter, state courts in several instances have enunciated the importance of education as provided in state constitutions and have, thereby, required strong assertion of the individual's educational and equal protection rights. In view of *Rodriguez*, cases challenging state school finance programs under the federal Constitution are not likely to reemerge unless the makeup and philosophy of the Supreme Court change or plaintiffs find some alternative federal constitutional basis for such actions.[46] The legacy of *Rodriguez* will, however, continue to be exhibited as actions are periodically brought under state constitutions challenging the equity of school finance legislation.

NOTES

1. Shaffer v. Carter, 252 U.S. 37 (1970).

2. *Ibid.*

3. Miller v. Childers, 107 Okla. 57, 238 P. 204 (1924).

4. Dickman v. Porter, 35 N.S. 2d 66 (Iowa 1948)

5. Morton Salt Co. v. City of South Hutchinson, 177 F. 2d 889 (10th Cir. 1949).

6. Newton Edwards, *The Courts and the Public Schools* (Chicago: University of Chicago Press, 1971), p. 256.

7. State v. Board of Commissioners of ELR County, 58 P. 959 (Kan. 1899).

8. Leroy J. Peterson, Richard A. Rossmiller, and Marlin M. Volz, *The Law and Public School Operation* (New York: Harper & Row, Publishers, 1978), p. 150.

9. Marion & McPherson Railway Co. v. Alexander, 64 P. 978 (Kan. 1901).

10. Stuart v. School District No. 1 of Village of Kalamazoo, 30 Mich. 69 (1874).

11. Union Refrigerator Transit Co. v. Kentucky, 199 U.S. 194 (1905).

12. Constitution of the United States, Article I Sec. 8, Cl. 3.

13. Freeman v. Hewit, 329 U.S. 249 (1946).

14. Henneford v. Silas Mason Co., 300 U.S. 577 (1937).

15. Welton v. Missouri, 91 U.S. 275 (1876).

16. Best & Co. v. Maxwell, 311 U.S. 454 (1940).

17. Shaffer v. Carter, *op. cit.* in f.1.

18. Wheeler v. Barrera, 714 U.S. 402 (1974).

19. Pennsylvania Association for Retarded Children v. Pennsylvania, 334 F.Supp. 1257 (Pa. 1971); Mills v. Board of Education of the District of Columbia, 348 F.Supp. 866 (D.C. 1972).

20. Shepheard v. Godwin, 280 F.Supp. 869 (1968).

21. Everson v. Board of Education, 330 U.S. 1 (1947).

22. *Ibid.*; Board of Education v. Allen, 392 U.S. 236 (1968).

23. Lemon v. Kurtzman, 403 U.S. 602 (1971).

24. Walz v. Tax Commission, 397 U.S. 664 (1970).

25. Committee for Public Education and Religious Liberty v. Nyquist, 413 U.S. 756 (1973).

26. See also Sloan v. Lemon, 413 U.S. 825 (1973).

27. Wolman v. Walter, 433 U.S. 229 (1977).

28. Bell's Gap Railroad Co. v. Pennsylvania, 134 U.S. 232 (1890).

29. Sawyer v. Gilmore, 109 Me. 169, 83 A. 673 (1912).

30. 79 Corpus Juris Secundum sec. 411.

31. 81 S.D. 140, 131, N.S. 2d 700 (1964).

32. See also Board of Trustees v. Board of County Commissioners of Cassia County, 83 Idaho 172, 359 P. 2d 635 (1961) and Rice v. Cook, 22 Ga. 499, 150 S.E. 2d 822 (1966).

33. Miller v. Childers, 107 Okla. 57, 238 P. 2d 204 (1924).

34. Horton v. Meskill, 172 Conn. 615, 376 A.2d 359 (1979). See also Board of Educ., Levittown Union Free School v. Nyquist, 443 N.Y.S.2d 843 (App. Div., 1981).

35. Seattle School District No. 1 v. Washington, 90 Wash. 2d 476, 585 P. 2d 71 (1978).

36. Pauley v. Kelly, 255 S.E. 2d (W.VA. 1979).

37. Shofstall v. Hollins, 110 Ariz. 88, 515 P. 2d 590 (1973).

38. Milliken v. Green, 390 Mich. 389, 212 N.W. 2d 711 (1973).

39. Board of Education of Cincinnati v. Walter, 52 Ohio St. 2d 368, 390 N.E. 2d 813 (1977).

40. See Thompson v. Engelring, 96 Idaho 793, 536 P. 2d 635 (1975); People ex rel. Jones v. Adams, 40 Ill. App. 3d 189, 350 N.E. 2d 767 (1976); Knowles v. State Board of Education, 219 Kan. 271, 547 P. 2d 699 (1976); State ex rel. Woodahl v. Straub, 164 Mont. 141, 520 P. 2d 776 (1974); Olsen v. Johnson, 276 Or. 9, 554 P. 2d 139 (1976).

41. Arthur Wise, *Rich Schools, Poor Schools* (Chicago: University of Chicago Press, 1968).

42. Burruss v. Wilkerson, 310 F.Supp. 572 *affirmed mem.*, 397 U.S. 44 (1970).

43. McInnis v. Shapiro, 293 F.Supp. 327 *affirmed mem.*, 394 U.S. 322 (1969).

44. *Ibid.*

45. San Antonio Independent School District v. Rodriguez, 411 U.S. 1 *rehearing denied* 411 U.S. 959 (1973).

46. See Kern Alexander, "The Potential of Due Process for School Finance Litigation," *Journal of Education Finance*, 6, No. 4 (Spring 1981).

SELECTED REFERENCES

ALEXANDER, KERN.   *School Law.* St. Paul: West Publishing Company, 1980.

ALEXANDER, KERN, and K. FORBIS JORDAN.   *Constitutional Reform of School Finance.* Lexington, Mass.: D.C. Heath & Company, Lexington Books, 1973.

COONS, JOHN E., WILLIAM H. CLUNE, III, and STEPHEN C. D. SUGARMAN.   *Private Wealth and Public Education.* Cambridge, Mass.: Harvard University Press, Belknap Press, 1970.

LEHNE, RICHARD.   *The Quest for Justice: The Politics of School Finance Reform.* New York: Longman, Inc., 1978.

PETERSON, LEROY J., RICHARD A. ROSSMILLER, and MARLIN M. VOLZ.   *The Law and Public School Operation.* New York: Harper & Row, Publishers, 1978.

WISE, ARTHUR E.   *Rich Schools, Poor Schools.* Chicago: University of Chicago Press, 1968.

CHAPTER SEVEN
THE POLITICS
OF SCHOOL FINANCING

Lasswell's famous definition of politics as "who gets what, when and how" seems particularly applicable to the politics of school financing.[1] Mosher and her coauthors defined politics as "The authoritative allocation of social values. . . . Since resources are seldom or never adequate to satisfy the claims made upon them, the imbalance between demands and resources underlies the conflicts that constitute the seedbed of politics."[2] Lasswell's definition of politics seems to emphasize power, and Mosher's values. Power and values are both important in understanding the politics of school financing.

Many leaders of the public schools in the past have considered the word "politics" to be an opprobrious term. Keeping politics out of the public schools was considered a desirable goal. Politics under this older concept were conceived of as graft, corruption, nepotism, partisan control by ward bosses, and similar undesirable practices. Of course, public schools and other public services should be sheltered from these negative aspects. However, the public schools are part of the public economy, and in a democracy all major decisions on educational policies, including public school financing, must be made by political processes. Effective educational leaders must understand the political processes by which decisions on educational policy are made. This is especially true in the area of public school financing.

Decisions on school financing are made at the federal, state, and local levels. Lasswell's definition of politics could well be expanded to include "where," so it would read "who gets what, where, when and how." Financing the public schools involves the allocation of resources available to the public economy. Applying the expanded definition to the public schools: (1) *what* means what share of the public economy will be allotted to each public service, including education; (2) *where* means the political unit that will receive the funds; (3) *when* means at what time the resources will be made available; and (4) *how* means how the necessary revenue will be provided. Politics of school financing at the three levels will be discussed in order. But let us first take a look at some of the depressants on school financing at all three levels of government.

SOME DEPRESSANTS ON SCHOOL FINANCING

The following three factors contribute heavily to an unfavorable climate for school financing.

Condition of the Economy

In Chapter 4, it was pointed out that historically the greatest advances in school financing have occurred during periods of high economic growth and relatively low inflation and the least advances have been made in times of depression or high inflation. In times of high inflation or depression public demands develop for cuts in taxes, reduction of services, or both. For example, the Advisory Commission on Intergovernmental Relations in 1977 made a study of the public attitude toward taxes and services. That was a year of high inflation and relatively low economic growth. In response to the question "Considering all governmental services on the one hand and taxes on the other, which of the following statements come closest to your view?" Following were the results: (1) keep taxes and services about where they are—52 percent, (2) decrease services and taxes—31 percent, (3) increase services and raise taxes—4 percent; (4) no opinion—13 percent.[3]

In June 1980 the National Retired Teachers Association–American Association of Retired Persons (NRTA–AARP) made a survey of the opinions of persons 55 years of age and over on taxes and government services. June 1980 was a time of high inflation and little or no economic growth.[4] In reply to a question on balancing the budget—"Would you rather see the government take in more money by raising taxes or cutting back on services and programs?"—the following results were received: (1) raise taxes—10 percent, (2) cut services—67 percent, (3) neither— 9 percent, (4) both—4 percent, (5) depends/don't know—10 percent.[5] As pointed out in Chapter 4, the population is growing older and that is a depressant to improvement of school financing.

Policy of the News Media

The news media, including the press, radio, and television, tend to throw a spotlight on the sensational and the negative. That is particularly true of news concerning government in general, which includes the public schools. The ongoing good things in the public schools are not emphasized as much by the media as the negative events. This is not the fault of the media, because the public is primarily interested in the sensational and the negative, and in our market economy, private enterprise must satisfy the public demand.

Negative subjects concerning the public schools that the media tend to report include the following: malfeasance or misfeasance of school officials, discipline infractions by pupils, riots by pupils, strikes by teachers, controversies of school boards, controversies between administrators and teachers, declining standardized test scores, drug use by pupils, drug sales by pupils, increased sexual activity by teen-age pupils, attacks on teachers by pupils, race related conflicts, and similar items. Wise school administrators attempt to counteract these negative influences by maintaining an open rather than a closed school system. "Open" means that the system is open to the media, welcomes the participation of the public in decision making, and makes available to the media favorable and unfavorable information. The media are not much interested in "canned handouts." But they will accept favorable items if they can enter the school system freely and discover for themselves favorable items that make interesting news.

Negative Attitudes toward the Public Schools

The Twelfth Annual Gallup Poll of the public's attitude toward the public schools showed that attitude had not improved between 1974 and 1980.[6] In 1974, 11 percent of the public gave a "D" or "FAIL" rating to the public schools, and in 1980 that rating had increased to 18 percent. In 1974, 48 percent of the public gave an "A" or "B" rating to the public schools, but in 1980 that rating had declined to 35 percent. Whether the decline in attitude toward the public schools was due to general dissatisfaction with economic conditions, to negative factors reported by the media, or to other factors is unknown. It is likely that the decline was due to a number of factors. For example, the same Gallup survey found that 26 percent of public school parents considered lack of discipline an important problem; 12 percent, use of drugs; 10 percent, poor curriculum; 10 percent, integration and busing; 8 percent, large school overcrowding; and 6 percent, pupils' lack of interest and truancy. They listed other problems, but these are the ones which are most likely to influence the public's attitude toward the public schools. That same poll surveyed the public's attitude toward a number of American institutions. The following percentages of negative replies were received in answer to the question, "How much confidence do you, yourself, have in these American institutions to serve the public's needs?": Very little confidence (1) 15 percent for the church, (2) 20 percent for the public schools, (3) 28 percent for the courts, (4) 23 percent for the local government, (5) 24 percent for state government, (6) 31 percent for national government, (7) 30 percent for labor unions, and (8) 36 percent for big business. On the positive side, the replies of those expressing a fair amount or a great deal of confidence were as follows: (1) 82 percent for the church, (2) 74 percent for the public schools, (3) 64 percent for the courts, (4) 71 percent for local government, (5) 69 percent for state government, (6) 61 percent for the national government, (7) 55 percent for labor unions, and (8) 55 percent for big business. Although the public is critical of the public schools, it has a greater confidence in them than any other American institution studied except the church.

POLITICS OF SCHOOL FINANCING AT THE LOCAL LEVEL

At this writing, about 42 percent of school revenue receipts were obtained from local sources. About 97 percent of the local school tax revenue was obtained from the property tax and the remainder from other types of local school taxes. The levy of any type of local tax involves political decision making. Local taxes for schools are levied either by direct vote of the electorate or by vote of the board of education in districts that are fiscally independent. In districts that are fiscally dependent, the tax must be approved by other local governing bodies. The levy of a tax, either for current expenses or to service a bond issue, gives the public an opportunity to express its approval or disapproval of the allocation of its resources to support the service requesting the tax levy. The Gallup poll mentioned earlier revealed that 82 percent of the public believed that schools are very important to one's success; 15 percent, fairly important; 2 percent, not too important; and 1 percent, no opinion. Despite this overwhelming belief in the value of education, taxpayers must be convinced that the tax levies requested are necessary to finance needed school services. Many requests for both school operating tax levies and bond issues were rejected by the electorate in the 1970–1980 decade.

Part of the opposition to local school taxes is no doubt due to the unpopularity of the property tax, from which approximately 97 percent of local school tax revenue is derived. The Advisory Commission on Intergovernmental Relations made a study in 1977 of what the public considered the "least fair" tax. In that study, it was found that 33 percent of the people believed that the property tax was the least fair tax; 28 percent, the federal income tax; 17 percent, the state sales tax; 11 percent, the state income tax; and 11 percent couldn't decide. Some of the factors affecting local school financing are discussed in the following paragraphs.

Community Influentials

Numerous studies have shown that each community contains groups of people who possess more than average influence in affecting public policy.[7] Johns and Kimbrough found that school districts had different types of power structures but that all districts studied had some type of power structure.[8] In that study, six school districts of above 20,000 population were selected from each of four states. Three of the districts in each state had been districts of high local financial effort for a period of years and three, low financial effort. Four types of power structures were found among these 24 districts: (1) monopolistic elite—districts in which a few powerful influentials cooperate to control decision making; (2) multigroup, noncompetitive structure—districts in which two or more groups of powerful influentials exist but have approximately the same values, goals, and beliefs and usually agree on most issues; (3) competitive elite—districts in which two or more elite groups compete for power; and (4) segmented pluralism—districts in which many groups compete and there is wide citizen participation in decision making. Johns and Kimbrough found that of the 24 districts studied, 6 had monopolistic elite structures; 9, multigroup, noncompetitive; 6, competitive elite; and 3, segmented pluralism. They found that 10 of the 15 monopolistic elite and multigroup, noncompetitive districts combined had made a low local financial effort over a period of years, and 5 had made a great effort. Of the 9 districts with competitive elite or segmented pluralism structures, 7 were high local financial effort districts and 2 were low effort districts.

The study showed that, although most districts with noncompetitive power structures were low effort districts and most districts with competitive power structures were high effort districts, districts with any type of power structure could be either low effort or high effort districts. Therefore it would seem advisable for local school administrators, who desire to be politically effective in presenting the needs of the school, to do the following: (1) become aware of the community power structure and identify the values, goals, and beliefs of the different groups within it, and (2) communicate with the influentials in the power structure—parent groups, teacher organizations, taxpayer groups, chambers of commerce, labor unions, lay advisory committees, and other community groups—to give all of them the opportunity to communicate with the board of education and its administrators. Communication is a two-way process and the public cannot gain an understanding of the financial needs of the schools unless there is effective two-way communication. The school administrator is no longer the "philosopher king" of Plato's *Republic*. The public needs the leadership, advice, and counsel of the professionally trained school administrator. As the educational level of the public rises, the school administrator who attempts to rule will become less and less politically effective. If the modern school administrator is a leader, he or she must be politically effective.

Conflict within the School System

Unfortunately an adversary relationship between teachers and administration has developed in many school systems since the growth of collective bargaining and the unionization of teachers' organizations. Bitter controversies among teachers' organizations, boards of education, and school administrators do not facilitate improvement in local school financing. Frequently those controversies produce teachers' strikes, charges by teachers that the school system has too much administrative overhead and charges by administrators that teachers are producing less and demanding more pay. The public tends to believe both and this produces an unfavorable political climate for school financing. Collective bargaining is a reality and will not go away. Collective bargaining developed primarily because present-day teachers are well-educated professionals and they demand the right to participate in decision making that affects them. This is a rational expectation in a democracy, and sound administrative leadership of both the board of education and teachers' organizations will create and follow policies that engender a cooperative relationship rather than an adversary relationship. This will produce a favorable climate for local school financing.

School Centralization

The movement toward consolidation of districts and schools within districts has created much controversy. Fifty years ago there were approximately 130,000 school districts in the United States, and at this writing there are approximately 16,000 school districts. The public school enrollment declined by 4 million pupils between 1974 and 1980, and it is expected to decline further until about the middle of the 1980s. This has resulted in the closing of many schools. The shifts of population within a district have also caused many schools to close.

The consolidation of school districts usually resulted in fiscal economies and improvement of educational opportunity, but it reduced lay participation in school governance and sometimes reduced school support. The closing of a school due to a decline in enrollment frequently causes opposition from parents living in the area served by the school.

The larger the school district, the less the opportunity for lay citizens to participate in public school decision making. Furthermore, the larger the individual school, the less opportunity parents have to participate in school decision making. There is no evidence that a school district with a population of 1 million is more efficient either fiscally or educationally than a district with a population of 100,000. Also, there is no evidence that a senior high school with an enrollment of 5,000 is more efficient either fiscally or educationally than a high school with an enrollment of 1,000 or 1,500. People tend to give political support to services they understand and feel that they own. Therefore as we organize school districts and individual schools in the future, it is advisable to recognize that *politically* "bigger is not always better," although it may be better *financially*.

Special Interest Groups

Boards of education frequently are pressured by special interest groups including some religious sects, veterans groups, patriotic societies, extreme rightists, extreme leftists, and others—to change the curriculum or to censure textbooks and library books. Frequently these groups oppose each other. For example, some parents' groups want the schools to go back to basics and others want an enriched curriculum. The board receives all of these inputs, but obviously it cannot please all of these competing groups. Politically it is good policy to give all of these groups a hearing, but if a critical value is involved, the board should have the courage to make the decision that is in the best interests of the people, even though it may be unpopular with some groups. If the board does not do so, it is not fit to govern.[9]

POLITICS OF SCHOOL FINANCING AT THE STATE LEVEL

In 1930 about .3 of 1 percent of public school revenue was provided from federal funds; 17.0 percent, from state sources, and 82.7 percent, from local sources. Fifty years later, the federal government provided an estimated 9.3 percent of school revenue; the state, 48.1 percent; and local sources, 42.5 percent.[10] This change in the percent of school revenue was caused primarily by the following factors: (1) unpopularity of the local property tax, (2) unequal distribution of wealth among school districts, (3) public demand for equalizing educational opportunity, and (4) accessibility of the state to tax sources not available to local school districts.

This shift in school support from local taxes to state taxes has been accompanied by much political controversy. Wealthy areas of states have objected to a policy that results in their contributing more in state taxes than is received in state grants. State legislators from wealthy school districts have frequently opposed state equalization formulas which apportioned state school aid in inverse relationship to local taxpaying capacity. Such legislators in many states have either opposed increases in state support of the public schools or insisted that if state aid were provided, it should be apportioned on a flat grant basis without taking into consideration variations in local taxpaying capacity. An examination of methods used by the states for allocating state funds[11] shows that political compromises have been reached in many states by allocating part of state funds on a flat grant basis or by guaranteeing a minimum of state funds to wealthy school districts, to secure passage of a state equalization appropriation.

Another political factor involved in increasing the percentage of school revenue from state sources is fear of the erosion of local control of education if state financing is increased. The virtues of local control are continually extolled by politicians seeking office. They also inveigh against the dangers of central controls, despite the fact that public school education is a state responsibility. It has become folklore to believe that "He who pays the fiddler will call the tune." There is *some* truth in this assumption. However, the state constitutionally can establish state controls over education without providing any state financing. It can also allocate state funds for the schools with few or no controls, or it can attach many controls.

There is some evidence that establishment of state controls may result in an increase in state financing, and an increase in state financing may result in an increase in state controls. In 1972 Wirt made an extensive study of the relative amount of centralized state control in all 50 states and developed a score of the relative amount in each state.[12] The authors of this book correlated the amount of state control in the 50 states in 1972 with the percentage of school revenue received from the state in 1972–73. The Pearson coefficient of correlation was .4743, and the Spearman rank order correlation was .38. The authors also correlated the amount of state control in the 50 states in 1972 with the percentage of school revenue received from the state in 1979–80. The Pearson coefficient of correlation was .5198, and the Spearman correlation was .49. This increase in correlation between 1972–73 and 1979–80 suggests either that when state controls are established political pressures demand that the state provide the revenues to meet increases in state requirements, or that the states with a high amount of state controls in 1972–73 continued the policy of supplying a relatively high percentage of revenue from state sources in 1979–80.

If the state establishes standards which reduce pupil-teacher ratios, requires the provision of kindergartens, or requires the provision of additional educational opportunities for the handicapped, the demand arises for the state to meet the increased revenue needs. At this writing, there is a strong demand for better quality education in the public schools. The states are under pressure to increase minimum standards. For example, some states have established minimum test scores for students to attain before receiving a high school diploma. Pressure is then brought on the state to provide increased revenue to meet these higher standards.

Although there seems to be a significant correlation between amount of state control and percent of revenue provided from state sources, the correlation is relatively low. A Pearson coefficient of correlation of .5198 explains only 27 percent of the association between amount of state control and percent of state revenue. Therefore some states supply state funds with few controls, others with many controls.

Politics of school financing at the state level deals with many issues, as pointed out above. The principal actors in the politics of state school financing include teachers' organizations, parent-teacher associations, school administrators' organizations, school board organizations, the chief state school officers, state boards of education, and governors and legislatures. Other groups such as chambers of commerce, the Farm Bureau, labor unions, associations of industries, and antitax groups also participate in the politics of school financing from time to time, especially when matters involving the levy of taxes arise.

The State Education Agency

The state education agency consists of the state board of education, the chief state school officer, and the state department of education.[13] Campbell and Mazzoni made an extensive study of policy making at the state level in 10 states.[14] They found that state boards of education were minor participants in setting educational policy, and that some chief state school officers had considerable influence with governors and state legislators while others had little. All chief state school officers had great influence on the state board of education and the state department of education. Chief state school officers and their associates in state departments of education frequently exercise influence by lobbying state legislatures for improvement in school financing.

Educational Interest Groups

Campbell and Mazzoni requested legislators in twelve states to list certain education interest groups in the order of their influence with the state legislature.[15] All of these states listed teachers' associations as having more influence with the legislature than any other interest group. States differed somewhat in their ranking of school board associations and associations of school administrators. However, a majority of the states ranked school board associations second and administrators' associations third.

The education power structure is no longer monolithic in most states. Some years in the past, administrators' associations, school board associations, teachers' associations, parent-teacher associations, and state education agencies commonly worked together on state school financing proposals. This is no longer true. Teachers' associations for many years have insisted that administrators had too much influence on educational policy. As pointed out earlier, an adversary relationship has developed among teachers, school administrators, and boards of education in many states. Consequently, these different interest groups have frequently advocated conflicting fiscal policies. This conflict has no doubt retarded progress in school financing in a number of states. In some states, the primary legislative goal of school finance reform has not been to improve school financing, but rather to reform taxation. This conflict of goals of state legislatures with goals of education interest groups makes it all the more politically desirable that education interest groups compromise their differences and form a coalition that speaks to the governor and the legislature with one voice.

The Governor

The governor has a powerful influence on school financing in all states. He or she can initiate fiscal policy and veto legislative bills. Campbell and

Mazzoni found that "Governors were crucial in the formulation and initiation of fiscal legislation affecting school finance and tax reform."[16]

Governors, as well as state legislators, are influenced by education interest groups and other special interest groups. In some states, education associations have become politically active in supporting or opposing candidates for the governorship or seats in the legislature. When they happen to support successful candidates, their influence is augmented, but if their candidates do not win, their influence is diminished.

It is particularly important that the state education agency and education interest groups work cooperatively with the governor in developing the fiscal program he or she presents to the legislature. Competing state services will certainly present their needs to the governor and the legislature. It is highly important that the governor have a full understanding of the fiscal needs of education before presenting a fiscal program to the legislature.

The State Legislature

The legislature plays the most important role in determining state school fiscal policy. It first must pass a bill before the governor can approve or veto it. The legislature deals with school fiscal matters through a committee structure. Usually there is an education committee in both houses of the legislature. There will also usually be a finance committee, a ways and means committee, or a committee on taxation, as well as an appropriations committee in one or both houses. Those interested in educational finance, if they are to be politically effective, must lobby all of these committees as well as individual legislators. The term "lobby" should not be considered derogative. It is the constitutional right of all groups and individuals to present their needs and interests to the legislature. In order for the democratic process to be successful, it is essential that lobbyists be ethical in their activities. If all lobbying were prohibited by law, the legislature would have insufficient information with which to make intelligent decisions.

POLITICS OF SCHOOL FINANCING
AT THE FEDERAL LEVEL

The public school revenue provided by the federal government increased from 3 percent of revenue receipts in 1950 to approximately 9 percent in 1980. Political activity for increased federal support of education is increasing. The National Education Association has recently been advocating that the federal government provide 30 percent or more of the public school revenue. Experts on school finance have supported increased financial contributions from the federal government primarily for two reasons: (1) to equalize educational opportunity throughout the nation because the states vary considerably in wealth; and (2) to improve the equity of taxation because federal taxes in general are more progressive than state and local taxes.

Educational leaders and organizations have generally advocated general federal aid with no federal control other than requiring that the federal grants received for the public schools be expended by the states for the public schools. Congress, however, has provided all federal funds for the public schools through a series of categorical grants which specify the purposes for which the funds must be expended, except for federal impact funds. Congress has followed this policy primarily in order to achieve certain goals that its members believe are not attained adequately by the public schools. Examples of these federal grants are ones earmarked for compensatory education, education for the handicapped, and vocational education. Federal grants for education are described in more detail in Chapter 15.

When the federal government makes a categorical grant for such purposes as vocational education or education of the handicapped, a special interest group is created that lobbies actively for its federal appropriation. These special interest groups in general oppose the consolidation of their categorical grants into a general aid grant with no specification by the federal government of the purposes for which it can be expended. Members of Congress are also reluctant to abolish categorical grants supported by strong special interest groups.

The National Education Association actively supported the Democratic candidate for president in 1976. He was elected, federal funds for education were increased during his administration, and a Department of Education was established. In 1980, the National Education Association again supported the Democratic candidate for president, but the Republican candidate was elected. In a number of states education associations support or oppose candidates for governor and the legislature. The long-term effect of these political activities on school financing at the federal and state levels is unknown at the present time.

Federal control of education is opposed by practically everyone. However, the appropriation of federal funds through categorical grants is a powerful federal control. Furthermore, court decisions and certain federal laws establish federal controls that affect school financing.[17] As a matter of fact, establishment of a federal requirement sometimes results in political pressure being brought on Congress to provide additional federal funds to meet the new requirement. Examples are court ordered busing, resulting in the emergency school aid appropriation to assist in racial integration, and federal requirements with respect to the education of the handicapped, resulting in large increases in the federal appropriation for the handicapped.

Increasing the amount of federal aid for the public schools is opposed by many lay interest groups and political conservatives. Such powerful organizations as the National Association of Manufacturers, the U.S. Chamber of Commerce, and the Farm Bureau Federation generally oppose federal aid for the public schools. Certain religious sects also oppose federal aid for education unless they share in it. The federal government during recent years has usually had a deficit, which many believe has added to inflation. Political conservatives generally support a reduction in federal expenditures for any function of government that can be provided for by the states or local units of government. It will require strong and effective leadership in support of federal aid for the public schools if that aid is to be increased substantially in future years.

Finally, academic political activists have had a major influence on school finance reform almost from the beginning of this century.[18] Teachers College, Columbia University produced George D. Strayer, Paul R. Mort, and Elwood P. Cubberley. Strayer and Mort became professors at Teachers College, and Cubberley became a professor at Stanford University. These men were the pioneer developers of school finance theory. They trained students of school finance who became professors at various universities throughout the nation, and they in turn also produced students of school finance. This process has continued to the present time. Strayer, Mort, Cubberley and many of their successors have been political activists. Through their consultancies, surveys, research, and writing they have had a major impact on school finance reform. They have served many times as consultants to state education agencies, state legislatures, state governors and committees of Congress. These academicians have also frequently been effective lobbyists for school finance reform. The academic political activists will no doubt continue to have a significant influence on the improvement of school financing at the federal, state, and local levels.

SOME POLITICAL STRATEGIES

As pointed out earlier in the chapter, the allocation of financial resources among competing public services involves political activity at the federal, state, and local levels. Some of the political strategies that have proven effective in enhancing the financing of education are described in the rest of this chapter.

Advocacy

Buchanan states,

> In a complex decision-making structure where final results emerge only from an interaction of divergent groups, it is functionally appropriate that there should exist a set of advocates, an advocacy group. That is to say, some group should present the case for "needs" with little or no regard being given to costs or the economic restraints.[19]

The advocates of education should conduct the research necessary to demonstrate that the needs presented are actual needs, not only of the pupils involved, but also of the total society. Emphasis should be given to what programs and services are to be bought and benefits to be received, rather than to immediate costs.

Although professional educators usually take the lead in advocacy of school support, it is frequently good political strategy for "blue ribbon" citizens' committees to assume the advocacy role after they have made extensive studies of educational needs. Such committees at the federal, state, and local levels have frequently made substantial contributions to the advancement of public education.

Coalitions

Major favorable decisions on school financing at all levels have usually been achieved through a coalition of interest groups with common goals. However, sometimes education groups have formed effective coalitions with non-education groups in political trade-offs whereby both groups attain different but nonconflicting goals.[20]

The Education Finance Center, Education Commission of the States, in its publication *State Education Politics: The Case of School Finance Reform,* stated the following:

> Different individuals and groups bring different interests and objectives to state education policy reforms. Interest groups vary in their mutual compatibility, partly as a consequence of the substantive form they take, but also as a consequence of the alternative combinations of policies and options already before state government. In many ways the essential quality of a state education leader is the ability to build political coalitions.[21]

The governing bodies of both counties and municipalities have state organizations in each state, and these organizations all seek revenue from state and federal governments. It is not good political strategy for education leaders to attempt to get more money for education by questioning the needs of the counties and municipalities for financial assistance. Frequently it is a better political strategy to form coalitions with those groups rather than to attack them.

As pointed out, the subgroups in education are no longer in coalition in many states. It would be good political strategy to eliminate conflict among education groups and to form coalitions of organizations of teachers, administrators, boards of education, parents and the state education agency to support mutually developed financial goals. In some states, advocates of the public elementary and secondary schools and advocates of higher education have been in conflict. The result has usually been to minimize the additional support provided each system. It would be better political strategy for these two interests to be in coalition than in conflict.

NOTES

1. Harold Lasswell, *Politics: Who Gets What, When and How?* (New York: McGraw-Hill Book Company, 1936).

2. Edith K. Mosher, Anne Hastings and Jennings L. Wagoner, Jr., *Pursuing Equal Educational Opportunity: School Politics and the New Activists* (New York: ERIC Clearinghouse on Urban Education, 1979), p. 1.

3. Advisory Commission on Intergovernmental Relations,*Changing Public Attitudes on Governments and Taxes, 1977* (Washington, D.C.: U.S. Government Printing Office, 1977).

4. The NRTA–AARP commissioned the firm of Hamilton and Staff, Inc. of Washington, D.C. to make this survey.

5. NRTA–AARP, Research and Data Resources Unit, "Nationwide Survey of Opinions of Older Americans" (Washington, D.C.: NRTA–AARP, 1980).

6. The results of their poll were reported in *Phi Delta Kappan*, September 1980, Vol. 62, no. 1.

7. Two of the most important of these early studies were made by Floyd Hunter, *Community Power Structure* (Chapel Hill, N.C.: University of North Carolina, 1953) and Robert H. Dahl, *Who Governs?* (New Haven, Conn.: Yale University Press, 1961).

8. Roe L. Johns and Ralph B. Kimbrough, *The Relationship of Socioeconomic Factors, Educational Leadership Patterns and Elements of Community Power Structure to Local School Fiscal Policy.* Final Report, Office of Education, Cooperative Research Project No. 1324 (Gainesville, Fla: University of Florida, 1968).

9. See Chapter 8 of Edgar L. Morphet, Roe L. Johns, and Theodore L. Reller, *Educational Organization and Administration: Concepts, Practices, and Issues*, 4th ed. (Englewood Cliffs, N.J.: Prentice-Hall, Inc., 1981).

10. Estimate made by National Education Association.

11. See *Public School Finance Programs*, periodically compiled by the Department of Education, U.S. Office of Education (Washington, D.C.: U.S. Government Printing Office).

12. Frederick M. Wirt, "What State Laws Say about State Control," *Phi Delta Kappan*, Vol. 59, no. 8, (April, 1978), 517–520.

13. One state—Wisconsin—did not have a state board of education at this writing.

14. Roald F. Campbell and Tim L. Mazzoni, Jr., *State Policy Making for the Public Schools* (Berkeley, Calif.: McCutchan Publishing Corporation, 1976).

15. *Ibid.*, p. 207.

16. *Ibid.*, p. 169–171.

17. See Chapter 6 of this book.

18. For a more complete discussion of this topic, see Stephen K. Bailey and others, *Schoolmen and Politics* (Syracuse, N.Y.: Syracuse University Press, 1962) and Chapter 4 of Roe L. Johns, *Education in the States: Nationwide Development Since 1900*, eds., Edgar Fuller and Jim B. Pearson (Washington, D.C.: National Education Association of the United States, 1969).

19. James M. Buchanan, in *Economic Factors Affecting the Financing of Education*, eds. Roe L. Johns and others (Gainesville, Fla.: National Educational Finance Project, 1970), p. 266.

20. Susan Fuhrman assisted by Joel Berke, Michael Kurat and Michael Usdan. *State Education Politics: The Case of School Finance Reform, Report No. F7912* (Denver Education Finance Center, Education Commission of the States, 1979), p. 7.

21. *Ibid.*, p. 7.

SELECTED REFERENCES

BINGHAM, RICHARD D., BRETT W. HAWKINS, and F. TED HERBERT. *The Politics of Raising State and Local Revenue*. New York: Praeger Publishers, Inc., 1978.

CAMPBELL, ROALD F., and TIM L. MAZZONI, JR. *State Policy Making for the Public Schools*. Berkeley, Calif.: McCutchan Publishing Corporation, 1976.

GOVE, SAMUEL K., and FREDERICK W. WIRT, eds. *Political Science and School Politics: The Princes and Pundits*. Lexington, Mass.: D. C. Heath & Co., Lexington Books, 1976.

IANNACCONE, LAWRENCE. *Problems of Financing Inner City Schools: Political and Cultural Restraints upon Improved Urban Education and Proposals to Overcome Them*. Washington, D.C.: President's Commission on School Finance, U.S. Government Printing Office, 1972.

KIRST, MICHAEL W., ed.   *The Politics of Education at the Local, State and Federal Levels*. Berkeley, Calif.: McCutchan Publishing Corporation, 1970.

LEHNE, RICHARD.   *The Quest for Justice: The Politics of School Finance Reform*. New York: Longman, Inc., 1978.

MOSHER, EDITH K., ANNE H. HASTINGS, and JENNINGS L. WAGONER, JR.   *Pursuing Equal Educational Opportunity: School Politics and the New Activists*. New York: ERIC Clearinghouse on Urban Education, 1979.

SCRIBNER, JAY D., ed.   *The Politics of Education*. The Seventy-sixth Yearbook of the National Society for the Study of Education. Chicago: University of Chicago Press, 1977.

WILLIAMS, MARY FRASE.   *Government in the Classroom: Dollars and Power in Education*. New York: Proceedings of the Academy of Political Science, Vol. 33, No. 2, 1978.

CHAPTER EIGHT
FISCAL CAPACITY AND EFFORT TO SUPPORT PUBLIC SCHOOLS

The United States is the richest large nation in the world today. This wealth is due to a great extent to the development of the nation's human resources and to the nation's willingness to commit a reasonable proportion of its resources for education. However, the wealth both among and within states in this country varies considerably. These variations have definite implications for the educational opportunities provided by the state and, to some extent, may reflect the attention—or lack of it—devoted to the development of human resources in the past.

Disparities in physical and human resources among states and school systems produce a substantial unevenness in ability to support public schools. The major role of public school finance policy is to address the educational needs of both by redistributing financial resources. Both federal and state governments bear the responsibility of helping to overcome fiscal disparities which deny equality of educational opportunity. This is accomplished by making funds more uniform through various equalization measures available. This is not a simple task in a country which has some 16,000 school systems in 50 states, all with different physical and human characteristics.

At first glance, it appears to be a relatively simple matter to use resources from the federal level to fill in incapacities at the state level and to use state resources to supplement the revenues of poorer local school districts. The problem, though, is actually more complex, since there is little agreement on how fiscal capacity is to be measured and how much is needed for educational services. The matter is further complicated by the myriad social and economic conditions which lead some states or localities to put forth greater financial effort than others to support their educational programs.

MEASUREMENT OF STATE FISCAL CAPACITY

Fiscal capacity is the ability of state and local school systems to obtain revenues from their own sources through taxation.[1] Or, fiscal capacity may be broadly defined as a quantitative measure of economic resources within a governmental unit which can be used to support public functions. Relative capacity among states or localities is determined by dividing the measure of capacity by some unit such as per capita or per pupil.

Traditionally, policy makers have relied on personal income and tax revenues as economic indicators of capacity. Personal income is most commonly used among states because the data are kept current by the U.S. Bureau of Commerce.[2] Data for tax revenues are also collected annually by various departments of the federal government and by several independent agencies.

Personal Income

When the income of the people of each state is known, it is possible to determine the per capita income, the income per child of school age (ages five through seventeen, are generally used), or the income per pupil in average daily membership or attendance. The ratio of children to total population varies considerably from state to state, depending on which pupil measure is used. The personal income per average daily attendance or average daily membership is probably the superior measure for determining the state capacity to support the public schools. This is a more accurate measure if one is concerned about accurate capacity measures for financing the public schools. To use a school-age population broadens the measure by including children in nonpublic schools, thus inflating the divisor. The relative capacity of states with large nonpublic school enrollment would thus be substantially reduced.

Personal income is the amount of current income received from all sources, including transfer payments from government and business but excluding transfer payments from other sources. The major part of personal income is derived from labor income, proprietors' income, rental income, dividends, interest, and transfer payments.

Personal income, however, does not reflect the total fiscal capacity of the state for two basic reasons. First, personal income represents a measure of the flow of capital and does not capture the stock of wealth that a state might possess. Personal and real property are not included. Income is not wealth; wealth constitutes the total value of the stock of all assets, physical and financial, held at a particular time—less liabilities.[3] Second, resident personal income does not capture the potential capacity which a state may have from its ability to export its tax burden to other states, such as Florida and Nevada's ability to tax tourists through sales, hotel, and amusement taxes, or the ability of Alaska, Louisiana, West Virginia, Texas, New Mexico, and Wyoming to tax oil and mineral deposits.

Further, some contend that since people throughout the United States must pay federal income tax, the amount paid by individuals should be deducted from the personal income in each state when determining ability to support schools. There seems to be considerable merit in this contention. Still another point has been advanced for consideration: Before the people of a state can support other than incidental education, they must have an income above the required for the bare necessities of living. A good case can be made for subtracting some figure representing the actual cost of living. Perhaps a reasonable and conservative figure would be the $1,000 exemption currently taken into consideration in calculating the federal income tax. If personal income is to be used, the difference between the most and the least wealthy states would be somewhat greater than would be indicated by total personal income.

Tax Revenues

Tax revenues are an inferior measure of fiscal capacity, because they reflect taxpayer effort as well as capacity. For example, a poor state could put forth great effort and show a high revenue base, while a rich state could exert little tax effort and show low revenues. Neither measure, nor personal income or tax revenues, represents a true and accurate measurement of a state's fiscal capacity.[4]

Representative Tax System

Another measure, which largely corrects for the aforementioned deficiencies, is the representative or uniform tax system method. This approach, developed by the Advisory Commission on Intergovernmental Relations, derives data by using the following methodology:

> (1) Determining for each of the various kinds of state and local taxes a national average rate which, if applied throughout the nation, would have produced the same total amount of revenue that state and local governments actually obtained from the particular type of tax in (a base year); (2) estimating by state the potential yield of each type of tax, if imposed at this uniform nationwide rate; and (3) aggregating these potential-yield amounts for each state to arrive at an estimate of its total tax capacity.[5]

Other researchers have developed other methods of determining state fiscal capacity. Quindry annually reports on state fiscal capacity for the Southern Regional Education Board. He computes potential tax collections by using personal income as the representative base measure and supplementing it with alternative bases, such as the value of natural resources severed from land and waters of a state as the measure for severance tax potential or the number of registered motor vehicles as a measure of ability to collect motor fuel and license taxes.[6]

Akin developed another measure, which makes allowance for the interaction among sources of revenue as a result of actual tax impact. He maintains that since all taxes are actually paid from either income or wealth, heavy use of a particular tax prevents full use of another tax. Akin's method involves the use of a regression analysis to estimate tax rates that result in revenues a particular jurisdiction might expect if taxes behaved in a normative manner as in other taxing jurisdictions.[7] Another measure, developed by Charlesworth and Herzel—gross state product—is the state counterpart of gross national product and measures the value of all goods and services produced in a state.[8]

Of the various measures, however, probably the most accurate and complete is that of Halstead, published in 1978 by the National Institute of Education. Derived from a 1962 ACIR study, this approach involves four steps:

> (1) identifying for each of the various kinds of state and local taxes the tax *base* or "allocator" which represents the degree to which the taxable activity exists within the jurisdiction, (2) with these allocators and the amount of taxes actually collected, determining for each tax a national average rate, which if applied throughout the nation would have procured the same total amount of revenues that state and local governments actually obtained, (3) estimating by state the potential yield of each type of tax by imposing the aforementioned uniform nationwide rates to the state allocator bases, and (4) aggregating the potential yield amounts for each tax to derive the total capacity of a given state.[9]

The allocator, the key to this methodology, must indicate within permissible limits the base or extent of the activity subject to a tax within the state. With the sales tax, for example, the allocator is the dollar value of the retail sales in the state.

CAPACITY COMPARISONS AMONG STATES

During the decade from 1970 to 1980 the nation's overall per capita personal income rose 143 percent. Every state showed an increase in income greater than the decade's 93.4 percent inflation increase. In 1980 Alaska ranked first in per capita personal income ($12,406), followed by Connecticut ($11,445), California ($10,856), and New Jersey ($10,755). Mississippi ranked last in 1970 and remained there in 1980, with $6,508.[10] Arkansas was next lowest with $7,180 in 1980.

The gap between the richest and poorest states narrowed, with the states below average increasing at a rate of 153 percent and the states above average showing a 10-year increase of 138 percent. States in the Northeast and the West still have the highest income, while the poorest are located in the Southeast and Rocky Mountain regions. States in the Far West had 113 percent of the national average in 1980, compared with 111 percent in 1970. The mideast region, which includes Delaware, Maryland, New Jersey, New York, and Pennsylvania, showed a decline in percentage of the national average from 113 percent in 1970 to 106 percent in 1980. Southeastern states remained the poorest, but increased from 82 to 86 percent of the national average.

These data indicate that there has been a relative decline in the preeminence of some states, but overall there still remains a substantial difference between the richest and the poorest. In comparing Connecticut with Mississippi, the richest and poorest states in 1970, we find that at the beginning of the decade Mississippi's per capita personal income of $2,547 was 52 percent of Connecticut's $4,871, a difference of $2,324 per person. By 1980, Mississippi's per capita personal income of $6,508 was 56 percent of Connecticut's $11,445, a difference of $5,937 per person. Although there has been a small decline of 4 percent, the difference remains quite substantial.

Comparisons of fiscal capacity among states using the representative-tax system, also show a narrowing of the gap between the richest and poorest. Data available from Halstead's 1975 study show that Nevada, with its tax potential from gambling and other sources, has the highest capacity in the nation, with 151 percent of the national average. Next is Wyoming at 147 percent; followed by Delaware, 122 percent; Illinois, 114 percent; and Connecticut, 113 percent. Nevada, Connecticut, and Delaware were also listed among the five wealthiest in per capita personal income in 1975, and again in 1980. The representative-tax system, though, greatly enhances the picture of Nevada's and Wyoming's fiscal capacity.

With the representative-tax system, as with personal income, Mississippi has the lowest capacity, only 70 percent of the national average. Next comes Maine, with 74 percent; South Carolina, 77 percent; Alabama, 78 percent; and Arkansas, 78 percent. These same five states were also the lowest in per capita personal income in 1975. By 1980, these five still remained the lowest in per capita personal income.

The decline in the differential between the most and least able states has been more gradual with the representative-tax system than with personal income (see Figure 8–1). If we do not consider Alaska, maintenance of the high percentage differential for the richest states with the representative-tax system may be largely attributed to Nevada's, Wyoming's and Delaware's relative affluence.

Insofar as financial support relates to educational opportunity, the wealthiest states have a decided advantage. The most able states can finance a reasonably adequate quality of education with a lower tax effort than can the least able. This means that if schools were to be financed entirely from state and local funds, either the people in the least able states would have to make a much greater effort to support their schools than the people in the most able, or the children in the states with the lowest capacity would inevitably have to attend schools that were inadequately financed. Thus, the national interest inevitably requires equalizing of funds from federal sources.

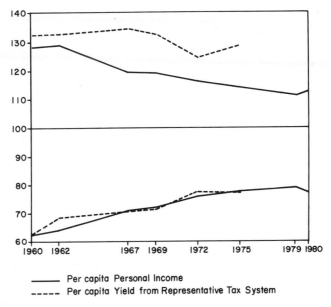

```
140
130  ┄┄┄┄┄┄┄┄┄┄┄┄┄┄┄
120
110
100
 90
 80
 70
 60
   1960 1962      1967 1969    1972    1975      1979 1980
```

━━━━━ Per capita Personal Income
┄┄┄┄┄ Per capita Yield from Representative Tax System

FIGURE 8–1 DECLINE IN DIFFERENTIAL BETWEEN MOST AND LEAST ABLE STATES FOR 1960–1980 BY ALTERNATIVE MEASURES OF CAPACITY. Note that richest and poorest are defined as the five richest and five poorest by each capacity measure.

VARIATIONS IN EFFORT AMONG STATES

The effort made by each state to support public schools is influenced by many factors: the people's interest in and attitude toward public education, the proportion of students in nonpublic schools, the people's "feeling" about government and taxes, the tax structure of their state, the amount of taxes they pay for purposes other than public schools, whether they have children or grandchildren in school, their reaction to the program offered by the schools in their community, and probably their reaction to the party in power and to the leadership of prominent legislators and the governor, and so on. No one has been able to determine, up to this time, the entire effect of any one factor, or any combination of factors such as these, upon the effort made by any state to support its public schools.

Tax effort is defined as the extent to which a state utilizes its fiscal or tax capacity to support the public schools. Computation of expenditures per pupil or of state and local revenues per pupil is insufficient to indicate tax effort accurately. With either of these measures, a richer state putting forth the same effort as a poorer state will always appear to be making a greater effort. Thus, tax effort must be expressed in terms of a percentage relationship between expenditures (from state and local sources), or state and local revenue, and the state's tax capacity.

Tax effort—is a relative measure based on average national practice and may be used to compare various classifications of states to each other—high to low, rich to poor, and so on. The denominator for the effort ratio may be any fiscal capacity measure—personal income per unit or tax yield from a representative tax system per unit. Table 8–1 shows tax capacity and tax effort for

TABLE 8–1   Interstate Differentials in Tax Capacity and Effort to Support Public Schools

States	CAPACITY MEASURES		EFFORT MEASURES	
	Personal 1979 Income per Pupil Enrolled 1978–79, As Percent of U.S. Average	Yield from Representative Tax System 1978–79, per Pupil Enrolled 1978–79, As Percent of U.S. Average	State and Local Public School, Revenue, 1978–79, As Percent of Personal Income 1979, of U.S. Average	State and Local Public School Revenue 1978–79, As Percent of Yield from Representative Tax System 1979, of U.S. Average
United States	100.0	100.0	100.0	100.0
High				
New Jersey	120.0	112.7	1.12	1.19
California	118.8	102.2	.81	.95
New York	118.0	102.5	1.18	1.36
Illinois	116.7	113.8	.94	.96
Delaware	116.4	136.8	1.06	.91
Middle				
Wyoming	99.4	140.1	1.23	.87
Nebraska	98.8	100.3	1.05	1.03
Iowa	99.0	103.1	1.12	1.08
Virginia	94.6	91.6	.95	.98
North Dakota	95.0	94.2	1.01	1.02
Low				
Maine	72.6	75.8	1.16	1.11
Idaho	72.5	75.7	.98	.94
New Mexico	71.8	97.8	1.28	.94
Arkansas	71.3	72.2	.94	.93
Mississippi	68.0	67.9	.89	.89

Sources: Personal income data from Department of Commerce, Bureau of Census, *Survey of Current Business* (April 1980), (Washington, D.C.: U.S. Government Printing Office), Table I, p. 25. Representative tax system data from D. Kent Halstead, *Tax Wealth in Fifty States* (Washington, D.C.: National Institute of Education, U.S. Government Printing Office, 1978) as projected in *Determining an Appropriate Teacher Salary*, James A. Richardson and J. Trent Williams, (paper delivered at American Education Finance Association Conference, New Orleans, 1981). Pupil enrollments from *Rankings of the States, 1980* (Washington, D.C.: National Educational Association, 1980), Table B–2, p. 11.

public schools in selected states. State and local revenues per pupil are the numerators while personal income per pupil and yield from the Halstead representative tax system per pupil are the denominators.

VARIATIONS IN LOCAL FISCAL CAPACITY

Variations in the fiscal capacity of school districts are generally much greater than capacity among the states. The range of capacity among districts in states where districts have been reorganized is much less than in states with many small districts. This is inevitably the case because when several small districts with wide differences in wealth per pupil are combined to form one district, differences within the area are eliminated.

Recent studies in a number of states have indicated a range in ability in county unit and other large district states of from about 9 to 1 up to about 20 or 25 to 1. Thus, even when all districts are reasonably adequate in size, it is apparent that there is a considerable difference among the districts in ability to finance an educational program. If no state aid were provided in these states, the least wealthy districts would have to make from nine to twenty-five times the effort made by the wealthiest to finance an equitable program of educational opportunity. The situation in the small-district states is, of course, much more serious, with the range exceeding 100 to 1 in several of them. The information, inadequate as it is in a number of states, points definitely to the following conclusions:

1. In no state can the least wealthy districts finance a reasonably satisfactory program of education from local funds without an unreasonable tax effort and, in many districts, the effort required would be prohibitive.
2. The differences in wealth in small district states are so great that no program involving state and local support is likely to solve all the financial equality problems until further reorganization occurs.
3. Until further progress is made in many states in district organization and provisions for financing schools, inequalities in educational opportunity are certain to continue. Substantial numbers of students in many states cannot expect to have even reasonably adequate educational opportunities under present conditions.

MEASUREMENT OF LOCAL FISCAL CAPACITY

Equalization of educational opportunity hinges on the appropriate measurement of local taxpaying ability. The need to equalize the disparities in local capacity has long been recognized, and each state has taken steps to ameliorate the problem. In 1906 Cubberley observed that "any attempt at the equalization of opportunities for education, much less any attempt at equalizing burdens, is clearly impossible under a system of exclusively local taxation."[11] The state must take action to overcome the disparities inherent in the diverse economic conditions which characterize different local school districts. This issue has persisted as one of the most complex questions facing states in their attempts to meet the educational needs of all children regardless of where they attend school.

Early analysis showed that equalization could not be accomplished without the state assuming greater responsibility for financing the schools. It was a recognized function of state government to provide for a uniform educational program among all local school districts. The mechanisms for accomplishing this are equalization formulas that allocate state funds in inverse relationship to local taxpaying capacity. (Chapter 12 details types of state aid formulas.) The basic dilemma is, of course, how to best measure local fiscal capacity in order to bring about optimal equalization. This subject has been much discussed in school finance circles in recent years. Three basic approaches have been used to address the problem: (1) tax base, (2) tax base surrogate, and (3) economic indicator.

The *tax base* approach simply determines taxpaying ability by using the available tax base(s). For example, if property is the school tax base, then equalized valuation of property is used as the measure of fiscal capacity. If a sales tax or other nonproperty source is used as the tax base then it is used as the measure of fiscal capacity.

The second approach, the *tax base surrogate*, was used in several states in an earlier era, when property tax assessments were too unevenly administered to be a reliable measure of ability to pay. This method, sometimes called an index of taxpaying ability, utilized selected variables which were predictive of equalized valuation of property at some point in time. The problem, of course, was to find a time in which property values were reasonably well assessed, in order to set up a predictive equation. This approach served as a stopgap measure while property-tax administration was in the process of being improved.

Mississippi still employs this surrogate or index approach, using the county's percentages of each of the following: assessed valuation of public utilities; total motor vehicle license receipts; state value of farm products; total state personal income; total state gainfully employed nonfarm, nongovernment workers; and state retail sales tax paid. The index has served a useful purpose in Mississippi and a few other states. Its basic fault is that it may have tended to detract from the state's need to develop better and more uniform property assessments.

The *economic indicator* approach is a theoretical determination of fiscal capacity utilizing measures of income, wealth, and consumption, regardless of whether they are accessible through local taxation. It is not a proxy or surrogate measure for equalized assessed valuation of property. It departs materially from the two above measures in that it presumes that a capacity measurement does not need to be tied to an accessible local tax base. This approach suggests that since all taxes must be paid out of income or accumulated wealth, it really does not matter what particular tax base is used locally to actually collect the revenues.

Opponents of this approach maintain that local taxing units actually only have taxpaying ability relative to their accessibility to legislatively designated tax bases. If there is inequality of local resources it is created by variations in the ability of taxpayers to pay the particular, available tax. Equalization of funding must, therefore, be directed toward erasing disparities created by the revenues from legally levied taxes. If full equalization is to be attained, taxpaying ability must be determined by each and every one of the locally available tax bases.

The tax base approach addresses this issue by determining the actual ability to pay for schools, rather than using a theoretical measure of capacity such as the economic indicator. Burrup has observed that the economic indicator is inappropriate for comparing fiscal capacities of localities unable to tap major wealth bases.[12] Other authorities agree, maintaining that the fiscal capacity of a community is its access to legally permissible taxes.[13]

The quest for better measurement of local fiscal capacity is not new; in fact, in 1923 Strayer and Haig suggested that economic indicators could be used as an alternative to property valuations for purposes of school fund equalization. They recommended that local fiscal capacity be determined in New York by summing taxable income with one-tenth of the full value of real estate, then dividing by two. Reasoning that this measure was more comprehensive, since the relative position of localities was much different with each measure, they suggested that the combination would give a more accurate picture of overall economic resources.[14]

Ten years later, Mort criticized Strayer and Haig's economic indicator, observing that it defined theoretical taxpaying ability under an ideal system of taxation, not the actual situation. Mort noted that the power to tax rests with the legislature, not the local taxing unit. He said,

> the true criterion of the relative ability of local units to pay for education is the ability-to-pay under the taxing system established by the state rather than the ability-to-pay under an ideal taxing system.

Mort pointed out the shortcoming of the economic indicator approach:

> Since we must deal with communities which have no power over their tax systems except through state action, we cannot consider their ability as it would be under an ideal tax system. To build our system of state aid on such a foundation would throw excessive burdens upon actual taxpayers in some communities, simply because there happened to be wealth in those communities that was not taxable under the existing system of taxation.[15]

Mort's position on the use of a theoretical measure of fiscal capacity is apparently the prevailing view today. Most states use only those measures of ability which relate directly to taxable sources. These states have implicitly followed the philosophy which maintains that local taxpaying ability should, appropriately, be a measure of accessibility to local tax revenue. This position is enunciated by the authors of this text in a National Educational Finance Project report:

> The local taxpaying ability of school districts in reality is not their theoretical taxpaying ability, but rather a measure of their accessibility to local tax revenue. If a district only has the authority to levy property taxes then its local taxpaying ability (or effort to support schools) should be measured only in terms of the equalized value of the taxable property of that district. However, if a district has the power to levy local nonproperty taxes, such as payroll taxes, sales taxes, utility taxes, etc., then the yield of such local nonproperty taxes can justly be incorporated in the measure of the taxpaying ability of that district.[16]

At this writing, some states, including Virginia, Pennsylvania, Maryland, Kansas, Arkansas, Rhode Island, Connecticut, and Missouri, utilize a measure of local capacity other than property valuations: Virginia uses an index of property valuations, sales and income; Pennsylvania incorporates 60 percent weighting for property valuation per pupil and 40 percent weighting for personal income per pupil; Maryland defines local fiscal capacity in terms of property valuation and taxable income per pupil; Kansas utilizes a four-year average of adjusted property valuation and taxable resident incomes; Arkansas, because of poor property assessments, switched to an income measure entirely for the 1979–80 school year; Rhode Island has for many years used an index of property valuations and family income as a measure of local capacity; Connecticut uses the ratio of district median family income to state median family income as a property valuation adjustment; Missouri has an income adjustment applied to property valuation to determine the required local effort. Notably, in Virginia, Arkansas, Rhode Island, Missouri, and Connecticut the income tax is not available locally for taxation, and the use of income is purely a theoretical measure of ability of local school units to pay for education.

Pros and Cons of Economic Indicator Approach

Proponents of the economic indicator approach maintain that it is not necessary for an income tax to be accessible locally for it to be used as a measure of fiscal ability. They advance three propositions in support of this argument. First, personal income is generally accepted as the best available indicator of ability to pay, regardless of the tax being levied. Second, several studies have shown that property wealth and income are not similarly distributed among school districts usually having a low correlation. Third, evidence is increasing that income is a significant factor in the determination of local fiscal effort to support education.

Effect on Ability.   It is helpful here to remind ourselves that wealth and income measure two entirely different aspects of fiscal resources. Wealth is a stock, while income is a flow of capital. Real property constitutes only a portion, possibly 35 percent, of the wealth of a state. Table 8–2 shows the impact on selected Florida school districts when real property, total wealth, and total wealth plus personal income are used as measures of local fiscal capacity. Real property valuation alone tends to overstate the relative fiscal capacity of some of the counties and understate others.

School districts rich in income may be relatively poor in property valuations or vice versa. Examples may be found of very high property values in metropolitan areas that have moderate or low per capita personal income. The Plains states have long experienced the dilemma of property rich farmers who are barely able to meet their tax obligations because they have such low annual income in relation to wealth.

Thus, school districts rich in income may be relatively poor in property valuations or vice versa. Fisher found that in the 28 largest Standard Metropolian Statistical Areas (SMSA) several central cities showed greater relative fiscal capacity when the measure was adjusted gross income per pupil rather than when the measure was equalized assessed valuation of property per pupil.[17] Thus, the inclusion of personal income as an indicator of fiscal capacity would show these central cities to be relatively better off than if property valuations alone were used. The relative fiscal capacity effects of use of a personal income measure as opposed to equalized assessed valuation of property are shown in Table 8–3. Here Fisher shows that while central cities are generally relatively better off than other school districts in their own SMSA's, by either the personal income or property measure, the use of income does not consistently enhance the position of cities for equalization purposes.

TABLE 8–2   Nonexempt Real Property, Total Wealth, and Wealth plus Income for Small and Large School Districts

	Percent of State Nonexempt Real Property	Percent of State Total Wealth	Percent of State Total Wealth Plus Personal Income
Smallest school districts			
Union	.028	.026	.031
Gilchrist	.059	.040	.040
Glades	.123	.082	.075
Liberty	.032	.024	.025
Lafayette	.041	.028	.028
Largest school districts			
Dade	20.323	19.602	19.737
Broward	13.425	11.115	11.292
Hillsborough	4.249	5.575	5.750
Duval	4.798	6.583	6.643
Orange	5.673	4.109	4.348

Source: Kern Alexander, "The Wealth Tax as an Alternative Revenue Source for Public Schools," *Journal of Education Finance*, Vol. 2, No. 4 (Spring 1979) 474.

TABLE 8–3 **Rank of Central Cities according to Adjusted Gross Personal Income and Equalized Assessed Valuation of Property per Pupil**

Central City	Number of School Districts in SMSA	Rank of City in SMSA According to Adjusted Gross Personal Income per Pupil	Rank of City in SMSA According to Equalized Assessed Valuation of Property per Pupil
Atlanta	9	2	1
Baltimore	6	3	3
Birmingham	10	5	5
Boston	84	5	21
Buffalo	44	3	4
Chicago	327	7	16
Cincinnati	75	6	9
Cleveland	57	10	7
Dallas	62	2	2
Detroit	97	6	6
Houston	48	1	13
Kansas City	92	4	13
Los Angeles	69	6	17
Louisville	9	6	2
Milwaukee	85	8	11
Minneapolis-St. Paul	43	2	1
New Orleans	4	2	1
New York	198	5	9
Newark	86	17	21
Clifton	97	5	4
Philadelphia	219	5	5
Phoenix	56	4	10
Pittsburgh	135	3	4
St. Louis	108	8	15
San Diego	51	5	18
San Francisco	90	2	14
Seattle	36	1	4
Washington	9	5	9

Source: Jack E. Fisher, "A Comparison between Central Cities and Suburbs on Local Ability to Support Public Education," (Ed.D. dissertation, University of Florida, 1972), pp. 184–5.

Statewide, Fisher's data indicate that the inclusion of income in a local capacity index will not materially help city school districts. Both measures indicate that central cities are above average for the state and for suburbs in their SMSA.

Correlation between Income and Property.   Correlation studies have shown that property values and income usually have a rather low relationship. James, Thomas, and Dyck found a low correlation between property valuation and income in the following states: Wisconsin, .57; New York, .40; Oregon, .34;

California, .34; Massachusetts, .20; New Jersey, .26; New Mexico, .09; Washington, .01; and Nebraska, −.18. Kimbrough and Johns also found rather low correlations in Kentucky, Florida, Georgia, and Illinois. Farner and Edmundson similarly found little or no correlation between equalized value of property per pupil and income per pupil among counties in eleven western states.[18]

Advocates of the use of an income factor to determine local fiscal capacity maintain that these low correlations evidence the need to combine income with property valuations to arrive at a more comprehensive measure of fiscal capacity. On the other hand, critics of this approach say that income merely measures a different type of tax base than property, and to assume that you should use income as a measure of fiscal capacity when you cannot tax it would violate the principle of horizontal equity.

Income and Local Effort.   The most cogent argument yet presented for the use of income as a measure of local taxpaying ability is given by McMahon.[19] After observing that higher-income school districts usually levy higher property taxes, McMahon recommends broadening the measures of ability to pay to include income, even though the income tax may not be locally accessible. His rationale is as follows:

> . . . equity on the tax side, is addressed by broadening the measures of wealth and effort for the simple reason that wealth incorporates human capital and financial assets (i.e., an income factor) is a better measure of the true ability-to-pay than is a measure of wealth that is limited to real property. All taxes go back to the individual taxpayer's ability-to-pay, which are basic to both the state's and the district's fiscal capacity, irrespective of whether the tax handle used is consumption (for state sales taxes) or real property (for property taxes). Each school district has access to income through the tax handle of real property.[20]

The taxpayer equity issue bears close examination if only property or consumption taxes are accessible and income is used as a measure of ability. Horizontal tax equity is the widely accepted principle of taxation which maintains that individuals with equal ability to pay should bear equal tax burdens (see Chapter 5). The horizontal inequity of an income factor is seen where two equally poor, low-income families with homes of the same value live in two different local school districts, one rich in income, the other poor. The poor family in the high-income school district must put forth greater tax effort to support a similar school program than the poor family in the low-income school district, because the income factor would make the high-income district appear more affluent for state equalization purposes.

Thus, use of income or any other inaccessible measure may unfairly burden individual taxpayers in school districts which show high ability when measured by untaxable indicators. Noting this horizontal inequity in 1933, Mort observed that, "A district may be the situs of great wealth, yet if a large part of it cannot be taxed locally, the part that is taxed is penalized heavily."[21]

In a 1979 study of school finance in North Carolina it was found that the use of a theoretical fiscal capacity measure where the local school district did not have the legal authority to tap the tax source tended to create inequity:

> Where property is the only locally available tax base, use of theoretical taxpaying ability in a state equalization program requires that districts with a high ratio of income-to-property levy higher property tax rates than other districts. This disparity in tax rates . . . violates the horizontal equity principle as applied to the individual taxpayer. . . . Those who live in a district whose average incomes are low pay lower property tax rates for a given expenditure guarantee than taxpayers with the same income living in districts where average incomes are high.[22]

Although strong arguments are found on both sides of this issue, it seems that standard practices among the states, coupled with the difficulty of accommodating the principle of horizontal taxpayer equity, weigh against the use of the economic indicator approach. The more appropriate and prevailing view seems to be that if a tax source is not locally accessible then it should not be used as a measure of local fiscal capacity for state aid purposes. Correspondingly, where the tax source is available it should certainly not be left out of the determination of local fiscal capacity.

Equalized Assessment of Property Value

The aforementioned tax base approach largely pertains to taxation of real property, since the major portion of local revenues for schools comes from this source. Because property is the major resource of local public school funds, the state aid formulas of most states use the equalized assessed valuation of property as the sole criterion for equalization of state funds. Difficulty with property-tax administration is a traditional problem that continues to be inextricably linked to public school financing.

If all property in every state were assessed at full value, or even at a uniform percentage of full value, the problem of determining local ability would be much simpler than it is under present conditions. However, the assessment practices in most states traditionally have been far from uniform. Studies of assessment ratios within states show a range of from less than 2 to 1 in percent of true value up to more than 8 to 1. Such variations result in many complications, not only in attempts to determine local ability, but also in efforts to devise an equitable and satisfactory state plan for financing schools.

One difficulty arises from the wide differences of opinion about the method that should be used to determine the full value of property. It cannot be the original cost, because in many areas purchase price or the original cost of construction represents only a small percentage of current value. It cannot in all instances be the sales price, because there may be sales, among relatives or under enforced conditions, at a price far below that for which similar properties are being sold.

The goal in every state undoubtedly should be to attain uniform assessment procedures, but thus far few states have made satisfactory progress in that direction. Existing assessed valuations in most states, therefore, do not provide a satisfactory basis either for determining local ability or for prescribing local uniform effort.

Four possible measures for accurately determining local property wealth are (1) equalized valuation based on partial or full value of property, (2) assessed valuation determined largely by local policy, (3) a sales-ratio plan supplemented by appraisals, and (4) an index of taxpaying ability (the aforementioned property tax base surrogate approach).

Many believe that state-equalized property values offer the only satisfactory solution to the problem. However, there is much local resistance in many states to the implementation of this concept. When assessors are voted into office by the people of the county where they reside, they are likely to oppose any state effort to equalize or raise assessments in the county, regardless of how low they may be.

Some contend that there should be no effort to establish any sort of foundation program plan for financing schools until assessments are equalized. Many who are seriously concerned about inequalities in educational opportunity insist that improvements in state support need not wait until some uncertain date when assessments can perhaps be equalized. They point out that if this policy were followed, children in many parts of the state would be penalized and handicapped merely because their elders had not been able to work out a satisfactory political solution to a difficult problem. They insist that as far as school support is concerned, the same purposes that might be attained through equalized assessment can generally be accomplished through a formula. That is the reason many insist that the state adopt and use a sales-ratio plan.

During the past few years, leaders in several states, acting on the assumption that assessments at full value probably will not be politically feasible in the near future, have helped to establish an assessment, or sales-ratio plan for use as a basis for determining local ability and prescribing uniform local effort.

Unfortunately, in all but a few jurisdictions, sales-ratio studies are sporadic and inaccurate. California is an example of a state in which considerable progress has been made. There, computerized assessment of single-family homes has produced differences between assessments and selling prices that are only half as much as the most accurate assessors have been able to achieve in other states. However, of sixty jurisdictions nationwide that are considered to have the potential for computerized assessment studies, only eight are using them in assessment administration.

The sales-ratio plan, of course, has some weaknesses. Unless considerable sums are invested in a continuing study of the relationship of sales price to assessed value of property and in appraisals of types of property not frequently sold, and unless there is an adequate sampling, the ratio may not be fair and equitable. Some hold that sales-ratio studies in certain states may be subject to political manipulation. There also may be a tendency for the legislature to pass a law freezing ratios or assessments to those of a certain year. In fact, such laws have already been passed in a few states.

When sales-ratio studies are properly made and supplemented by competent appraisals, especially for commercial and industrial properties, the following procedures can be used, not only in determining local ability but also in prescribing uniform local effort to finance the schools:

1. The state agency responsible for making the study certifies to the state board of education, at a designated time each year, the ratio for each county.
2. The state board of education uses this ratio as a basis for determining the funds that would be available if a uniform tax levy were made in each county on property assessed at full value or at a designated percentage of full value.
3. The ratio for a county is then applied to the school districts in the county, by finding the percentage of the county's total valuation that the assessed valuation of the district represents and multiplying this by the amount of funds that would be available if equalized valuation and a uniform levy were used.
4. The districts in each county are required to make whatever levy is necessary to provide the funds required, on the basis of a uniform effort (by levying either a higher or a lower millage than the rate based on uniform assessment practice), until the county brings its assessments in line with state standards.

VARIATIONS IN LOCAL FISCAL EFFORT

There are several possible measures of effort. Expenditures may constitute a very rough indication of effort, but they do not accurately measure it because a district with high ability may be able, with little effort, to expend a larger amount of funds than a less wealthy district could expend with much higher effort. Expenditures therefore give some indication of the investment in education, but not necessarily of the effort being made to support the schools.

Local tax levies likewise are often considered an indication of the effort made by a school district. However, a relatively high levy in a district having a low ratio between assessed and actual valuation may constitute less effort than a much lower levy in a district with a relatively high assessment ratio.

Due to variations in assessment practices, relative levels of local effort are difficult if not impossible to determine in many states. A high millage (a mill is one-tenth of a cent) levy in a district may or may not represent high effort, depending upon the assessment ratio in the district as compared with that in other parts of the state. In some states, laws limiting the levy for school purposes may mean that the people in a number of districts are levying far less than they would be willing to make available if the laws permitted.

In spite of these factors, it is not uncommon to find districts in a state that are levying from two to six or eight times as much for support of schools as other districts. Undoubtedly, in many cases this represents a major difference in effort. In addition, districts in states where the laws permit may be receiving funds from other local tax sources, such as payroll or sales taxes. In some cases, however, these other sources of revenue are used in lieu of levies that otherwise would be made on property. Consequently, property levies are lower in those districts than in districts which are not permitted, or do not choose, to use nonproperty taxes as a source of revenue.

If local support is to be utilized, equality of opportunity might theoretically be attained in either of two ways: (1) limit the effort that may be made by school districts, and perhaps take away and distribute to other districts some of the state funds now received by districts with sufficient revenue to provide a reasonably adequate program, or (2) provide sufficient funds from state sources to enable all districts to have as large an amount available per pupil as is now available in the more favored districts.

The possibility of limiting local effort or of taking funds from some of the more wealthy districts might appeal to a number of people who are concerned about high taxes and believe that too much money is now being devoted to education. People usually want to effect improvements where they are needed instead of limiting opportunities that are now available in the more favored districts and states, although even those people who favor equitable distribution of educational funds might change their opinion if they lived in some of the more favored districts. With local effort, the more wealthy districts will always have more local funds available per student or per classroom unit than the less wealthy. Thus, unless some limitation is imposed on these wealthy districts, there will continue to be some inequality in educational opportunity.

Why tax effort varies among school districts is a question of great interest to educators and economists alike. Why some populations have higher aspirations for education and are willing to pay for it is probably a more complex issue than was suggested earlier with the argument that variation in income is the determinant. Kay, for example, found that urbanized school districts tended to have higher tax effort.[23] While urbanization had a higher relationship with property wealth and income, Kay also discovered that population mobility and educational level were important factors.

School districts with less property wealth often put forth greater fiscal effort than their wealthier counterparts. Presumably, the greater effort is in many instances necessary in order to provide acceptable educational programs. Other factors, however, can play an important role in the level of tax effort of a community to support public schools. Meyers, for example, found that defeat of a millage proposal by Detroit voters in 1963 was attributable in part to opposition of private and parochial school patrons who had no children in public schools. McLoone found that areas with good schools and high taxes tended to have a relatively rapid turnover of young families with children in public schools.[24] Voters over age 50 are less likely to vote for higher tax rates, and professional and white-collar workers are more likely to approve increased school taxes than blue-collar workers and retirees.[25] Too, cyclical economic effects, beyond mere income levels, may have an effect on taxpayers' willingness to pay taxes. In times of rapid inflation, resistance to additional taxes intensifies.[26]

Willingness to provide tax support for public schools is also influenced by the politics and power structure of the community. Districts with competitive power structures tend to make higher local financial effort in proportion to ability than do districts with noncompetitive or monopolistic power structures. Education appears to benefit from a pluralism of competing power structures, that is, where various power groups are forced to seek allies in order to be politically effective. Educational advocates in such a setting have been found to be effective political allies. Where a school district is dominated by a monolithic, noncompetitive power structure influenced largely by economics, the political effectiveness of educational interests is substantially reduced.[27]

Thus, the nature of local fiscal effort is quite complex, with factors as diverse as the political, educational, social, and economic conditions of each community. Undoubtedly, the wealth and income of the people is an important element, but this alone does not explain why two school districts of the same relative economic level will have greatly different local school fiscal effort. The answer can only be found in the myriad pluralistic conditions of our democratic system of government.

NOTES

1.   See Advisory Commission on Intergovernmental Relations, *Measures of State and Local Fiscal Capacity and Tax Effort of State and Local Areas* (Washington, D.C.: U.S. Government Printing Office, 1962) p. 3.

2.   See U.S. Department of Commerce, Bureau of the Census, *Finances of Public School Systems in 1978–79* (Washington, D.C.: U.S. Government Printing Office, 1980), p. 9.

3.   C.T. Sandford, J.R.M. Willis, and D.J. Ironside, *An Annual Wealth Tax* (New York: Holmes & Meier Publishers, Inc., 1975), p. 3.

4.   See William E. Sparkman, "Tax Effort for Education," in *Educational Need in the Public Economy*, eds. Kern Alexander and K.Forbis Jordan (Gainesville, Fla.: University of Florida Press, 1976), pp. 299–336.

5.   Advisory Commission on Intergovernmental Relations, *op. cit.*

6.   Kenneth E. Quindry, *State and Local Revenue Potential 1976* (Atlanta: Southern Regional Education Board, 1977), pp. 6–7. See also, Kenneth E. Quindry and Niles Schoening, *State and Local Tax Performance 1979* (Atlanta: Southern Regional Education Board, 1980).

7.   John Akin, "Fiscal Capacity and the Estimation Method of the Advisory Commission on Intergovernmental Relations," *National Tax Journal*, Vol. xxvi, No. 2 (June, 1973).

8.   Harold K. Charlesworth, and William G. Herzel, *Kentucky Gross State Product, 1969* (Lexington, Ky.: University of Kentucky, 1972).

9.   Kent D. Halstead, *Tax Wealth in Fifty States* (Washington, D.C.: Government Printing Office, 1978), p. 5.

10.   U.S. Department of Commerce, Bureau of the Census, *Survey of Current Business* (Washington, D.C.: Government Printing Office, May, 1981).

11.   Ellwood P. Cubberley, *School Funds and Their Apportionment* (New York: Teachers College Press, Teachers College, Columbia University, 1906).

12.   Percy E. Burrup, *Financing Education in a Climate of Change* (Boston: Allyn & Bacon, Inc., 1974).

13.   Roe L. Johns and Edgar L. Morphet, *The Economics and Financing of Education*: A Systems Approach, 3rd ed. (Englewood Cliffs, N.J.: Prentice-Hall, Inc., 1975).

14.   George D. Strayer and Robert Murray Haig, *The Financing of Education in the State of New York* (New York: Macmillan, Inc., 1923).

15.   Paul R. Mort, *State Support for the Public Schools* (New York: Teachers College Press, Teachers College, Columbia University, 1926), p. 16.

16.   Roe L. Johns, "The Development of State Support for Public Schools," in *Financing Education: Fiscal and Legal Alternatives*, eds. Roe L. Johns, Kern Alexander, K. Forbis Jordan (Columbus, Ohio: Charles E. Merrill Publishing Company, 1972). See also James A. Hale, "Measuring School District Fiscal Capacity," *Texas Tech Journal of Education*, Vol. 7, No. 3 (Fall 1980).

17.   Jack E. Fisher, "A Comparison between Central Cities and Suburbs on Local Ability to Support Public Education," (Ed.D. dissertation, University of Florida, 1972).

18.   Thomas H. James, Alan J. Thomas, and Harold J. Dyck, *Wealth Expenditure and Decision Making for Education* (Washington, D.C.: U.S. Office of Education, Cooperative Research Project #1241, 1963), pp. 7–8; Ralph B. Kimbrough and Roe L. Johns, *The Relationship of Socioeconomic Community Power Structure to Local Fiscal Policy*, Final Report, Office of Education, Cooperative Research Project #1234 (Gainesville, Fla.: University of Florida, 1968); Frank Farner and John Edmundson, *Relationships of Principal Tax Bases for Public School Support in the Counties of the Eleven Western States* (Eugene, Oreg.: University of Oregon, 1969), p. 11.

19.   T. R. Melcher, "The Relationships between Alternative Local Fiscal Capacity Measures and Selected School Finance Equity Standards" (Ph.D. dissertation, University of Florida, 1978).

20.   W. W. McMahon, "A Broader Measure of Wealth and Effort for Educational Equality and Tax Equity," *Journal of Education Finance*, 4 (Summer 1978), 65–88.

21.   P. R. Mort, *State Support for Public Education* (Washington, D.C.: American Council on Education, 1933).

22.   Kern Alexander and T. R. Melcher, "Alternative Measures of Local Fiscal Capacity," in *Access to Equal Educational Opportunity in North Carolina*, The Report of the Governor's Commission on Public School Finance (Raleigh, N.C.: North Carolina Department of Education, 1979), p. 75.

23.   Harold B. Kay, "A Study of the Relationship between Selected Socio-Economic Variables and Local Tax Effort" (Ed.D. dissertation, University of Florida, 1973).

24.   Alfred Victor Meyers, "The Financial Crisis in Urban Schools: Patterns of Support and Nonsupport among Organized Groups in an Urban Community" (Ed.D. dissertation, Wayne State University, 1964; Eugene McLoone, *Background Paper on State and Local Taxation* (Albany, N.Y.: New York Educational Conference Board, July, 1969).

25.   Irving M. Witt and Frank C. Pearce, *A Study of Voter Reaction to a Combination Bond-Tax Election* (San Mateo, Calif.: San Mateo College, 1968).

26.   James M. Buchanan, "Taxpayer Constraints on Financing Education," in *Economic Factors Affecting the Financing of Education*, eds. Roe L. Johns, and others (Gainesville, Fla.: University of Florida, 1970), pp. 278–82.

27.   Kimbrough and Johns, *op. cit.*, pp. 187–90.

SELECTED REFERENCES

ADVISORY COMMISSION on INTERGOVERNMENTAL RELATIONS.   *Measures of State and Local Fiscal Capacity and Tax Effort*. Washington, D.C.: U.S. Government Printing Office, 1962.

ADVISORY COMMISSION on INTERGOVERNMENTAL RELATIONS.   *Measuring the Fiscal Capacity and Effort of State and Local Areas*. Washington, D.C.: U.S. Government Printing Office, 1971.

DUE, JOHN F., and ANN F. FRIEDLANDER. *Government Finance: Economics of the Public Sector.* Homewood, Ill.: Richard D. Irwin, Inc., 1977.

HALSTEAD, D. KENT. *Tax Wealth in Fifty States.* Washington, D.C.: U.S. Government Printing Office, 1978.

MUSGRAVE, RICHARD A., and PEGGY B. MUSGRAVE. *Public Finance in Theory and Practice.* 3rd ed. New York: McGraw-Hill Book Company, 1980.

QUINDRY, KENNETH E., and NILES SCHOENING, *State and Local Tax Performance, 1978.* Atlanta: Southern Regional Education Board, 1980.

SPARKMAN, WILLIAM E. "Tax Effort for Education," in Kern, Alexander, and K. F. Jordan. *Educational Need in the Public Economy.* Gainesville, Fla.: University of Florida Press, 1976.

CHAPTER NINE
INEQUALITY
IN OPPORTUNITY AND
REDISTRIBUTION EFFECTS
OF PUBLIC EDUCATION

Equality of educational opportunity is a goal to which practically every American citizen has subscribed in theory for many years. But practical application is a different matter. Vigorous and emotionally charged arguments occur periodically in every community, in every state legislature, and in Congress concerning the desirability of taking additional steps to implement this concept.

Equality of opportunity for all does not mean that every student should have the same program of education. Nor, as the courts have emphasized, does it mean that all students must have the same amount of money expended on them. Instead, it means that every person should have the opportunity for the kind and quality of education that will best meet his needs as an individual and as a member of the society in which he lives. There should be no controversy about implementing a concept such as this in a democracy; yet there frequently is. Why? Apparently, it is because many people are complacent about what has been accomplished and are not willing to recognize the serious problems that still exist.

In the future, these problems must be faced by every citizen more realistically than they have been in the past. Many studies have shown, and numerous authorities have commented on, the tragedy inherent in wasted human and natural resources. There can be no doubt that the nation has been seriously handicapped by this neglect or that it cannot be afforded in the future. The

EDUCATIONAL QUALITY AND FINANCIAL SUPPORT*

Two basic questions have directly or indirectly been involved in most of the discussions and controversies about public education in the various states of this nation from the beginning: (1) What should be accomplished through public education and how can it best be done? (2) How much should the programs of education cost and how should they be financed?

These two questions obviously are interrelated. Any agreements and policies relating to the first have implications for the second, and any solutions agreed upon for the second question are likely to have implications for the first. When the quantity or the quality of education is increased, financial support generally needs to be increased. When the financial support is restricted, the quantity and the quality of education are likely to be limited. In fact, the financial provisions for education establish the limits within which schools and educational institutions must operate; they also determine whether or not certain kinds of decisions may be made about the quantity and the quality of education to be provided.

Some people begin their consideration of these problems with the assumption that any reasonable quantity and quality of education that most people find desirable can and should be financed. Others begin with the assumption that taxes are high and that financial support must be limited, and conclude that educational provisions and programs must be limited accordingly.

Cost-Quantity Relationships

It is much easier for most people to understand the relationships between quantity and educational expenditures than between quality and expenditures, or costs. Probably there are only a limited number of situations in which, if quality is to be maintained, increased quantity does not require increased expenditures. In some school systems, a few students could be added to certain classes or beneficial changes could be made in organization or programs without increasing costs appreciably. However, in most local or state school systems, if the enrollment increases by 10 percent, the costs probably increase in nearly the same proportion, provided the same quality is maintained. Likewise, it should be obvious that if a larger proportion of the student population attends high school or college, if vocational and other classes are added to an academic program, if special classes are organized for disadvantaged or exceptional children, if transportation is provided for students who previously have been transported by their parents, or if any similar changes are made that increase the quantity of education or educational services, the cost is likely to increase.

The quantity of education provided in most state and local school systems has increased considerably over a period of years. That is one of the reasons

*This section was prepared with the collaboration of Russell B. Vlaanderen, Director, Research and Information Services, Education Commission of the States, Denver, Colorado.

school expenditures have increased. Still further increases to meet emerging needs may be expected in many areas. The expenditures for education, therefore, will tend to increase somewhat proportionally in these areas unless there are significant changes in quality, in organization and operation (including increased utilization of the new technologies), or in the purchasing power of the dollar.

Cost-Quality Relationships

When it comes to the quality of education as related to cost, there are usually greater differences of opinion. Many people would agree that increasing the quality is likely to add somewhat to the cost, but fewer would agree that increasing the cost would necessarily result in better quality.

Cost Not Always Related to Quality. Before analyzing cost-quality relationships, it is desirable to call attention to certain conditions under which there are no necessary relationships between cost and quality:

1. Small schools tend to cost more per pupil than larger schools, even though the quality of education provided in the smaller schools is frequently found to be lower. Thus, increasing the number of small schools could add to the cost without increasing, or perhaps even while decreasing, the quality. On the other hand, in certain areas it might be possible to decrease the cost or improve the quality by eliminating small schools and organizing larger schools. However, there is some evidence to indicate that where small schools have to be maintained, the quality in many cases could be improved by increasing the services and expenditures.

2. In some school systems, the quality of education may be adversely affected by inept leadership and administration. For example, teachers and other employees may not be carefully selected, with the result that a large proportion may not be very competent. In other systems, employment policies may be unusually good, and only the most competent persons may be selected for service in the system. Although the cost may not be any greater in the second system than in the first, the quality of education provided may be higher. Similarly, factors that contribute to low morale may result in relatively low quality of service in one district, whereas in other districts high morale may result in higher quality. In individual school systems, therefore, quality may be affected to some extent by a number of factors that are not directly related to finance.

3. In some instances, state laws or local board policies may require the continuation of outmoded policies or practices that limit or do not add to the quality of education provided. A change in law or in board policy in such instances should result in the improvement of quality without any material change in financial support.

4. In many state and local school systems, it may become possible to effect some increases in quality, at least for certain students, without adding appreciably to the costs. Tirrell has stated, "The answer to the question, 'Must Quality Education Cost More,' could be *no*, but it would require the adoption of new policies and procedures utilized today in only a small number of educational institutions, although quite widely accepted in business, industry and the military."[1]

Quality Difficult to Measure.   Aside from situations such as those just discussed, however, is there any relationship between the cost or expenditures and the quality of education provided? A few contend that despite greatly increased expenditures for the schools, the quality or standard of education generally has not been raised in this country. Others hold that the quality of education has improved, partly because there are more well-prepared teachers, better facilities and services, and, in general, better learning conditions and opportunities.

One problem arises from the fact that it is difficult to define or to measure the quality of education. The measurement of *quantity* is relatively easy. Different people define the term *quality* in different ways. Some think of quality only in terms of academic achievement by pupils in schools, whereas others insist that quality be judged by the all-round development and progress of pupils. Where different bases are used for judging, the judgments are bound to differ.

On the basis of numerous studies, it seems that the following conclusions are justified.[2]

1. The quality of education provided by the schools today is generally superior to that of a few generations ago. This does not mean that the quality is as good as it should be or that there are no weaknesses to be corrected. In fact, there are many communities throughout the nation where the quality undoubtedly is much lower than it should be. Unquestionably, there have been weaknesses in the programs for the disadvantaged and for some of the more able students, and there have been failures to provide for the individual needs of many others. The evidence does not indicate that educational standards generally have declined, but that they are not as high as they should be.

2. In spite of some reports to the contrary, the products of the public schools generally compare favorably with those of private and parochial schools. In fact, public school graduates in college generally do at least as well as, and perhaps even better than, graduates of many other schools, and the quality of education in public schools is at least equal to that in other schools.

3. The quality of education provided in school systems where expenditures are low is far less satisfactory than that in systems where expenditures are above the national average. Low expenditures tend to result in inadequate leadership, large classes, poor teachers and teaching, and other features that contribute to low quality.

INEQUALITIES IN OPPORTUNITY

The desirability of equality of educational opportunity has not even been accepted in theory in certain parts of the world. It seems impossible to attain adequacy under present conditions in many of the underdeveloped areas. However, considerable progress has been made. A larger proportion of the people of the world than a generation ago now realize the importance of at least some education for all. More and more people want more from life than mere survival. Many have begun to learn that in any nation human beings need not be handicapped by diseases that can be prevented or cured, by malnutrition, by poverty, by inadequate education, or by exploitation. Most people have begun to recognize that education can and should constitute the key that may make available to them, their children, and their neighbors some of the better things life has to offer. However, the task of educating people so that each person may make a constructive contribution to society has become vastly bigger, more challenging, and much more complex than it was a few years ago. There is more to learn, greater need for learning, and greater cost as well.

Most people in this country have assumed that we have been providing reasonably adequate programs of education. In many respects, the record has been impressive. For example, at the turn of the century the most educated fifth of the population received an average of 14 years of schooling, while the least educated fifth received only 3.7 years. Thus, the most educated person has spent almost four times as much time in school as the least educated.[3] By the mid-1970s, this differential had been reduced to the point that the most educated fifth had about 40 percent more years of schooling. During the period from 1870 to 1978, the number of high-school graduates per 100 persons 17 years of age rose from 2 to 75.[4] Meade has observed the progress of education, noting that in early stages of education, financed entirely by taxation, the burden has always fallen "at least somewhat more heavily on the rich than the poor," and expenditure on the education of the poor "has been an equalizing factor of greatest importance."[5] Yet the evidence that has been accumulated during recent years clearly shows that the needs of substantial numbers of people have been grossly neglected. Blacks in the South (many of whom have moved to urban ghettos), Chicanos, Indians, Orientals, poor whites of Appalachia and many other areas, and the less academically minded students in most parts of the nation have had inadequate opportunities to develop their talents.

A fairly recent phenomenon has been the apparent disenchantment of a number of the more able students. Some have not continued their education through or after high school graduation, and many have become a part of the nation's youth who drop out at a disturbing rate. Gross inequalities and inadequate opportunities for people of all ages have retarded the development of the nation. The price of indifference and neglect has exceeded the cost that would have been necessary to ensure adequate and equitable opportunities for everyone.

Inequalities among States

Some of the differences in equality of educational opportunity among the states in this country are difficult to demonstrate convincingly, perhaps partly because only limited objective evidence has been available. This may be one reason why many people have not seemed to be seriously disturbed about the existing situation.

One difficulty comes from the fact that state averages do not indicate variations within each state. The educational opportunities in the best school system in some of the handicapped states may compare reasonably well with those in the best systems in other states. In some of the poorest school systems, however, the deficiencies are striking but are not obvious to those who note only the averages. State statistics do not create a visual and dramatic impression of the hundreds or thousands of people who are, and will continue to be, seriously handicapped during their lifetime because of inadequate educational opportunities in the communities in which they have lived.

Another difficulty arises from the fact that most of the evidence available deals with factors that, although important, only indirectly reveal variations in educational opportunity. For example, the percentage of adults who have completed four or more years of college work does not give any indication of the number who might have completed college had better educational opportunities been provided in their public schools.

The income of the citizens of a state affects their potential expenditure for education and other governmental services. The expenditures for education on a state-wide basis seem to relate rather directly to the quality of education provided or, at any rate, have a positive correlation with selected indicators of quality, as evidenced by the data presented in Table 9–1. These data, however, do not justify a conclusion that the cause-and-effect relationship exists because of high correlations.

Table 9–1 lists in the first column the five states ranking highest in estimated current expenditures per child of school age in average daily attendance and the five states ranking lowest on this basis in 1979–80. The second column shows that the average expenditure per school-age child ranged from $1,414 in Georgia, to $3,041 in New York. Each of the five states ranking highest on this measure had expenditures per child in excess of $2,600, and each of the five ranking lowest had expenditures below $1,600. The measurement and extent of variations in fiscal ability are considered in another chapter of this text.

The third column gives the median number of school years completed in each of these states by persons 18 years of age or older in 1976. The data indicate a narrowing of the gap between states with highest and lowest expenditures, on this measure of differences in educational opportunity.

The fourth column gives the percentage of draftees that failed the mental tests for induction into the armed services in 1972. The average for the five states of lowest expenditures was more than twice that of the five top states of expenditures. In terms of personal income per child of school age in 1978,* the highest ranking state, California, showed 1.7 percent of its draftees fail the

*"Rankings of the States," (Washington, D.C.: National Education Association, 1980), Table D–11.

TABLE 9-1   Differences in Educational Opportunities Among High- and Low-Income States

STATES (BASED ON ESTIMATED CURRENT EXPENDITURES PER CHILD OF SCHOOL AGE) ADA 1979-80 (1)	ESTIMATED CURRENT EXPENDITURES PER PUPIL (ADA) 1979-80 (2)	MEDIAN YEARS OF SCHOOL COMPLETED BY PERSONS 18 YEARS OLD AND OLDER IN 1976 (3)	PERCENT OF DRAFTEES FAILING MENTAL TESTS 1972 (4)	PERCENTAGE OF ILLITERATES 1972 (5)
Five highest:				
New York	$3,041	12.5	2.2	1.4
New Jersey	2,893	12.4	2.8	1.1
Massachusetts	2,737	12.6	1.0	1.1
Connecticut	2,755	12.6	1.2	1.1
Delaware	2,644	12.5	5.5	.9
Five lowest:				
Idaho	$1,542	12.6	1.4	.6
New Hampshire	1,515	12.6	.6	.7
Alabama	1,503	12.2	8.6	2.1
Arkansas	1,502	12.2	7.7	1.9
Georgia	1,414	12.3	11.6	2.0

Sources: National Education Association, *Rankings of the States,* (Washington, D.C.: National Education Association, 1980) Table H–10 (Columns 1 and 2); *Digest of Education Statistics* (Washington, D.C.: National Center for Education Statistics, 1980), Table 13 (Column 3) and Table 14 (Column 5) ; and *Digest of Education Statistics (Washington, D.C.: National Center for Education Statistics, 1979), Table 15 (Column 4).*

mental tests while the lowest ranking state, Mississippi, had a failure rate of 17.1 percent.

The illiteracy percentage for the state ranking lowest in expenditures per child, Georgia, was 2.0. The highest-ranking state, New York, showed 1.4 percent.

Complicating factors in any analysis arise from (1) the mobility of the population within the United States, (2) migration and the places where large proportions of immigrants have settled, and (3) the composition of the population in each of the states as between rural and urban dwellers, whites and nonwhites, and so on. These data cannot show, therefore, the educational situation in any state at present. Nor do they give an exact picture of the situation as it was a few years ago. However, even without further refinement, they indicate some important differences among states. These differences seem to be related to some extent to the differences in expenditures per pupil and fiscal ability.

Considerable additional information indicating differences in educational opportunity could readily be presented. Whereas no single set of figures based on one factor should be considered significant, the fact remains that all data tend to show that, in the past, there have been significant differences in educational opportunity among many of the states and that these differences are still sufficient to warrant considerable concern.

With the great mobility of population at the present time, it is evident that inadequate educational opportunities in a state not only handicap the people in that state but constitute a problem for other states to which some of these people migrate. It is evident that under modern conditions, the nation cannot afford the losses resulting from the presence of substantial numbers in the total population who have had inadequate educational opportunities.

Inequalities within States

The evidence indicates rather clearly that the range in educational opportunities available within most states is considerably greater than the interstate differences indicated by the averages for the various states. In a few states, a majority of children seem to have reasonably adequate educational opportunities. Generally speaking, the states with the greatest extremes are small-district states in which only limited state support supplements local funds. In some of the small poverty-stricken districts and the urban ghetto areas, educational opportunities are tragically inadequate. The fact that blacks and other minority children who have attended schools in the South, in the urban ghettos, and in many other impoverished areas have had inadequate educational opportunities has been widely publicized during the past few years and, as a result, some improvements have been made. However, the opportunities for many other children, regardless of race or similar factors, have been, and continue to be, far from satisfactory, even in many of the more affluent school districts and states.

There are many indications that the quality of education provided in most school systems of adequate size tends to be reflected in the level of expenditure. The significant differences that are found in most states in expenditure for education among districts, as noted later, tend to reflect important differences in the educational opportunities that are provided. However, these differences are brought out more clearly and more meaningfully for many people by studies that provide evidence for each district in a state on items such as the following:

1. The percentage of eligible children in early childhood education programs including kindergarten
2. The number and percentage who drop out before completing high school
3. The extent to which compensatory and remedial programs are being provided for the educationally disadvantaged
4. The percentage who attend college

5. The percentage of students who are engaged in educational programs and activities during the summer months
6. The nature and extent of programs in vocational, career, and adult education
7. The extent to which provision is made for various kinds of special education and the percentage of students who are involved in such programs
8. The nature and extent of health, counseling, and other services provided
9. Indications as to the achievement and progress of students at all levels
10. The extent to which staff and patrons are willing to utilize promising innovative programs and methods

Inequalities within Local School Systems

There is greater equality of educational opportunity within many local school systems than within most states. In each local school system, a uniform tax base is available for support of the educational program, and all schools are operated under the policies established by the board. As indicated earlier, the educational opportunities available may be reasonably adequate or quite inadequate, but inequities usually have not been particularly obvious, except in the poverty or ghetto areas.

Evidence accumulated during the past few years, however, has helped to focus national attention on the fact that the inequalities within many school systems are more serious than most people had considered probable.[6] The federal funds authorized under the Economic Opportunity Act, Title I of the Elementary and Secondary Education Act of 1965, and other related acts and provisions have facilitated and stimulated the development of programs that have alleviated the situations in many areas. However, the problems are complex and deep-seated, and only the first steps have been taken toward their solution. Not all solutions have been the result of voluntary action on the part of the schools, however. The courts have intervened both in finance and segregation issues. The issue of *de jure segregation* was settled in *Brown*, in 1954, and in 1973 the Supreme Court of the United States issued a decision on *de facto segregation* in *Keyes* v. *School District No. 1, Denver, Colorado.*[7] Since the court ruled for the first time on a case involving segregation in a school district that had never operated under a constitutional or statutory provision that mandated or permitted racial segregation, northern school districts will no longer be able to rely on the "neighborhood schools" policy as a defense against segregation suits.

REASONS FOR INEQUALITIES IN OPPORTUNITY

Why are serious inequalities in educational opportunity permitted to exist year after year in a country in which a majority of the people seem dedicated to the concept of equality? Some of the background factors involved are:

1. Many people do not realize the extent or implications of inequalities;
2. Some people have become accustomed to the existing situation and accept it as normal;
3. Substantial numbers seem to be more concerned about their own personal problems and the rising costs of living and government than about variations in educational opportunity that do not seem to affect them immediately;
4. Until comparatively recent years, the procedures needed to solve certain aspects of the problem had not been satisfactorily developed or understood;
5. Most important of all, there are wide differences among local school districts in wealth per pupil.

Some of the important reasons for differences in educational opportunity, in addition to the general background factors listed above, are briefly discussed on the following pages.

Inadequate School Districts

Many studies have shown that both small schools and small school districts usually offer less satisfactory educational programs, are less efficient, and are more expensive to operate than larger schools and districts.

Despite the fact that the number of school districts in the United States has been reduced to about one-sixth of the number that existed only 35 years ago, there were still sixteen thousand in 1980. Three states had more than one thousand districts each. However, practically all small districts have been reorganized in some states during the past few years.

It is not possible to operate an effective and economical school system in a district having only a few hundred students. Where districts of this size are maintained, the costs per student are high, and some of the needed services cannot be provided, except, perhaps, through an intermediate or area service unit. A district having at least five to ten thousand students has many potential advantages and can provide a more adequate program than any small district.

Any state with a large number of small districts has marked differences in local ability to finance schools. In such states, the development of an equitable finance plan that would make possible adequate schools in all districts is difficult if not impossible. However, as districts are reorganized and larger districts evolve, the problem becomes simpler, and a satisfactory solution is more practicable. In fact, in several states, district reorganization would probably contribute at least as much or more to the equalization of financial support and of educational opportunity than has been accomplished thus far though improvements in state provisions for financial support.

Financial Effect of Reorganization.   If five small districts with wide differences in ability were to combine into one larger district, the extremes in that area would be eliminated. If similar reorganizations were to be effected throughout a state, the range in local ability would be greatly reduced—probably to 10 or 15 to 1. The effect of reorganization on differences in local ability is illustrated in Figure 9–1.

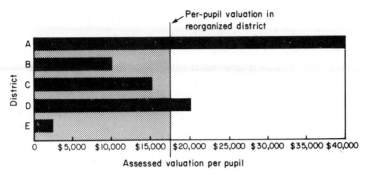

FIGURE 9-1

Let us assume that District A, with 2,500 pupils, had $40,000 per pupil in equalized valuation of property; District B, with 1,500 pupils, had $8,500; District C, with 3,500 pupils, had $15,000; District D, with 500 pupils, had $20,000; and District E, with 2,000 pupils, had $2,000. If a new district comprising these five districts were to be organized, the range of 20 to 1 in ability would be eliminated and the valuation per pupil in the new district would be a little under $18,000.

Small Schools

Although few, if any, small school districts can be justified under any conditions, some small schools are necessary and probably will be necessary for some years to come, because they are isolated. Relatively small high schools are even more expensive and probably less satisfactory than small elementary schools. The small number of pupils per teacher usually found in such schools is the greatest single factor contributing to high costs, but the limited range of offerings tends to limit the adequacy of educational opportunity. Where small isolated schools are necessary, higher costs can be justified, but not otherwise. The per capita costs of education tend to be higher and the quality of the educational program less satisfactory in elementary schools having fewer than 175 to 200 pupils and in high schools having fewer than 300 pupils, than in larger schools.[8]

Differences in Ability and Effort

Some of the variations in ability and effort to support schools among and within the states, together with certain implications for financial support, are discussed in Chapter 8. The important point to note here is that marked differences in ability are found among school systems within states and that these are maximized by faulty district structure. In small-district states, it is not possible to provide reasonable equity for taxpayers and consequently to assure anything closely approaching equality of educational opportunities for the children, except perhaps through a system of complete state support. Inadequate and expensive small schools often are perpetuated by the district structure,

191

and as long as such schools exist in nonisolated areas, the problem of equitable and adequate financial support is not likely to be solved.

Inadequate district structure is likewise one of the important reasons for differences in effort. In districts with extremely limited wealth, adequate educational opportunities cannot be provided unless the taxpayers make an excessive effort, and not even then unless the state develops an adequate and equitable plan of financial support. Even if substantial state support is provided, marked variations in effort will be necessary if anything approaching equality of educational opportunity is to be assured.

It must be recognized, however, that even if all districts should be properly organized and a sound state plan of financial support developed, there would still be variations in effort due to differences in the people's interest in their schools, in their attitude toward taxes, and in their willingness to provide the financial support needed for a satisfactory program of education.

Unsound Legal and Financial Provisions

Legal provisions, in addition to those relating to district organization, frequently result in inequalities in opportunity. The intent of the law probably is not to create or to perpetuate inequalities, but the net effect of certain types of laws is definitely to do so. Many illustrations could be given, but a few should suffice to bring out some of the implications. For instance, when the laws of a state provide that all or practically all state funds for schools are to be apportioned on a flat-grant basis, there are certain to be inequities for taxpayers and inequalities in educational opportunity, even in states in which all districts are reasonably adequate in size. Laws providing different tax limits for different types of school districts also tend to result in marked inequities. If property on which school taxes may be levied is assessed at a low percentage of actual valuation, adequate financial support may be impossible, especially when local levies are limited by law. When assessment ratios vary in different parts of a state, the inequities are likely to be particularly serious, because the assessing practice will result in much lower support in proportion to ability in some parts of the state than in others. The Education Commission of the States issued the results of a study on assessment practices in March 1973 in which it concluded that "school revenue systems in the state suffer because of poorly drawn laws, inadequate laws and antiquated laws dealing with real property taxation."[9]

Even laws providing for the election of county superintendents or the state superintendent by popular vote may indirectly have considerable bearing on both the adequacy and the quality of educational opportunities in the various states. In fact, any legal provisions that result directly or indirectly in handicapping or preventing the citizens of properly organized districts from establishing and operating the kind and quality of schools needed to permit and assist every child to develop to his or her maximum potential have some effect on both the quality and the adequacy of educational opportunity.

REDISTRIBUTION EFFECTS
OF EDUCATION*

Because of the complexity of the many tax structures and allocation systems, studies of educational finance traditionally have not attempted to determine the income redistribution effect derived from governmental policies in education. Generally, studies have been concerned with the equality of expenditures of the fiscal ability of local school districts to produce revenues for education. The school district itself has been the basic unit with which the data have been associated. Attempts to break down the clientele of the school districts as to contribution of the taxpayers and benefits thereto are uncommon. The paucity of redistributional studies may be partially attributed to the belief that public education is free, compulsory, and its benefits the same to everyone who participates.

In viewing public schools as a redistributional tool to bring about greater equality, one must analyze the school fiscal structure from two aspects. First is the simple redistributive effect of the state tax structure and the school allocation system with regard to their impact on low-, middle-, and high-income families. If low-income families are receiving more educational benefits in terms of dollars for their education than they pay in taxes for education, there is a positive redistribution effect. Second, the taxation and allocation system may be viewed from a position of equality both within and among income classes.

Politics of Inequality

Where education is concerned, the governmental response of providing better services to low-income families in low-wealth school districts has been very gradual. Expenditure variations among states and school districts were much greater thirty years ago, but wide differences still persist. A theory of redistribution politics in education must recognize that, although each person has one vote, the significance and power of each vote is not equal, even after reapportionment. In analyzing the educational power structure, it quickly becomes apparent that redistribution of income through education probably is not the strategic basis on which most voters make fiscal decisions. The people who pay into the system and those who receive the benefits back may not be allied on the same economic basis.[10] Families sending their children to parochial schools, or older persons who have very low incomes, may see no benefit to be derived personally from voting for greater taxes to equalize resources among school districts; this will generally reflect adversity to both redistribution and equalization of expenditures. Thus, voters may join the wealthy at the voting

*This section is an excerpt from Kern Alexander, Thomas Melcher, and Stephen Thomas, "Income Redistribution Effect of Public Schools on Low Income Families," in *Educational Need in the Public Economy*, eds. Kern Alexander and K. Forbis Jordan (Gainesville, Fla.: University Presses of Florida, 1976), pp. 84–112.

booths and retard a positive reallocation of resources to assist low-income children in poor school districts.

Another condition which tends to inhibit the egalitarian motive of public education is the lack of political power of those who are poor and live in poor school districts. With regard to legislative influence, it is true that the more populous school districts in this country are also the ones with the greatest average wealth per pupil.[11] It is to their disadvantage to encourage state governments to fiscally equalize among school districts. Some argue quite rationally that for sheer numbers, more persons are actually found in wealthier than in average or below-average school districts, thereby including a low-income voter response which may seek redistribution locally but retard similar stress at the state level. This problem is magnified by unreasonably large numbers of school districts in many states, a variable in the redistribution context which holds important implications for equality.

Even where a majority of low-income voters exercise their franchise in poor school districts, the overall political power structure of the state responds to varying coalitions with divergent goals. Equality through redistribution becomes a cloudy objective. As Buchanan and Tullock have explained, the taxpayer/voter may respond differently over a series of issues.[12] In one situation, a voter as beneficiary may be in the minority, but with another issue, he/she may derive no benefits and yet stand in the voting majority. Certain individuals may do very well with particular outcomes but badly with others.

The pattern of redistribution cannot, therefore, be specified under the present democratic method of financing public education. Redistribution through education requires a concerted political effort at the state or federal level to form coalitions with mutual interests encompassing the ideal of public education and advancing both the social and economic desirability of greater equality.

Redistribution Studies

Analysis of the equity of public investment in education centers on the distribution of benefits and costs. The costs of public investment in education are the taxes which support it, and the distribution of the costs is the incidence of these taxes. While private costs of education, such as foregone income and tuition payments, are of considerable importance, especially in higher education, only public costs, measured by the taxes supporting the program, are relevant in determining the redistributive effect of public investment.

The benefits of public investment in education are more complex, involving difficult conceptual problems. However, direct benefits may be defined as the subsidy allocated to each person participating in the program. Direct benefits are the difference between the per-pupil cost of the program and the amount paid by each pupil in fees or whatever other charges may be assessed. This hopefully is little or nothing in public schools. Indirect benefits are both public and private. As explained more fully in Chapter 3, public indirect benefits include a wide variety of intangible benefits to society, as well as increased tax collections resulting from the greater earnings of the individual. Private indirect benefits include nonmonetary benefits to students and their families, as well as monetary benefits to students in the form of increased lifetime earnings, discounted to present value. While the indirect benefits of public investment in education are of tremendous importance, conceptual and empirical problems have to date prevented reliable, accurate measurement of these benefits, and most distributional studies have considered only the direct benefits.

Most studies of the redistribution effects of public investment in education have been concerned with the effects of higher education. Considerable controversy has arisen in this area; some writers have concluded that present higher educational finance systems tend to redistribute wealth from low-income to high-income families, while others have concluded the reverse.

Public Higher Education. Hansen and Weisbrod compared the average subsidies received by families with children in the California public higher education system with the average total state-local tax burden levied on those families. They concluded that

> Some low-income persons have benefited handsomely from the availability of publicly subsidized higher education. But on the whole, the effect of these subsidies is to promote greater rather than less inequality among people of various social and economic backgrounds, by making available substantial subsidies that low-income families are either not eligible for or cannot make use of because of other conditions and constraints associated with their income position.[13]

The Hansen-Weisbrod conclusion that the California system for financing public higher education "leads to a sizeable inequitable redistribution of income from lower to higher income families" has been challenged by several writers, most notably Joseph Peckman.[14] Peckman questioned the Hansen-Weisbrod methodology in several respects, and, in reanalyzing the data, found that the California public higher education finance system did result in a redistribution of income from the upper-income classes to the low- and middle-income classes.

Windham estimated the distribution of costs and direct benefits of the Florida system of public higher education, concluding that the Florida system results in a redistribution of income from lower- to higher-income groups.[15] Unfortunately, his findings are of questionable validity, due to the inadequacies of the data and procedures used in estimating the distribution of tax burdens. While the tax burden estimates in the California studies were made specifically for that state, Windham's tax burden estimates were based on extrapolations from national data.

These studies have common ground in at least three conclusions:

1. Poor people pay taxes but very few participate in higher education. Those who do, attend less expensive community colleges.

2. Middle-income people are heavy users of the public higher education system, and the taxes they pay do not cover the costs.

3. Rich people pay more taxes, but also are usually enrolled in the higher cost public institutions. Those who do not attend public schools get no direct benefits.

Public Schools. While most research on the redistribution effects of public education has dealt with higher education, three particular studies have focused on the public school level. Holland and Grubb, in studies of the Oklahoma and Boston public schools, respectively, measured the distributional effects of these systems, following procedures similar to those developed in the higher education studies.[16] Johns, in a National Educational Finance Project study, established procedures for evaluating state school finance programs in terms of the extent to which financial equalization of educational opportunity is provided and the extent to which taxes used to finance the programs are regressive or progressive.[17]

Holland found that the Oklahoma public school finance system resulted in a redistribution of income from the upper-income classes to the lower-income classes. Income classes below the $5,000 family income level received positive net transfers, while income classes above the $5,000 family income level received negative net transfers.

In his study of redistribution in Boston, Grubb analyzed the redistribution effect of education for both whites and nonwhites and found a positive redistribution to low-income persons when using expenditure per pupil as a measurable benefit.

Overall conclusions from these studies are fairly obvious. Regardless of how the redistribution effect is calculated, aid to public elementary and secondary schools has a positive redistribution effect. This is true whether the redistribution effect is determined from the benefits of present common school expenditures or whether the benefits are presumed to derive from increased lifetime earnings. Either measure supports governmental investment in the lower levels of education as a means of eradicating poverty and equalizing governmental benefits among the income classes.

It should be borne in mind that a major boost to the benefits to elementary and secondary education is given by the mere fact that compulsory attendance laws require the poor to attend school, and since public schools have no tuition, the poor can afford to partake of the benefits.

Institute for Educational Finance Study. A major redistribution study at the University of Florida drew conclusions from a sample of 60 school districts in 12 states, representing a wide range of economic, social, and geographical conditions. The amount of funds for public schools varied substantially among states. In 12 states—Arkansas, California, Delaware, Iowa, Kentucky, New Hampshire, New York, Oregon, South Dakota, Utah, Virginia, and Wisconsin—there were a great variety of tax structures as well as different types of school finance structures. New Hampshire and South Dakota were included because they represented states with low percentages of state aid, which relied to the greatest degree on local property taxes, while Delaware was selected as one of the states with the highest percentages of state aid.

Tax burdens on families at each selected income level varied widely among both states and local school districts.[18] For example, a family in the $25,000 income category in Beverly Hills, California, paid $487.59 in state and local taxes for education, while the same income group in Alexis I. Du Pont, the wealthiest school district in Delaware, paid $886.35. A family of $25,000 income in Brookhaven, the wealthiest district among the selected districts in New York, paid $1,276.99, while the family of the same income in the wealthiest district in Oregon paid only $418.64. These wide differentials were caused by a combination of regressive versus progressive tax systems and varying state and local effort for support of the public schools. This phenomenon tends to exist within states as well.

States which relied on local property taxes to support the schools established a taxation pattern which reduced the positive redistribution impact of the public schools. Reliance on local property taxes also appeared to make the incidence of tax payments fluctuate to a much greater degree within income classes, although with the interplay of local fiscal effort, it is difficult to absolutely confirm this observation from the data presented.

The direct benefits of public schools can be easily quantified in terms of dollar subsidies or the amount of expenditures which government allocates for the education of each child. Direct benefits are used here as the measure of benefits offered through school services.

Wide disparities between rich and poor school districts were found in California, where the wealthy district had 2.6 times the revenue of the poorest, and Virginia, where the richest had 2.1 times the poorest. The benefits available varied greatly among both states and school districts, with the greatest per-pupil benefit found in New York and the lowest in Arkansas.

Redistribution of Income.   Families in the $3,500 income category in all states examined derived a substantial positive redistributional effect when taxation for education was compared with benefits received. As shown in Table 9–2, the redistribution effect for a low-income family was much greater on the average than for a middle- or high-income family. In Beverly Hills, California, a poor family received $10.42 in education benefits for every dollar paid for public school taxes at both state and local levels. A poor family in Governor Wentworth, the wealthiest school district in New Hampshire, in the sample, received $8.00 worth of benefits for every dollar in taxes. The state with the lowest ratio for a poor family in a wealthy school district was Arkansas, where the benefit-tax ratio was 2.82.

The positive redistributional effect in the poor school districts, while much less than in the rich districts, was found to be substantial. In poor districts,

TABLE 9–2 Redistribution Effect of the Public School as Measured by the Revenue-Tax Ratio for a Model Family of Four with One Child in Public School

SCHOOL DISTRICT AND STATE	BENEFIT RATIO		
	FAMILY WITH $3,500 INCOME	FAMILY WITH $10,000 INCOME	FAMILY WITH $25,000 INCOME
Arkansas			
Crossett	2.82	1.47	0.72
Little Rock	3.03	1.61	0.78
Pulaski	1.94	1.03	0.50
Cabot	1.79	0.94	0.46
Gosnell	1.31	0.69	0.34
California			
Beverly Hills	10.42	5.63	2.58
Lake Tahoe	6.77	3.69	1.68
Los Angeles	4.48	2.46	1.12
Ceres	3.94	2.16	0.98
Travis	3.28	1.79	0.82
Delaware			
Alexis I. Du Pont	5.55	2.42	1.05
Wilmington	4.88	2.10	0.92
Mt. Pleasant	4.07	1.85	0.81
Woodbridge	3.86	1.61	0.70
Caesar Rodney	2.51	1.05	0.46
Iowa			
Pleasant Valley	6.42	2.93	1.71
Jefferson	4.15	1.92	1.10
Des Moines	3.45	1.67	0.90
Anamosa	2.98	1.42	0.78
Council Bluffs	2.29	1.13	0.60
Kentucky			
Bardstown	3.68	1.62	0.91
Franklin	3.17	1.41	0.79
Jefferson	2.92	1.34	0.73
Letcher	2.67	1.15	0.66
Breathitt	2.96	1.26	0.73
New Hampshire			
Gov. Wentworth	8.00	4.83	2.43
Berlin	4.40	2.64	1.30
Manchester	3.56	2.14	1.06
Fall Mountain	2.76	1.63	0.75
Merrimack Valley	2.50	1.48	0.68
New York			
Brookhaven 6	4.78	2.40	1.08
Hempstead 21	4.69	2.37	1.07
New York City	4.92	2.43	1.10
Salamanca	3.48	1.75	0.79
Fort Covington	4.94	2.41	1.09
Oregon			
Klamath	6.79	2.78	1.41
Reedsport	4.90	2.31	1.11
Portland	4.10	1.95	0.93

Table 9–2 (continued)

	BENEFIT RATIO		
SCHOOL DISTRICT AND STATE	FAMILY WITH $3,500 INCOME	FAMILY WITH $10,000 INCOME	FAMILY WITH $25,000 INCOME
Oregon (cont'd)			
South Umpqua	2.58	1.32	0.61
David Douglas	2.16	1.13	0.52
South Dakota			
Mitchell	3.72	2.18	1.03
Lake Central	3.28	1.93	0.91
Sioux Falls	3.00	1.67	0.83
Pierre	2.08	1.22	0.57
Utah			
San Juan	3.29	1.55	0.83
Iron	2.56	1.22	0.65
Grand	2.07	0.99	0.52
Weber	2.06	0.98	0.52
Davis	2.06	0.98	0.52
Virginia			
Arlington	4.98	2.46	1.18
Fluvanna	3.01	1.47	0.71
Fairfax	2.44	1.26	0.59
Smyth	2.06	1.04	0.49
Wise	1.78	0.91	0.43
Wisconsin			
West Allis	5.29	2.66	1.24
Madison	3.80	1.93	0.90
Milwaukee	3.40	1.75	0.81
Antigo	3.03	1.54	0.72
Tomah	2.70	1.39	0.64

the greatest redistribution for a low-income family was found in New York, where benefits received were $4.94 for every dollar paid in taxes. The lowest redistribution effect was found in Wise County, Virginia, where a poor family received benefits worth only 1.78 times as much as the taxes it paid.

The redistribution effect of the public schools was uniformly positive when all three income levels were analyzed. For middle-income families ($10,000) the benefit-tax ratio was lower than for poor families. A middle-income family living in Beverly Hills, California, received $5.63 for every dollar paid, while a middle-income family in Travis, the poor district in California, received benefits at a 1.79 ratio. Wealthy families tended to receive a negative benefit return on the tax dollars they paid if they lived in poor school districts.

The implications of this redistribution analysis suggest that the public schools are an effective vehicle for redistribution of income, even if only the direct benefits are considered. A primary reason for this positive redistribution effect is the common and free nature of public schools, wherein low-income classes participate as fully and equally as high-income groups. Compulsory attendance laws contribute to the positive income redistribution, since poor children must attend school and receive its benefits. The positive outcomes of governmental investment in public schools suggest that federal and state governments should increase resources for public schools in order to provide poverty-level families with a greater share of tax subsidy benefits.

Equality of Benefits.   Measurement of redistribution of income presents a picture of fiscal inequality which is familiar in other studies, but it adds a new dimension. Here one sees inequality of treatment within income classes created by location of residence—horizontal inequality. With regard to taxation only, the burden of taxation is greater on poor families living in poor school districts. In addition, the benefits measured in terms of school revenues are much less. Combine this with a greater reliance on local property taxes, and the net result is substantial inequality within income classes. A poor family in a poor district paid more taxes in 9 of the 12 states studied; the benefit-tax ratio was nevertheless lower. In Arkansas, for example, poor families in a poor school district paid $187.06 in taxes for education, while poor families in a rich district paid only $160.05; the poor family in the rich district received $2.82 for each dollar in taxes, while the poor family in the poor district received only $1.31 for each of its tax dollars. This phenomenon was uniform, with one exception: New York, where the poor family in the poor district actually received a greater benefit ratio than did its counterpart in the rich school district.

The general pattern of inequality of benefits within income classes was also found in the middle-and high-income groups. It is easy to conclude that it is much better to be poor in a rich school district than to be poor in a poor school district, or one may conclude that it is simply better, from a redistribution point of view, to live in a rich school district regardless of income level. The implications of this within-class inequality are difficult to pinpoint; however, one may suspect that the despair which characterizes many of the nation's poor school districts emanates from this economic condition.

The remedy for the economic plight of taxpayers in low-wealth school districts can be found in greater equalization of state resources for education. The school districts with low fiscal ability must be buoyed up with increased state equalization of resources.

Further, movement away from the local property tax would have a desirable two-fold effect. First, it would create a more progressive tax structure, whereby low-income families would use less of their income for taxes, and second, it would allow a more uniform distribution of benefits to local school districts, whether they are rich or poor. The tendency would then be to have greater equality, not only within income classes, but also among income classes in all school districts.

The overall conclusion of the University of Florida study is that public schools vertically equalize among income classes with substantially greater benefit ratios for the poor than for the wealthy, but lack of fiscal equality in the distribution system between rich and poor school districts perpetuates a problem of horizontal inequality.

NOTES

1. John E. Tirrell, "Quality Education Does Not Have to Cost More," *Compact* (February 1968), (Denver: Education Commission of the States), p. 23.

2. For example, the illiteracy rate was cut in half from 1930 to 1960. National Society for the Study of Education, *Mathematics Education* (Chicago: University of Chicago Press, 1970); and National Society for the Study of Education, *The Elementary School in the United States* (Chicago: University of Chicago Press, 1973).

3. Christopher Jencks and others, *Inequality: A Reassessment of the Effect of Family and Schooling in America* (New York: Basic Books, Inc., Publishers, 1972), p. 20.

4. National Center for Education Statistics, *Digest of Education Statistics, 1980* (Washington, D.C.: U.S. Government Printing Office, 1980), p. 64.

5. J.E. Meade, *Efficiency, Equality, and the Ownership of Property* (Cambridge, Mass.: Harvard University Press, 1965), pp. 32–33.

6. James S. Coleman, *Equality of Educational Opportunity* (Washington, D.C.: U.S. Government Printing Office, 1966).

7. Brown et al. v. Board of Education of Topeka, 347 U.S. 483; Keyes v. School District No. 1, Denver, Colo. 413 U.S. 189 (1973).

8. Leslie L. Chisholm and M.L. Cushman, in *Problems and Issues in Public School Finance*, eds. Roe L. Johns and Edgar L. Morphet (New York: Teachers College Press, Teachers College, Columbia University, 1952), p. 103.

9. Alan C. Stauffer, *Property Assessment and Exemptions: They Need Reform* (Denver: Education Commission of the States, 1973), p. 38.

10. James D. Rodgers, "Explaining Income Redistribution," in *Redistribution through Public Choice*, eds. Hochman and Peterson (New York: Columbia University Press, 1974), p. 169.

11. Jack E. Fisher, "A Comparison between Central Cities and Suburbs on Local Ability to Support Public Education" (Ed.D. dissertation, University of Florida, 1972).

12. J.M. Buchanan and G. Tullock, *The Calculus of Consent* (Ann Arbor, Mich.: University of Michigan, 1962).

13. W. Lee Hansen and Burton A. Weisbrod, *Benefits, Costs and Finance of Public Higher Education* (Chicago: Rand McNally & Company, Markham, 1969).

14. Joseph Peckman, "The Distributional Effects of Public Higher Education in California," *Journal of Human Resources* 5 (Summer 1970), 361–70.

15. Douglas M. Windham, *Education, Equality and Income Redistribution* (Lexington, Mass.: D. C. Heath & Company, 1970).

16. David W. Holland, "The Distribution of the Costs and Benefits of Public Schooling," *Southern Journal of Agricultural Economics* 5 (July 1973), 71–79; and W. Norton Grubb, "The Distribution of Costs and Benefits in an Urban Public School System," *National Tax Journal* 24 (1971), 1–12.

17. Roe L. Johns, "Criteria for Evaluating State Financing Plans for the Public Schools," in *Alternative Programs for Financing Education*, eds., R. L. Johns and Kern Alexander, vol. 5 (Gainesville, Fla.: University of Florida, 1971), pp. 231–63.

18. Tax data are from Stephen E. Lile, *Family Tax Burdens Compared among States and among Cities Located within Kentucky and Neighboring States* (Frankfort, Ky.: Kentucky Department of Revenue, 1975). See also Stephen E. Lile, *Interstate Comparisons of Family Tax Burdens with Residence Location Based on Each State's Largest City* (Frankfort, Ky.: Kentucky Department of Revenue, 1978).

SELECTED REFERENCES

ALEXANDER, KERN, and K. FORBIS JORDAN, eds. *Educational Need in the Public Economy*. Gainesville, Fla.: University of Florida Press, 1976.

BOWLES, SAMUEL, and HERBERT GINTIS. *Schooling in Capitalist America*. New York: Basic Books, Inc., Publishers, 1976.

BURKHEAD, JESSE. *Input and Output in Large City High Schools*. Syracuse, N.Y.: Syracuse University Press, 1967.

CHENERY, HOLLIS, and others. *Redistribution with Growth*. London: Oxford University Press, 1974.

HOCHMAN, HAROLD M., and GEORGE E. PETERSON. *Redistribution through Public Choice*. New York: Columbia University Press, Teachers College, Columbia University, 1974.

JENCKS, CHRISTOPHER and others. *Inequality: A Reassessment of the Effect of Family and Schooling in America*. New York: Basic Books, Inc., Publishers, 1972.

JENCKS, CHRISTOPHER, and others. *Who Gets Ahead? The Determinants of Economic Success in America*. New York: Basic Books, Inc., Publishers, 1978.

JOHNS, ROE L., KERN ALEXANDER, and DEWEY H. STOLLAR, eds. *Status and Impact of Educational Finance Programs*, Vol. 4. Gainesville, Fla.: National Educational Finance Project, 1971.

JOHNS, ROE L., and KERN ALEXANDER, eds., *Alternative Programs for Financing Education* Vol. 5. Gainesville, Fla.: University of Florida, 1971.

LILE, STEPHEN E. *Interstate Comparisons of Family Tax Burdens with Residence Location Based on Each State's Largest City*. Frankfort, Ky.: Kentucky Department of Revenue, 1978.

MOSTELLER, FREDERICK, and DANIEL P. MOYNIHAN, eds. *On Equality of Educational Opportunity*. New York: Random House, Inc., 1972.

OWEN, JOHN D. *School Inequality and the Welfare State*. Baltimore: Johns Hopkins University Press, 1974.

POLE, J.R. *The Pursuit of Equality in American History*. Berkeley, Calif: University of California Press, 1978.

CHAPTER TEN
DEVELOPMENT
AND IMPACT
OF CONCEPTUAL
THEORIES
OF STATE SUPPORT

State support for the public schools has a long history. It probably began in the early part of the nineteenth century. Unfortunately, authentic financial reports are not available through which the evolution of state support during the nineteenth century may be traced. However, by 1890 the states collectively provided $33,987,581 in financial aid for the public schools. This amounted to 23.8 percent of total school revenue in 1890.[1] Undoubtedly, much of the state aid reported was derived from income from sixteenth section land grants from the federal government, which could be strictly interpreted as federal rather than state aid. In fact, Mort, in the study from which these data are quoted, referred to the revenue as "state and federal," revenue although the federal government did not make any direct appropriations for the public schools until the Smith-Hughes Bill was enacted into law in 1917.

The sixteenth section land grants, provided in the Ordinance of 1787 and the action of Congress in 1802, continuing the policy of making land grants for public education in all states newly admitted to the Union, undoubtedly stimulated state support. State agencies handled these land grants and distributed funds derived from them. This set a precedent of providing funds for the public schools from the state level. Some of these land grants proved to be valuable and productive of income, and others worthless. The demand was made in some states during the nineteenth century that the state provide funds for the schools in the townships that had happened to receive worthless land grants. This was probably the beginning of the concept of financial equalization for the purpose of equalizing educational opportunity.

Although it is generally conceded that education was a state responsibility under the Tenth Amendment to the federal Constitution, most states during the nineteenth century exercised that responsibility, primarily by authorizing the levy of local school taxes for support of the public schools. No integrated plans of school finance were developed during the nineteenth century. No conceptual theory of school finance was developed. Such state funds as were distributed were generally apportioned on a school census basis with little consideration given to equalization of educational opportunity or the provision of at least a minimum program of education for all children. In the remainder of this chapter, primary attention will be given to the development of conceptual theories of state support and the extent to which those concepts have been accepted by the states. The terms *state support* and *state aid* will be used interchangeably.

DEVELOPMENT OF THEORIES
OF STATE SUPPORT[2]

All important social movements have had an intellectual leader or leaders. These people, who are almost always theorists, are sometimes considered impractical by the general public. However, it is the theorists who shape social policy and social organization more than any other group in society. Politicians and public officials usually base their policies on theoretical assumptions of some kind. Politicians such as Jefferson, Hamilton, and Madison, who were also theorists, have had a profound effect on governmental policy in the United States.

The early theorists on state school finance were not politicians or holders of public office. All of them were university professors, but they have had a profound influence on political policy in the United States with respect to state school financing. These theorists dealt with some of the crucial values, issues, and problems in American society. Therefore, what they had to say was of great interest to the public. Some of the values and issues involved in determining policies on state school financing follow: Is equalization of educational opportunity a function of a democratic government? What level of education should be guaranteed to everyone in order to promote the general welfare? To what extent should the states exercise control over the public schools? To what extent should "home rule" in school government be encouraged? Are nonproperty taxes more equitable than local property taxes? What percent of school revenue should be provided from state sources?

The central stream of state school finance theory in the United States originated at Teachers College, Columbia University, at the beginning of the twentieth century. The chief participants in this stream and their principal concepts are discussed in the following sections.[3]

Ellwood P. Cubberley[4]

The development of the theory of state school support began with Cubberley, who was a student at Teachers College, Columbia University, near the beginning of the twentieth century. His famous monograph, *School Funds and Their Apportionment*, a revision of his doctoral dissertation, was published in 1906.[5] It is interesting to note that George D. Strayer, Sr., who is discussed later, also received his doctor's degree at Teachers College in 1905. These two were among the first professors of educational administration. Strayer stayed at Teachers College and Cubberley went to Stanford University. These two giants were largely responsible for developing the early literature of educational administration. The conceptualizations of school finance developed by these two men, their students, and students of their students have dominated the thinking on educational finance during the first three-quarters of the twentieth century.

Cubberley's work was so fundamental in formulating the basic concepts of state school financing that several quotations from his original study published in 1906 are included here. He studied the historical development of education in the United States, the legal arrangements provided for public education, the effect of the Industrial Revolution on the distribution of wealth, and the inequalities of educational opportunity among the several districts of a state. He then formulated his concept of the state's responsibility for providing educational services as follows:

> The state owes it to itself and to its children, not only to permit of the establishment of schools, but also to require them to be established—even more, to require that these schools, when established, shall be taught by a qualified teacher for a certain minimum period of time each year, and taught under conditions and according to requirements which the state has, from time to time, seen fit to impose. While leaving the way open for all to go beyond these requirements the state must see that none fall below.[6]

He applied his basic concept of state responsibility to the apportionment of state school funds in the following words:

> Theoretically all the children of the state are equally important and are entitled to have the same advantages; practically this can never be quite true. The duty of the state is to secure for all as high a minimum of good instruction as is possible, but not to reduce all to the minimum; to equalize the advantages to all as nearly as can be done with the resources at hand; to place a premium on those local efforts which will enable communities to rise above the legal minimum as far as possible; and to encourage communities to extend their educational energies to new and desirable undertakings.[7]

These concepts were stated by Cubberley in 1906, but they seem quite applicable today. Numerous books, monographs, and articles have been written on state responsibility for education and state financing, but it is difficult to find in all the literature on this subject a better or clearer statement than Cubberley's conceptualization. It is true, as will be pointed out later in this chapter, that Strayer and Mort at a later date criticized one part of Cubberley's conceptualization; but the differences that arose were on the technology of state distribution of school funds rather than the values or goals. The differences arose over the implementation of the phrase "to place a premium on those local efforts which will enable communities to rise above the legal minimum as far as possible. . . . "

After formulating his conceptualizations of sound policy in state school financing, Cubberley used them as criteria to evaluate the methods used by the states to distribute school funds at the beginning of the century. As Cubberley's study was the first comprehensive one to be made of state school funds, and as it was made at the very beginning of the twentieth century, his findings provide a valuable benchmark for measuring progress in state school financing. Therefore, some of his principal findings are set forth below:

1. That due to the unequal distribution of wealth, the demands set by the states for maintaining minimum standards cause very unequal burdens. What one community can do with ease is often an excessive burden for another.

2. That the excessive burden of communities, borne in large part for the common good, should be equalized by the state.

3. That a state school tax best equalizes the burdens.

4. That any form of state taxation for schools fails to accomplish the ends for which it was created unless a wise system of distribution is provided.

5. That (judged by Cubberley's criteria) few states (at the beginning of the twentieth century) had as yet evolved a just and equitable plan for distributing the funds they had at hand.[8]

Harlan Updegraff[9]

Updegraff is not as well known as some of the other theorists in state school financing, but his contributions are important. Although he accepted the concepts of Cubberley for the most part, he did make some important additions to Cubberley's model. Updegraff, a professor of educational administration at the University of Pennsylvania, made a survey of the financial support of rural schools in New York state in 1921 in which he presented some new concepts of state support.[10] These are the principles of state support he proposed:

1. Local support is fundamental.

2. The local units for the support of schools should contain, insofar as practicable, enough property taxable for school purposes to raise that portion of the expenses of the school which it is believed should be borne by the local districts without an undue burden upon the owners of property.

3. Some portion of the support of local schools should come from the state government, the amount being dependent upon certain factors, exact standards for which have not been scientifically determined, but which will vary in the different states.

4. The administration of state aid should be such as to increase the efficient participation of citizens in a democratic form of government.

5. The purpose of state aid should be not only to protect the state from ignorance, to provide intelligent workers in every field of activity, and to educate leaders, but also to guarantee to each child, irrespective of where he happens to live, equal opportunity to that of any other child for the education which will best fit him for life.[11]

Those were the days in which the word efficiency was greatly emphasized in administration. Therefore, it is not surprising that Updegraff presented a set of criteria for determining the efficiency of state support, a summary of which follows:

1. The efficient participation of citizens in the responsibilities of citizenship should be promoted by making the extent of the state's contribution dependent upon local action.

2. The state should neither be timid nor autocratic in withholding state funds because of deficiencies in local action.

3. Special grants should be provided to encourage the introduction of new features into the schools.

4. The districts should receive support in inverse proportion to their true valuation per teacher unit.

5. Efficiency in the conduct of schools should be promoted by increasing the state grant whenever the true tax rate is increased and by lowering it whenever the local tax is decreased.

6. The plan of state aid should be so framed that it will measure precisely the elements involved and will respond promptly and surely to any change in the local district.[12]

Updegraff not only proposed principles and criteria for state support, but he also developed techniques for the distribution of general school aid that embodied his ideas. He proposed a sliding scale that provided increased amounts of state aid per teacher unit for each increase of ½ mill of school taxes levied ranging from 3½ to 9 mills,[13] but he provided proportionately more state aid for a district with a low true valuation per teacher unit.

Under Updegraff's plan, the state would support variable levels of minimum programs ranging from $840 per teacher unit to $2,160, depending upon the amount of local tax effort. He attempted to incorporate the concepts of equalization of educational opportunity and reward for effort within the same formula. As will be pointed out below, both Strayer and Mort opposed that approach. Updegraff justified his proposal for encouraging additional local effort on the basis of efficiency. Updegraff's ideas fell into disfavor for many years following the emergence of the concepts advanced by Strayer and Mort. However, today Updegraff's concept of a variable level foundation program depending upon the level of local effort is being utilized in some state support programs. It is interesting to note that Updegraff's model for state support was rediscovered fifty years later by John E. Coons, William H. Clune, III, and Stephen D. Sugarman and named "power equalizing" in their book *Private Wealth and Public Education.*

Updegraff introduced another idea, the teacher unit, which today is incorporated in many state support programs. He suggested that instead of using teachers employed as a basis of state distribution, standard numbers of pupils per teacher should be fixed for different school levels, for urban and rural districts, and for different types of classes.[14]

George D. Strayer, Sr.[15]

Strayer, like Cubberley, was interested in the total area of educational organization and administration, and he made major contributions in every sector. In none, however, did he make a greater contribution than in state school finance, for he advanced the theoretical basis of school financing. Strayer first advanced his theories of school finance in volume 1 of the Report of the Educational Finance Inquiry Commission, which was published in 1923. This volume, *The Financing of Education in the State of New York,* by Strayer and Haig, devoted four pages to a theoretical conceptualization of the equalization of educational opportunity that has had a major impact on educational thought and policy.[16]

So important has been the effect of this report that some selected excerpts from it are set forth here. The concept "equalization of educational opportunity" that prevailed at that time was described as follows:

> There exists today and has existed for many years a movement which has come to be known as the "equalization of educational opportunity" or the "equalization of school support." These phrases are interpreted in various ways. In its most extreme form the interpretation is somewhat as follows: The state should insure equal educational facilities to every child within its borders at a uniform effort throughout the state in terms of the burden of taxation; the tax burden of education should throughout the state be uniform in relation to tax-paying ability, and the provision for schools should be uniform in relation to the educable population desiring education. Most of the supporters of this proposition, however, would not preclude any particular community from offering at its own expense a particularly rich and costly educational program. They would insist that there be an adequate minimum offered everywhere, the expense of which should be considered a prior claim on the state's economic resources.[17]

Strayer and Haig stated that to carry into effect the principle of "equalization of educational opportunity" or "equalization of school support" it would be necessary

> (1) to establish schools or make other arrangements sufficient to furnish the children in every locality within the state with equal educational opportunities up to some prescribed minimum; (2) to raise the funds necessary for this purpose by

local or state taxation adjusted in such manner as to bear upon the people in all localities at the same rate in relation to their tax-paying ability; and (3) to provide adequately either for the supervision and control of all the schools, or for their direct administration by a state department of education.[18]

Strayer and Haig then presented the following conceptual model for formulating a plan of state support, which incorporated the principles they had outlined:

(1)   A local school tax in support of the satisfactory minimum offering would be levied in each district at a rate which would provide the necessary funds for that purpose in the richest district.

(2)   The richest district then might raise all of its school money by means of the local tax, assuming that a satisfactory tax, capable of being locally administered, could be devised.

(3)   Every other district could be permitted to levy a local tax at the same rate and apply the proceeds toward the cost of schools, but

(4)   since the rate is uniform this tax would be sufficient to meet the costs only in the richest district and the deficiencies would be made up by state subventions.[19]

It will be noted that Strayer and Haig emphasized the equalization of the tax burden to support schools as well as the equalization of educational opportunity. However, they did not incorporate the reward for effort or incentive concepts in their state support model. They attacked these concepts, which had been advanced by Cubberley and Updegraff, in the following words:

Any formula which attempts to accomplish the double purpose of equalizing resources and rewarding effort must contain elements which are mutually inconsistent. It would appear to be more rational to seek to achieve local adherence to proper educational standards by methods which do not tend to destroy the very uniformity of effort called for by the doctrine of equality of educational opportunity.[20]

Paul R. Mort[21]

Mort was one of Strayer's students and later became his colleague at Teachers College, Columbia University. Strayer and Haig referred to a "satisfactory minimum program" to be equalized, but they offered no suggestions concerning how to measure it. Mort assumed the task of defining a satisfactory minimum program as his doctoral problem. His doctoral dissertation, *The Measurement of Educational Need*, was published in 1924.[22]

Mort perhaps should be classified a disseminator and developer,[23] but he was a theorist as well. Although he accepted completely the conceptualization of Strayer and Haig, he somewhat clarified their theories, and he advanced some concepts of his own concerning the formulation of a state minimum program. Therefore, some of the key ideas developed by Mort in his dissertation are presented here.

Mort presented an advanced concept of what should be included in the state-assured program. These are the elements he recommended for inclusion:

1. An educational activity found in most or all communities throughout the state is acceptable as an element of an equalization program.
2. Unusual expenditures for meeting the general requirements due to causes over which a local community has little or no control may be recognized as required by the equalization program. If they arise from causes reasonably within the control of the community they cannot be considered as demanded by the equalization program.
3. Some communities offer more years of schooling or a more costly type of education than is common. If it can be established that unusual conditions require any such additional offerings, they may be recognized as a part of the equalization program.[24]

Mort modestly stated that "it cannot be hoped that these will prove exhaustive as the thinking in this field develops."[25] However, his concepts of the elements to include in a minimum program are as valid today as when they were written. For example, his third element includes compensatory education for the disadvantaged, which is a comparatively recent extension of the educational offering.

Mort defined a satisfactory equalization program as follows:

A satisfactory equalization program would demand that each community have as many elementary and high school classroom or teacher units, or their equivalent, as is typical for communities having the same number of children to educate. It would demand that each of these classrooms meet certain requirements as to structure and physical environment. It would demand that each of these classrooms be provided with a teacher, course of study, equipment, supervision, and auxiliary activities meeting certain minimum requirements. It would demand that some communities furnish special facilities, such as transportation.[26]

Mort sought objective, equitable measures of educational need that could be used by a state legislature in determining the amount of the state appropriation for equalization. He also wished his measure to be used by officials in the state department of education for apportioning state school funds with a minimum of state control.

Mort used complicated sets of regression equations to estimate on the basis of average practice the typical number of teachers employed in elementary schools that varied in numbers of pupils. He assumed that sparsity of population would make it necessary for some districts to operate certain small schools that would not have the economies of scale provided by larger schools. In other words, he assumed that a greater number of teachers for a given number of pupils would need to be employed in the small schools than in the large schools. His statistical studies, based on average practice in New York state at that time, showed that more teachers were employed per pupil in elementary schools with an average daily attendance of less than 142, but that the average number of teachers per pupil employed for larger elementary schools did not vary substantially. He found that the number of pupils per teacher varied in high schools up to 518 in average daily attendance but did not vary substantially in high schools above that size. He developed separate regression equations for both elementary and high schools. One could take the average daily attendance of any size school, substitute it in the appropriation equation, and compute the number of either typical elementary teachers or typical high school teachers.[27]

Mort's concept of "weighting pupils" was later extended to include weighting pupils enrolled in vocational education, exceptional education, and compensatory education, in order to provide for the extra costs of these special programs.

Most foundation programs today use some form of the adjusted instruction unit or weighted pupil measure.[28] The weights, of course, have changed, as well as the methods of determining them, but the concept of making allowance for necessary cost variations beyond the control of local boards of education is generally recognized as sound policy.

Mort directed a national study of state support in 1931. The report of this survey, entitled *State Support for Public Education*, contained a summary of the status of state support at that time. Following is a brief summary of Mort's findings concerning the condition of state support in 1931–32:

1. In all but a few states, the actual minimum status of education was determined by the economic ability of local districts to support schools rather than the social needs for education.
2. The minimum program actually guaranteed was in nearly every state far below the program provided in communities of average wealth.
3. An analysis of the methods used by the different states to measure educational need revealed that no state was using as refined measures as were available. Measures in use were inequitable in one or more of the following respects: treatment for variation of size of school, treatment of districts of the same size, caring for the higher costs of high schools, caring for non-residence, consideration of costs of living, consideration of transportation, and consideration of capital outlays.[29]

Henry C. Morrison[30]

Morrison is sometimes forgotten by those studying the theory of state school financing. He is perhaps more noted for his theories of instruction and curriculum than for his theories of school finance. However, Morrison wrote an important book, *School Revenue*, in which he made some significant contributions to the literature on school finance.[31] He noted the great inequalities of wealth among school districts that caused great inequalities in educational opportunity. He observed that constitutionally education was a state function and that local school districts had failed to provide that function efficiently or equitably. He asserted that attempts to provide equal educational opportunities by enlarging school districts, by offering state equalization funds—such as those advocated by Mort—or by offering state subsidies for special purposes had failed. He theorized that those measures would continue to fail to meet educational needs and, at the same time, to provide an equitable system of taxation to support schools. Therefore, Morrison proposed a model of state support whereby all local school districts would be abolished and the state itself would become the unit both for taxation and for administration of public schools. He suggested that the most equitable form of tax for the state to use for the support of schools was the income tax.

Morrison's ideas on state school finance were not well received. At that time, great emphasis was being given to local initiative and local home rule. In fact, local self-government was almost equated to democracy itself in the political thought of Morrison's time. The Cubberley-Updegraff-Strayer-Haig-Mort axis of thought was in the mainstream of American political thought and, therefore, widely accepted.

However, the defects that Morrison saw in local school financing are as evident today as in his time. Furthermore, educational opportunities are far from being equalized among school districts within most states, and there is more complaint about the inequities of local property taxes for schools than ever before. It is interesting to note that, in recent years, Hawaii has established a state system of education with no local school districts that is similar to the model advocated by Morrison.

PROGRESS TOWARD ATTAINING GOALS
ADVOCATED BY THEORISTS

It is noticeable that all of the principal theorists of state support advocated (1) equalization of educational opportunity by the process of equalizing financial support, and (2) provision of an equitable system of taxation for school financing. What progress have we made toward attaining these goals? The record is mixed. We have made some progress, but wide differences in educational opportunity still exist in most states.

Cubberley in 1905, Updegraff in 1921, Strayer in 1923, Morrison in 1930, Mort in 1933, The Committee for the White House Conference on Education in 1956, The National Educational Finance Project in 1971, The President's Commission on School Finance in 1972, and the Education Finance Center of the Education Commission of the States in 1979—all pointed out that educational opportunity had not been equalized at the times the studies were made. The Education Finance Center of the Education Commission of the States pointed out that considerable improvement had been made in equity in school financing between 1970 and 1979 but that many inequities still exist.[32]

Some recent studies of individual states have shown wide differences among school districts in the per-pupil financial support available in the states studied. Examples of those studies are (1) Hickrod and others, *Equity Measurements in School Finance: Indiana, Iowa and Illinois*, (2) Adams, *Analyses and Comparison of Fiscal Response in Four States* (Colorado, Wisconsin, Kansas and Maryland), and (3) Carroll, *The Search for Equity in School Finance: Results from Five States* (California, Florida, Kansas, Michigan, and New Mexico). [33]

Despite this rather gloomy picture of public school financing, considerable progress has been made both in equalizing educational opportunity and providing a more equitable system of taxation for education. In 1930, about .4 of 1 percent of school revenue was provided by the federal government; 17.0 percent, from state sources; and 82.6 percent, from local sources. In 1980, the federal government provided an estimated 9.3 percent of school revenue; the states, 48.1 percent; and local sources, 42.5 percent. This fifty-year trend of providing a higher percentage of school revenue from state and federal sources not only tended to equalize the tax burden for the support of the public schools, but it also tended to reduce the disparities among school districts in per-pupil expenditures.

Tron reported that in 1978–79 all but two states allocated some state funds according to the following models: (1) minimum foundation program, (2) percentage equalizing, (3) guaranteed yield, or (4) guaranteed tax base. State funds under these models are allocated in inverse relationship to local taxpaying capacity. [34] The policy tends to reduce the disparities of expenditure per pupil among the districts of a state. The two states that did not allocate state funds by equalization methods include Hawaii, which has a complete state support system (excluding federal aid), and North Carolina, which usually provides about three-fourths of state-local revenue from state sources. Provision of a high percentage of school revenue from state sources tends to equalize school financial support, because the districts of less per-pupil taxpaying capacity in general receive more state school funds proportionately than they contribute in state taxes.

EVALUATION OF A STATE'S SCHOOL FINANCE PROGRAM

A comprehensive evaluation of a state's school finance program involves at least the following studies: (1) variations in the access of pupils to needed educational programs and services, (2) variations among the districts of the state in fiscal equalization, and (3) equity of tax structure.

Variations in Educational Programs and Services

In evaluating a state's school finance program, it seems logical to start by analyzing the variations among districts in the educational opportunities and services provided. [35] Illustrations of studies of this type are (1) Kern Alexander and James Hale, *Educational Equity: Improving School Finance in Arkansas*, 1978, (2) C. Cale Hudson, *Nebraska Public School Finance Study*, 1978, and

(3) J. Alan Thomas, *School Finance and Educational Opportunity in Michigan*, 1968.[36] These researchers found that educational programs and services available to pupils varied widely among the districts of a state, due largely to variations in fiscal resources and size of district.

Following are some of the studies that should be made of the educational programs of each district of a state of at least of an adequate sample of the school districts of a state:

1. Percentage of eligible children in early childhood education programs, including kindergarten
2. Variety of educational programs and courses provided in middle schools and high schools
3. Number and percentage of pupils who drop out before completing high school
4. Extent to which compensatory and remedial programs are being provided for the educationally disadvantaged
5. Percentage of students engaged in educational programs and activities during the summer months
6. Nature and extent of programs in vocational, career, and adult education
7. Extent to which provision is made for various kinds of exceptional education and the percentage of students involved in such programs
8. Nature and extent of health, counseling, and other services provided
9. Availability of library and instructional materials resources.

These items relate primarily to *access of pupils to educational programs*. Note that performance of students as measured by standardized tests is not included. Numerous studies have shown that student performance as measured by standardized tests is largely a function of the socioeconomic status of parents. Students will not achieve equally, regardless of the financial resources available. However, all students should have *equal access* to the educational programs which meet their individual needs.

Measuring Fiscal Equalization of Educational Opportunities[37]

It is generally assumed that fiscal equalization results in equalization of educational opportunity. This is true only when the plan recognizes necessary differences in per-pupil costs of programs such as vocational education, exceptional education, education for the culturally disadvantaged, and so forth. Furthermore, variations in sparsity of population and in cost of living should also be included.

The most commonly used method of comparing the fiscal resources of school districts is to compare the per-pupil expenditures for current operations. Lay persons, including some legislators, frequently conclude that educational opportunity throughout a state would be perfectly equalized if the same amount of money were expended per pupil. No valid comparison of school expenditures of school districts can be made unless cost differentials are recognized. Pupils should be weighted in order to take into account these cost differentials. The

National Educational Finance Project developed cost differentials for different types of educational programs.[38] Differentials of this type can be used to weight pupils in proportion to cost variations. These weightings should be supplemented by weighting due to variations in sparsity of population and, theoretically, in cost of living. Unfortunately, valid tools for measuring variations in the cost of the same standard of living have not yet been developed.

Some Statistical Tools. Following are some statistical tools useful for analyzing fiscal equalization.

1. The *Pearson coefficient of correlation* or the *Spearman rank order correlation* can be used to determine the relationship between per-pupil wealth and per-pupil expenditure. According to this technique, the higher the correlation, the less the fiscal equalization.

2. The *Lorenz curve* and the *Gini coefficient* have been used recently by a number of researchers to measure the extent of fiscal equalization in a state.[39] The Lorenz curve is developed by plotting data for cumulative proportions of pupils and cumulative proportions of spending expenditures on coordinate axes. Figure 10–1 shows this curve.

The districts are sorted by ascending order of wealth per pupil. The cumulative proportions of pupils in the districts are represented by the horizontal axis and the cumulative proportions of total operating expenditures accounted for by these districts are represented by the vertical axis. The curve thus plotted would be a straight line if the operating expenditures per pupil were the same in all districts. A sagging curve represents lesser expenditure in poorer districts. The measure of its inequality as defined by Gini Coefficient G is given by the following formula:

$$G = \frac{\text{Area A}}{\text{Area (A + B)}}$$

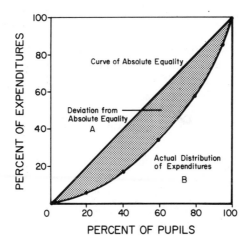

FIGURE 10–1 Lorenz Curve——Distribution of School Expenditures

In this formula, A is the area between the sagging Lorenz curve and the line marking the 45 degree angle and B is the area below area A and above the horizontal axis. When the Gini index is equal to 1.0, complete inequity exists; when the index is 0.0, complete equity exists. This simple technique can readily be programmed for computer simulation. It does not provide any information concerning the variation among districts of fiscal equalization, but it can be assumed that the Gini index correlates positively with the coefficient of variation among districts in fiscal equalization. If the Gini index is computed on the basis of weighted pupils, it is a measure of fiscal equalization rather than fiscal neutrality. For example, in a state using the power equalizing formula it would be impossible to attain a Gini index of 0 if different types of districts make varying levels of local effort.

3. The *coefficient of variation* is useful for comparing the fiscal disparities in one state with the fiscal disparities of other states. This is a very simple measure. The current expenditure per weighted pupil (excluding expenditures for transportation and school food service) is computed for each district in the state. The mean and standard deviation for the distribution are computed. The coefficient of variation is computed by dividing the standard deviation by the mean and multiplying the quotient by 100.

4. Various measures of range have been used to analyze variations among school districts in per-pupil expenditures. The *Restricted Range* is the difference between the per-pupil expenditure at the 95th and 5th percentiles. The Restricted Range Ratio or the *Federal Range Ratio* is the restricted range divided by the per-pupil expenditure at the 5th percentile.

A number of other measures are available, but the above list includes most of the commonly used measures of fiscal equalization.

Equity of School Taxes

The various theories and principles of taxation have been discussed in chapter 5. If the relative progressivity of a tax is considered the best single measure of equity, the most equitable taxes are federal taxes; the next most equitable, state taxes; and the least equitable, local school taxes. The four major types of taxes listed in order of progressivity are personal income taxes, corporate income taxes, sales taxes and property taxes. The federal government obtains most of its revenue (excluding social security taxes) from personal and corporate income taxes; the states, from sales and income taxes; and local school districts, from property taxes. Therefore, the higher percentage of revenue the public schools of a state receive from federal and state sources, the more progressive the tax structure, and hence the more equitable, assuming that the progressivity of a tax is a valid measure of equity.

Another important concept of the equity of school taxes is that the quality of a child's education should not be a function of the per-pupil wealth of the school district. Furthermore, the school finance plan should not make it necessary for the taxpayers of a school district to tax themselves excessively to provide educational opportunities for their children comparable to those more wealthy districts provide with much lower school taxes.

In this chapter we have presented the origin of school finance theory and some measures of the equalization of educational opportunity. These measures are not adequate for the overall evaluation of a state's school finance program. In Chapter 12 alternative school finance plans are analyzed and comprehensive criteria for the evaluation of a state's school finance plan are presented.

NOTES

1.   Paul R. Mort and Research Staff, *The National Survey of School Finance: State Support for Public Education* (Washington, D.C.: American Council on Education, 1933), p. 24–26.

2.   This section is abstracted largely from Roe L. Johns, "State Financing of Elementary and Secondary Schools," in *Education in the States: Nationwide Development since 1900*, eds. Edgar Fuller and Jim B. Pearson (Washington, D.C.: National Education Association, 1969), Chap. 4.

3.   *Ibid.*, pp. 182–83.

4.   This section on Cubberley was abstracted or quoted from Johns, *Ibid.*, pp. 183–86.

5.   Ellwood P. Cubberley, *School Funds and Their Apportionment* (New York: Teachers College, Columbia University, 1906).

6.   *Ibid.*, p. 16.

7.   *Ibid.*, p. 17.

8.   *Ibid.*, adapted from the summary presented on pp. 250–54.

9.   Abstracted from Johns, *Ibid.*, pp. 185–86.

10.   Harlan Updegraff, *Rural School Survey of New York State: Financial Support* (Ithaca, N.Y.: By the author, 1922).

11.   *Ibid.*, p. 117.

12.   *Ibid.*, pp. 117–18.

13.   *Ibid.*, pp. 134–35.

14.   *Ibid.*, p. 155.

15.   Abstracted from Johns, *Ibid.*, pp. 186–88.

16.   George D. Strayer and Robert Murray Haig, *The Financing of Education in the State of New York*, Report of the Educational Finance Inquiry Commission, Vol. 1 (New York: Macmillan, Inc., 1923).

17.   *Ibid.*, p. 173.

18.   *Ibid.*, p. 174.

19.   *Ibid.*, pp. 175–76.

20.   *Ibid.*, p. 175.

21.   Abstracted from Johns, *Ibid.*, pp. 188–92.

22.   Paul R. Mort, *The Measurement of Educational Need* (New York: Teachers College, Columbia University, 1924).

23.   See Stephen K. Bailey and others, *Schoolmen and Politics: A Study of State Aid to Education in the Northeast* (Syracuse, N.Y.: Syracuse University Press, 1962).

24.   Mort, *Ibid.*, pp. 6–7.

25.   *Ibid.*, p. 7.

26.   *Ibid.*, p. 8.

27.   In later years, Mort's "typical teacher" came to be known as "weighted teacher" or "instruction unit" in some states.

28.   Today the term *foundation program* is more commonly used than the terms *equalization program* or *minimum program*.

29.   Paul R. Mort and Research Staff, *op. cit.* in f.l.

30.   Abstracted from Johns, *Ibid.*, p. 192.

31.   Henry C. Morrison, *School Revenue* (Chicago: University of Chicago Press, 1930).

32.   Cubberley, *op. cit.*; Updegraff, *op. cit.*; Morrison, *op. cit.*; Mort, *op. cit.* in f.l.; Neil H. McElroy, *A Report to the President* (Washington, D.C.: U.S. Government Printing Office, 1956); Roe L. Johns, Kern Alexander, and Dewey Stollar, eds., *Status and Impact of Educational Finance Programs* (Gainesville, Fla.: National Educational Finance Project, 1971); Neil H. McElroy, *Schools, People and Money: The Need for Educational Reform* (Washington, D.C.: U.S. Government Printing Office, 1972); Allan Odden, Robert Berne, and Leanna Stiefel, *Equity in School Finance* (Denver, Colo.: Education Commission of the States, 1979).

33.   G. Alan Hickrod, and others *Equity Measurements in School Finance: Indiana, Iowa and Illinois* (Normal, Ill.: Center for Study of Educational Finance, 1980); E. Kathleen Adams, *Analyses and Comparison of Fiscal Response in Four States* (Denver: Education Finance Center, Education Commission of the States, 1979); Stephen J. Carroll, *The Search for Equity in School Finance: Results from Five States*. Prepared for the National Institute of Education (Santa Monica, Calif.: The Rand Corporation, 1979).

34.   Esther O. Tron, *Public School Finance Programs 1978–79* (Washington, D.C.: U.S. Government Printing Office, 1980).

35.   Much of the material in this and the following sections was adapted from Roe L. Johns, "Analytical Tools in School Finance Reform," *Journal of Education Finance*, Spring 1977.

36.   Kern Alexander and James Hale, *Educational Equity: Improving School Finance in Arkansas*. Report to the Advisory Committee of the Joint Interim Committee on Education (Little Rock, Ark.: Joint Interim Committee on Education, Arkansas Legislature, 1978); C. Cale Hudson, *Nebraska School Finance Study* (Lincoln, Neb.: Nebraska State Department of Education, 1978); J. Alan Thomas, *School Finance and Educational Opportunity in Michigan* (Lansing, Mich.: State Department of Education, 1968).

37.   Adapted from Roe L. Johns, *op. cit.* in f.35.

38.   Roe L. Johns and Kern Alexander, *Alternative Programs for Financing Education*, vol. 5. (Gainesville, Fla.: National Educational Finance Project, 1971), p. 272. See also chapter 12.

39.   For other measures see Carroll, *Ibid.*, pp. 30–31; and Johns, Alexander, and Stollar, *Ibid.*, Chap. 4. Vol. 4.

SELECTED REFERENCES

ALEXANDER, KERN, and K. FORBIS JORDAN, eds.   *Constitutional Reform of School Finance*. Lexington, Mass.: Lexington Books, D. C. Heath & Company, 1973.

FULLER, EDGAR, and JIM B. PEARSON, eds.   *Education in the States Nationwide Development since 1900*. Washington, D.C.: National Education Association, 1969, Chap. 4.

JOHNS, ROE L., KERN ALEXANDER, and DEWEY STOLLAR, eds.   *Status and Impact of Educational Finance Programs*, vol. 4. Gainesville, Fla.: National Educational Finance Project, 1971.

U.S. DEPARTMENT of COMMERCE, BUREAU of the CENSUS.   *Historical Statistics of the United States: Colonial Times to 1979*. Washington, D.C.: U.S. Government Printing Office.

U.S. Office of Education.   *Profiles in School Support*, published deciannually since 1930, and *Public School Finance Programs*, published periodically. Washington, D.C.: U.S. Government Printing Office.

WISE, ARTHUR E. *Rich Schools, Poor Schools*. Chicago, Ill.: University of Chicago Press, 1968.

CHAPTER ELEVEN
PLANNING
AND DEVELOPING
THE SCHOOL FINANCE
PROGRAM

Comprehensive planning of a state's school finance program involves critical decision making in the following major areas:

1. the educational program to be financed
2. the system of taxation used to finance the program
3. the system for allocating the state funds to local school districts

This chapter examines the planning of the educational program to be financed.[1] Planning of the state's educational program involves fundamental policy decisions with respect to the following:

1. Who should be educated? That is, what target populations should be served? (For example, prekindergarten, kindergarten, grades 1–12, and special categories such as exceptional or handicapped, those with vocational needs, culturally disadvantaged, and adult.)
2. What educational goals and objectives should be established for each of these target populations?
3. What kinds of educational programs are needed for these different target populations?

When appropriate decisions have been made concerning these important matters, the next steps would be:

1. To ascertain the present numbers of pupils in the different target populations in the state and to project for at least a five- to six-year period the estimated number in each category
2. To determine the numbers and percent of the pupils in each target population that are presently being served by a program designed to meet the needs of those in that category
3. To determine the variations among districts in the percent of each target population served
4. To determine the extent to which the overall educational goals and the goals and objectives of each target population are being attained.

This may seem like a large order indeed, but it is impossible to develop rational fiscal policies for educaton without first establishing educational policies and goals and determining, insofar as possible, the extent to which those policies and goals are being attained. As pointed out in Chapter 7, decisions on policies and goals must be made through political processes. They are made by direct vote of the people, by local boards of education, by the state board of education and by the legislature. Although educators have access to the decision makers on education policy and make valuable inputs into the decision-making process, they do not make and should not make the final decisions on fundamental policies. Obviously these decisions cannot be made wisely by uninformed persons. Those making the policy decisions should have access to the information necessary to choose between policy alternatives. However, the more the educational policy makers are involved in making the studies needed to make policy decisions, the greater the possibility they will use the information produced in these studies in their policy decisions. All too often in American education, policy decisions have been made by those who are unaware of the possible consequences of the decision at the time it was made. This chapter is devoted largely to the determination of educational need and the measurement of the cost of the state-assured basic program or foundation program.

DETERMINATION OF EDUCATIONAL NEED

When an operating concensus has been reached on who should be educated at public expense, what goals and objectives are appropriate for the different target pupil populations, and what educational programs are needed for attaining those goals and objectives, it is then possible to determine needs and to make certain evaluations of how well a state is meeting its educational needs. Procedures for doing this are presented next.

Ascertaining the Numbers of Potential Students in Different Target Pupil Populations

It is essential in long-range fiscal planning to know the present and projected numbers of pupils in different age groups with differing educational needs. For example, what is the present census of children and youth in the following age groups: (1) prekindergarten, ages three and four; (2) kindergarten, age five; (3) elementary school age; (4) middle school or junior high school age; and (5) senior high school age? How many of these pupils at each age level (1) are physically or mentally handicapped,[2] (2) are culturally disadvantaged, (3) need different kinds of vocational programs? The numbers of pupils in each of these target populations and in other appropriate groups with special needs should be projected for at least five years into the future. This information should be provided for each district as well as for the state as a whole.

Ascertaining the Percent of Each Target Population That Is Served

In order to determine the state's unmet educational needs, it is necessary to ascertain the numbers and percent of pupils in each pupil population category who are presently served by educational programs appropriate to their needs and the numbers and percent of pupils who are not so served. This information should be obtained for each district in the state and for the entire state. For example, what programs for the mentally or physically handicapped are available in each district, and how many pupils in each handicapped category are served and how many unserved? The same kind of studies should be made of vocational education, education for the culturally disadvantaged, and programs needed for adults.

Studies should also be made in each district of the adequacy or inadequacy of counseling and guidance services, instructional supervision, instructional materials, libraries, science laboratories, vocational shops, learning environments, and so on. Studies of this type should be made by competent personnel in state departments of education and institutions of higher learning in cooperation with knowledgeable personnel employed by local boards of education. This is extremely important information to make available to study groups and decision makers on school finance, because it not only reveals the unmet educational needs of the state but it also reveals existing inequalities in educational opportunities.

Determining the Extent to Which the Goals and Objectives of the Different Target Pupil Populations Are Being Met

This is probably the most difficult problem of all. It is essentially a measure of the quality and appropriateness of educational programs provided for each category of pupil needs. It is possible to measure the attainment of certain knowledge and skills by appropriate objective tests, but the results of such tests should be used with great caution in inferring satisfactory or unsatisfactory goal attainment for different target groups. For example, a given score on a reading test taken by sixth-grade culturally disadvantaged pupils in an urban ghetto might be considered a satisfactory goal attainment for that population, but the same score might be considered an unsatisfactory goal attainment for sixth grade culturally advantaged pupils in an upper-middle-class suburb. Extreme caution should be exercised in comparing the measurable educational attainment of districts that differ widely in socioeconomic and cultural levels of parents.

Frequently, school districts with a low socioeconomic level also have low taxpaying ability and, because of the heavy reliance on local property taxes for school support in some states, the districts with the lowest socioeconomic level provide less than adequate educational programs for their children.

PROJECTION OF EDUCATIONAL COSTS
BASED ON NEED

Those engaged in a study of school finance in a state should make alternative projections of educational costs by biennial or annual periods for at least five to six years in advance. These alternative projections of educational costs should be based on alternative assumptions with respect to at least the following variables:

1. Birth rates and grade survival ratios from grade to grade
2. Amount of immigration to the state or migration from the state
3. Types of educational programs to be provided for target populations with differing needs and the numbers of pupils that will be in these programs
4. Cost differentials for different types of educational programs
5. Numbers of pupils who probably will transfer from nonpublic schools to public schools and vice versa
6. Cost differentials needed for sparsity or density of population
7. Quality level of education to be provided
8. Purchasing power of the dollar

These cost projections should include proposed expenditures for all items of current expenses, capital outlay, and debt service. Data needed for some of these alternative assumptions are readily available. Much research is needed to obtain the necessary data to make alternative projections for other factors. It has been pointed out that it is desirable to compute and project the pupil target populations with varying educational needs and to develop programs that will meet these needs. The next step is to compute the cost differentials needed to provide for the different kinds of educational programs needed.

Computation of Cost Differentials
for Different Kinds of Educational Programs

Educational programs designed to meet the needs of various categories of pupils vary widely in per-pupil cost. Special programs for exceptional (handicapped) children, vocational students, and culturally disadvantaged are "high-cost" programs compared with the typical elementary and secondary instruction programs.

The Weighted Pupil Method. One widely used method of comparing the differences in cost is the so-called weighted pupil technique. This procedure is based on the assumption that pupil-teacher ratios are lower, and operating and capital outlay costs are greater, for special education programs. When the weighting procedure is used, the weight of "1" is assigned to nonexceptional, nonvocational pupils at certain grade levels that have the lowest cost per pupil. The cost per equivalent full-time pupil for the high-cost programs is then computed in relation to the cost per pupil of the lowest cost pupils.[3]

Researchers associated with the National Educational Finance Project studied the per-pupil cost differentials for different types of programs in a number of states. These studies were based primarily on average practice in what was reported to be exemplary programs in each state. It was found that the cost differentials for different types of programs varied considerably from state to state but that programs for exceptional education, vocational education, and the culturally disadvantaged cost more per pupil in all states than the per-pupil cost of the basic program for pupils in grades 1–12.

In a 1981 study conducted for the U.S. Department of Education, Kakalik and others, using a large sample of school districts in several states, found that the cost of educating the average handicapped child was 2.17 times as much as to educate the average nonhandicapped child.[4] The cost difference varied by age level from 1.98 at the elementary level to 2.48 at the secondary level. It also varied by type of handicap from 1.37 for speech impaired children up to 5.86 for functionally blind children.

Similarly, vocational education and compensatory education programs have high cost differentials when compared with regular educational programs. Alexander and others found great variations in costs among hundreds of vocational education courses in Florida.[5] When these courses were grouped into programs, the cost factors between vocational and regular programs ranged from .93 to 2.41 with variations fluctuating depending on how the courses were grouped into programs.

Table 10–1 presents a set of cost differentials used by the state of Florida in 1980–81 for allocating state foundation program funds for different types of educational programs. School district boards in Florida utilize program accounting extensively, and the cost differentials in the state school finance program are based largely on the experience of local boards of education.

TABLE 10–1   Educational Cost Differentials Used by Florida in 1980–81 for Allocating State Foundation Program Funds

EDUCATIONAL PROGRAM	WEIGHTING PER EQUIVALENT FULL-TIME PUPIL
I. Basic programs	
1. Kindergarten and Grades 1, 2, & 3	1.234
2. Grades 4, 5, 6, 7, 8, & 9	1.00
3. Grades 10, 11, & 12	1.08
4. Educational alternatives*	2.00
II. Special programs for exceptional students	
1. Educable mentally retarded	2.12
2. Trainable mentally retarded	2.78
3. Physically handicapped	3.52
4. Physical and occupational therapy—part-time	6.02
5. Speech and hearing therapy—part-time	7.39
6. Deaf	3.71
7. Visually handicapped—part-time	11.15
8. Visually handicapped	3.56
9. Emotionally disturbed—part-time	5.59
10. Emotionally disturbed	3.26
11. Specific learning disability—part-time	4.96
12. Specific learning disability	2.56
13. Hospital and homebound—part-time	14.76
14. Profoundly handicapped	6.50
III. Special vocational-technical programs— job preparation	
1. Agriculture	2.26
2. Office	1.78
3. Distributive	1.61
4. Diversified	1.34
5. Health	2.23
6. Public service	3.12
7. Home economics	1.65
8. Technical, trade, industrial	2.10
9. Exploratory	1.49

*A school or program for disruptive or disinterested pupils who disturb other pupils in the regular schools. This may frequently be an alternative to expulsion.

Note that the weighting is based on full-time equivalency. This means that if a student spends part of the day in a special highly weighted program and part of the day in the basic program, the weighting for that student is proportionate. For example, if a vocational agriculture student spends one half of the school day in the basic program for grades 10, 11 and 12 and half of the day in vocational agriculture, that student is counted as half of an equivalent full-time student in the basic program, with a weight of 1.08 and half of an equivalent full-time student in agriculture, with a weight of 2.26.

It is possible that Florida has gone into more detail than necessary in weighting pupils. However, the concept is sound. The weights presented in Table 10–1 should not be considered scientifically determined weights. They represent only average practice in the state of Florida at the time they were computed. Cost-effective studies may show that different methods of teaching, new technology, or improved managerial procedures change these cost differentials. In fact, the chief danger of using cost differentials in a school finance program is that they may become a "self-fulfilling prophecy." That is, boards of education may tend to spend in accordance with the cost differentials included in the finance program instead of what is needed to be expended to obtain the goals of the program. Therefore each state should establish its own cost differentials in terms of what is needed in that state. Ideally, program cost differentials should be based on cost-effective studies instead of an average of reported best practice.

In order to plan the state finance program, it is necessary to compute the cost of the state-assured basic program or foundation program. The term "foundation program" is now generally used to designate the state-assured program financed jointly by the state and local school districts in proportion to their relative taxpaying ability. Originally, the term was used to designate the state-assured program regardless of whether it was supported jointly by the state and local school units or entirely by the state. For this reason the authors generally use the term *basic state program* or *state-assured program* regardless of whether it is financed entirely by the state or jointly, and the term *foundation program* to designate equalization plans of state support financed jointly.

The current expense cost of the state-assured basic educational program or foundation program, except expenditures for school transportation and school food service, can readily be computed from weighted pupils. Let us assume that the current expense allotment that the state decides to make for a student with a weight of 1 is $1,600. The total cost of the state-assured or foundation program can be computed as follows:

> Multiply the number of equivalent full-time pupils in each program category by the weight assigned to that category. For example, referring to table 10–1, assume that a school system has 500 full-time pupils in average daily membership in kindergarten and grades 1, 2 and 3. Then 500 pupils times a weight of 1.234 equals 617 weighted pupils. Follow the same procedure for each program category, find the total of weighted pupils for the district, and multiply by $1600. The product equals the current expense cost of the basic or foundation program, excluding transportation and school food service, guaranteed by the state. The $1600 allotment per weighted pupil is used solely for the purpose of illustration. It could be more or less than that amount.

The basic allotment of $1,600 per pupil can be adjusted for differences among school districts in the cost of living (or better still, differences in the cost of education) and higher costs due to the sparsity of population that forces some boards to maintain small schools at a higher per-pupil cost than large schools. For example, let us assume that the cost of living for the same standard of living varies from 5 percent of the average cost to 5 percent above the average cost. The total cost of the state-assured program for a district with the lowest cost of living in the state would be reduced to 95 percent of the amount computed above, and the amount for a district with the highest cost of living in the state would be increased to 105 percent of the amount computed above.

The adjustment for sparsity can be computed in the same manner. In practice, these adjustments may partially cancel each other. For example, a sparsely settled district may have a low cost of living factor and a high cost due to sparsity.

The Adjusted Instruction Unit Method.   Another method being used by a number of states to provide for program cost differentials is the adjusted instruction unit method. This method actually is based on the weighted pupil method, because it assumes that the necessary pupil-teacher ratio varies for different types of programs. If we assume that one instruction unit, supplemented by such instructional service units as librarians, principals, counselors and supervisors is needed for every twenty-four non-high-cost pupils, the pupil-teacher ratio for each type of program can be computed simply by dividing 24 by the appropriate weight shown in table 10–1. For example, in table 10–1 the weight for pupils in grades 4, 5, 6, 7, 8, and 9 in the basic program is 1.00. Since one instruction unit is allotted for every 24 equivalent full-time pupils in the basic program for those grades, the total full-time equivalent students in the basic program in grades 4, 5, 6, 7, 8, and 9 is divided by 24 in order to determine the instruction units allotted for those students. From table 10–1 it can be seen that Florida assigns a weight of 2.12 for educably mentally retarded students. The basic 24-pupil allotment divided by 2.12 equals 11.32. The total equivalent full-time membership of educable mentally retarded students is divided by 11.32 in order to determine the number of instruction units allotted for that category. Similar computations are made for all categories.

The state allotment per instruction unit under this plan is equivalent to $1,600 times 24, or $38,400. The total current expense cost of the state-assured program (excluding transportation and school food service) is determined by multiplying the total number of instruction units by $38,400. The cost of the state-assured program under the instruction unit plan is exactly the same as under the weighted pupil plan, provided that the same cost differentials are used.

Choice of Plan.   Which is the better plan for determining the cost of the state assured program, the weighted pupil or the instruction unit? As pointed out, the two plans are mathematically equivalent, provided the same cost differentials are recognized. It would seem advisable to use the plan that is politically preferred in a state. If a state has been accustomed to using the instruction unit, it may be politically advisable to continue using it. With continued inflation, there may be a psychological political advantage in computing the cost of the basic or foundation program in terms of weighted pupils rather than instruction units. To some legislators, $1,600 per weighted pupil may not seem excessive, whereas $38,400 per instruction unit may seem like a lot of money. The authors have noted that in states where the state teachers' association has come into disfavor because of alleged aggressive tactics, legislatures have urged that the emphasis be placed on children rather than teachers, and they prefer some type of weighted pupil measure. Both the weighted pupil and the adjusted instruction unit methods are sound in principle, and it is good policy on the part of the educatonal leadership in a state to accept the method preferred by the legislature of that state.

Much emphasis is being given at the present time to accountability. Both methods provide for a type of administrative accountability, because a district would not receive weighted pupils or adjusted instruction units for a high-cost program unless it offered that program.

Compensatory Education for the Culturally Disadvantaged

Cost differentials for the culturally disadvantaged should be included in the program of state support. Studies made by the National Educational Finance Project revealed that school systems with well-developed programs for pupils in this category were spending about twice as much per pupil for culturally disadvantaged as for non-high-cost pupils. This is not to suggest that a weight of 2.0 should be given to these pupils in allocating state funds. Much additional research is needed to determine proper weighting for these pupils.

The federal government, through Title 1 of ESEA, provides funds for culturally disadvantaged pupils but not enough to meet the need. Culturally disadvantaged pupils are not evenly distributed among the districts of a state. They tend to be concentrated in most large cities, in some small cities, and even in some rural districts. Problems have arisen in state funding of compensatory education because of the difficulty of classification of pupils. Many culturally handicapped pupils could also be classified as handicapped exceptional pupils. Much additional research is needed on compensatory education for the culturally disadvantaged. However, the states cannot afford to wait for the results of cost-benefit studies before funding programs for compensatory education. Experience with such programs will produce evidence upon which satisfactory cost differentials can be established.

Computing the Cost of Transportation for Inclusion in the Basic State Program of School Financing

As pointed out earlier, the cost of transportation to include in the state basic program or foundation program cannot be computed in terms of weighted pupils or adjusted instruction units. However, the cost per pupil transported varies widely among the school districts of a state, due primarily to variations in the density of transported pupils. State formulas for allocating state funds for transportation commonly use density of transported pupils per one-way mile of bus route or density of transported pupils per square mile of area served as a measure of density. Either measure is satisfactory.

Before computing the cost of transportation to include in the state aid program, it is necessary for the state to adopt policies with respect to what pupils are entitled to transportation for inclusion in the state finance program. Following are the types of policies usually adopted for inclusion:

1. Pupils living beyond a specified walking distance from the school they attend. The states vary in the distance they set, the range being usually from 1.0 to about 2.0 miles, with the average being about 1.5 miles. Some states set shorter distances for elementary pupils than high school pupils.
2. Physically handicapped pupils living any distance from school.

The cost of transportation to include in the basic state program is usually determined by computing average costs for districts with similar densities of transported pupils. This can be done either graphically or mathematically.

The desirable cost differentials due to variations in density of transported pupils can be computed graphically by plotting cost per pupil transported on the X axis and density per bus mile of transported pupils on the Y axis of coordinate axes. A smoothed curve can be drawn which will best fit the plotted data. The relationship between cost per pupil transported and density is curvilinear. The state allotment per pupil transported for different degrees of density can be determined by noting from the curve the allotted cost per pupil at the point where a line drawn vertically from the density measure intersects the curve.

A more precise method of determining an equitable allotted cost per pupil transported is to use a mathematical formula for this purpose. The following formula is satisfactory for that purpose: The allowable or allotted cost per pupil transported $-Y = A + BX + CX^2$, in which X is the density of transported pupils per bus mile and A, B, and C are constants determined by a statistical method known as "least squares" which can be programmed on a computer for ease of computation. Other mathematical formulas can be used for this purpose provided they accurately depict the relationship between the two variables—cost per pupil transported and density. Some states include other factors such as road conditions and topography in their formulas for allocating state funds for transportation, but these two factors have only a very slight effect on variations in cost per pupil transported in most states.

The transportation of pupils is an important item in the school budget. At this writing, more than 56 percent of all public school elementary and secondary pupils were transported to school at a cost of approximately $3 billion. But the percent of local school budgets expended for school transportation varies greatly, due primarily to variations among districts in scatter of population. Therefore the state must include financial assistance for school transportation in its state financial support program if it is to discharge its responsibility for equalizing the financial support of the public schools.

School Food Service

The school food service program has become a major operation in recent years. In 1978, approximately 60 percent of the pupils enrolled in the public schools participated in the school lunch program.[6] The school food service program also includes the school breakfast program and the Special Milk Program. The total expenditures of the school food service program increased from $2.4 billion in 1970 to an estimated $8.1 billion in 1980.[7] This includes expenditures from the federal, state, and local governments and children's payments. Data presented by the National Center for Education Statistics indicate that in 1975 approximately 44 percent of the cost of a school lunch was funded by the federal government, 35 percent by children's payments, and 20 percent by state and local governments.[8]

How should the school food service program be funded? The major part of that program is the school lunch program. At this writing, the amount a pupil is charged for a lunch depends upon the income of his or her parents. Pupils with parents who have an income below a specified level are given free lunches, pupils with parents who have an income between the lowest level and the next specified level pay a reduced price for their lunches, and pupils with parents who have an income above a specified level pay the highest price charged pupils. However, pupils charged the highest price for their lunches do not pay the full cost of their lunches, primarily because of the funding contributed from tax sources. Boards of education must ascertain the income of parents of pupils receiving free or reduced price lunches. Furthermore, records must be kept and reports made of expenditures and payments received from pupils in each category. This involves extensive accounting and much paper work.

It is obvious that the present system of funding the school lunch program is cumbersome, inequitable, and fiscally inefficient. It is inequitable because it is impossible for local school authorities to ascertain accurately the income level of the pupils' parents. Furthermore, some low-income parents have too much pride to apply for a free or reduced price lunch. It is inefficient because of bureaucratic paper work and because full economy of scale cannot be attained in a school lunch program with only 60 percent of the enrollment participating. In order to have an efficient and equitable program for financing school lunches, it must be made a part of the total school program and funded entirely from federal, state, and local tax sources. The school lunch program should certainly be considered as much a part of the total school program as pupil transportation. When school transportation became a major program, it was found to be more efficient to fund it entirely from public funds. It would be relatively simple to integrate state funds with federal and local funds and include the school lunch program as a part of the total state-assured program.

In 1978–79, thirty-three states provided some state aid for the school food service program, and practically all school districts maintaining a school lunch program provided financial assistance for the program by making facilities and utilities available or by direct cash assistance.[9]

Other Items of Current Expense

All items of current expense should be included in a *program budget* of state support. This policy facilitates provision of a balanced program of state support. The extensive use of categorical grants by a state invariably results in an unintegrated program of state financing. Following are some objects of school expenditure that are frequently supported by special-purpose grants.

Driver Education.   Driver education is a relatively new service for many school systems. In a few states it is required by law. These states usually have provided a special-purpose appropriation designed to help meet the expenses of conducting this program. Since this new service involves considerable additional expense, many are inclined to think the only way to meet the financial need is through a special appropriation. However, since every child in certain high-school grades should participate in and benefit from a properly developed program of driver education and training, the financial need can be readily determined and probably can be met most satisfactorily merely by increasing the amount per unit included in the foundation or basic program. This should be more equitable than another special-purpose appropriation.

Textbooks, Library Books, and Other Instructional Materials.   State policies relating to the provision of textbooks vary considerably. In some states, the parents of pupils in all grades are expected to buy the textbooks. Other states provide the cost of textbooks for elementary grades but not for high school grades. Still others provide textbooks or funds intended to meet the cost of textbooks in all grades.

Library books, films, slides, and other instructional materials generally are expected to be provided at public expense, but the funds available in a number of small districts have been so limited that the unsatisfactory policy of soliciting book donations to meet part of the library needs has been followed. Several states, recognizing that the cost of providing an adequate supply of library books from local funds would require greater effort on the part of poor than of wealthy districts, have established special funds for that purpose. There are now many other kinds of essential instructional materials that will need to be provided by school systems.

If the cost of textbooks and library books and other appropriate materials is to be met from public tax funds, it should be included in the foundation or basic program. Again, in this instance there seems to be no need for a special fund or appropriation. The cost of textbooks and library books per pupil can be determined and added to the basic or foundation program.

Sick Leave and Retirement. A few states have established special funds for sick leave or for salaries of substitute teachers. This need, of course, must be recognized, but there should be no reason for a special fund. Studies have been made in a number of states, and can be made in others, to determine the percentage allowance that should be made for payment of substitute teachers. This need, of course, must be recognized, but there should be no reason for a special fund. Studies have been made in a number of states, and can be made in others, to determine the percentage allowance that should be made for payment of substitute teachers. Provision can readily be made to include this amount in the foundation or basic program allowance per instruction unit or per weighted pupil.

Provisions for retirement and Social Security seem to need further attention. In some states the practice has been to expect each local school system to finance costs other than those paid by the employee. Obviously this is not equitable, because the least wealthy districts are in a less satisfactory position to meet these costs than are the more wealthy. The most equitable plan is to include in the state program for each district the amount required to finance these aspects of the program, rather than to charge each district with its share of the cost.

Extended School Term and Summer Programs. Many progressive school systems in the nation are now extending the school term for all students beyond the customary 9-month or 180-day term. Some school systems divide the school term into four quarters or quinmesters extending throughout the calendar year; students may attend any of the quarters or quinmesters totaling 180 days, and those desiring acceleration may attend all quarters or quinmesters. Still other systems use schemes such as the 45 day in school and 15 on vacation for four different sections of pupils extending throughout the year, in order to reduce the school plant space required but not to provide more than 180 days of instruction for any one pupil. Another plan is to divide the calendar year into quarters and have three quarters of the pupils in school at any one time and one quarter on vacation. This plan has usually been met with strenuous parental objections. None of the plans that has as its objective the reduction of building space needed by spreading the 180-day term throughout the calendar year has been shown to increase the quality of instruction, and the money saved has usually proven to be negligible.

Many school systems provide summer enrichment and makeup programs for students who desire them. Unfortunately, many systems finance these programs largely through fees, and this policy of course discriminates against the pupils from low income families. However, a number of states are beginning to finance, at least in part, the summer school program. There is no sound reason why it should not be fully financed from public funds.

A study made by a research team at the University of Florida showed that over time a school term of 210 days would increase the educational opportunities provided for pupils without increasing costs, because it would reduce enrollment by reducing the years in elementary and high school from twelve to eleven and would also provide almost a full year of enrichment.[10]

The formula for state support should make it possible for boards of education to extend the school term beyond 180 days for all pupils or for the number of pupils who desire the extended term. It should also provide for the financing of the summer enrichment and makeup programs and be flexible enough to make it possible for boards of education to experiment with such scheduling plans as the 45–15 year.

Technically, this is relatively easy to accomplish by the following procedures:

1. At 5 hours per day for 180 days, an equivalent full-time student would have 900 hours of instruction. If a student is in attendance for 210 days, he or she would have 1,050 hours of instruction, which amount divided by 900 equals 1.17 equivalent full-time students. Weighted pupils or adjusted instruction units can readily be computed from equivalent full-time students. This policy would provide financing both for the extended school year and or summer programs.

    Equivalent full-time students can be computed for systems operating on schedules extending throughout the school year for 180 days or days beyond 180 by the same method.
2. State allotments for transportation can be determined similarly by computing the allotment for 180 days and proportionately more for pupils transported more than 180 days.

The Florida School Finance Law of 1973 incorporated all of these provisions in the foundation program for that state.

Sparsity Adjustment

Small schools do not have the economies of scale possible for large schools, therefore the cost per pupil for an equivalent quality of education is higher than in large schools. This is particularly true of high schools. Therefore all unnecessary small schools should be consolidated with larger centers. Small schools cost more per pupil than large schools, primarily because they must be operated with lower pupil-teacher ratios than in large schools in order to provide the educational programs needed.

In many states, there are areas so sparsely settled that it is not possible to establish schools of economical size. The state should make allowance for the necessary extra costs of such schools in its program of state support. This can readily be done by appropriate weighting of the pupil in small schools or by decreasing the number of pupils per allotted instruction unit. However, the state should carefully avoid subsidizing unnecessary small schools. This can be accomplished by establishing a "formula of necessity" for small schools based on a minimum required distance by the nearest traveled road to another school of the same grade level. Another alternative would be to determine the necessity for the small schools in a district by a survey made by the state department of education in accordance with regulations of the state board of education.[11]

Adjustment for Variations in the Cost of Living

The proposals set forth above provide for necessary differentials in the unit costs of different types of educational programs, differences in the unit costs of transportation, and differences in costs due to sparsity of population.

Are there other differences in the unit costs of delivering an equivalent quality of educational services? The most important item in school current expenditures is instructional salaries. Excluding transportation, instructional salaries amount to approximately 70 percent of current expenditures. What must instructional personnel and other school employees be paid in different areas of the state in order to assure an equivalent quality of personnel? Are there differences in the cost of living that would favor one district over another? Are there any real differences among the districts of a state in the cost of living for the same standard of living? Are some districts more attractive places in which to live than other districts? Are the districts with the highest cost of living also the districts with a more attractive living environment? Are the districts with the lowest living costs also the districts with the least attractive living environment? What is the net effect on teachers of differences in the cost of living versus differences in community attractiveness and living conditions? Available research does not provide answers to these questions. Until research indicates the effects of these factors on the ability of boards of education throughout the state to recruit an equivalent quality of personnel, it does not seem advisable to allow for cost-of-living or community hardship factors. When we have valid evidence of the effect of these factors on the cost of delivering an equivalent quality of educational services, appropriate weightings for these factors should be used in computing the cost of the state basic or foundation program. Research to answer these questions is greatly needed.

Adjustment for Municipal Overburden

During recent years many large, core cities have experienced great increases in municipal costs, resulting in major increases in municipal taxes. This, in turn, has resulted in taxpayer resistance to both municipal and school taxes in those cities. Political pressure is being brought in some states to adjust the state school finance formula so as to allot proportionately more state school funds to cities with high municipal taxes. It is argued that high municipal taxes reduce the financial ability of cities to provide local tax support for the public schools.

The National Educational Finance Project made the following statement on municipal overburden:

> It has been suggested by some that the financial ability of large urban districts as measured by the equalized value of property be reduced appropriately in the state's apportionment formula because of the extra costs as compared with many suburban and rural areas. However, the costs of those cities for public safety, welfare, sewage disposal, control of air and water pollution, transportation and other services are so great that they cannot be substantially met by manipulations of the school apportionment formula. The cities should be provided direct financial aid in accordance with their needs for municipal services and their relative financial ability. Both the federal and state governments should contribute financial aid to the cities for this purpose.
>
> Core cities as a rule have a higher percent of high cost pupils than surrounding suburban districts. It has already been recommended in this chapter that pupils should be weighted appropriately in order to provide for the extra costs of culturally disadvantaged pupils.
>
> These provisions, if implemented, would solve the problem of municipal overburden without inserting special provisions in the school apportionment formula for that purpose.[12]

RESPONSIBILITY FOR PLANNING THE SCHOOL FINANCE PROGRAM

School finance planning at this writing needs to be improved. Decisions on school finance are made at the federal, state, and school district level. Decisions at all three levels are frequently made on the basis of expediency, without the benefit of sound planning. All too often financial decisions at these levels are not integrated into a sound finance program. If educational finance planning is integrated, it is obvious that school finance decision makers at the federal, state, and local levels must plan cooperatively. The federal education agency should not make decisions on school finance programs without consulting with state education agencies, and state educational agencies should not make decisions on school finance programs without consulting with local educational agencies. Furthermore, school employees, including administrators, teachers, and support personnel, must be brought into the planning process if the most efficient planning is to be attained. Lay citizens have a vital interest in determining educational goals and in the fiscal planning for those goals. Members of Congress, state legislatures, and local boards of education will make better decisions on school finance if representatives from those bodies participate in planning the programs. Ad hoc lay committees appointed by federal and state officials and local boards of education have frequently made valuable contributions to school finance planning.

Finally, the importance of research and adequate information for school finance planning cannot be overemphaszed. No group or agency can make sound decisions on school finance planning unless it is able to anticipate the consequences of those decisions. Therefore the decision makers on school finance policy should have available the services of competent researchers on school finance who can assist them in evaluating the consequences of alternative policies. Research on school finance should be one of the continuing activities of the federal education agency, the state education agencies, the institutions of higher learning, and the local school systems staffed to conduct research.

NOTES

1. The first part of this chapter is abstracted or adapted from Roe L. Johns and Edgar L. Morphet, *Planning School Finance Programs* (Gainesville, Fla.: National Educational Finance Project, 1972).

2. Numbers of pupils with different types of handicaps should be identified.

3. For detailed information on the methodology of computing education cost differentials, see Roe L. Johns, Kern Alexander, and K. Forbis Jordan, eds., *Planning to Finance Education*, Vol. 3 (Gainesville, Fla.: National Educational Finance Project, 1971).

4. J. S. Kakalik, W. S. Furry, M. A. Thomas, and M. F Carney, *The Cost of Special Education* (Santa Monica, California: The Rand Corporation, 1981).

5. Kern Alexander, William Dickey and Douglas Forth, *Cost of Vocational and Adult Education Programs in Florida* (Gainesville, Florida: Institute for Educational Finance, University of Florida, 1975).

6. U. S. Department of Commerce, Bureau of the Census, *Statistical Abstract of the U.S.*, 100th edition (Washington, D.C.: U.S. Government Printing Office, 1979), p. 138.

7. Unpublished paper presented by Task Force VII of the American School Food Service Association at the AFSA Seminar, Williamsburg, Va., December 7–11, 1980.

8. W. Vance Grant and Leo J. Eiden, *Digest of Education Statistics, 1980*. (Washington, D.C.: U.S. Department of Health, Education, and Welfare, Education Division, National Center for Education Statistics, 1980), pp. 198–99.

9. Esther O. Tron, *Public School Finance Programs 1978–79*, (Washington, D.C.: U.S. Government Printing Office, 1980), p. 15.

10. J. B. White and others, *Year-Round Schools for Polk County, Florida* (Gainesville, Fla.: Florida Educational Research and Development Council, College of Education, University of Florida, 1966).

11. For an extensive discussion of the sparsity adjustment see Roe L. Johns, "An Index of the Extra Costs of Education Due to Sparsity of Population," Vol. 1, No. 2, *Journal of Education Finance*, (Fall, 1975). Note: This periodical is sponsored by the American Educational Finance Association.

12. Roe L. Johns and Kern Alexander, eds., *Alternative Programs for School Financing*, Vol. 5, (Gainesville, Fla.: National Educational Finance Project, 1971), pp. 344–45.

SELECTED REFERENCES

ALEXANDER, KERN and K. FORBIS JORDAN, eds. *Educational Need in the Public Economy*. Gainesville, Fla.: University Presses of Florida, 1976

BENSON, CHARLES S. *The Economics of Public Education*, 3rd ed., Boston: Houghton Mifflin Company, 1978

JOHNS, ROE L., and EDGAR L. MORPHET. *Planning School Finance Programs*. Gainesville, Fla.: National Educational Finance Project, 1972.

JOHNS, ROE L., KERN ALEXANDER, and K. FORBIS JORDAN.   *Planning to Finance Education*, Vol. 3. Gainesville, Fla.: National Educational Finance Project, 1971

MORPHET, EDGAR L., DAVID L. JESSER, and ARTHUR P. LUDKA.   *Planning and providing for Excellence in Education*. Denver, Improving State Leadership in Education Project, 1971.

REISCHAUR, ROBERT D., ROBERT W. HARTMAN, and DANIEL J. SULLIVAN.   *Reforming School Finance*. Washington, D.C.: Brookings Institution, 1973.

THOMPSON, JOHN THOMAS.   *Policy making in American Education: A Framework for Analysis*. Englewood Cliffs, N.J.: Prentice-Hall, Inc., 1975.

CHAPTER TWELVE
STATE PROVISIONS
FOR SCHOOL SUPPORT

All states, with the lone exception of Hawaii, have chosen to finance public schools by using both state and local tax revenues. States have historically placed substantial reliance on local funding even though it is a well-established legal principle of our government that "the whole state is responsible for education of all children of the state."[1] Use of local tax revenues marked the first step toward a sound financial base for the public schools in America. While local taxation gave a stable means of support, it nevertheless created vast equalization problems, especially in those states with large numbers of small school districts. As a result it has been necessary for states to design various types of state-aid formulas which redistribute money from areas with above average wealth to areas with below average wealth. In this chapter these equalization programs are discussed along with various criteria and assumptions which are relied on to justify them.

REVENUE AND ALLOCATION DIMENSIONS

The extent of equalization among school districts provided in a state is a function of both the method of revenue collection and the process by which funds are distributed back to local school districts. Thus, any state school-aid model has two dimensions, *revenue* and *allocation*. Within the revenue dimension, consideration is given to taxpayer equity. This is affected by the particular model of state support used, ranging from a complete state-support model to complete local support. Since state taxes, generally, are considered to be more progressive than local property taxes, the more a state shifts toward state aid the less regressive the system. See Chapter 5 of this text for more discussion of this aspect of the various taxes.

The allocation dimension refers to the principal methods utilized to distribute funds to local school districts. A state may choose to allocate a flat amount of funds per pupil, per teacher, or by some other standard unit of measure, without taking local fiscal capacity into account. A flat grant may also be made, based on a variable unit of need which addresses costs of educational programs. In most cases, though, the allocation dimension represents a large equalization program whereby funds are distributed in inverse proportion to local fiscal capacity. In other words, school districts with less wealth are given more state money per unit of need than more able districts. Units of educational need may vary, depending on whether costs of education programs are considered, just as may be done in the aforementioned flat-grant programs.

The degree of equalization may be assessed, taking into account both the revenue and allocation dimensions, by using a typology developed by the National Educational Finance Project. The NEFP typology classifies all state-aid programs according to an equity score.[2] Using this approach, one can fully evaluate the equity of a school finance program for both student and taxpayer.

Policy decisions regarding state school fund distribution affect both dimensions, as formulas are adopted which increase or decrease the utilization of certain taxes or increase or decrease the percentage of state funding, thereby shifting the reliance placed on various types of taxes. Further, when the impact of both revenue and allocation dimensions are considered, poorer school districts will have a net inflow of funds, as they pay a smaller per-capita portion in state taxes in the revenue dimension and receive back a larger amount per pupil through the equalization effects of the allocation dimension. This flow equalizes educational opportunity while serving as a positive force in the overall redistribution of the state's wealth.

STATE SUPPORT IN RELATION
TO STATE CONTROL

The statement is frequently made that "control follows the dollar." If this statement were inevitably true, it would mean that any amount of state funds provided for schools would result in some state control of the educational program and, presumably, that the larger the proportion of state funds, the greater the amount of state control.

While various aspects of control are discussed in other appropriate places in this book, it seems desirable to review developments briefly here as a background for further consideration of the problem of state support. In the first place it should be recognized that state controls or requirements for schools did not originate with state aid. In fact the general assumption for many years was that local school systems could assume full responsibility for financing their schools. As Burke points out,

> After decentralized school systems were once established, states found that there were wide differences in school attendance, length of term, qualifications of teachers, and physical facilities . . . States generally attempted to attain minimum standards at first through local support which resulted in very unequal tax burdens.[3]

The fact is that most states were not much concerned about the inequalities in local tax burdens until after the beginning of the present century. They were, however, increasingly concerned about assuring a minimum amount of education (primarily elementary education at first) for all children be financed through public tax funds rather than through discriminatory rate bills, fees, and tuition charges.

States eventually learned that minimum standards could not be established and enforced in all districts unless sufficient funds were provided by the state to enable the districts to meet the expenses of attaining these standards. The attempt to enforce standards for one aspect of the program in various communities often resulted indirectly in lowering other standards. Some districts simply could not make the tax effort necessary to meet state prescribed minimum standards and at the same time maintain satisfactory standards for all levels and aspects of the program. The burden on a number of districts finally became so obviously intolerable that state after state found it necessary to provide some state support.

While no conclusive studies have been made of state controls in relation to state support, there is considerable evidence to indicate that *the amount of state control is not determined as much by the amount of state support as by the procedures and policies followed by the state in providing the support.*

If a state assumes that only limited funds can be provided to assist the districts in financing their schools, it is likely to be greatly concerned with assuring maximum "economy" in the use of those funds. Moreover, if the legislature or officials of a state assume that local school systems are not to be trusted to plan sound procedures for meeting minimum standards and expending state and local funds, they will insist on a maximum of control.

In 1956, Fowlkes and Watson studied state financial support of schools in relation to local educational planning in a number of midwestern states. Some of these states provided very little support for schools, while others made a substantial contribution through state funds. The authors decided that "No conclusion is justified that increases in state support result in an increased number of controls."[4] The following observations seem to be justified:

1. There would be some state controls and requirements even if there were no state aid
2. Controls may be advantageous and desirable or may be limiting and undesirable
3. Increased state support does not necessarily result in increased state controls
4. Undesirable controls are likely to develop when the problem is ignored or when maximum emphasis is placed on economy and efficiency in a narrow and restricted sense
5. No control should ever be established at the state level that can more appropriately be handled at the local school level
6. The objective in every state should be to devise a system of support that is adequate to meet needs throughout the state and to restrict controls and requirements to those necessary to assure adequate and equitable educational opportunities.

ELEMENTS OF STATE EQUALIZATION PROGRAMS

State school finance programs must have three primary structural elements: measurement of educational needs, of costs, and of local fiscal capacity.

Educational Needs

Educational needs of pupils must be determined by using some measure which is uniformly quantifiable for all school districts in the state. Such measures have traditionally included counts of census or school-age children, of school-attending children, of enrollment, of average daily membership and average daily attendance. Quite different effects may evolve from each of these choices of basic measures. Census of school-age children constitutes the entire population in this particular age group, whether they are attending school or not. Cubberley early inveighed against the use of census because, as he said, it "has no educational significance in that it does not place a premium on any effort that makes for better education."[5] School-attending children takes into account those attending nonpublic schools. Enrollment includes those children who register for school attendance. Average daily membership is the average of aggregate days of membership, and average daily attendance is the aggregate number of days attended for a given period of time divided by the number of days in the period. Practically all states use either average daily membership or average daily attendance. Advocates for average membership maintain that the school districts must maintain a place in the schools for all children in membership, whether they are actually present or not, and the state and local school district should share in costs associated with each of these student places.

Proponents of average daily attendance argue that the state should not pay local school districts for the education of children for days when they are not in attendance. It is further maintained that the use of average daily attendance as a measure of need gives the school district financial incentive to enforce compulsory attendance laws. Thus, use of ADM would tend to enhance the flow of state funds to districts which experience high rates of absenteeism, usually the urban areas of a state.

Another measure of educational need, the full-time equivalent (FTE) pupil, has been used in some states in recent years. Here a pupil count is taken a few times during the school year, but the school day or week is broken down into hours or minutes in which pupils are assigned to certain of the school programs. Thus, a student who is assigned a one-half day in the regular school program and attends, say, an area vocational school the other one-half day, is counted as .5 FTE in each school and duplication of pupil count, in ultimate funding, will not occur.

Costs

The second element of the state school finance program is a determination of costs of the educational program. What are the budgetary amounts needed to operate the school programs throughout the state? A state may prescribe various cost allocations per pupil count of educational need or it may simply utilize the expenditure level of the local school district as the basis of costs. If the former method is used, the state is confronted with annually establishing what the educational costs should be, where with the latter the state merely responds to levels of costs determined by local expenditure levels. The choice has much to do with the type of state-aid formula in use. This will be discussed in more detail later in this chapter. Chapter 11 fully explains the process of establishing costs by weighting FTE pupils, as is done in Florida; by weighting classroom or teacher units; by varying pupil-classroom or pupil-teacher ratios, as is done in Kentucky and several other states. Regardless of method, each state-aid formula must establish a cost or dollar amount to be applied to the measure of educational need, in order to establish the level of the educational program to be funded.

Local Fiscal Capacity

The third element of a state-aid formula is the determination of local fiscal capacity. This element is not present in a flat grant. Equalization grants require the determination of local fiscal capacity. Measurement of local fiscal capacity is discussed extensively in Chapter 8. Suffice it here to note that most states use equalized assessed valuation of property as the measure of fiscal capacity, with a few using the economic indicator approach. Mississippi still uses the tax base surrogate or ability index. Implicit in the measurement of fiscal capacity for purposes of equalization is a determination of effort. The state must see to it that a child's education is not inhibited by lack of educational effort, resulting in the child being unable to succeed because of low educational aspiration or political restraints of a particular community.

These three elements of a state school finance program are combined in various ways, no two states utilize the same method. All, though, are necessary in order to construct an equalization program.

DESIGN OF STATE-AID PROGRAMS

There are an infinite number of alternative models of state school financing. No two of the fifty states use exactly the same model in all respects. Furthermore, some change in each state's school finance plan is made in practically every general session of the legislature of that state.

A very broad classification of grants may be unit[6] or flat grants, as opposed to equalization grants.

A third group of grants may be called nonequalizing or even antiequalizing. With such grants, the state would give more funds to those school districts with more funds. For example, a grant which provided matching funds based simply on local expenditure levels would be the antithesis of equalization, would not establish uniformity of educational opportunity, and would do nothing to encourage efficiency.

Acknowledging the difficulty in classification, the following is as useful as any:

   I.   Flat (unit) grants
        A.   Uniform flat grants per distribution unit
        B.   Variable flat grants reflecting unit cost variations

  II.   Equalization grants (cost units uniform or reflecting cost variations)
        A.   Strayer-Haig-Mort (foundation) programs
        B.   Percentage equalization, state-aid ratio, or guaranteed valuation programs
        C.   District power-equalizing programs

 III.   Nonequalizing matching grants

The two main types of grants, flat and equalization, require further explanation.

Flat Grants

Under this type of model, state grants are allocated to local school districts without taking into consideration variations among the districts in local taxpaying ability. There are two major variations of this model, as follows:

1. A uniform amount per pupil, per teacher, or some other unit of need is allotted without taking into consideration necessary variations in unit costs of different educational programs and services.
2. Variable amounts per unit of need that reflect necessary variations in unit costs are allocated to local school districts.

Equalization Grants

Under this type of model, state funds are allocated to local school districts in inverse proportion to local taxpaying ability. In other words, more state funds per pupil, per teacher, or per other unit of need are allocated to the districts of less wealth than to those of greater wealth. As in the flat grant models, there are two main variations in the equalization models, as follows:

1. In computing the cost of the program equalized, a uniform amount is allowed per pupil, per teacher, or per other unit of need, without giving consideration to necessary variations in unit costs of different educational programs and services.
2. Variable amounts per unit of need that take into consideration necessary variations in unit costs are used in computing the cost of the foundation or basic program.[7]

For purposes of discussion in this chapter, the primary methods for distributing state funds will be divided into flat grants, full state funding, foundation programs, percentage-equalizing grants, and district power-equalizing grants.

EFFICACY OF THE FLAT GRANT

As shown earlier, a flat grant is an amount of money per unit of need which does not take into account the fiscal capacity of the local school district. To say, though, that flat grants do not equalize is not accurate, because the extent of equalization of a flat grant depends on the size of the grant and in what ratio it stands to local funds. If, for example, there were no local revenues for education and all funds came from the state level, then a flat grant would be fully equalizing. Or if a flat grant represented a substantial percentage of all state and local funds, then a considerable amount of equalization would be achieved.

The basic arguments against flat grants are that they may reduce efficiency and equality. It is highly inefficient for states to try to equalize their education programs by heaping flat grants on school districts which already have substantially more resources than other districts in the state. In fact, it is difficult for most states to find sufficient resources to equalize local inability even when fiscal capacity is taken into account.

Full fiscal equalization can never be attained with a flat grant system so long as local revenues supplement state funds. Equalization grants, in addition to having the potential for obtaining full fiscal neutrality, provide a more efficient method by redistributing state dollars from the more affluent areas to the less fortunate school districts.

The effects of a flat grant as a basic state aid can be illustrated by using the hypothetical NEFP prototype state shown in Figure 12–1.[8] Here we assume that the flat grant is distributed per weighted pupil, which effectively adjusts for educational needs but not for fiscal capacity of the school district. A legal limit of 12 mills is allowed for each school district, which we assume is levied, producing only $267 per weighted pupil in the least wealthy school district and $1,554 in the most wealthy. Without a required local effort or a charge-back, the state funds flow in the same amount to rich and poor alike. The modest equalization effects of the flat-grant approach are revealed by the rich-poor ratio. With only 12 mills of local funds, excluding the state flat grant, the revenue ratio between most and least wealthy districts is about 6 to 1, but when the flat grant is included the revenue ratio is reduced to about 2 to 1. Obviously, equalization has taken place but full fiscal equalization cannot be achieved.

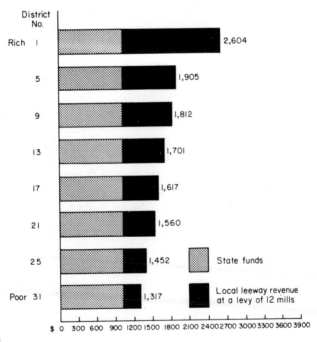

FLAT GRANT MODEL (dollars per weighted pupil based on 12-mill local levy plus state funds)

FIGURE 12–1

The economic inefficiency of flat grants alone has been sufficient to drive many states toward more equitable means of distributing funds. At the turn of the century, flat grants were used extensively, basing a given amount on the census of children of school age in a school district or county.[9] Today North Carolina and Kentucky have major grant programs which could be defined as types of flat grants. Both states, though, provide for various types of pupil need weightings which prevent their programs from being simple dollar per scholar financing. Thus, both states would be classified as having variable flat grants. North Carolina has traditionally provided such a high percentage of state aid that it has much greater fiscal equalization than most states which distribute funds by taking local fiscal capacity into account.

Flat grants are commonly used by many states as supplementary categorical aid to the basic or general state school finance program. Such categorical funds are usually either "pupil targeted instructional programs" or "pupil support services." Among the former are support for handicapped children, compensatory education for culturally deprived, vocational and bilingual education programs. Categorical flat grants for "pupil support services" are usually for transportation, textbooks, materials, educational television and school food services.

If these categorical flat grants become too numerous, they may significantly detract from the equalization of the basic state equalization formula, particularly if monies are placed in categorical flat grants in lieu of the basic state equalization program. While flat grants may have some equalizing tendencies, they are certainly less effective than the same amounts of money channeled through a program which equalizes local fiscal capacity. Thus, if state monies are distributed through flat categorical funds rather than through the basic aid program, the equalization effects of the total program may be substantially reduced.

THE FOUNDATION PROGRAM

The foundation program concept embodies the ideal that all students throughout each state, regardless of where they live, should be entitled to participate and receive maximum benefits from a program of education designed to meet their needs.

The terms *foundation program* and *equalization program* are often used interchangeably. Generally, the term foundation program has been preferred during recent years. In reality, it signifies the essential educational opportunities which should be provided through the public schools for all students, regardless of the wealth of the district in which they live or attend school. It is the program which should be supported throughout the state on a partnership basis by an equitable combination of state and local funds. The use of this term is designed to center attention on the program of essential educational opportunities, but it necessarily has important implications for the provisions for financing schools. On the other hand, the term equalization program tends to center attention on the financial provisions rather than on the educational program itself.

The foundation program has proven to be the most commonly acceptable method of state school financing. Today 29 states use foundation program formulas to distribute basic state school funds.[10]

In practical terms, the foundation program concept implies a plan for financing schools that requires equity for taxpayers as well as equity and adequacy of opportunity for students. It means that the resources of each state—and, by implication, of the nation—must be used to provide the financial support required to meet basic educational needs. Thus, the wealthiest citizens and people in the wealthiest communities should be expected to make as much financial effort to support the foundation program of education as the poorest. To attain this objective would mean a change in the customary way of doing things for people in a number of states and communities.

The concept of the foundation program was first introduced in the Strayer-Haig Educational Finance Inquiry in New York in 1923.[11] This study showed the inconsistency between reward for effort and the principle of equalization. The contributions of Strayer and Haig were discussed in detail in Chapter 10.

Strayer and Haig, in reality, presented a new theory in educational finance, which constituted the basis for studies and developments that have resulted in revolutionizing provisions for financing schools in a number of states. The foundation program plan has provided a partnership basis for supporting aspects of the educational program included in the plan. Both the state and districts provide on an equitable basis the funds needed to support the foundation program level of educational opportunity financed throughout the state. Beyond this program, each district may provide funds to finance additional or higher quality services in accordance with the desires of the board and the citizens of the district, but within the limits of state laws or constitutional provisions.

The following statements regarding the foundation program concept are of interest:

> The concept of the foundation program has proved highly useful as a device for differentiating the responsibility of the state as a whole from the additional responsibilities assumed by local communities on their own initiative.[12]

> The foundation program is more than a device for apportioning state aid for schools. In effect, it determines the level of education available to children in local units which have so little taxpaying ability that they can supplement it very little from local resources, no matter how great a tax effort they make.[13]

> Early systems of raising state revenues and apportioning them to schools lacked a rationale. Modern systems of state school finance are those which are based on research and planning. This provides a rationale which in its simplest form consists of sensibly determining: (1) What is to be financed. (2) How much it will cost.

(3) What sources of revenue are available. (4) How the revenues may be tapped to meet the costs. (5) How to apportion state school revenue.[14]

The concept of the foundation program is that of establishing an equitable fiscal partnership between the state as a whole and the individual school systems charged with the responsibility and privilege of operating the public schools.[15]

The foundation program should constitute an expression of, and a plan for implementing, the state's responsibility for the essential educational opportunities to be provided through its public elementary and secondary schools. In reality, no aspect of the educational program which is considered essential should be omitted in any state. In practice, however, only a few states have thus far developed a comprehensive foundation program plan.

A comprehensive foundation program plan has decided advantages, if properly developed, over a partial or special-purpose foundation program. As pointed out by Mort and Reusser, the foundation program should include "(1) all the activities the state wishes to assure the communities of least ability to support schools, and (2) the whole range of expenditure involved."[16]

There is a difference between excluding important elements that are found only in some of the districts of a state and excluding features that are distinctly experimental or pioneering in nature. For example, let us assume that generally only the wealthier districts in a state have provided services for exceptional children or have established kindergartens. If such services are considered essential, they should be included in the foundation program, even though they are not provided in all districts. To exclude them would mean that they could not be provided in many of the poorest districts. It would be unrealistic in the light of the needs and demands of a modern program of education.

If most foundation programs are unsatisfactory as far as scope is concerned, even more are unsatisfactory in terms of adequacy of financial support. Several still have the characteristics of the obsolete "weak district" plan for state support which is based on the false assumption that if a state provides some "equalization aid" for the poorer districts, it has established a foundation and therefore has met its major responsibility.

Educational Need and Fiscal Equalization in the Foundation Program

The foundation program has two basic aspects: (1) the program level of services established by the state, and (2) the fiscal equalization aspect, which combines state and local resources to fund the program. Greater elaboration regarding the establishment of the desired level program is given in the preceding chapter of this book, where measurement of need and application of costs are discussed. As indicated in that chapter, program level is generally measured in terms of weighted classroom units, weighted average daily attendance or membership, or full-time equivalent (FTE) pupils. State methodology varies considerably.

As mentioned above, the foundation program level can also be established without a great elaboration of educational needs and program costs, by the state simply establishing an amount per pupil. The fiscal equalization aspect of the foundation program constitutes the combining of state and local tax funds to finance the established program. Quite simply, the formula is Foundation Program Level (Educational Needs and Costs) *minus* Required Local Effort (or charge back) *equals* state aid. The required local effort is the tax effort each school district must make to supply its share of the foundation program. The term charge back may be used in some states where the state does not require a particular tax levy but instead merely deducts an amount determined to be the district's share, based on the fiscal capacity of the local school district.

To explain and simplify, let us assume that we have two school districts, the state's richest (A) and the poorest, (B); the richest district, A, has seven times the wealth of the poorest. Suppose they both had 2,000 pupils in average daily membership but district B had more handicapped and compensatory needs, resulting in a greater weighting of educational needs. After weighting the number of children with special needs and multiplying them times the costs of programs, it is found that district A had only 2,100 weighted average daily membership (WADM) to district B's 2,400. If the value of the weighted unit is say $2,000, then district A's foundation program allotment would be 2,100 WADM *times* $2,000 = $4,200,000, while district B's foundation program allotment would be $4,800,000. Let us further assume that a 10-mill levy in district B will raise only $300 per WADM, but will raise $1,800 per WADM in district A. Then district A's state aid per WADM would be $2,000 *minus* $1,800 or $200 per WADM. While district B's state aid per WADM would be $2,000 *minus* $300, or $1,700. The foundation level established in this hypothetical situation would provide all school districts with some money, even the richest, district A. The foundation program, therefore, fully equalizes for educational needs, as defined by the state, and fully fiscally equalizes up to the state prescribed level, in our example, $2,000. The foundation program approach does not, however, equalize beyond that state prescribed level.

The foundation program formula is computed as follows:

$$S_i = P_iF - rV_i$$

where:

S_i = state equalization aid to ith district
P_i = pupils, ADA, ADM, or FTE weighted for costs of program, in ith district
F = foundation program dollar value
r = mandated tax rate
V_i = assessed valuation of property of the ith district.

Combining State and Local Revenues

There are two major problems in determining the proportion and amount of the total cost of the foundation program to be provided by local effort and by state effort. The first pertains to the percentage of the total cost of the program to be provided from the state and from local funds; the second pertains to development of procedures for assuring uniform and equitable local effort.

In most states, practically all state funds are derived from sources other than property taxes, whereas most local funds for schools are provided through local property-tax levies. Theoretically, therefore, except in those states which have state property taxes or substantial sources of local revenue derived from other than property taxes, the percentage of local funds to be used toward the cost of the foundation program on a state-wide basis should be somewhat related to the sources of income of the people of the state. If most of the income of the residents is derived from sources other than property, the largest percentage of funds for support of the foundation program should come from state sources. However, there is another factor to be considered. All or most districts levy some taxes for the current program in addition to those required for the foundation program, and many also have tax levies for bond retirement. Most of these revenues are derived from levies on property. This suggests, therefore, that the largest percentage of funds for support of the foundation program in all states should come from state sources. This percentage will vary from state to state, but probably in most states from 70 to 80 percent or more of the cost should come from state sources.

Equalization Effect of Required Local Effort

Fiscal equalization of the foundation program can be increased or decreased by adjusting the level of required local effort. If required local effort is increased, the revenue from local tax leeway is decreased, reducing the disparity between rich and poor school districts. Using the NEFP prototype state of 32 school districts referred to earlier, the equalization impact of a 5-mill increase in required local effort can be illustrated. Figure 12–2 shows Model A as having a program with the same total dollars as Model B, but B has a required local effort of 10 mills, while A has only 5 mills. The equalization effect shows where revenues of the wealthiest district, No. 1, are reduced from $2,226 per weighted pupil in Model A to $1,845 in Model B, while the least wealthy school district, No. 31, has an increase of revenues from $1,473 per weighted pupil in Model A to $1,629 in Model B. Keep in mind that the state has not increased its contribution, and the value of the total program is the same; the funds have been merely redistributed by the change in required local effort.

From this comparison, one can see how politically difficult it may be to raise the required local effort without increasing the total amount of funds in the foundation program. Without raising the overall level, the process becomes one of "leveling down" in order to increase equalization. Experience in several states has shown that "leveling up," that is allowing the wealthiest district to maintain or slightly increase its revenue per weighted pupil, is much more politically feasible. The difficulty with the foundation program concept is manifest, though, in this dilemma, and more often than not equalization is severely

EQUALIZATION EFFECT OF AN INCREASE IN REQUIRED LOCAL EFFORT
UNDER FOUNDATION PROGRAM

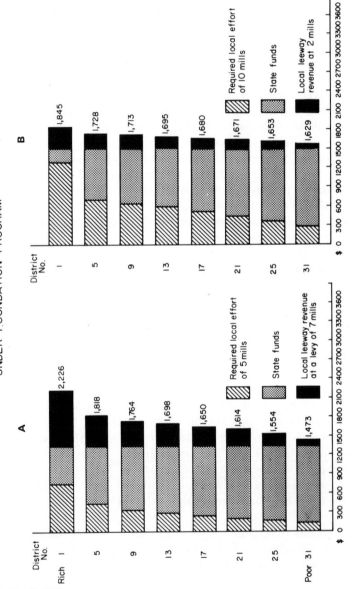

FIGURE 12-2

limited because the state is not willing to provide the additional resources required to fully equalize.

FULL STATE FUNDING

Full state funding assumes that the state government should be responsible for raising all of the revenue for support of the public elementary and secondary schools. Local school districts would not have taxing authority, and thus, could not supplement state funds with locally derived revenues. In the early 1970s the concept of full state funding was looked upon favorably in some quarters. For example, the Fleischmann Commission in New York State recommended full state funding as an effective means of accomplishing fiscal equalization.[17] As observed in an earlier chapter of this text, the concept of full state funding is credited to Henry C. Morrison, who, in his 1930 book, *School Revenue*, proposed that all school funds be collected and distributed from the state level. Morrison reasoned that education is a state and not a local function and as such, should not allow local fiscal capacity to affect educational opportunity. Morrison noted that education is different from most other local functions in that the benefits and costs of education programs "spill over" from one district to another throughout a state. He maintained that if education was viewed as a local function, then rich districts would always acquire greater resources than poorer urban slums and underprivileged rural areas. He said, "Our people still largely think of public education as a purely individual and local benefit . . . poor school districts are looked upon as poor relations at best, and perhaps not even that relationship is acknowledged."[18]

State legislatures, though, have not been enthusiastic about moving to full state funding. Today, only Hawaii can be classified as having such a system. Hawaii has a single, unified, state school system under the fiscal control of the governor and the legislature. Revenues to support the public schools are generated from state sales and personal net income taxes.

Full state funding as considered here does not in its pure sense allow any low taxing leeway. Some people speak of almost full state funding, which could actually be interpreted to be a program similar to that of North Carolina. Some maintain that, since the state controls the level of required local effort, the entire state foundation or equalization program constitutes state funding. Too, it would be possible to have full state funding of current operation and allow funds for capital outlay and debt service to derive from local taxation. Full state funding, though, in the context in which we discuss it, assumes all funds would flow from state revenue sources, and state legislation would provide complete fiscal control. In this regard, the Advisory Commission on Intergovernmental Relations has observed that "nearly" full state funding could quickly detract from the entire concept. In so commenting, the ACIR has stated that: "failure to circumscribe the amount of local enrichment—by limiting it to 10 percent of the state grant, for example—would undermine its . . . objective—[to create] a fiscal environment more conducive to educational opportunity."[19]

Full state funding would not guarantee absolute equality of educational opportunity, since the vagaries of state politics would still play an extremely important role. Legislators could still advance various rationales for assisting their own local constituencies to the detriment of children in other school districts. It would, however, remove the extraneous variables of local fiscal capacity and effort from considerations of equal educational opportunity. As Lindman has observed: "Perhaps the most obvious result of complete state support or of state operation of schools would be the equalization of school tax burdens."[20]

But certainly many problems are manifest in such a drastic change in school financing in this country. Advantages may be self-evident from an equalization perspective, but other considerations may also weigh heavily on such a decision.

Rossmiller has observed that: " . . . full state funding will not be a panacea for all the ills which afflict elementary and secondary education. Full state funding would eliminate or reduce some problems, but probably would aggravate other problems."[21] Full state funding would produce equal dollars per weighted pupil among all school districts. With all local taxes abolished, local revenue disparities would be eliminated, thus complete equalization would be attained. Should the state use distribution criteria that would concentrate resources in certain types of school districts, for example, the Florida cost of living factor, then the amounts per pupil would vary.

Methods of fund allocation under full state funding could also vary. A state may choose to distribute funds using a general or block grant approach that allows substantial local autonomy. At the other extreme, the state could budget all educational expenditures directly or follow the Hawaiian approach, whereby the state education agency prepares the state budget after reviewing and approving budget requests from each of the seven administrative school districts.

Or a state could follow the approach used in North Carolina to fund its state-aid program. North Carolina fully funds its basic support program, which consists of a state teacher-salary schedule and an administrators' salary schedule in addition to several additional programs for pupil targeted instructional programs and pupil support services. These various allocations are so numerous that, when combined, they constitute practically all elements of the budget for school operation. Such an approach is more confining than general or block grants and more restrictive than most foundation programs, but less restrictive than that of Hawaii. North Carolina, while having a funding program that could be a model for full state funding, is itself actually quite far from full state funding, since local funds in North Carolina account for about 25 percent of school revenues.

The most overt advocacy position toward full state funding yet was by the aforementioned Fleischmann Commission in New York in 1972. Its recommendation called for use of full state funding to "remove disparities in educational spending that are unrelated to educational requirements of students or geographical differences in prices of educational services."[22]

PERCENTAGE EQUALIZING

With a percentage equalizing formula, the state responds to local financial initiative for support of the public schools. Each local school district establishes its own expenditure level within state limits, and the state equalizes the expenditure by providing state funds based on the district's relative fiscal capacity. Philosophically, this is quite different from the foundation program, wherein a uniform level of assured funding is established by the state in terms of uniform cost units provided in the foundation program. The foundation program is, thus, a fixed unit formula, whereas percentage equalizing is a variable unit formula. Variable in the sense that the dollar level to which the equalizing percentage is applied may vary with each school district according to its expenditure level.

In theory, percentage equalizing does not mandate a minimum level of effort as does the foundation program, but instead simply equalizes the level of effort reflected by each local school district's expenditure level. Similarly, percentage equalizing is capable of fully equalizing all local tax revenues up to the richest in the state. Contrarily, the foundation program only equalizes up to the state-established dollar level of the foundation program, and local revenue above this creates disparities in relation to the fiscal capacity and effort of each school district. If implemented in its unrestrained form, the percentage equalizing formula fully neutralizes differences in fiscal capacity, while giving incentive for increasing local tax effort. Under this approach, the dollar level of the local educational program is a function of local tax effort but not of fiscal capacity. A poor school district with a high level of effort will be able to maintain the same quality educational program as a wealthy school district putting forth the same effort. In other words, if all districts tax themselves at 10 mills, each will have the same state and local resources regardless of local fiscal capacity.

The arithmetic of percentage equalizing is computed as follows:

$$S_i = ADM \left(1 - C \times \frac{V_i}{V_s}\right) E_i$$

where:

S_i = state aid to the ith district
C = constant arbitrarily selected having value between 0 and 1.0
V_i = assessed valuation per pupil in ith district
V_s = assessed valuation per pupil in state
E_i = educational expenditure level selected in the ith district

The constant C may be set at whatever percent the total local share is of the total school support in the state. Therefore, $1-C$ will represent the state share. To illustrate, let us assume that the local assessed valuation of property is $20,000 per pupil ($V_i$) and the state assessed valuation per pupil is $40,000 ($V_s$). We set the constant (C) at 0.6, and further, we assume this school district has 2,000 pupils in average daily membership and expends $1,500 ($E_i$) per pupil per year.

$$S = 2000 \left(1 - .6 \times \frac{\$20,000}{\$40,000}\right) \; \$1,500$$

State aid would then equal .70 × $1,500, or $1,050 per pupil in ADM times 2,000 pupils in ADM, or $2,100,000 state aid for the school district.

Now compare this result with a school district with the same number of pupils in ADM, 2,000; the same expenditure level, $1,500; the same constant (C) of 0.6, but with a school district with a greater wealth of $30,000 assessed valuation per ADM. The result is as follows: The state aid would equal .55 times $1,500, or $825 per pupil in ADM times 2,000 pupils in ADM or $1,650,000 total state aid for the school district.

The impact of variation in local wealth can be readily seen from this example. The feature, though, which distinguishes percentage equalizing from the foundation program is the ability to apply the wealth ratio to differing local expenditure levels. Therefore, if the .55 ratio in the latter example were applied to a $2,200 per-pupil expenditure, this school district would have received $1,210 per pupil in ADM, a total in state aid for the school district of $2,420,000. Greater local fiscal effort is rewarded at the same level for both wealthy and less wealthy school districts.

But what if the percentage constant (C) is raised to, say, .80; how does this affect equalization?

Then the state-aid-percentage is less, and consequently the school district would get a smaller portion of funds from the state. Thus, the constant (C), if established at 0.5, will result in the state providing 50 percent of the funds for the school district with average wealth; at 0.6, 40 percent; at 0.8, 20 percent, and so on. The lower this constant is set, the greater the potential for equalization.

Figure 12–3 shows a profile of a hypothetical state where the state grant is percentage equalizing. Here it is assumed that rich district No. 1 and poor district No. 31 put forth the same effort and thereby acquire fully equalized results. Too, the local districts in this model are limited to a total of 17 mills. Such limitations are in theory unnecessary, but, as a practical matter, legislatures have felt compelled to place such limitations on local school board prerogatives. Of course, most states give some leeway above such limits, to be invoked by voter approval. In this idealized version, the state is completely fiscally equalized. Too, it assumes that the poor districts put forth as much or more local fiscal effort than the rich school districts. This assumption probably has little

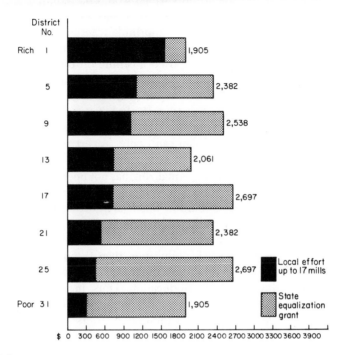

PERCENTAGE EQUALIZING GRANT
(dollars per weighted pupil)

District No.	
Rich 1	1,905
5	2,382
9	2,538
13	2,061
17	2,697
21	2,382
25	2,697
Poor 31	1,905

Local effort up to 17 mills

State equalization grant

$ 0 300 600 900 1200 1500 1800 2100 2400 2700 3000 3300 3600 3900

FIGURE 12–3

validity, since most studies indicate that the very rich put forth low effort because they don't need the extra money, and the middle and very poor often put forth low effort for a variety of economic, social, and political reasons. Thus, incentive grants of this type have not been shown to fiscally equalize as the chart shows, because of idiosyncracies in effort.

Since the percentage equalizing formula was first seriously advanced by Updegraff and King in 1922, only seven states have adopted it for use as a basic aid formula: Iowa, Massachusetts, Maine, New York, Pennsylvania, Rhode Island, and Vermont. The plan has not been short of academic adherents,[23] yet state legislatures have never been enthusiastic over the concept. The reasons for this can probably be reduced to four. First and foremost, it places the state in a reactive rather than a proactive mode. State appropriations must respond to local tax effort in each district of the state. Such uncertainty makes legislatures uncomfortable in tight budgetary periods, which is most of the time.

Second, no educational plan is prescribed at the state level and no attempt is made to measure local educational needs or costs. Advocates of local control are comfortable with such a scheme, but legislators tend to want to exercise more authority over use of the funds than percentage equalizing in its raw form permits.

Next, a system of full fiscal equalization is extremely difficult to implement because of the great state expenditures which would be required to bring the poorest district up to the level of the richest. Consequently, limitations have been placed on the percentage equalizing formula where it has been adopted, which basically changes its nature to something more akin to the foundation program. For example, New York imposed a ceiling on the local expenditure level beyond which the state would not equalize. Such modification effectively negates the perceived benefit of local determination and results in reversion to a type of foundation program. This is particularly true where all districts are at or near the state-prescribed expenditure level. Polley noted this in New York when he pointed out that such a plan can easily "revert back to a foundation program."[24]

The last reason that percentage equalizing has not been popular is because it does not mandate a required level of local effort. Anyone who has studied the politics of education realizes that low financial effort for the public schools may result from a myriad of social and economic issues, few of which have anything to do with children or education. Too, it is widely held that the poor and ignorant have less aspiration for education than the better educated and more affluent. More and better education generally breeds a demand for higher quality education. Education derives education. Thus, in many cases it is necessary for the state to intervene to demand a uniform level of effort for education, to bring the poor- and low-aspiration districts upward. Percentage equalizing does not lend itself to such state action.

DISTRICT POWER EQUALIZING

District Power Equalizing (hereinafter called DPE) is a method of equalizing district tax bases so that all school children will have access to the same resources. It is a method of distributing state funds, which is a *very* close relative of percentage equalizing in theory and may be the same as percentage equalizing under certain circumstances. In theory, DPE has three important characterizations. First, disparities in fiscal capacity among school districts are entirely equalized, so that a child's education is not a function of local school district capacity but of the state's as a whole. Second, local school districts are allowed to levy whatever tax rate they desire and are fully equalized. Under this approach, a child's education is a function of local tax effort but not of wealth. Third, a recapture provision controls the amount of equalizing funds which a state grants to local school districts. This provision mandates that the very wealthy school districts which raise funds above a certain revenue limit with a prescribed local tax rate will have to pay the extra back into a central state education fund for redistribution to other school districts. While the recapture feature is not new and has, in fact, been used in Utah in concert with its foundation program, the proponents of DPE have popularized the concept.

This scheme of financing was devised by Coons, Clune and Sugarman in 1970 as an alternative during the era when state school-aid formulas were under increasing judicial scrutiny.[25] It was Coons and his colleagues who provided the conceptual basis for the plaintiffs in the famous California Supreme Court case, *Serrano* v. *Priest*, where that state's system of school finance was held to violate the California constitution.[26]

DPE premises the removal of wealth as a determinant to use of local school revenues to completely equalize tax resources among all school districts. In theory this is no different from either the foundation program or percentage equalizing, because if both were geared to the wealthiest district in the state as the "key district," then full equalization would take place. The practicality of financing, though, has never allowed this to happen in either case, because to level-up to the richest requires an inordinate amount of tax resources in most states. Of course, another alternative is full state funding, as previously discussed, and yet another alternative, a nonfiscal one, is to reorganize the school districts of the state in such a way as to give each the same or approximately the same resources per pupil. DPE seeks to do this with a formula which guarantees all districts a resource base of equivalent value.

DPE works as follows. Let us assume that we have two school districts; district A has $10,000 per pupil assessed valuation and district B has $20,000. If they both levy a property tax of 10 percent, then district A will raise $1,000 per pupil, while district B raises $2,000 with the same effort. If the goal were to equalize resources to the $20,000 assessed valuation per-pupil level, then the state would supplement district A's revenues in the amount of $1,000.

This, alone, is not dissimilar from the foundation program or percentage equalizing, but DPE has two additional features. First, it is designed to place no or few limits on local tax effort, high or low. In theory, a district could levy as little or as much as it chooses, and the state would equalize. Coons and his coauthors do acknowledge that the state may want to require a statutory minimum tax effort below which a school district would not be allowed to go; "it should represent merely a sound educational base,"[27] not so high that it would deny effective local decision making, but high enough to assure equal opportunity.[28] But they admonish against "overambitious use of both minimum and maximum rates"[29] for fear that local control would be diminished.

Second, the recapture feature provides that if a district's revenues exceed the prescribed dollar-per-pupil limit, then the recapture is invoked. In the earlier example, let us assume that all districts were equalized to the level of district B. Then, where a district with $30,000 assessed valuation per pupil raises $3,000 with a 10 percent tax, it would have to rebate $1,000 back to the state general education fund, bringing it back in line with the resources of district B. This money would, of course, help ameliorate the state's revenue problems, and would theoretically make DPE more fiscally feasible.

To implement DPE, the state establishes a schedule which shows local property-tax rates corresponding to expenditures per pupil. When a district levies a particular tax rate, it will obtain the revenues necessary from local and state sources to sustain the prescribed expenditure. If it collects less than the expenditure level, the state supplements; if more, the state recaptures.

Table 12–1 represents a hypothetical DPE schedule. It shows a linear relationship between tax rate and level of expenditure. The assumption here is that each school district's resources are equalized to $30,000 assessed valuation per pupil. A school district which raises more from the prescribed tax rate than the established expenditure will be subject to the recapture provision. For example, suppose a school district chooses the $5.00 tax rate in the first column but has an assessed valuation of $35,000 per pupil, resulting in revenues of $1,750 per pupil, this would exceed the $1,500 in the second column (Schedule A) by $250, which would then be recaptured. If, though, a school district chooses the $5.00 tax rate but has only $10,000 of assessed valuation per pupil, then it would raise only $500 per pupil, resulting in a state grant supplement of $1,000.

Several modifications of the basic DPE concept have been advanced by school finance theorists. One which Coons and his colleagues suggested originally was that the DPE expenditure schedule be based on weighted pupil units rather than simple per-pupil count. This would introduce the educational needs and costs aspects of the traditional foundation program into the DPE determinations. Further, it has been proposed that the relationship between the tax rate and expenditures per pupil should flatten out at the higher expenditure levels, producing a "kink" in the relationship. (See the second Schedule B in Table 12–1.) Districts with tax rates below the "kink," $1,400, gain substantially as they move up to that predetermined point, but those above gain revenues at a more reduced level per increase in tax levy. In other words, expenditures would not be allowed to rise as fast as the revenues the tax rate would produce above a given point. Such a restraint would presumably discourage a continued upward climb of school tax rates after a certain level.[30] This type of limitation, if too severe, would effectively cap off the local tax rate, producing the type of limitation that legislatures have generally required but have traditionally dealt with in a more direct and simple manner, by prohibiting the local levies beyond a given maximum tax rate.[31]

To date, only Wisconsin among the 50 states has adopted a plan which could be characterized as DPE as envisioned by Coons and his fellow theorists. The Wisconsin plan was enacted in 1973 and included a negative aid or recapture provision with a "kinked" schedule.* The Wisconsin experiment with pure DPE was, however, short-lived because the recapture provision was held to be unconstitutional by the Wisconsin Supreme Court before the law became effective.

Several states have enacted small supplementary programs which probably could be classified as either DPE or percentage equalizing. An example of a program entitled DPE, but actually percentage equalizing, is found in

---

*The authors wish to express appreciation to Richard A. Rossmiller, University of Wisconsin, for his comments regarding the nature of the Wisconsin formula.

Kentucky. The Kentucky plan, though, only amounts to 4 percent of state foundation program funds for public schools and only equalizes up to a total tax rate of about seven cents per hundred dollars of assessed valuation. The fund was only $31 million per pupil in 1981–82, a very small amount compared with Kentucky's major aid program, through which $780 million was distributed in the same year. Other states have usually used the DPE approach only in a similar limited way, to supplement a much larger education fund.

Reluctance on the part of states to adopt DPE as their primary or major general state-aid formula may be attributed to several reasons, First, there persists a feeling the DPE, to a large extent, abdicates the state's responsibility to establish an efficient and uniform basic educational program throughout. Further, legislatures like to know what they are funding. In many instances, the legislative concern is for specific educational needs—the handicapped, compensatory education, vocational education, or teachers' salaries. This type of identification is not feasible with DPE.

Second, the state's legal responsibility to provide for education extends beyond fiscal equalization to adequacy of educational programs. Adequacy of funding is not guaranteed by the state in the DPE program; it merely provides that the state will equalize whatever the locality decides to do. Third, the recapture provision,* which is a prominent difference between percentage equalizing and DPE, in its idealized form, is not popular. Politically, it is difficult to restrict state aid to wealthy school districts and practically impossible, Utah withstanding, to enact legislation which forces them to pay their excess revenues into a state general education fund. The theory of recapture is good, but to believe that it is generally practicable may well be naive in most political settings.

Fourth, as mentioned previously, a child's education should not be a function of wealth of the locality, but neither should it be entirely a function of tax effort. The philosophy of minimal local restraint, which supports DPE, does not recognize the state's responsibility to assure children that their education will not be a function of the vagaries of local politics or of general community disregard for the value of education. Fifth, to allow local school districts nearly complete autonomy in setting their own tax rates and fully equalizing the fiscal disparities places state legislatures in a reactive mode when allocating state revenues. This, of course, as observed earlier, would be the same in an unlimited version of percentage equalizing grants. The uncertainty about how much money will be required from year to year to fund such a program makes legislatures extremely uncomfortable. Some legislators believe

*It should be noted that although a recapture provision is a feature of a pure DPE formula, such a negative-aid feature could actually be part of a foundation program or a percentage equalizing plan, if the program level were set high enough by the state. A recapture has been used with a foundation program in Utah for many years. See David Alexander, Richard Salmon & Van Mueller, "Alternative State Fiscal Equalization Systems," *The Foundation Program*, Indiana 93–380 Section 842 Study, directed by William Wilkerson (Indianapolis: Indiana Department of Education, 1977), pp. 37–50.

TABLE 12–1 District Power Equalizing of Basic Dollar Guarantee per Pupil

LOCAL TAX RATE PER $100 OF ASSESSED VALUATION	GUARANTEE PER PUPIL SCHEDULE (EXPENDITURE LEVEL)	
	SCHEDULE A	SCHEDULE B
$2.00 (minimum)	$ 600	$ 600
2.25	675	700
2.50	750	800
2.75	825	900
3.00	900	1000
3.25	975	1100
3.50	1050	1200
3.75	1125	1300
4.00	1200	1400
4.25	1275	1450
4.50	1350	1500
4.75	1425	1550
5.00	1500	1600
5.25	1575	1650
5.50	1650	1700
5.75	1725	1750
6.00	1800	1800

that DPE is tantamount to giving local school districts a blank check. With such a perception, a negative legislative response may well be predicted.

Last, to attempt to evaluate the success or failure of DPE in terms of its legislative acceptance is to realize that DPE is not a discrete type of formula at all, but rather so closely akin to percentage equalizing and to guaranteed valuation formulas that attempting to identify it as a separate formula is rather fruitless. Its main distinguishing features, the almost limitless local effort and the recapture provision, are so widely objectionable that it may well never be enacted in its originally intended form.

RADICAL SCHOOL FINANCE ALTERNATIVES

Lately, educational literature has been deluged with books and articles alleging the failure of the public schools. It is maintained by some reformers that the public schools are stultifying, intellectually limiting, and restrictive of opportunity.[32] Others assert that the public schools are capitalist tools to control the working class, vocationalizing the children into lower levels of blue-collar employment. Yet, others of essentially the same school of thought propose the complete deschooling of society—a kind of educational nihilism.[33]

On the opposite end of the political spectrum, we have *laissez-faire* economists and capitalists criticizing the public schools because they are said to limit individual choice and freedom.[34] Most vocal among this latter group is Milton Friedman, who sees the school system of the United States as an "island of socialism in a free market sea," wherein the state monopoly is unduly restrictive of educational liberty.[35] He acknowledges the value of education for maintenance of democratic society and observes that educational gain to children accrues not only to the benefit of the child and parent but to members of society at large (the "neighborhood effect"). This "neighborhood effect," as he calls it, justifies governmental action to finance education, but he quarrels with the present methods used to finance the schools.[36] It is his position that both compulsory attendance laws and the system used to finance the schools create a monolithic educational structure which resists change and limits individual choices and freedoms.[37]

Vouchers

Friedman's solution is the "voucher system," which he first advanced in 1955, when he proposed that government finance the schools but not administer them.[38] He points out that the implicit assumption that government's role is to provide schooling by paying, subsidizing, and administering the schools is not necessarily valid. The two steps, he claims, can be separated, with government financing the schools through vouchers but not actually conducting the educational program. Under such a system, government would give parents a voucher redeemable at a specified maximum sum per child per year, if spent on approved educational services. Parents could supplement, or "add on," to the voucher in any amount they desire, to buy more expensive educational services. Government's role would be limited to insuring that the schools meet minimum standards similar to those minimum sanitary standards required of restaurants.[39] Presumably, under this scheme, public schools would continue to exist but would enter the marketplace on the same footing with private and parochial schools. In other words, government could continue to administer certain schools, hire teachers, and conduct programs, but these schools would receive only the resources they could acquire from vouchers or, in the alternative public schools, that could be administered and financed directly by the state. But the state would be required to provide the same financing for students who choose to attend approved schools, private and parochial.

According to Friedman, the voucher plan would improve education by (1) giving parents greater freedom to choose a desirable educational program for their children, (2) doing away with the educational monopoly of public education, and (3) increasing competition among schools, so that each would become more effective and efficient.

Today, 26 years after Friedman first proposed the voucher system, no state has seen fit to adopt it. Problems with the voucher are numerous, not the least of which is the likelihood that it would allow more affluent parents to "add on" resources and send their children to better quality schools, leaving the poor and middle classes more limited choices among the less expensive lower or minimally approved schools. Coons and Clune have disagreed with Friedman with regard to the "add on" and have proposed what they consider to be an improved system, family power equalizing.[40]

Family Power Equalizing

In the same vein as the voucher, this approach, it is said, "makes the consumer king" and gives the parents freedom to shop for the type of education they desire for their children.[41]

The difference between the two is that the Friedman voucher is a flat grant, where family power equalizing is equalized, based on the individual family income. In keeping with its equalization purpose, family power equalizing would not allow the "add on" of the voucher system.

This type of voucher would require that each family contribute to the educational support of its child in accordance with the family's ability to pay. Ability to pay would be measured in terms of the income level of the family, and the voucher would vary according to both the income and the expenditure of the school. Every school would be required to establish an expenditure per pupil per year falling into one of four expenditure catagories set by the state. The expenditure of the school would not be allowed to fall below or rise above its chosen expenditure level. Secondary schools could adopt a higher expenditure level than elementary schools. The family would be assessed a special income tax in accordance with the chosen expenditure level. A progressive rate structure for such a tax would force families who are better off financially to pay a greater percentage of the selected expenditure level than families from poorer circumstances. Thus, if a family with $10,000 income selected a school with a $2,000 per-pupil expenditure level, it could pay only $200 per pupil, receiving an $1,800 voucher. If a family with $40,000 income selected the same school, it would pay possibly $1,600 and receive only a $400 voucher. The extent of equalization would depend on the relationship between the expenditure levels selected by the school and the extent to which the tax structure is graduated.[42]

Even though this plan addresses the income inequality issue, it has met with no more success than the Friedman proposal. In the 11 years since it was first advanced, state legislatures have remained uninterested.

Tax Credits

A third type of financing scheme which could be classified along with vouchers is tax credits. Tax credits have been proposed at the federal level, yet they have important implications for state school finance. Should tax credits be enacted by federal legislation, the level of funding of traditional federal categorical aids would almost certainly decline, and the impact of such credits would undoubtedly tend to restructure the American education system. Tuition tax credits were introduced in the 1977–78 Congress by Senators Moynihan of

New York and Packwood of Oregon. The bill was defeated in 1978, but re-emerged in 1981 and is currently under serious consideration by the Congress. As introduced in 1981, the bill calls for a federal personal income tax credit to parents consisting of $250 or up on one-half of a student's tuition in private or parochial elementary or secondary schools. If enacted, the tax credit would increase to $500 the second year. Estimates of the cost to the federal treasury are difficult to estimate, but a good guess is that a $250 tax credit for one year would cost the U.S. Treasury from $1.5 to $3.0 billion.

The philosophical basis for tax credits is the same as for vouchers; they would increase parental choice and strengthen education through competition. Such proposals are attractive to many because they conjure up the picture of unfettered liberty in the pursuit of equal opportunity, yet many are convinced that the pitfalls of vouchers and tax credits may be much more injurious than beneficial to education.

OBJECTIONS TO VOUCHERS AND TAX CREDITS

Both vouchers and tax credits represent such extreme changes in the government's role in financing education that enactmant of such measures could basically restructure the American system of education. As discussed elsewhere in this text, the public schools of this country are both "free" and "common." Education should be free, because the societal benefits of education are so great that all should pay through general taxation for the education of all youth. Public schools were to be "common" in order to transmit "a common language, heritage, set of values, and knowledge. These are necessary for appropriate political functioning in our democratic society."[43] Public schools were designed to be places where all classes, privileged and underprivileged, rich and poor, regardless of religious or ethnic background, were to learn to work and live together in justice and harmony.[44]

Social Cohesion

Vouchers and tax credits will tend to create educational conditions contrary to the public, common-school purpose of social cohesion, mutual understanding, and socialization. Vouchers and tax credits may well encourage separation and balkinization of society through intensification of competition and distrust among individuals grouped by school, religious sect, and social and economic stratum.

Parental Limitation

Parental choice in all educational matters may not always be in the best interest of the child. The law is replete with hundreds of cases where parents of limited perspective or intelligence have sought to contract the spectrum of knowledge which their own and other children could acquire by seeking to purge the public school libraries of great works of art and literature and to restrain instruction regarding important scientific developments. In a system of vouchers and tax credits, the state would not be in a position to expand and extend the scope of knowledge; in fact, the voucher and tax credit would put state financial assistance in the service of the narrow political, religious, and ideological views of society. What parents do choose, under such systems, is likely to be a direct extension of the beliefs and values they already hold, "with little opportunity for students to experience the diversity of backgrounds and viewpoints that contribute to the democratic process."[45] An editorial in the *Washington Post* in 1978 probably best summarizes this objection to vouchers and tax credits.

> Most Americans understand that it takes a strong sense of national community to hold this huge and heterogeneous country together. That sense of community arises, above all, from public schools—the experience that a child shares with others of widely differing backgrounds and conditions for twelve years or so while growing up. Subsidies that encourage parents to take their children out of public schools will inevitably diminish this strength.[46]

Class Orientation

A person's choice of life-styles or education is limited by his or her awareness of the options. A prerequisite to the exercise of liberty to choose is the acquisition, by education, training, or experience, of knowledge of available alternatives. What constitutes success in life to the lower-middle-class, blue-collar parent may be much more limited than that of the upper-middle class. Poorer working-class parents appear to emphasize conformity in their children, while parents in higher income positions tend to stress independence of thought and expansiveness of thinking.[47] A tendency exists to select options which one's own experiences indicate are most rewarding; thus, limited experiences produce limited choices. Under the voucher or tax credit system, parental choices would be restricted to class orientations. The commonality and equality fostered by the public schools, where rich or poor alike attend school together, would be lost. Vouchers and tax credits would tend to foster a system of closer correspondence between children of parents of the same social class, reinforcing caste and class and reducing social mobility.

Church and State

One of the basic and unique tenets of the Constitution of the United States is that church and state should be held separate. The burden falls on the state to assure that children receive at least a minimum of secular education, yet have the freedom to acquire sectarian instruction as well. According to the U.S. Supreme Court, the state cannot inhibit, enhance, or become excessively entangled with religion. Since most of the private schools in this country have religious affiliation, aid to private schools generally means enhancement of religion. As discussed in an earlier chapter of this text, state grants or assistance which give incentive to parents to send their children to sectarian schools violates the Establishment Clause of the First Amendment.[48] Thus, both vouchers and tax credits are probably unconstitutional.

Friedman, more or less acknowledges this and suggests that the U.S. Supreme Court would accept a voucher plan which "excluded church-connected schools but applied to all other private and public schools."[49] Under such a condition, undoubtedly the voucher and tax credit movement would lose much of its political potency.

Equity

Vouchers and tax credits are probably deficient from the standpoint of both equality and social justice. Former Secretary of Health, Education and Welfare, Joseph Califano, in arguing against tax credits, pointed out that the rich are helped more than the poor. He said: "We cannot afford poverty programs for people who aren't poor."[50] Tax credits are inequitable for several reasons, but most obviously because they are given to rich and poor alike. Although equity could be increased by a negative tax provision, whereby parents not paying taxes would be paid directly by the federal government for the amount of the credit, the overall impact of the plan would still tend to favor the rich.

Too, no tax credit benefits whatsoever would go to any of the poor families who send their children to public schools. The vast majority of poor people in this country send their children to public schools. Children of the wealthy are often found in private, high tuition schools where tax credits would be most valuable. Tax credit benefits are skewed toward the wealthy.[51] Presently, 80.4 percent of the nonpublic-school families have incomes of over $15,000 per year. Catterall observes that "The recipients of the tuition tax credit dollars will tend to be higher income, whiter Americans; the recipients of current federal dollars for schools tend to be lower income and minority children."[52]

Friedman's voucher would have virtually the same inequitable impact as the tax credit. Coons' voucher, however, would correct this inequity by tying the voucher to family income level.

Segregation

Vouchers, both Friedman's and Coons', and tax credits would tend to segregate the schools along racial lines. Quite early in the desegregation era, the state of Virginia sought to use tuition grants and tax credits to maintain segregation in the public schools. The Supreme Court struck down this system, and state courts did likewise.[53]

Vouchers and tax credits would, undoubtedly, give new impetus and financial leverage to segregation of the educational system. Jacobs has shown that benefits from the Moynihan-Packwood tax credit scheme would flow disproportionately to white families.[54] Black enrollment makes up 15.7 percent of the public school enrollment, but only 6.4 percent of private school enrollment. Black families in the public schools would receive no tax credit benefits.[55]

Experience shows that the "freedom of choice" which proponents of vouchers and tax credits advance does not serve well to integrate the schools.[56] Black and white parents probably would not choose the same schools because of gaps between the two in educational attainment, aspiration, and social and economic conditions which permeate our society. At the present time, the public schools are the most integrated organ of American society. Neither the voucher nor the tax credit have features which would encourage integration; on the contrary, they give incentive to separating and division.

State Action in Private Schools

Perhaps one of the most important effects of either vouchers or tax credits would be to introduce state action into the private elementary and secondary schools. State action is a legal concept which declares that where private entities receive government benefits or have close governmental relationships, federal and state statutes and constitutional provisions apply equally with public schools. Where state action exists, government regulation legitimately enters the private sector. Many oppose vouchers and tax credits as aid to private and parochial schools, because it would bring these schools under state control. This type of state intervention has already transpired in higher education, where the federal government's primary aid mechanism is student-oriented tuition grants and loans. Ironically, Moynihan has complained bitterly of this kind of governmental intervention into private higher education, while at the same time proposing similar federal programs to assist private elementary and secondary schools.[57]

Summary

Thus, vouchers and tax credits would appear to have detrimental effects on both public and private elementary and secondary schools. Effectively, both approaches to funding could restructure education in this country, to the extent that no schools would be either public or private, but either quasi-public or quasi-private. The question is whether the benefits to be gained by movement toward a financing scheme which would allegedly enhance competition ultimately result in more losses than gains to individual, society and the economy. Ultimately all financial alternatives must be weighed in terms of their costs and benefits, and in the case of both vouchers and tax credits, the costs appear to far outweigh the benefits.

CRITERIA FOR EVALUATING
A STATE'S FINANCE PLAN

A comprehensive state school finance plan must deal with at least three major kinds of public policy issues:

1. The scope, content, and quality of the public school program
2. The organizational arrangements for providing public schooling
3. The level and method of financing the public school program

An adaptation of the criteria proposed by the National Educational Finance Project for the evaluation of a state's provisions for school financing is presented below.

Criteria Relating to Programs. The state school finance plan should:

1. Provide educational programs that meet the needs of all the educable and trainable children and youth of the state
2. Include provisions for innovation and improvement in instructional programs
3. Include provisions for the identification and evaluation of alternative methods of accomplishing educational objectives
4. Provide a system for local districts to develop program and financial data that permit accountability to the public
5. Give children access to needed educational programs throughout the state
6. Provide appropriate programs for adults

Criteria Relating to Organization. The state school finance plan should financially penalize or at least not financially reward:

1. The establishment or continuation of small inefficient school districts
2. The establishment or continuation of small inefficient enrollment centers, except in cases resulting from geographical isolation
3. The continuation or establishment of school districts that segregate pockets of wealth, or leave pockets of poverty in the state, or result in the segregation of pupils by race or socioeconomic class
4. The continuation or establishment of school enrollment centers that result in the segregation of pupils by race or socioeconomic class

Criteria Relating to Finance. The state school finance plan should:

1. Provide for equalization of educational opportunity by equalizing the financial resources of school districts in accordance with educational needs. The quality of a child's education should not be made dependent on the wealth of the district in which he lives nor should it depend substantially on the aspiration level of the people of that district.
2. Include all current expenditures and capital outlay and debt service in order to facilitate equitable budgetary planning for all phases of each district's educational program
3. Recognize variations in per-pupil program costs for local school districts associated with specialized educational activities needed by some but not all students, such as vocational education, education of exceptional or handicapped pupils, and compensatory education
4. Recognize differences in per-pupil local district costs associated with factors such as sparsity and density of population, e.g., pupil transportation, extra costs of isolated schools, and other necessary variations in the cost

of delivering educational services and facilities of equivalent quality throughout the states

5. Be funded through an integrated package that facilitates equitable budgetary planning by local school districts

6. Utilize objective measures in allocating state school funds to local school districts

7. Be based on a productive, diversified, and equitable tax system

8. Integrate federal funds with state funds and allocate them to local districts in conformance with proposed criteria, to the extent permitted by federal laws and regulations[57]

SUMMARY OF FINDINGS OF THE NATIONAL EDUCATIONAL FINANCE PROJECT CONCERNING ALTERNATIVE FINANCE MODELS

The National Educational Finance Project tested all of the commonly used models (plans) of state support. Following is a summary of the conclusions derived from these tests:

1. State funds distributed by any model tested provide for some financial equalization, but some finance models provide more equalization than others. Even the flat grant model provides for some equalization despite the fact that under this model each district, regardless of wealth or necessary variations in unit costs, receives the same amount of state money per pupil or other unit. This is due to the fact that the less wealthy districts receive more state aid per pupil than the revenue per pupil they contribute to the state treasury.

2. A flat grant model by which state funds are apportioned on the basis of a flat amount per pupil unit or other unit that does not take into consideration necessary variations in unit costs or variations in wealth per unit of need of local districts provides the least financial equalization for a given amount of state aid of any of the state-local support models tested.

3. A flat grant model under which necessary cost variations per unit of need are provided for but variations in the per pupil wealth of local districts are ignored provides for more equalization than the flat grant model described in 2 above but it does not equalize financial resources as well as the equalization models providing for cost differentials and variations in wealth.

4. Equalization models under which necessary unit cost differentials are provided for in computing the cost of the educational program equalized, and which take into consideration differences in the wealth of local school districts in computing state funds needed by a district, are the most efficient models examined for equalizing financing resources in states that use a state-local revenue model for financing schools.

5. In equalization models, the greater the local effort required in proportion to the legal limit of local taxes for schools, the greater the equalization.

6. In equalization models, the greater the local tax leeway above the required local tax effort required for the support of the foundation program, the less the equalization.

7. Complete equalization is attained only under full state funding or under an equalization model that requires school districts to contribute the full legal limit of local taxes to the cost of the foundation program.

8. The higher the percent of school revenues provided by the state, the greater the equalization of financial resources under both flat grant and equalization models, but there is always more equalizaton under an equalization model than a flat grant model for any given amount of state funds apportioned.

9. As full state funding is approached (100 percent of school revenue provided by the state) the difference between the equalizing potential of flat grant models and equalization models begins to disappear, assuming that cost differentials are provided for under each model. For example, with 90 percent or more state funding of schools, the differences between flat grant models and equalization models in equalizing financial resources would not be significant, but the equalization models would always be slightly superior until full state funding is reached.

10. As the percent of unequalized local revenue is increased, the possibility of equalizing financial resources decreases.

11. A complete local support model provides for no equalization whatsoever.

12. The higher the percent of state funds provided in relation to local revenue, the greater the progressivity of the tax structure for school support.

13. The higher the percent of federal funds provided in relation to state and local revenues, the greater the progressivity of the tax structure for school support. This is due to the fact that federal taxes are on the average more progressive than state taxes and state taxes are generally more progressive than local taxes.

14. Many states can increase the progressivity of state taxes by increasing the proportion of state revenue obtained from relatively progressive taxes.

15. A state support model that provides exclusively for unlimited percentage equalizing or district power equalizing in proportion to increases in local tax effort may tend to disequalize educational opportunity in a state, because the educational opportunities for children are made dependent upon the willingness of their parents to vote for local taxes for schools.[58]

SELECTING THE BEST MODEL

Which school finance model is the best model? That depends entirely on the values and goals of those making decisions on school fiscal policies. Following are some options:

1. If one believes that educational opportunities should be substantially equalized financially among the districts of a state, but that districts should be left with some local tax leeway for enrichment of the foundation program, an equalization model is the best model. However, the higher the priority one gives to equalization, the more he or she will prefer the equalization model that provides the most equalization.

2. If one believes that educational opportunities should be completely equalized financially among the districts of a state, the complete state support model is the preferred model.

3. If one believes that all children, regardless of variations in ability, talent, health, physical condition, cultural background, or other conditions that cause variations in educational needs, have a right to the kind of education that meets their individual needs, he or she will select school finance models that incorporate the programs needed and that provide for necessary cost differentials per unit of need.

4. If one believes that educational opportunity should be substantially equalized among the states, he or she will support a revenue model that provides a substantial percent of school revenue in general federal aid apportioned in such a manner as to tend to equalize opportunities among the states.

5. If one believes that the taxes for the support of the public schools should be relatively progressive rather than regressive, he or she will prefer revenue models that provide a high percent of school revenue from federal and state sources.

6. If one believes that public, financed education should tend to remove the barriers between caste and class and provide social mobility, he or she will oppose any plan of school financing that promotes the segregation of pupils by wealth, race, religion, or social class.

7. If one believes that all essential functions of state and local government should be equitably financed in relation to each other, he or she will oppose any finance model for any function of government, including education, under which either federal or state funds are allocated to local governments on the basis of "the more you spend locally, the more you get from the central government" rather than on the basis of need.

8. If one believes that the educational output per dollar of investment in education should be maximized, he or she will support finance models that will improve efficient district organization and efficient organization of school centers within districts.

9. If one believes in a federal system of government, he or she will support finance models that will not require a decision governing public education to be made at the federal level when it can be made at the state level, and he or she will not require a decision to be made at the state level when it can be made efficiently at the local level, regardless of the percent of revenue provided by each level of government.

10. If one believes that education is essential to the successful operation of a democratic form of government in a free-enterprise society, and if one believes that education is essential to the economic growth of the nation and to the fulfillment of the legitimate aspirations of all persons in our society, he or she will support revenue models sufficiently financed to meet educational needs adequately.[59]

NOTES

1. See Ellwood P. Cubberley, *School Funds and Their Apportionment* (New York: Teachers College, Columbia University, 1906), p. 15.

2. Roe L. Johns and Richard Salmon, "Criteria for Evaluating State Financing Plans for the Public Schools," in *Alternative Programs for Financing Education, Vol. 5,* eds. Roe L. Johns

and Kern Alexander (Gainesville, Fla.: National Educational Finance Project, 1971), pp. 231–63.

3. Arvid J. Burke, *Financing Public Schools in the United States*, rev. ed. (New York: Harper and Row Publishers, Inc. 1957), p. 395.

4. John Guy Fowlkes and George E. Watson, "A Report on State Financial Support and Local Educational Planning," mimeographed (Madison, Wisc.: University of Wisconsin, 1956), p. 80.

5. Cubberley, *op. cit.*, p. 123.

6. D.S. Lees, *Local Expenditure and Exchequer Grants* (London: Institute of Municipal Treasurers and Accountants, 1956), pp. 3–7, 156–60, 168–77, in *Perspectives of the Economics of Education*, ed. Charles S. Benson (Boston: Houghton Mifflin Company, 1963), pp. 354–63.

7. Johns and Alexander, eds., *op. cit.*, pp. 265–67.

8. Note: *Testing Proposals Graphically.* The National Educational Finance Project constructed a prototype state consisting of thirty-two actual school districts selected from more than one state. The most wealthy district had approximately six times the equalized valuation per weighted pupil as the least wealthy district, which is considerably less than the variation in most states. A number of alternative models were tested on the prototype state, few of which are presented in the charts in this chapter.

9. Cubberley, *op. cit.*, p. 100.

10. Esther O. Tron, *Public School Finance Programs 1978–79* (Washington, D.C.: U.S. Government Printing Office, 1980). Note: Since Tron's report, Kentucky has begun to collect the required local effort at the state level and distribute it back through the state aid formula. Although this does not make a difference in the level of equalization, it does change the technical classification of their funding scheme from a foundation to a variable flat grant.

11. George D. Strayer and Robert M. Haig, *The Financing of Education in the State of New York*, Report of the Educational Finance Inquiry Commission (New York: Macmillan, Inc., 1923), p. 173.

12. Paul R. Mort and Walter C. Reusser, *Public School Finance*, 2nd ed. (New York: McGraw-Hill Book Company, 1951), pp. 400–1.

13. Burke, *op. cit.*, pp. 445–46.

14. Francis G. Cornell and William P. McLure, "The Foundation Program and the Measurement of Educational Need," in *Problems and Issues in Public School Finance*, eds. R. L. Johns and E. L. Morphet (New York: Teachers College, Columbia University, 1952), p. 195.

15. National Education Association, Committee on Tax Education and School Finance, *Guides to the Development of State School Finance Programs* (Washington, D.C.: The Association, 1949), p.11.

16. Mort and Reusser, *op. cit.*, p. 397.

17. Fleischmann Commission, *The Fleischmann Report* (New York: Viking Press, 1973), pp. 61–73.

18. Henry C. Morrison, *School Revenue* (Chicago: University of Chicago Press, 1930), p. 164.

19. Advisory Commission on Intergovernmental Relations, *Urban America and the Federal System* (Washington, D.C.: U.S. Government Printing Office, 1969), p. 23.

20. Erick L. Lindman, "The Conant Plan: Shall the States Take over the Financing of Schools?" *School Administrator* (February 1970), 11–12.

21. Richard A. Rossmiller, "Full State Funding: An Analysis of Critique," in *Constitutional Reform of School Finance*, eds. Kern Alexander and K. Forbis Jordan (Lexington, Mass.: D.C. Heath & Co., Lexington Books, 1973), p. 72.

22. *The Fleishmann Report on the Quality, Cost, and Financing of Elementary and Secondary Education in New York State*, Vol. 1 (New York: Viking Press, 1973).

23. Charles S. Benson, *The Economics of Public Education* (Boston: Houghton Mifflin Company, 1961), pp. 242–46.

24. John Polley, *Studies of Public School Support 1966 Series: Vital Issues in Public School Finance* (Albany, N.Y.: University of New York, State Education Department, Bureau of Educational Research, 1967), pp. 10–11.

25.   John E. Coons, William H. Clune III, and Stephen D. Sugarman, *Private Wealth and Public Education* (Cambridge, Mass.: Harvard University Press, Belknap Press, 1970), pp. 201–12.

26.   5 Cal. 3d 584, 96 Cal. Rptr. 601, 487 P.2d 1241 (1971).

27.   *Ibid.*, p. 210.

28.   One may observe here that Coons and others begin to back their way into a feature of both the minimum foundation program and percentage equalizing.

29.   *Ibid.*, p. 211.

30.   See Benson, *op. cit.*, p. 353, for elaboration on DPE manipulations.

31.   No profile chart is shown for DPE because of its similarity to percentage equalizing.

32.   Jonathan Kozol, *Death at an Early Age* (Boston: Houghton Mifflin Company, 1967).

33.   Samuel Bowles and Herbert Gintis, *Schooling in Capitalist America* (New York: Basic Books, Inc., Publishers, 1976), pp. 203–13; Ivan Illich, *Deschooling Society* (New York: Harper and Row, Publishers 1971).

34.   E.G. West, *Education and the State* (London: The Institute of Economic Affairs, 1970). See also Joel H. Spring, *Education and the Rise of the Corporate State* (Boston: Beacon Press, 1972).

35.   Milton Friedman and Rose Friedman, *Free to Choose* (New York: Harcourt Brace Jovanovich, 1980), p. 154.

36.   Milton Friedman, *Capitalism and Freedom* (Chicago: University of Chicago Press, 1962), pp. 86–87.

37.   Friedman and Friedman, *op. cit.*, p. 162.

38.   Milton Friedman, "The Role of Government in Education, in *Economics and the Public Interest*, ed. Robert A. Solo (New Brunswick, N.J.: Rutgers University Press, 1955), pp. 127–28.

39.   Friedman, *op. cit.*, in f. 36, p. 89.

40.   John E. Coons and Stephen D. Sugarman, *Family Choice in Education: A Model State System for Vouchers* (Berkeley, Calif.: Institute of Governmental Studies, University of California, 1971), pp. 10–11.

41.   *Ibid.*, pp. 256–83.

42.   *Ibid.*, p. 259.

43.   Henry M. Levin, "Educational Vouchers and Social Policy" in *Care and Education of Young Children in America*, Ron Haskins and James J. Callagher (eds.) (Norwood, N.J.: Ablex Publishing Corp., 1980), p. 119.

44.   R. Freeman Butts, "Educational Vouchers: The Private Pursuit of the Public Purse," *Phi Delta Kappan*, 61, No. 1 (1979), 7.

45.   Levin, *op. cit.*, p. 17.

46.   *Washington Post*, February 27, 1978, editorial.

47.   Melvin R. Kohn, *Class and Conformity* (Homewood, Ill.: Dorsey Press, 1969). See also Levin, *op. cit.*.

48.   *Committee for Public Education and Religious Liberty v. Nyquist*, 413 U.S. 756, 93 S.Ct. 2955 (1973).

49.   Friedman and Friedman, *op. cit.* p. 163.

50.   *Plain Dealer* (Cleveland), February 14, 1978, editorial.

51.   Martha J. Jacobs, "Tuition Tax Credits for Elementary and Secondary Education," *Journal of Education Finance*, Winter, 5, No. 3 (1980).

52.   James Catterall, *Tuition Tax Credits for Schools: A Federal Priority for the 1980's* (Palo Alto, Calif.: Institute for Research on Educational Finance and Governance, Stanford University, 1981).

53.   *Griffin v. County School Board of Prince Edward County*, 377 U.S. 218, 84 S.Ct. 1226 (1964); *Poindexter v. Louisiana Financial Assistance Commission*, 275 F.Supp. 833 (E.D. La. 1967), *affirmed*, 389.

54.   Jacobs, *op. cit.*, pp. 238–41.

55. Catterall, *op. cit.*

56. Green v. County School Board of New Kent County, 391 U.S. 430, 88 S.Ct. 1689 (1968).

57. Daniel Patrick Moynihan, "Government and the Ruin of Private Education," *Harper's Weekly*, (April 1978), 28–38.

58. Adapted from Johns and Alexander, *op. cit.* in f. 2, pp. 232–34.

59. *Ibid.*, pp. 346–49.

SELECTED REFERENCES

ALEXANDER, KERN, and K. FORBIS JORDAN, eds. *Constitutional Reform of School Finance*. Lexington, Mass.: D.C. Heath & Co., Lexington Books, 1973.

ALEXANDER, KERN, and K. FORBIS JORDAN, eds. *Educational Need in the Public Economy*. Gainesville, Fla.: University Presses of Florida, 1976.

BENSON, CHARLES S. *The Economics of Public Education*, 3rd ed. Boston: Houghton Mifflin Company, 1978.

BERKE, JOEL S., ALAN K. CAMPBELL, and ROBERT T. GOETTEL. *Financing Equal Educational Opportunity: Alternatives for State Finance*. Berkeley, Calif.: McCutchan Publishing Corporation, 1972.

BURRUP, PERCY E. *Financing Education in a Climate of Change*, 2nd ed. Boston: Allyn & Bacon, Inc., 1977.

COHN, ELCHANAN. *The Economics of Education*. Cambridge, Mass.: Ballinger Publishing Company, 1979.

COMMISSION ON ALTERNATIVE DESIGNS FOR FUNDING EDUCATION. *Financing the Public Schools*. Bloomington, Ind.: Phi Delta Kappa, 1973.

COONS, JOHN E., WILLIAM H. CLUNE III, and STEPHEN D. SUGARMAN. *Private Wealth and Public Education*. Cambridge, Mass.: Harvard University Press, Belknap Press, 1970.

GUTHRIE, JAMES, ed. *School Finance Policies and Practices*. Cambridge, Mass.: Ballinger Publishing Company, 1980.

HACK, WALTER G. *Economic Dimensions of Public School Finance: Concepts and Cases*. New York: McGraw-Hill Book Company, 1971.

JOHNS, ROE L., and KERN ALEXANDER, eds. *Alternative Programs for Financing Education*. Gainesville, Fla.: National Educational Finance Project, 1971.

JOHNS, ROE L., KERN ALEXANDER, and K. FORBIS JORDAN. *Financing Education: Fiscal and Legal Alternatives*. Columbus, Ohio: Charles E. Merrill Publishing Company, 1972.

MORPHET, EDGAR L., and DAVID L. JESSER, eds. *Emerging Designs for Education*. New York: Scholastic Magazines, Inc., Citation Press, 1968.

MORT, PAUL R., WALTER C. REUSSER, and JOHN W. POLLEY. *Public School Finance*, 3rd ed. New York: McGraw-Hill Book Company, Inc., 1960.

PINCUS, JOHN, ed. *School Finance in Transition*. Cambridge, Mass.: Ballinger Publishing Company, 1974.

PRESIDENT'S COMMISSION ON SCHOOL FINANCE. *Schools, People and Money: The Need for Educational Reform*. Washington, D.C.: Government Printing Office, 1972.

REISHAUER, ROBERT D., ROBERT W. HARTMAN, and DANIEL J. SULLIVAN. *Reforming School Finance*. Washington, D.C.: Brookings Institution, 1973.

CHAPTER THIRTEEN
FINANCING
CAPITAL OUTLAY

The proportion of total expenditures allocated to capital outlay and interest on indebtedness for capital outlay in the public schools of the United States has varied greatly in different decades.[1] Expenditures for capital outlay and interest on indebtedness[2] comprised 19.1 percent of total expenditures in 1949–50; 20.1 percent in 1959–60; 14.4 percent in 1969–70; 11.3 percent in 1975–76; and 9.1 percent in 1979–80.[3] It is notable that expenditures for capital outlay plus interest have constituted the highest percentages of total expenditures in years when the school enrollment was increasing and declined when the enrollment became static or decreasing. Enrollment increased rapidly in the 1950s and 1960s, became static in 1970, and started declining in 1975. It is anticipated that enrollment in the public schools will not start increasing again until about 1985.[4]

The construction of new buildings is a major financial undertaking for most boards of education. It is financially impossible for most of them to finance major capital outlays from current revenue receipts. Boards of education commonly issue serial bonds that mature annually, usually over a period of twenty to twenty-five years. Therefore, the annual debt service for capital outlay plus the capital outlays made from current revenue receipts is the best national measure of the annual tax burden for capital outlay.

Since only a small part of capital outlay comes from current revenue receipts, the proportion of revenue receipts expended for debt service annually is a fairly good measure of the annual tax burden for capital outlay. Expenditures for debt service for capital outlay amounted to 6.1 percent of revenue receipts in 1949–50; 10.8 percent in 1959–60; 8.1 percent in 1969–70; and 8.1 percent in 1973–74.[5] These data show that the annual tax burden for capital outlay, as measured by the percentage of revenue receipts allocated to debt service, has not fluctuated nearly as much as the percentage of total expenditures allocated to capital outlay plus interest. The smoothing of the annual tax burden for capital outlay is sound fiscal and sound educational policy.[6] It would not have been possible to provide the school facilities needed from current revenue during the period of rapid growth in school enrollment from 1950 to 1970. However, as will be pointed out in this chapter, many boards of education do not have the bonding capacity or the taxpaying ability to provide for their capital-outlay needs by issuing bonds. Unfortunately, far less progress has been made in school finance reform for capital outlay than in school finance reform for current expenditures. For example, in 1978–79 state grants for capital outlay amounted to only 18 percent of total expenditures for capital outlay plus interest, whereas the state provided 47 percent of total public school revenue receipts for that year.[7]

There are many indications that the tradition of relying almost entirely on the current and anticipated (through bond issues) revenues from local property taxes to finance school plant construction and other major capital outlay costs is no longer tenable. Even when districts are reorganized in rural and suburban areas, there will be many school systems that will not have the local resources needed to provide adequate school housing in addition to helping to support modern programs of educaton. The problems of providing modern school plants, not only in the ghetto areas of cities but also in many rural and metropolitan area school districts, cannot be resolved until appropriate new designs, provisions, and procedures for financial support are developed and implemented.

The tradition of local responsibility for financing school sites, buildings, equipment, and other capital costs is still strongly entrenched in many states. Many people believe that if the state assists in financing the current costs of operating schools, local school districts should be expected to provide their own buildings and meet other capital-outlay needs. In many parts of the nation, however, there are serious shortages and inadequacies, and many school systems cannot provide suitable facilities from local resources.

Even in the large-district states there will continue to be problems in providing satisfactory facilities in all communities if the construction has to be financed entirely from local funds. In county-unit states, the range of ability is much less than in small-district states, but it is still ten or more to one in most of these states. If little state support is provided for current operating programs, the problem of financing school buildings will be more acute both in small-and in large-district states than would be the case if satisfactory and adequate state support programs had been developed and fully financed in those states.

In most communities, when school buildings are financed with local funds, the costs must be paid entirely from the proceeds of property taxes. However, in many districts, especially in urban and suburban areas, many parents who have children attending school may not own any property. Many residents who have considerable taxpaying ability are likely to derive much of their income from sources other than property. If school buildings are to be financed from the proceeds of property taxes, those who are not property owners may escape much of their responsibility for helping to finance the cost of facilities needed for the students of the community.

Thus, the tradition of local responsibility for financing school plant construction is neither sound nor realistic in any state. The wealthy school systems may have ample resources to provide excellent facilities for all students. The districts of average wealth may be able to provide reasonably satisfactory facilities if they are willing to make a high tax effort. The least wealthy, however, will not be able to afford satisfactory facilities unless funds from state and perhaps federal sources are provided to assist in meeting the costs.

At this writing the federal government provides only a negligible amount of aid for capital outlay. Therefore most boards of education have only two sources of revenue available for financing capital outlay—local and state. In some states, boards of education have only local revenue available. The options available to boards of education under local financing and under state financing are discussed in order below.

FINANCING CAPITAL FACILITIES: LOCAL OPTIONS[8]

Prior to the twentieth century, financing of public school facilities was the total responsibility of local governments in the United States. The schools were an integral part of American frontier life, and the actual construction of buildings often proved to be one of the year's biggest social events.[9] Initially, public school facilities were financed by private donations of sites and materials and erected by volunteer workers. Later, special local property taxes were levied in order to finance construction of needed facilities. By the latter part of the nineteenth century, local communities found it necessary to borrow funds, and state legislatures enacted laws which permitted the issuance of bonds for school construction by specific school districts or municipalities.[10] Even though the population of the country was burgeoning and the costs of providing public school facilities were rapidly increasing, most states were reluctant to have their state governments assume major responsibility for financing the construction of local public school facilities. Although an examination of current public school support programs will show a myriad of state capital-outlay and debt-service-assistance programs, the tradition of financing public school facilities *primarily* by local governments exists in most states today.

With the exception of the limited funds available from state-supported, capital-outlay and debt-service programs, local school districts in most states have relatively few options available for obtaining the funds necessary to finance the construction of their school facilities. In essence, local school districts are faced with one, or a combination, of the following three choices.

Current Revenues

Often referred to as "pay-as-you-go" financing, the ability to finance the construction of school facilities from current revenues is an alternative available only for the large and/or very affluent school districts. In essence, the entire cost of a project or projects is accrued from the proceeds of one fiscal year's local tax levy, which usually results in sharp increases in the local tax rate. According to Burrup, for those districts with the available resources, financing the construction of school facilities through current revenue " . . . is an ideal way to finance capital outlays. It is the quickest and perhaps the easiest way to getting the necessary resources from the private sector of the economy. It eliminates expenditure of large sums of money for interest, the costs of bond attorney fees, and election costs.[11]

In opposition, there are those who argue that the use of current revenue for financing capital facilities results in: (1) creation of tax friction among both taxpayers and governmental agencies because of increased school taxes, (2) failure to distribute capital costs among the generations who benefit from the school facilities, and (3) failure to realize the economic advantages of borrowing in periods of inflation. Therefore, the use of current revenue to finance the costs of constructing public school facilities has been minor when compared with the total amount expended for capital purposes in the United States.[12]

Reserve Funds

Some states permit school districts to accumulate tax funds for the purpose of funding the construction of future school facilities. The reserve building funds are kept separate from the school districts' current operating funds and are commonly financed by special tax levies. Generally, state laws stipulate that reserve building funds can only be invested under very controlled conditions, and the interest yield normally does not keep pace with inflation. Critics of the reserve fund option claim that changes in school district leadership often result in diversion of reserve funds to purposes other than those intended when the funds were collected. Also, critics contend that many of the taxpayers who contribute to the reserve funds will not realize any benefits. Most importantly, although reserve funds and current operating funds usually are financed and maintained separately, the taxpayer is only concerned with the total cost of the school district's budget. Consequently, the higher tax rates required to finance reserve building funds may create taxpayer resistance and result in a reduction of the current operating budget.[13] However, there are serveral advantages to the use of the reserve fund option. After sufficient funds have been accumulated, the project can be constructed without the delays and expenses associated with gaining voter approval for the issuance of bonds. Debt service charges are avoided and legal restrictions on taxing or debt limitations will not interfere with the project.[14] Reserve building funds are used by many states in this country but currently provide only a relatively small amount of the total funds used for construction of public school facilities.

General Obligation Bonds

The vast majority of public school facilities are constructed through the sale of general obligation bonds by local school districts. School bonds, generally referred to as municipal bonds, are legal papers issued by the borrower as evidence of debt, which specify interest rates, payment periods, and security.[15] Municipal bonds enjoy tax-exempt status from the federal income tax and from state income taxes in most states. The tax-exempt status makes the purchase of municipal bonds particularly desirable for investors with high incomes.

Probably one of the most desirable features of municipal bonds from the vantage of the investor is its relative safety of principal. According to the New York Stock Exchange,

> . . . They are considered second only to obligations of the Federal Government. During their severest test—The Great Depression—only about ⅓ of 1% suffered any loss of principal and less than 2% defaulted, that is, failed to pay interest or principal on time. In most of these cases, bondholders eventually received their interest and principal.[16]

One variety of municipal bonds, general obligation, is secured by the full faith, the credit, and generally the unlimited taxing power of the issuer. In effect, the borrower promises to use every available means to meet interest payments when due and to return the full face value of the bonds to the investors at maturity. General obligation bonds are usually recognized as the most secure of the municipal bonds.

Municipal bonds, including general obligation, are normally rated by one of the national rating companies for the purpose of alerting potential purchasers of municipal bonds of the relative security of the issue.[17] The rating awarded the school district by the rating company significantly influences the interest charged the issuer.

Most general obligation bonds issued by school districts are in the form of serial bonds chronologically arranged so that the bonds comprising the issue mature at regular intervals, usually annually or semiannually. Therefore, balanced debt service can be arranged over the life of the total issue. In contrast, the term bond is rarely used and actually prohibited in some states, due to a history of poor management practices. The term bond is used in conjunction with a sinking fund and is designed to meet interest payments at regular intervals, but delays repayment of the principal until the end of the indebtedness period.

The constraints that school districts operate under regarding the issuance of general obligation bonds vary considerably among the states and even among districts in some states. Most states have enacted school district debt limitations in the form of percentage of locally assessed valuation of real property which cannot be exceeded. Restrictive debt limitations have proved particularly troublesome for those states or school districts with limited local tax bases. There is also considerable variation among the states regarding the approval process required prior to the sale of general obligation bonds by the school districts. Some states require a simple majority of those voting at referendum, while other states require considerably more than a simple majority. The lack of uniform property assessment practices resulting in inequitable tax rates plagues some states, while voter-initiated property tax limitations confront other states. Nevertheless, despite the many problems inherent in the sale of general obligation bonds, this method remains the primary option for many, and the only option for some, school districts for financing public school facilities in the United States.

At this writing, municipal bonds, including school bonds, are being sold at the highest interest rate in this century. It is not sound fiscal policy for boards of education to bind themselves to taxpayers with these high interest rates for twenty to twenty-five years. If interest rates decline in the future, the boards should be able to call their long-term bonds bearing the highest interest rates and refund the bonded debt at a lower interest rate. Bonds issued for a period of twenty to twenty-five years usually carry a sliding scale of interest rates, the earlier-maturing bonds bearing a lower interest rate than the longer-maturing bonds. Municipal bonds are now commonly subject to call, with a small premium, ten years after date of issuance. Bonds with this provision are usually sold at nearly the same price as noncallable bonds. However, if bonds are issued callable at any time after issuance, the issuing body will have to pay a higher interest rate than on noncallable bonds or bonds subject to deferred call at a premium.

The number of years over which a bond issue matures should not exceed the life of the facility for which the bond was issued. This is not a problem for a school building, which usually has a life of from 40 to 50 years, for bonds are usually issued to mature over a period of 20 to 25 years. Most states prohibit school bond issuance for more than 20 to 25 years, because it would be difficult to market 40 to 50 year bonds without paying excessive interest rates. However, certain types of equipment such as school buses have a life of only approximately 10 years. Some boards of education finance school buses by separate bond issues, and such bonds should mature in not more than 10 years.

As pointed out, it is good fiscal policy to have a school bond rated by a national rating company such as Moody's Investor Service, Inc., or Standard & Poor's Corp. However, these rating agencies sometimes will not rate a small bond issue that is issued by a small district or will give it a low rating. An unrated bond issue or one with a low rating will be marketed at a higher interest rate than a highly rated issue. Boards of education issuing bonds which might otherwise be unrated or low rated can obtain a high rating if the issue is insured with a municipal bond insurance company such as the Municipal Bond Insurance Association or the American Municipal Bond Assurance Corporation. Such insurance will guarantee the payment of principal and interest on an insured bond issue. This insurance will cost the board of education a fee, but the lower interest rate obtained by the board will usually make it a good investment.

As pointed out, most boards of education under present financial arrangements must obtain most of the funds needed for financing school facilities by the issuance of bonds. However, due to inflation and taxpayer resistance, it is becoming progressively more difficult to secure the approval of electors for bond issues. For example, 72.2 percent of the bond issues submitted to the electors were approved in 1961–62 and 55.6 percent in 1976–77.[18]

The problems of boards of education in the 1970s and early 1980s were further increased by the increase per square foot in building costs and the increase in interest costs of bond issues. In the following section of this chapter, state policies for assisting in the provision of school facilities are presented.

FINANCING CAPITAL FACILITIES: STATE OPTIONS

As discussed previously, prior to the twentieth century, capital facilities for public elementary and secondary education were financed almost exclusively from local resources. Undoubtedly, some school districts experienced difficulty in providing adequate school facilities before 1900, but no state had seen fit to develop a continuing capital facilities assistance program until Alabama took the initiative in 1901 and established an aid plan for rural schools. Two years later, in 1903, Louisiana, by constitutional amendment, enacted a state plan in which bonds could be issued for the construction of school facilities in impoverished areas of the state. By 1909, South Carolina was providing state assistance for financing capital facilities serving black rural school children, while Virginia and North Carolina had established modest state loan funds.[19] The following twenty years saw several states implementing matching grants for the purpose of assisting and encouraging school consolidation, and in 1927, Delaware took the first major step toward a comprehensive state capital facilities financing program. The Delaware plan required that primary support for the financing of local public school facilities be borne by the state government, with only a small contribution required of the local school district.

During the years of the Great Depression and World War II, a shortage of both local and state resources virtually prohibited local school districts from engaging in extensive building programs. Burdened with the problems of aging facilities, inadequate and insufficient buildings, and a growing desire for more and better school facilities, the limited number of state assistance programs were either woefully inadequate, inequitable, or both. A report by Webber in 1941 indicated that of the twelve states that had established various forms of state-aid programs for helping local school districts finance their public school facilities, none had programs that could be regarded as equitable.[20] Such programs were either crude and inequitable distribution systems, in which the principles of equalization were neither recognized nor applied, or else were simple devices for easy-term loans to districts by the state.

Shortly after World War II, attention once again focused on the problem of providng necessary funds for financing the construction of capital facilities for public school children. In 1947 Florida became the first state to develop and adopt a plan based on the concept of determining the financial resources needed annually by each school district to replace its buildings at the end of their normal life expectancies. Stimulated primarily by the increased demand for school facilities due to the postwar baby boom, many more states enacted various forms of state capital facilities-assistance plans. By 1950, approximately twenty states had enacted some form of state-aid program for assisting at least some of their local districts in funding school construction programs.

After 1950, still greater effort was made to encourage state participation in financing the construction of local public school facilities. For many years, school finance experts had been urging state legislatures to enact a wide assortment of state capital-outlay programs.[21] Additional impetus was given to the drive for increased state funding of public school facilities when the United States Office of Education and the University of California at Berkeley cooperated in a national study of state public school capital-outlay programs. After analysis of the various state programs, the researchers recommended, in part, that the states should provide additional leadership and financial resources for comprehensive and efficient public school capital-outlay programs.[22]

According to Barr and Wilkerson, forty states had developed various forms of assistance programs for financing local public school facilities by 1965. A more recent study conducted by Augenblick identified thirty-five states that provided financial support through 5 primary mechanisms for local school district capital expenditures in 1975–76. Three years later, in 1978–79, Webb indicated that thirty-seven states fit into the Augenblick classification. A somewhat similar classification of state-assisted capital-outlay and debt-service programs as used by Augenblick and Webb was made for this chapter and the results are displayed in Table 13–1.[23]

The procedure used in this chapter classifies each of the 50 states into the following categories: (1) complete state support, (2) grants-in-aid (that is, subcategories of equalization grants, percentage-matching grants, and flat grants), (3) loans, (4) authorities, and (5) no state assistance. Each of these categories with the exception of "no state aid" are discussed below along with the relative advantages and disadvantages of each.

Complete State Support

As its name suggests, a complete state-support program requires that the funding of capital and debt-services expenditures of the public schools be borne by the state. It is apparent from an examination of Table 13–1 that only the three states of Florida, Hawaii, and Maryland are classified as having imple-

TABLE 13–1 State-Assisted Capital Outlay and Debt Service Programs in the United States, 1978–79

| STATE SUP-PORT | GRANTS-IN-AID | | | LOANS | AUTHORITIES | | NO STATE ASSIS-TANCE |
	EQUALI-ZATION	PERCEN-TAGE-MATCHING	FLAT		LOCAL	STATE	
Florida	Alabama	Alaska	Alabama	Arkansas	California	Georgia	Arizona
Hawaii	Illinois	Connecticut	Georgia	California*	Florida	Kentucky	Colorado
Maryland	Maine	Delaware	Illinois*	Indiana	Indiana	Maine	Idaho
	Massachu-setts	Georgia	Indiana	Michigan	Illinois	Maryland	Iowa
	Michigan	Missouri	Kentucky	Minnesota	Iowa	North Da-kota	Kansas
	New Jersey	New Hampshire	Mississippi	North Carolina	Kentucky	Pennsylva-nia	Louisiana
	New Mexico	Vermont	Missouri	North Da-kota	Massachu-setts	Virginia	Montana
	New York		Nevada		New York	Wyoming	Nebraska
	Pennsylvania		New Jersey	Virginia	Pennsylvania		Oregon
	Rhode Island		South Carolina	Wisconsin			Ohio
	Tennessee			Wyoming*			Oklahoma
	Utah						South Dakota
	Washington						Texas
	Wisconsin						West Virginia
	Wyoming						

Source: Ester O. Tron, *Public School Finance Programs, 1978–79.* (Washington, D.C.: U.S. Government Printing Office 1980.) Unnumbered and unpublished page proofs.

*Unfunded, or no school district has met eligibility requirements for participation.

mented complete state-support programs by 1978–79. It can be argued that none of the three completely meets the criteria of complete state support. According to Webb, neither Florida nor Maryland has seen fit to fully fund their capital outlay needs.[24] The local school districts have either had to supplement state funds, or the building needs have not been met. Hawaii, which is usually considered to have full state funding of both current and capital expenditures, permits a small local contribution for capital expenditures.

Advantages cited by proponents of complete state support usually include the following:

1. A higher degree of fiscal equalization is achieved within the state because the quality of facilities is not a function of the taxpaying abilities of local education agencies.
2. State governments normally have access to a greater variety and quantity of resources than do local governments and can avoid the over-utilization of a single resource.
3. A state government can develop an allotment mechanism based upon needs, which will provide a higher level of efficiency.
4. If it were necessary for the state government to acquire the necessary funds from the issuance of bonds, it is likely that the larger issue would result in overall savings in interest and service charges.

5. The restrictions placed on state governments are usually not as rigorous as those placed on local governments, and the long delays and costs incurred by local bond referendums would be avoided.

Disadvantages cited by opponents of the complete-state-support program usually include the following:

1. Additional concentration of power and control of the public schools will become focused at the state level, thereby further alienating local citizens from the public schools.
2. The centralization of power would result in uniformity of public school facilities throughout the state, and such facilities would not recognize the unique needs of varying localities. In addition, it is likely that the centralization of power would result in less experimentation and innovation in school facilities and in a high level of mediocrity.
3. Due to a high level of competition for resources at the state level, the construction of urgently needed public school facilities could be unnecessarily delayed.

Grants-in-Aid: Equalization

The primary purpose of the equalization grant-in-aid is to provide increased taxpayer equity within the state. In the absence of state support for the construction of public school facilities, taxpayers in school districts with low ability to pay are required to make a significantly greater fiscal effort to construct capital facilities than taxpayers in districts with high ability to pay. Consequently, equalization grants are designed to allocate revenues per unit of need inversely with the fiscal abilities of the local school districts. As can be determined by an examination of Table 13–1, approximately fifteen states in 1978–79 had enacted some form of equalization grant-in-aid for the allocation of state capital-outlay assistance to local school districts. The variety of equalization grants in use in 1978–79 was very extensive, ranging from an annual allocation in the manner of the Strayer-Haig equalization model for current expenses[25] to a varying percentage of state support based on the local school districts' relative ability-to-pay standard.

Advantages cited by proponents of equalization grants-in-aid usually include the following:

1. Comparable public school facilities can be provided throughout the state without the imposition of an excessive local tax burden on districts with low ability to pay.
2. Since some local contribution is required for participation in most equalization grants-in-aid, the frivolous use of state funds would be curtailed.
3. Reduced dependency on the local property tax for the construction of school facilities would provide local governments with additional resources for other governmental services and/or tax relief. In addition, the economic health of local governments would be strengthened and the marketability of municipal bonds for other than school purposes would be enhanced.

Disadvantages cited by opponents of equalization grants-in-aid usually include the following:

1. In order to guarantee funds for all school districts in a state, a substantial amount of state resources would have to be dedicated to this purpose, while inadequate appropriations would render the program ineffective.
2. A statewide system would not necessarily be responsive to the variety of local needs, and local schools initially might experience difficulty in responding to immediate construction needs.

Grants-in-Aid: Percentage-Matching

The percentage-matching grant is designed to provide a fixed percentage of state support for each local (usually state-approved) public school capital-facilities project. The fiscal capacity of the local school district is not taken into consideration, and the total amount of state assistance varies in accordance with the cost of the project. For the school year 1978–79, eight states had either enacted or were using a percentage-matching grant for distribution of state assistance for construction of local capital facilities.

Advantages usually cited by proponents of percentage-matching grants include the following:

1. Initiation of school construction projects remains the prerogative of local school districts, and the building programs can be tailored to meet the needs and desires of local citizens.
2. The state, through the use of its approval process, can encourage cost-effective construction practices and influence the design and location of school buildings.
3. State assistance would reduce the dependency of local school districts on the property tax, thereby freeing local resources for other governmental purposes. In addition, the economic health and the marketability of municipal bonds for other than school purposes would be enhanced.

Disadvantages usually cited by opponents of percentage-matching grants include the following:

1. A percentage-matching grant invariably penalizes local school districts with limited fiscal capacity to support school building programs. Local school districts with high fiscal capacity can obtain sufficient funds to qualify for state matching funds with relative ease, while districts with less taxpaying ability can only obtain the required matching funds through imposition of an extraordinary tax effort by their citizens. Of course, if the state's matching percentage were quite high (for instance, 90 percent state to 10 percent local) the disequalization effect of the percentage-matching grant would be neutralized, and the percentage-matching would take on the characteristics of an equalization grant-in-aid.
2. In order to guarantee funds for all local school districts with qualifying building projects, it would be necessary for the state to appropriate substantial resources. Insufficient appropriations would render the program ineffective.

3. School districts with sufficient capital facilities would not be eligible for state assistance, and citizens would see little direct benefit from their state taxes.

Grants-in-Aid: Flat Grant

As its title implies, the flat grant is designed so that the state allocates a fixed amount of funds per unit to the local school district, to be used to finance local capital construction. Some states annually allocate a fixed amount of funds per ADA or ADM, while other states allocate a fixed amount per state-approved project. Regardless of the unit of need used by the state, the flat grant procedure ignores the variation in fiscal capacity among the state's school districts. For the school year 1978–79, ten states were classified as either using or having enacted a flat grant for the distribution of state funds for construction of local capital facilities.

Advantages cited by proponents of the flat grant usually include the following:

1. Control of the local school building program generally remains with the local school district, thus the building program can be tailored to meet local needs or desires.
2. While usually viewed as nonequalizing, the flat grant does provide some measure of equity, since statewide resources are used for funding the flat grant program. Obviously, the greater the amount of the flat grant provided by the state (in other words, as the flat grant approaches complete state aid), the greater will be the equity provided the taxpayers.
3. State assistance in the form of a flat grant would reduce dependency of the local school districts on the property tax, thereby freeing local resources for other governmental purposes. In addition, the economic health of local governments would be strengthened and the marketability of municipal bonds for other than school purposes would be enhanced.
4. The flat-grant program can be easily administered, due to its simple allocation technique and the ability to accurately anticipate required funds.

Disadvantages cited by opponents of the flat-grant program usually include the following:

1. Most state flat-grant programs only supplement the local funds required to finance the school building program. Consequently, variation in the quality of school facilities among the states' school districts is considerable, coupled with an inequitable tax effort.
2. In those states that annually allocate funds on a per-unit basis without consideration of building needs, some school districts reserve unneeded funds while others have unfunded capital needs.

Loans

State capital-assistance loan funds have been established to provide direct financial assistance to local school districts. Commonly, states have established a permanent fund, or funds, often through the use of dedicated revenues, for the purpose of providing low-interest loans to local school districts. Unlike the previous state assistance plans, loans provided by the state contain the provision that the funds be repaid at some future date. With some exceptions, loans do not take into consideration the relative fiscal capacities of the local school districts, and as a consequence, do not provide for a high degree of fiscal equalization.[26] Funds available from state loan funds are usually modest, and states have either had to restrict all school districts to a certain amount per approved project or to control the number of eligible school districts by implementing certain qualifying criteria. Occasionally, a school district either has to be taxing or bonding itself at a certain level or it falls below the specified measure of fiscal capacity needed to qualify for a state loan. For the school year 1978–79, ten states either had enacted or were using loan funds as a means of helping local school districts finance construction of their capital facilities.

Advantages cited by proponents of state loan funds usually include the following:

1. The loan fund provides local school districts with an economical mechanism for borrowing necessary funds, due to the modest interest charged by the state.
2. Generally, state loans to local school districts are not charted against the local school district's debt limitation, thereby giving them access to additional resources.
3. The time required to acquire funds from state loan funds is usually considerably less than the time required to acquire funds through the sale of bonds.
4. The state, through the use of its approval process, can encourage cost-effective construction practices and influence the design and location of school buildings.

Disadvantages usually cited by opponents of state loan funds include the following:

1. Normally, state loan funds are extremely limited and serve only as a minor resource in the local school district's total building program.
2. Due to limited funds in most state loan funds, plus the common practice of permitting all school districts equal access to state loans, fiscal equalization is not enhanced.
3. The establishment of modest state loan funds often diverts the attention of the legislature from adequately funding the construction of public school capital facilities.
4. Local control of school construction may be diluted through use of the state approval process required for those school districts seeking state loans.

Authorities

A unique device designed to help local school districts finance the construction of their school facilities is the school building authority. Building authorities can be designed to function at either the local or state levels of government. In essence, a building authority is an agency established by the state for the purposes of circumventing restrictive taxing or debt limitations of local governments and/or facilitating the construction of essential local school facilities. According to Jordan,

> The authorities function as corporate bodies outside the regular governmental structure and secure their funds through the sale of revenue bonds. Facilities are constructed and the local school district then enters into a long-term rental agreement which serves as the legal document to guarantee repayment of the revenue bonds.[27]

Since the building authorities are separate agencies of government and do not operate schools, taxing or debt limitations of the local school district need not apply.

Advantages cited by proponents of building authorities usually include the following:

1. Many of the debt and taxing restrictions on local school districts are imposed by state constitutions, which often are difficult to amend. The use of building authorities permits the state to assist local school districts in financing the construction of needed facilities without constitutional amendment.
2. Unless prohibited by the state or federal governments, a combination of state, local, and federal current revenues may be used by the school district to pay the costs of lease-rental or lease-purchase agreements with the building authorities.
3. Often, building authorities can be used by the local school district without acquiring voter approval, thereby avoiding building delays and added expense.

Disadvantages usually cited by opponents of building authorities include the following:

1. The enactment of building authorities only ignores the more pressing problem of adequately financing the construction of public school facilities, by evading taxing and debt limitations.
2. Revenue bonds are generally used to finance building authorities, which results in higher interest costs than the interest costs of the more secure general-obligation bonds.
3. The right of the taxpayer and citizen to express his approval or disapproval is circumvented by the use of building authorities.

SUMMARY

The National Educational Finance Project made a national survey of the problems of financing school facilities in 1971. The problems identified then still existed in large part in 1980. The following is a summary of the findings of the study of school facilities made by the Project.[28]

In any general discussion of aid for public school construction throughout the nation, two paramount problems emerge: (1) many state-aid plans are only token in nature, and several states do not provide local school districts with any financial assistance for school construction; and (2) the federal government has not provided financial support for any general programs for school construction. Even though title for school buildings may legally reside with the state and education has historically and legally been considered a state function, the entire, or a major portion of, the financial burden for providing housing for educational programs and students has been placed upon the shoulders of the local school district in a great number of states.

This general pattern throughout the nation has resulted in a heavy drain upon local fiscal resources as a source of financial support for school construction. Various constitutional limitations and statutory provisions restrict the latitude available to the local school district by imposing constraints such as the following:

1. Unduly restrictive debt and tax rate limitations in some states, and wide variations among the states in these matters

2. Assessment practices in local districts which do not coincide with statutory or constitutional prescriptions, and wide variations in assessment levels among local districts, which result in property tax bases unrelated to the real fiscal capacity (as measured by property value) of the several districts

3. A property tax base which is heavily relied upon for school construction funds, is not immediately responsive to changes in the economy as a whole, does not necessarily coincide with taxpaying capacity, and is regressive in terms of assumption of the burden

4. Voter reactions to property tax rates which suggest that psychological limits may have been reached and that rates may have reached confiscatory levels in many districts

5. Unduly rigid voter qualifications and provisions which require more than a majority vote for passage, thereby making it extremely difficult to obtain approval in some states

6. An extremely rapid increase in school construction costs, without a uniformly corresponding increase in revenue potential from property taxes

7. Overdependence on the property tax, which is also heavily relied upon to support other local governmental functions

8. School-district geographical boundaries which result in the isolation of commercial and industrial taxable wealth, thereby creating residential areas with low revenue-generating capacity

9. Variations in local-district facility needs and fiscal abilities which are so extreme that many districts could not meet their needs even if all legal restrictions on local debt and tax rates were removed.[29]

It is obvious that an equitable plan of financing school plant facilities cannot be based exclusively on local school financing, even if all legal obstacles were eliminated, because of the wide variance among local school districts in wealth and taxpaying ability. It has already been pointed out in this book that school districts vary in equalized valuation as much as 10 to 1 in states with large school districts such as county unit states, and variations are much greater in states with many small districts. Therefore, an equitable plan for financing school facilities must involve either full-state financing or an equitable combination of local, state, and federal financing, if and when substantial federal assistance becomes available.

What are the characteristics of an equitable plan for financing school facilities? It is beyond the scope of this book to present the technical details of alternative equitable plans for financing school facilities. Following however are some of the characteristics of an equitable plan.

1. The quality of school facilities available to the pupils of a school district should not be determined by the wealth of the district. Either the state must fully finance the facilities needed or it must provide an equalization grant which substantially equalizes the financial resources of the school districts that are available for financing needed facilities. This is one of the principal criteria used for evaluating the equity of a state's plan for financial current expenses.

2. An equitable measure of need for school facilities should be utilized. The measure of need for school facilities should be based primarily upon the educational program needed. The measure of need should give consideration to at least the following factors.

    a.   The school buildings of all school districts depreciate at a rate of about 2 percent per year. Therefore all districts have a depreciation need of at least 2 percent of present replacement cost. The depreciation of equipment is still greater. Therefore the depreciation of buildings and equipment combined is probably about 2½ percent per year. Unit depreciation costs can readily be computed on a pupil- or teacher-unit basis.

    b.   The measure of need should include pupil growth, projected pupil growth, and capital-outlay needs resulting from a shift in the residence of the pupil population within a district.

    c.   Different types of educational programs cost varying amounts per unit. Furthermore school plants may cost more in some school districts than the state average, due to differences in site costs and other factors. These cost variations should be included in the measure of need.

    d.   Some districts may have issued bonds and provided the needed facilities without waiting for the state to develop an equitable plan of school financing. The debt service on such bonds should be included in the measure of need for such districts.

3. The finance plan should provide for financing school facilities by borrowing and by current revenue. Boards of education should have ample authority to issue bonds for school facilities and utilize annual state grants to pay all or part of the debt service on such bonds. If a district does not have the bonding capacity needed to finance the facilities needed, a state authority should be given the power to issue state bonds in behalf of the district and should utilize all or part of the annual state capital-outlay allotment to the district to pay the debt service on the bonds. School districts should also have the authority

to use current annual state allotments for capital outlay and current local revenue, in order to reduce interest costs of excessive borrowing.

4. The school plant program should be carefully planned and projected over a period of years. The state department of education should provide technical assistance to boards of education for this planning process.

5. The state should not exercise unnecessary state controls over the school plant program of a school district. It is recognized that the state should enforce minimum standards with respect to health and safety, but the state should not establish state plans for school buildings or require a uniform number of square feet per elementary or high-school pupil. The need for the school plant originates in the educational program, and local boards of education should be given a large measure of authority in determining the educational program needed in the district. Educational needs vary among the districts of a state and the same program in every district would not be equitable to the pupils. The school plant should facilitate the educational program needed, not control it.

6. The plan for financing the school plant should be an annual, continuing plan as contrasted with ad hoc, emergency plans.

NOTES

1. A considerable part of this chapter has been adapted from pages 2–28 of *Improving School Finance in Louisiana*, Vol. 2, prepared by Professor Richard G. Salmon (Virginia Polytechnic Institute) as part of a study of educational equity submitted to the Louisiana State Department of Education in 1980.

2. Less than 5 percent of interest payments made by boards of education is expended by them for nonbonded debt. See *Statistics of State School Systems 1971–72, National Center for Education Statistics*, p. 70. Therefore in order to estimate the total financial burden for capital outlay, it is necessary to add interest to expenditures for capital outlay.

3. Percentages computed from data presented in W. Vance Grant and C. George Lind, *Digest of Education Statistics, 1980* (Washington, D.C.: U.S. Government Printing Office) p. 73, except for 1979–80, which was computed from *Estimates of School Statistics 1979–80*, by the National Education Association.

4. Martin M. Frankel, ed., *Projections of Education Statistics to 1986–87* (Washington, D.C.: U.S. Government Printing Office), pp. 18–19.

5. Office of Education, U.S. Department of Health, Education and Welfare. *Statistics of State School Systems 1949–50, 1956–60, 1969–70 and 1973–74*. Unfortunately the Office (Department of Education) has not reported data on debt service since 1973–74.

6. Since the total value of bonds issued by boards of education began declining in 1975, primarily due to a decline in enrollment, it is estimated that only approximately 7 to 7.5 percent of revenue receipts was allotted to debt service in 1979–80.

7. Computed from data provided in *Public School Finance Programs 1978–79* (Washington, D.C.: Office of Education, U.S. Government Printing Office, 1980) pp. 14–15, and *Estimates of School Statistics 1979–80* (Washington, D.C. National Education Association, 1980) p. 35.

8. This and the following sections were largely abstracted from "Financing School Facilities," written by Richard G. Salmon as part of an unpublished report submitted to the Louisiana State Education Department in 1980 by the Economics and Education Institute and the Gulf South Research Institute.

9. W. Monfort Barr and others, *Financing Public Elementary and Secondary School Facilities in the United States*, Special Study Number Seven, National Educational Finance Project (Bloomington, Ind.: Indiana University, 1970), p. 25.

10.   *Ibid.*

11.   Percy E. Burrup, *Financing Education in a Climate of Change*, 2nd ed. (Boston: Allyn & Bacon, Inc., 1977), pp. 240–41.

12.   Barr and others, *op. cit.*, p. 127.

13.   Burrup, *op. cit.*

14.   K. Forbis Jordan, *School Business Administration*, 3rd ed. (New York: Ronald Press Company, 1969), p. 205.

15.   Barr and others, *op. cit.*, p. 100.

16.   New York Stock Exchange, *Understanding Bonds and Preferred Stocks* (New York: New York Stock Exchange, Inc., August, 1978).

17.   One of the most widely used of the rating companies is Moody's Investor Service, Inc., which rates each issue on an eight-scale continuum from Aaa to C. Standard & Poor's Corp. is also widely used.

18.   Grant and Lind, *op. cit.*, p. 72.

19.   M. David Alexander, "Financing Capital Outlay," in *Critical Issues in Educational Finance*, eds. Stephen B. Thomas and Koy M. Floyd (Harrisonburg, Va.: Institute for Educational Finance, 1975), p. 109.

20.   Gerald D. Webber, *State Equalization of Capital Outlays for Public School Buildings* (Los Angeles, Calif: University of Southern California Press, 1941), p. 5.

21.   Barr and others, *op. cit.*, p. 137.

22.   A total of 16 specific recommendations were made by the researchers. See Erick L. Lindman and others, *State Provisions for Financing Public School Capital Outlay Programs* (Washington, D.C.: U.S. Government Printing Office, 1951), p. 136.

23.   W. Monfort Barr and William R. Wilkerson, "State Participation in Financing Local School Facilities," in *Trends in Financing Public Education*, Eighth National Conference on School Finance (Washington, D.C.: National Education Association, 1965), pp. 224–32; John Augenblick, *Systems of State Support for School District Capital Expenditure* (Denver Education Commission of the States, 1977), p. 7; L. Dean Webb, *Financing Capital Outlay* (Tucson, Ariz.: Joint Select Committee on Tax Reform and School Finance of the Arizona Legislature, 1979), pp. 11–7 to 11–9.

24.   *Ibid.*, p. 11–6.

25.   See for example M. David Alexander, Richard G. Salmon, and Van Mueller, *Final Report of the Foundation Program Sub-Study* (Indianapolis, Ind.: Indiana School Finance Study, 1978), pp. 13–55.

26.   Some states have combined the techniques of loan funds and grants-in-aid by implementing loan-grants which are designed to assist school districts that cannot make full repayment in a reasonable time period without enacting a burdensome tax effort. In such cases, the state is authorized to cancel the unpaid portion after a certain number of years.

27.   Jordan, *op. cit.*, p. 207.

28.   Adapted from W. Monfort Barr and K. Forbis Jordan, "Financing Public Elementary and Secondary School Facilities," in *Planning to Finance Education*, eds. Roe L. Johns, Kern Alexander, and K. Forbis Jordan (Gainesville, Fla.: National Educational Finance Project, 1971), pp. 251–52.

29.   *Ibid.*, p. 252.

SELECTED REFERENCES

BARR, W. MONFORT, and WILLIAM R. WILKERSON. *Innovative Financing of Public School Facilities*. Danville, Ill.: Interstate Printers & Publishers, Inc., 1973.

BURRUP, PERCY E. *Financing Education in a Climate of Change*, 2nd ed. Boston: Allyn & Bacon, Inc., 1977, Chapter 10.

EDUCATIONAL FACILITIES LABORATORIES. *Guide to Alternatives in Financing School Buildings*. New York: The Laboratories, 1971.

GARMS, WALTER I., JAMES W. GUTHRIE, and LAURENCE C. PIERCE. *School Finance: The Economics and Politics of Public Education*. Englewood Cliffs, N.J.: Prentice-Hall, Inc., 1978, Chapter 14.

HACK, WALTER G. "School District Bond Issues: Implications for Reform in Financing Capital Outlay." *Journal of Education Finance*, Vol. 2 (Fall 1976).

JOHNS, ROE L., KERN ALEXANDER, and K. FORBIS JORDAN. *Planning to Finance Education*. Gainesville, Fla.: National Educational Finance Project, 1971, Chapter 7.

PIELE, PHILIP K., and JOHN STUART HALL. *Budgets, Bonds and Ballots: Voting Behavior in School Finance Issues*. Lexington, Mass.: D. C. Heath & Company, 1973.

CHAPTER FOURTEEN
PERSONNEL POLICIES
AND SALARIES

Issues concerning financial support as it relates to personnel probably have attracted more attention and taken more of the time of local citizens, board members, and school officials during recent years than most other problems relating to the schools. This attention was probably essential under the circumstances, and the issues should not be neglected in the future, primarily because the kind and quality of educational programs provided in any well-organized school system or school are largely determined by the qualifications and contributions of the personnel employed.

Even the best personnel policies, however, will not necessarily resolve some of the basic problems of education in a school system under modern conditions. An essential, but often neglected, first step is systematic and perceptive planning for the improvement of all aspects of education. Identification and agreement on appropriate goals, determination of needs and priorities, development and implementation of relevant programs and procedures, and other similar steps should establish a sound basis for developing defensible personnel and salary policies.

Although the best plans and policies that can be developed for improving education are essential, they have little meaning until they are implemented—that is, utilized intelligently as guides for decisions and actions by everyone concerned or involved. All factors and conditions in the external, as well as internal, environment for education should be reasonably favorable if significant progress is to be made. These include the attitudes and expectations of the staff, the community, the board, and the administration; the policies established by law and the state board of education; the quality of leadership provided; and many others, including the assurance that sufficient funds will be available to provide adequate and appropriate compensation for all members of the professional, facilitating, and managerial staff, as well as for facilities, equipment, and supplies.

Expenditures for personnel (certificated and noncertificated) in school systems constitute from 80 to 85 percent of the funds expended for the current operation of the schools. Policies relating to provisions for personnel and the expenditure of these funds significantly influence the quality of education in a school system. It is important, therefore, that not only boards of education and school officials but also the citizens in each community make every effort to ensure that all conditions are favorable and conducive to providing a high-quality program of education.

From time to time, various school systems have found themselves confronted with an especially difficult problem. If financial support has been so limited or if personnel policies have been so unsatisfactory that the schools have not been doing a good job, many people have become dissatisfied and critical. This tends to make it difficult or impossible to obtain additional local support. When inadequate funds are responsible for the difficulty, only exceptionally competent leadership on the part of the board, the citizens of the community, and the administrative staff, or the provision of additional funds from state sources, can establish a basis for resolving the dilemma. If, however, the difficulty has arisen primarily because of unsatisfactory or inadequate personnel policies, it seems apparent that prompt and effective attention to improvement of those policies should provide a sound basis for effecting improvements.

FACTORS AFFECTING PERSONNEL POLICIES AND ADMINISTRATION

Personnel policies are developed and administered in a changing socioeconomic context. They are influenced by many factors, including proposed new theories and concepts, conclusions based on recent research, new insights and understandings, and attitudes and expectations of members of the society as well as of those who are affected by the policies.

Theories Relating to Organization and Management

Theories relating to organization and management have been considerably revised during recent decades. Attention that was directed primarily to "scientific management" and "efficiency" some years ago has shifted increasingly during recent years to the consideration of factors involved in human welfare and relationships within the entire social system. Selznick, for example, has been concerned primarily with the functions of organizational goals in assisting the individuals involved to identify their own hopes and aspirations with the goals of the organization.[1] Argyris has proposed the following seven processes as essential if management is to make progress in resolving the fundamental conflicts that tend to exist between personal hopes and desires and the needs of the organization:

1. Precise assignment of responsibility
2. Appropriate evaluation and rewards
3. Authority that is binding on all who are in the organization
4. Perpetuation of the organization
5. Effective communication
6. Identification with the organization
7. Pacing the work of the organization[2]

The basic problem seems to be one of reconciling individual hopes and desires with organizational needs. McGregor has emphasized the need for acceptance of the principle of collegial collaboration between "superiors and subordinates"—the concept that subordinates are capable of self-discipline and self-improvement and that integration of organizational and personal goals is essential if the major goals of the organization are to be attained.[3]

Fawcett has stated:

> Persistent themes permeating the writings of these three men are (1) the need to establish clear goals for the organization . . . (2) the need to utilize intrinsic motivation for changes in employee behavior; and (3) the need to work together as colleagues to achieve co-operatively the goals of the organization . . . These ideas seem exceptionally well suited for use by educational governments during the next decade and a half.[4]

Important Recent Developments

The socioeconomic setting in which both professional (or certificated) and classified (noncertificated) personnel in education are operating has changed significantly and probably will continue to change for a number of reasons. These changes mean that the relations of management to employed personnel and of employees to management are viewed from a different perspective, not only by each group but also by the society in which they function. Although some board members and administrators may attempt to continue the traditional stance, they can no longer expect to play the autocratic role of "telling the employees" what they must do and how much they will be paid. Moreover, professional personnel no longer can afford to pretend that they are concerned only with teaching or with improving instruction and need not be concerned with policies or administrative decisions. The inevitable interrelationships are increasingly brought into sharp focus by accumulating experience as well as by empirical evidence. Some of the major related developments are discussed briefly in the following paragraphs.

A Collegial Situation.   All but a small proportion of teachers and other staff members are college graduates, and many hold a master's or a doctor's degree. Many of them are better prepared in their areas of specialization than are the principals or superintendents in the system in which they work. On the other hand, many know little about problems of management or aspects of education outside their areas of specialization. Thus, the need has developed for involving personnel, who have much to learn from working together as peers, and who (as a result of such collaboration) should be in a position to enhance their contributions to the educational process. Therefore, all should contribute to the development of policies and should benefit from the contributions of others regardless of their official status.

Mobility.   Under modern conditions, neither teachers nor members of the administrative or professional service staff need to be place-bound. Those who have succeeded—and sometimes those who have failed—can move to another location as readily as students and their parents. Thus, teachers who find a climate unfavorable for service have tended to seek one they consider more favorable. On the other hand, investments in retirement and other benefits may constitute constraining influences.

Professional Organizations.   The organizations for professional as well as for noncertificated personnel have increased considerably in numbers and in strength. If local conditions become very unsatisfactory, the state or national organization may be requested to assist in bringing about improvements. An employee is no longer an individual who has to wage a lonely battle for what he or she considers to be his or her rights. One can join with others in seeking justice, defending vested interests, or attempting to bring about changes. One's efforts may be combined with those of others, either in waging battles against those involved in other aspects of education or in planning strategies for the improvement of all aspects of education. The latter, of course, is much more constructive.

Bureaucratization.   Most school districts in metropolitan areas have been increasing in population and, in many situations, this increase will continue. Many rural districts are becoming larger in size and population through reorganization. Largeness tends to result in bureaucratization involving impersonality and red tape. Policies and regulations developed in an effort to ensure order and promote efficiency sometimes tend to discourage initiative and prevent needed adaptations. Personnel, therefore, may either resign themselves to the routines or struggle to create an organization that will develop policies designed to free them to make their maximum contributions to the educational program.

Programs Sponsored by State or Federal Governments.   Both the state and federal governments have become increasingly interested in education. Many states are taking the lead in encouraging research, in planning improvements in curriculum and instruction, and in other ways. Federal funds are provided for new programs designed to promote stated or implied national goals. These and other developments are resulting in many adjustments in local school systems, and some of them have important implications for personnel.

Technological Developments.   The introduction and use of technology already has resulted in many changes in business and industry and in some aspects of government. It has already had considerable impact upon education. Many authorities believe that the most significant changes in education are still to come and that these will have many important implications for which there has been comparatively little planning. Some of the implications that are already apparent include:

1. The possibility of more meaningful individualization of certain aspects of learning adapted to the needs of each student
2. Changes in many aspects of the traditional role of teachers that will enable them to function more nearly on a professional level
3. The need for more careful planning, utilizing a systems approach to ensure that the technological developments are utilized intelligently and effectively to enhance educational opportunities—and not merely to increase efficiency of operation
4. The emergence of many new kinds of roles and types of positions in education and of the apparent need to develop a team approach to deal with many aspects of the program
5. The probability that the concept of a single salary schedule will no longer be appropriate[5]

Harris and Boulding, among others, have directed attention to certain pertinent facts and conclusions:

1. The ratio of the amount required for salaries of personnel to the total budget requirement in education has changed very little during recent years.
2. There seems to be increasing resistance to rising costs, even though the need for more adequate education should be apparent to everyone.
3. Unless education can find an effective way to utilize some of the technological developments in an appropriate manner and to adjust personnel assignments realistically, we may be headed for serious difficulties that could handicap the development of the nation.[6]

Koerner believes many legislators, board members, and even educators have been asking the wrong questions about the use of technology in classrooms and that the basic questions should be concerned with what we should be doing, but cannot do under present arrangements, and how technology can help. He stated, "I look forward to the time when the quality of American education at all levels can catch up with the quantity" and concluded that technology, when properly developd and utilized, could help to bring that about.[7] Although there are some indications that the wise use of appropriate technologies should help to improve education, there are no definite indications that it would result in decreasing costs.

Laws and Court Decisions.   Many legal developments have transpired over the past few years which materially affect employment of school personnel. Court decisions have generally protected and expanded teachers' rights. Most notably, the courts have determined that a teacher does not shed his or her constitutional rights of speech and association when becoming employed, and if a teacher is unconstitutionally dismissed redress may be found in damages against school officials or the school board under the Civil Rights Act of 1871. Too, nontenured teachers may be entitled to procedural due process under the Fourteenth Amendment if the contractual relationship between the board and the teacher is so vague as to give the teacher an expectancy of reemployment.[8]

Possibly the greatest impact on school personnel matters in recent years has come from affirmative-action requirements which compel educational institutions to pay female teachers on the same scale with males and to give equal treatment in hiring practices. Title VII of the 1964 Civil Rights Act specifically prohibited employment decisions predicated on the basis of race, color, religion, sex or national origin.[9] Thus, to make employment decisions or to have salary differentials along the lines of any of these classifications is not only unconstitutional but is violative of federal statutes as well.

The courts have, however, held that reasonable classifications of teachers are not unconstitutional so long as there is a rational relationship between the school board's act and the educational result it is trying to achieve. In a case where the state of South Carolina used scores on the National Teacher Examination as a determinant of salaries to be paid public school teachers, a federal district court ruled, and the U.S. Supreme Court affirmed, that the practice did not violate either the Fourteenth Amendment or Title VII of the Civil Rights Act of 1964, as amended. The Court found no discriminatory intent on the part of the state and said that, "It was important to the State to use its limited resources to improve the quality of the teacher force and to put whatever monetary incentives were available in the salary schedule to that task."[10] This finding was made by the Court even though the facts of the case showed that the effect of the use of the test was to place the majority of the black teachers in lower paying salary categories than whites.

In cases of discrimination, the courts will look to "intent" rather than to "effect." If the state legislature is not motivated by an intent to discriminate then classifications of teachers based on examination scores will be allowed to stand.

Evaluation and Accountability.   The idea of "evaluating" teachers and others involved in the educational process is perhaps as old as the idea of providing schools. Unfortunately, the criteria for evaluation often were not stated and, consequently, at least some of the evaluations were unfair or subject to misinterpretation. Many people currently believe that the focus, the context, and the procedures should be changed, in an effort to deal effectively with modern conditions and needs.

The concept of accountability in and for education has been generally accepted during the past few years as useful and appropriate, primarily because it: (1) directs attention to the results of the educational process rather than to its components; (2) attempts to fix responsibility for these results; and (3) is concerned with the consequences of the results—that is, whether the results represent poor, fair, or satisfactory progress.

There are, however, many problems and cautions that should be carefully considered. Landers has listed several, including:

> Every writer or speaker should make clear his definition or point of view regarding accountability;
> It is impossible to discuss sensibly the problems of accountability without reference to the goals of education;
> It would appear necessary to relate the new concepts in accountability to existing procedures and practices; and
> There is a real danger that the aims of education will be increasingly restricted to those which can most easily be measured rather than those which are most important. [11]

The concept of accountability is not limited to teachers and students, nor to the results shown by scores on standardized tests. Almost everyone (ranging from legislators who may support helpful or handicapping laws through board members who establish policies, administrators, teachers, students, and parents) has an important role to play in facilitating or retarding progress in improving education and, therefore, has some responsibility for the outcomes of the accountability process.

POLICIES RELATING TO PERSONNEL AND FINANCE

The development of appropriate personnel policies is of crucial importance in every state and local school system. In fact, policy planning is a major aspect of comprehensive long-range planning, which is essential for the continuous improvement of education in any school system. These plans and policies should include careful consideration of: (1) the aims (the establishment and maintenance of instructional and instructional-support programs), (2) the organizational structure (concerned especially with positions generated by the aims structure), and (3) personnel processes (those designed to attract, develop, and retain personnel needed to maintain and improve the system generated by the aims structure). Each of these important personnel processes must, of course, be further subdivided into sequential tasks that are essential to achieving the purposes and goals of the system.[12] All of the major policies established through this process have important implications for the financial support that is essential if the system is to function effectively.

Policies relating to personnel may be stated in law, in state and local board regulations, and in administrative directives, or they may be unwritten and consequently somewhat intangible. Both written and unwritten policies are important in every community. Written policies serve as guidance and are expected to be observed until they are repealed or revised. Unwritten policies are often the most difficult with which to deal. They are expressed through the attitude of the people of the community, of the board, and of the administrative staff toward teachers and other employees. This attitude determines the climate or conditions under which school personnel have to work. It may indirectly affect, and in some cases determine, what is included and what is not included in written policy. If the attitude is favorable to schools and to school personnel, working conditions are likely to be better and morale much higher than if the attitude is one of distrust, suspicion, and criticism. In fact, the attitude of the people of a state or community may determine whether the funds provided for salaries and the salaries paid are adequate or inadequate, and it even may have a decided effect on whether these funds are used wisely or unwisely in terms of the personnel services provided.

Almost all policies developed in a state or local school system have some implications for personnel. For example, if a local school board—because of inadequate understanding of modern educational needs or a false concept of economy—authorizes the construction of inflexible school buildings or provides inappropriate equipment, it may be unable to attract or hold progressive-minded teachers, even though the personnel policies may be well formulated. Moreover, the scope of policies relating directly to personnel is much broader than many boards and administrators have realized. The failure to develop appropriate policies in any pertinent area eventually may result in difficulties.

Some of the areas in which policies in many school systems are likely to be lacking or inadequate are: employment, responsibilities, and relationships of instructional assistants, paraprofessionals, and interns; procedures and relationships in grievances and professional negotiations; and the role of teachers and other staff members in the development and revision of policies. In many school systems, the board has given relatively little attention to developing policies for noncertificated personnel and to the relationships between these policies and those for certificated personnel. Yet these relationships are likely to be of vital importance in developing the educational program.

Basis for Development of Policies

The procedure used in developing policies relating to personnel may be as significant as the policies themselves. If the board and superintendent do not respect the members of the staff enough to seek their cooperation in preparing statements that are vital to morale and to the satisfactory functioning of the program, the staff will become aware of their point of view, and this awareness is almost certain to affect their attitude and their work.

The procedures to be used in developing or revising statements of policy relating to personnel need to be carefully thought through in every school system. These procedures should be worked out with the cooperation of the staff, and if that is done, the members of the staff undoubtedly will have an opportunity to participate in developing the policy statements. The citizens of the community also should be vitally interested in these policies. Many boards, therefore, have involved lay citizens, along with staff members, in the process of developing or revising policies to be proposed for adoption. The board must adopt policies before they can become official, but the proposals should originate, or at least be worked through, with staff members and perhaps with leading citizens and should have their concurrence. This is essential if policies are to be satisfactorily implemented.

Factors Affecting Personnel and Finance Policies

As a result of recent developments, including those discussed in an earlier section, personnel administration in education has moved from a position of somewhat peripheral, and largely managerial, concern to one of central concern for the human condition as well as for organizational goals. Studies by psychologists, sociologists, and economists, and the resulting modifications in management theory, have contributed significantly to this development, which has had considerable influence in industry as well as in education. Modern concern both for employees and for students, therefore, has been directed increasingly to the maximum development and utilization of the potential of individuals and to efforts to encourage greater self-direction and responsibility.

Many factors today interplay with modern management theory, having important implications for financing of school personnel. Problems associated with urbanization and the unique problems of the large cities have been and continue to be of paramount importance. Demographic trends and the ebb and flow of teacher supply and demand along with employment and salary considerations in the collective bargaining context also have a strong effect on management personnel policies.

Collective Bargaining.   The demand for collective bargaining, not only on salary policies but also on other policies, has spread rapidly during the past few years. The force of the adversary process of collective bargaining has on one hand expanded the teacher's power to require teacher organization input into the policy process, while on the other hand it has introduced a new fervor on the part of administrators to preserve and enlarge management's rights and prerogatives.

Presently, 32 states have some type of state public employee labor-relations laws affecting education.[13] Some of these are meet-and-confer statutes, but most pertain to collective bargaining. Most public collective-bargaining laws generally follow the private sector's requirements under the Taft-Hartley Act to bargain "wages, hours, and other terms and conditions of employment." The overall scope of the area of bargaining, though, is difficult to define and is always fluctuating. Wages, we know, cover regular pay, overtime, and cost of living, while hours and conditions include fringe benefits, holidays, vacations, sick leave, pregnancy leave, and so forth. Teachers, though, are different from most other private and public sector employees in that they may also expand the scope of bargaining to include curriculum planning, textbook selection, and other issues of educational policy.[14]

The precise impact of collective bargaining on financing of the public schools is not fully understood. Whether it ultimately leads to improved quality of education or even to better wages and working conditions for teachers is a subject of much needed objective research.

In a few studies, which could hardly be called conclusive, it has been found that salaries increased in bargaining districts over nonbargaining districts from about 0 to 4 percent for the year in which the studies were conducted.[15] Yet other studies have found either no effect or an adverse effect of collective bargaining on teachers' salaries. Teacher militancy in Florida during a 1968 teacher walkout had serious detrimental effects on the political potency of the teacher organization, which was reflected in the legislative attitude toward teacher salary increases for several years thereafter. In an interstate study, Kasper found that "there is no statistically significant positive effect of teacher organizations on salaries, once other variables such as income and urbanization are taken into account," and Balfour found a negative association between salaries and collective negotiations. Similarly, Zuelke and Frohreich found that collective bargaining had a significant negative effect on teacher salaries in small- and intermediate-sized districts in Wisconsin.[16] It is important to note that this latter study was conducted in school districts where collective bargaining had been in effect for many years. Several of the studies showing increased salary effects of collective bargaining measured only the short-term positive impact of bargaining.

The array of research only suggests the inconclusiveness of this controversy. The research does not measure the other effects that bargaining may have on working conditions or the quality of education generally. Even more difficult to measure is the psychological effect of bargaining on teachers and the community. Presumably, the quality of the educational program is positively affected by an uplifting of teacher morale, and bargaining may well be good for teacher morale in that it provides them with a formal structure through which their voice can be heard at policy levels. Of course, little evidence exists to show that long-range improvements are achieved in this manner. Some maintain, to the contrary, that the adversary role implicit in collective bargaining may have an overall detrimental effect.

The educational efficacy of collective bargaining cannot be reduced to mathematical precision. It must suffice to conclude that teachers, generally, must feel that the benefits to the teaching profession and to education outweigh the detriments, as evidenced by the spread of collective bargaining in education during the past decade. Assuming this trend will continue, certain admonitions are appropriate with regard to teachers' salaries and the adequacy of financing.

1. There is danger that progress in improving the support of education will be retarded by a struggle between rival teachers' organizations and between these groups and administrators and boards of education.

2. The problem of effecting needed improvements in education will not be solved merely by increasing salaries of teachers. There are many other needs to be met, and educational organizations as well as lay citizens need to keep this in mind.

3 There are limits to increases that may be made in salaries on the basis of employment for nine or ten months. Moreover, this traditional concept is in urgent need of revision if the educational needs of modern society are to be met. If provision is made for longer terms, year-round operations, or appropriate programs during the summer months, more adequate education can be provided, and higher annual salaries probably will be recognized as essential.

Salary Increases

Education and other governmental services are in a much different position than those in business and industry. If salaries of public employees are increased, the cost must be met through the proceeds of taxes levied on and paid by the citizens. Almost everyone watches taxes carefully. Many assume that the more money they must use to pay taxes, the less they have for private use. However, as pointed out in Chapter 3, certain governmental services, and especially education, may contribute to the productivity and to the taxpaying ability of the people—a fact not commonly recognized. If salaries paid by business and industry are raised, the increases must come either from increased production per man-hour or from profits passed on to the consumer in price increases. There is very little the consumer can do directly about price increases for products he wants. Yet from one point of view, these increases may be similar to indirect taxes. The consumer has to pay these costs if he purchases the goods, but he, along with others, may have the means rather directly at hand to keep down or limit tax levies and price increases for public services.

For some reason, many citizens fail to realize that in a capitalistic society, the values people hold are reflected in part by the prices they are willing to pay for products and services. Thus, the salaries paid teachers and other educational personnel in the various states and communities are always partly a reflection of economic conditions and partly an indication of the importance attached by the citizens to education and teaching.

The question the American people are attempting to resolve in this respect is: *How much should teachers and other school employees be paid in order to attract to education sufficient people with adequate competence and qualifications to provide the kind of schools and education needed in this country?* It is apparent that this question has not been satisfactorily resolved. Salaries of teachers in particular have tended traditionally to lag behind those of equally well-prepared people in business and industry. As one result, insufficient numbers of highly competent people have been attracted to education, the schools have not accomplished as much as the people seem to expect, and many people have been critical. Criticisms of salary policies and other matters will be beneficial if they result in a reorientation of people's thinking and the development of better perspectives regarding the significance and role of public education but will be harmful if they result in decreased support and lowered morale.

Between 1966–67 and 1979–80 the average classroom teacher's salary went from $6,821 to $16,001. This increase, though, only amounted to a 2.4 percent real gain when the cost of living was taken into account for the 13-year period.[17]

Classroom teachers' salaries vary substantially among the states. In 1979–80, the state average salary varied from a low of $11,900 to a high of $26,173. Classroom teachers' salaries in 5 states averaged over $19,000, while 5 states averaged less than $13,000.[18]

Salaries for instructional staff are on the average somewhat higher than for classroom teachers. Instructional staff includes supervisors of instruction, principals, guidance personnel, librarians, psychological personnel, teachers, and others.[19] The average annual salary for instructional staff among the 50 states in 1979–80 was $16,813.

To compare average instructional salaries among states does not give a true indication of the state's effort for salaries unless the fiscal capacity of the state is taken into account. Calculation of the various measures of state and local capacity is discussed in an earlier chapter of this book. If one uses the representative tax system as the measure of capacity, then the state's true fiscal effort for instructional salaries can be determined as shown in Table 14–1.

These effort data show that although Massachusetts is near the national average in per-capita personal income and below average in capacity, according to Halstead's representative tax system, it is first in tax effort for instructional salaries. Maine, one of the poorest states in the nation as measured by either the personal income or representative tax system, is ranked third. The study by Richardson and Williams shows that Mississippi, consistently the poorest state in the nation regardless of measure of fiscal capacity, ranks eleventh among the states in effort for instructional salaries. While Alabama and Arkansas, which also rank among the least able states, are found to put forth low effort for instructional salaries, ranking thirty-second and thirtieth respectively, more fiscally able states, such as Florida and Louisiana, have the lowest efforts of all the states.

TABLE 14–1 State Effort for Instructional Staff Salaries and Rank among the 48 Contiguous States and District of Columbia, 1978–79

	AVERAGE SALARY	EFFORT INDEX	CAPACITY AS PER-CENT OF U.S. AV-ERAGE*	EFFORT RANK
Highest five states				
Massachusetts	$22,000	0.371	94	1
New York	19,000	0.246	102	2
Maine	16,628	0.246	74	3
Rhode Island	17,189	0.236	86	4
Vermont	12,331	0.227	84	5
Lowest five states				
Oklahoma	12,525	0.146	102	45
Wyoming	14,939	0.144	147	46
New Hampshire	12,200	0.141	97	47
Florida	14,590	0.137	98	48
Louisiana	13,254	0.136	103	49
United States	15,836	0.189	100	

Source: James A. Richardson and J. Trent Williams, "Determining an Appropriate Teacher Salary," (paper delivered at American Education Finance Association Conference, New Orleans, 1981), pp. 17–18.

*Halstead's representative tax system is used as the measure of capacity, as discussed in Chapter 8.

Supply and Demand

Teachers who complain that their salaries are too low may take some solace in the fact that their situation has not changed significantly over the last 200 years. In 1776, Adam Smith attributed the low compensation of teachers to oversupply, which was caused by the education of vast numbers of teachers for the clergy, who, then unable to find positions in churches, overflowed into the teaching profession. The education of these clergy was paid at "public expense" in England. Smith observed that:

> The usual reward of the eminent teachers bears no proportion to that of the lawyer or physician; because the trade of one (the teacher) is crowded with indigent people who have been brought up to it at public expense; whereas those of the other two (lawyers and physicians) are encumbered with very few who have not been educated at their own.

The parallels between Smith's world and today's world are tenuous at best, but the supply-and-demand analogy may well be appropriate for today.

In Smith's day, greater numbers of people went into the clergy and teaching because they could not afford to pay for the more expensive education required to become a lawyer or physician. Thus, the numbers of teachers swelled, and, according to Smith, their wages declined.

The supply-and-demand phenomenon explains why prices rise and fall in a free-market economy. The theory of supply and demand was adequately explained quite early by John Locke as he sought to describe the market phenomena:

> All things that are bought and sold, raise and fall their price in proportion, as there are more buyers or sellers. Where there are a great many sellers to a few buyers, there use what art you will, the thing to be sold will be cheap. On the other side, turn the tables, and raise up a great many buyers for a few sellers, and the same things will immediately grow dear."[20]

Whether teachers are held dear depends to a degree on their supply. Teachers' salaries may then be at least partially determined by the student population as representative of demand and the quantity of teachers as indicative of supply.

In its simplest form, the supply-and-demand principle may be applied to teacher salary determination as depicted in Figure 14–1. Demand, D_T, represents both the private demand for public education and the spillover demand of society generally. Private demand is the want of families with school-age children who desire education for individual benefit. At the same time, there are social or spillover demands to society by which everyone gains from having an educated citizenry. The curve indicates that at very high salaries, fewer persons will buy education and fewer teachers will be demanded. The supply curve, S_T, suggests that as teacher salaries rise, assuming other salaries stay the same, more persons will enter the teaching profession. On the other hand, as Adam Smith observed, as the supply of teachers dramatically increases salaries will fall.

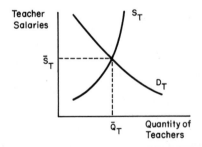

FIGURE 14–1   Supply of and Demand for Teachers

Source: James A. Richardson and J. Trent Williams, "Determining an Appropriate Teacher Salary," (paper delivered at American Education Finance Association Conference, New Orleans, 1981).

The simplicity of the marketplace model is, however, quite deceiving where public education is concerned. Of course, demand for teachers is greatly affected by the numbers of students to be educated, but beyond this, as Richardson and Williams observe, the value and significance that the public places on education must be taken into account if one is to relate salaries to demand.[21] In other words, the level of salaries or price may not relate directly to demand in public education as it does in Adam Smith's marketplace. In public education, salary levels are largely controlled by the legislature, particularly in states where various types of caps and limitations have been placed on local school districts to enhance overall statewide equalization. Too, the state legislature establishes certification standards, and regardless of numbers of students, can effectively regulate the supply of teachers through raising or lowering of the requirements to enter the teaching profession. Minimum accreditation standards for schools are also governed by the state, which may greatly influence the demand for teachers. Many other factors contribute to the state's influence on both supply of teachers and demand for their services. For example, the state may choose to expand services to certain types of students, such as the handicapped, and thereby create a substantial new demand for teachers trained in that area.

Thus, public school teachers' salaries are not established in the conventional sense of the marketplace. Hale suggests that the economic pattern has aspects of both an oligopoly and an oligopsony.[22] An oligopoly is a market structure where a small number of firms control a major portion of an industry's output. In education, the state legislature is in a position to control both certification of teachers and accreditation of schools, both of which can significantly affect supply. An oligopsony is a market structure where there are relatively few buyers with a high degree of concentration or interdependence.[23] Where the state can greatly influence demand for teachers through creation or deletion of programs, alteration of required pupil-teacher ratios, or other policy determinations, the result is a "kinked" demand curve deviating substantially from the curve which could be expected under unregulated market conditions.[24] States with greater numbers of local school districts and lower levels of state regulation could be expected to evidence greater adherence to the supply-and-demand characteristics of the marketplace than states with fewer school districts and more centralized control.

Regardless of how one classifies the teacher market, it is certain that it does not function and probably should not function in the traditional sense of the *laissez-faire* market. No one will deny, however, that the forces of the marketplace are present and undoubtedly influence teachers' salaries. As to whether they control them, it is highly debatable.

Throughout the 1950s and 1960s, the demand for teachers far exceeded the supply, but the great shortages became surpluses as the pupil enrollment of the later 1960s and the decades of the 1970s reflected the decision of families to have fewer children.

Demand for teachers is obviously influenced by the number of students, and the expected decline in student enrollment in grades K–12, as projected by the National Center for Education Statistics, U.S. Department of Education, will produce a decline in demand for teachers.[25] These data show that student enrollment in public schools has declined from a high of 46,081,000 in 1971 to an estimated 40,387,000 in 1981. Three alternative projections to 1986 show a low expectation of 38,193,000, a high of 43,068,000 and an intermediate of 40,244,000. All three would represent a decline from 1971 in demand for teachers.

Demand is also influenced by the pupil-teacher ratio, which has been on a steady decline for many years. In 1958 pupil-teacher ratio in public elementary schools was 28.7 to 1, and in public secondary schools it was 21.7 to 1. By 1980, the decline had reached 20.7 to 1 for elementary and 18.1 to 1 for secondary. If this trend continues, in 1986 the elementary will be 19.1 to 1 and the secondary will be 17.5 to 1. Taking such trends into account, Frunkel has estimated that by 1986 there will be a need for 2,180,000 teachers in the public schools of the United States.[26]

Supply of teachers is affected by their salary levels and college students' choices of profession. Using low alternative projections, the National Center for Education Statistics estimates that the total number of teachers will decline by 8 percent from 1976 to 1986. Prospective entrants into the teaching field may well be discouraged from choosing this profession as they observe that the fiscal rewards for teachers are even less in 1980 than they were in 1970. In 1969–70, average teachers' salaries were 2.33 times as great as per-capita personal income, and in 1980 were only 1.84 times as great.

Teachers have never been held in as high esteem by society in general as their knowledge and educational investment would seem to warrant. Hofstadter's documentation of the low status of the schoolmaster in America is as accurate today as it was 50 years ago. Before the 1970s, teachers were, however, compensated in accordance with a general rise in a vast and strong national economy which had almost unlimited potential to raise nearly everyone's standard of living. Since the oil crisis of 1973, we have seen a dramatic shift in the fortunes of the American economy. Society has been forced to make choices which were not necessary before. As Thurow has observed, "Our political and economic structure simply isn't able to cope with an economy that has a substantial zero-sum element."[27]

Zero-sum is an economic condition where the losses exactly equal the gains. If you aid poor people, you are taking the money from the richer ones. If you increase teachers' salaries, you are drawing greater tax resources from taxpayers who may be unable to bear the burden. Whether they can afford it or not, they believe that they have other priorities which are more important to their well-being than increasing the standard of living of the teaching force. Hard political decisions thus arise which require voters to evaluate their needs for education in light of other pressing priorities.

Teachers' salaries have declined relative to the per-capita personal income of the nation. The data in Table 4–3 of Chapter 4 show that the average salary of the instructional staff declined from $18,149 in 1969–70 to $16,813 in 1979–

80 in terms of 1979–80 dollars, whereas the per-capita GNP increased in the same period from $9,661 to $11,060 in terms of 1979–80 dollars. The public has not found teachers' salaries to be of high priority in a zero-sum economy. Teachers have absorbed economic losses because they have not had the political strength to maintain at least a stable economic condition. Such loss cannot be entirely attributed to a diminution of teacher political power, but is probably more accurately assessed as a decline in the relative value that the public places on educational aspiration. Too, a downward slide in the relative economic condition of teachers may well be attributed to a general belief that the public schools are not directly benefiting those who bear the brunt of the taxes. Economic choices are more difficult to make in a distressed economy, and the tendency is for voters to forget or lay aside the long-range social benefits of education in favor of more immediate short-range individual demands. Zero-sum, another explanation of Pareto-optimality, discussed in another chapter of this text, does not merely exist in a declining or a static economy, but in a growing one as well. In an expanding economy, however, the choices are easier to make, since the total pie gets larger and more benefits can be acquired by a greater percentage of the population.

Since 1973, inflation has created a psychological barrier to increased investment in public education. Everyone has watched the dollar decline in purchasing power, and, in the case of the poor and middle class, this has meant a drop in the standard of living. The upper economic echelons, however, have had no such decline in standard of living. Inflation does not produce an overall diminution in the resources of a nation, but does tend to shift money away from the poorer to the more affluent economic classes. From 1972 to 1980, the real GNP of the United States rose $260 billion.

The rise in the overall standard of living has been less since 1972 than before, yet the average real income gains have nevertheless continued upward. Thus, the effect of inflation has been for real income to shift about in the population creating more inequality among economic classes. Thurow says that a "money illusion" exists where everyone thinks that inflation is harming them personally."[28] Conditions of supply and demand create gains for some and losses for others in a period of inflation, but everyone, regardless, believes that he or she would personally have fared better if inflation had not occurred. This personal phenomenon becomes a social one in which all are generally reluctant to invest in such services as education, regardless of the fact that higher taxes may tend to stem inflation and increased investment in education could increase real economic productivity.

Teachers, unfortunately, fall into the category of the less economically able and have suffered substantially from the psychology of inflation. Teachers' relative economic condition is not likely to change significantly until inflation is controlled and the American people gain new confidence in the country's economic condition.

The pattern of relative decline in teachers' salaries as compared with per-capita personal income makes teaching less attractive as a future source of employment to college students. Evidence of a decline in the choice of teaching as a career goal is shown by changes of college study plans by high-school seniors between 1972 and 1980. In 1972, 12 percent of the college-entering seniors chose to work toward teaching degrees, but this figure had declined to only 6 percent in 1980. Substantial increases were found in the following fields: business—13 percent in 1972 to 22 percent in 1980; engineering—5 percent in 1972 to 10 percent in 1980; and communications—2 percent in 1972 to 4 percent in 1980.[29]

Such forces will continue to play an important role in the supply of and demand for teachers. While the leveling off of the student population may decrease demand for teachers, declines in pupil-teacher ratios and the increasing scope of the educational curriculum may tend to produce a corresponding increase in demand. Further, population mobility will continue to create uneven demands among the states. On the other hand, the supply of teachers may dwindle if salaries continue to fall in relation to other employment. Depending on the particular balance produced, the public schools could well face a teacher shortage in the latter half of the 1980s (see Figure 14–2).

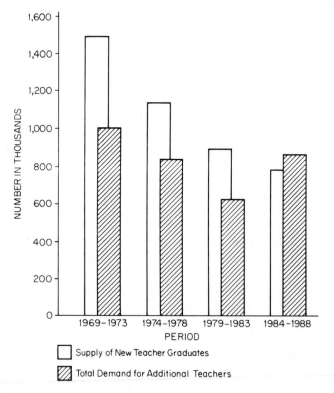

FIGURE 14-2

Source: National Center for Education Statistics, *The Condition of Education, 1980 Edition,* Washington, D.C., U.S. Government Printing Office, 1980, p. 73.

STATE PROVISIONS RELATING
TO SALARIES

As previously pointed out, state laws and regulations may affect rather directly salary provisions and other possibilities in the various school districts of the state. If only limited funds for schools are provided from state sources, the salary levels in each school system will be determined chiefly by the willingness and the ability of the citizens in the district to provide funds for schools. In such states, salaries in the least wealthy districts generally may be expected to be much lower than those in the most wealthy. However, when an adequate and realistic state foundation program has been established, all districts, regardless of their wealth, should be in a fairly satisfactory position (unless restricted by other state laws) to develop reasonably adequate salary schedules.

Many states, because of concern about this problem, have taken one step or another relating directly to salaries. Several have established state minimum salary schedules. West Virginia apparently established the first state minimum salary law in 1882. By 1937, twenty states had some kind of minimum salary legislation.[30] There are three major types of state minimum salary laws relating to teachers: (1) those that provide a state minimum salary schedule recognizing both training and experience, (2) those that fix a minimum salary on the basis of two or more flat rates but with no recognition of experience, and (3) those that fix a minimum salary as a single flat amount.

The interest of states in minimum salary schedules first developed largely because salaries paid in some districts obviously were totally inadequate. Those who were concerned with the problem apparently assumed that if a state minimum salary schedule could be established by law, the problem would be solved. However, it was soon discovered that many poor districts could not maintain a desirable pupil-teacher ratio or a satisfactory length of term and afford to pay the minimum salaries required for all teachers. Since state laws in many cases require a certain minimum length of term, the only alternatives for these districts were to maintain only the minimum term, increase the number of pupils per teacher, employ only teachers with minimum training, or levy excessive taxes.

The tendency in most states during recent years seems to be in the direction of attempting to develop an adequate and realistic plan for financing schools from state and local revenues. Progress in this direction facilitates provisions for reasonably adequate salaries, rather than emphasizing minimum salaries as the basic salary policy.

Determination of Salary Policy

Salary policies constitute one important aspect of general personnel policies. There has been a decided tendency during the past quarter of a century for districts to develop written statements relating to salary policy. These usually are developed with the cooperation of the staff or through the joint efforts of representatives from the staff and citizens of the community. These groups, however, can only *recommend* salary policy, and the boards may or may not approve the recommendations. However, when committees have done a good job of developing sound policies, the recommendations usually have been approved by the boards without major alteration.

The purposes of salary policies are to give assurance to the community that sound procedures will be observed in compensating employees, to give assurance to the staff that recognized policies rather than haphazard procedures will be followed, and to provide guidance to the administrator and his staff in developing satisfactory procedures for obtaining and retaining the services of competent personnel.

Suggestions for salary policies or schedules have been made in a number of studies. The suggestions set forth in the following paragraph, as adapted from those proposed for teachers by the Winnetka Citizens Advisory Committee twenty years ago, are more advanced in some respects than those adopted recently in many other school systems.

The salary plan should:

1. Meet reasonable competition for good beginning teachers without attempting to offer the highest starting salary
2. Assure dignified living standards for maturing personnel
3. Assure relief from hardship for heads of households
4. Contribute an uplifting influence to the dignity and prestige of teaching in the United States
5. Help to attract and hold teachers and principals of the highest quality
6. Stimulate increased graduate study through the master's degree
7. Encourage study, research, and travel beyond the master's degree
8. Provide adequate and dignified maximum salaries for teachers for whom teaching is only a part of their career
9. Provide markedly distinguished salaries for teachers who, in the tradition of the community, make substantial and measurable contributions to education in the district and in the United States
10. Provide a relatively long period for salary improvement before reaching maxima, but with safeguards against automatic advancement if a teacher's work is unsatisfactory
11. Provide annual increments of sufficient amount to be "felt"
12. Contrary to long-established tradition, provide an opportunity for teachers to achieve professional distinction and corresponding salary recognition without leaving teaching for administrative or supervisory personnel
13. Recognize any special economic factors in the community
14. Serve the long-term needs of the district, the board of education, and the faculty, and not be merely a temporizing, stopgap measure[31]

The Winnetka Committee also recommended policies that would include adequate leave for study, conferences, and travel and generous fringe benefits for all personnel. The importance of adequate provision for inservice education was likewise indicated as necessary board policy in addition to the salary policies proposed.

Some Trends in Developing Schedules

A salary schedule is simply a plan for compensating individual members of any group of employees, such as principals, teachers, secretaries, or custodians. This plan may be good or bad, satisfactory or unsatisfactory, in whole or in part. Givens noted some years ago that: "Salary schedules for teachers are social inventions that have been developed by insight and ingenuity to meet the problems of personnel administration in the schools."[32]

As previously indicated, there has been a distinct movement toward the development of salary schedules for all groups of school employees. Some additional trends are discussed briefly below.

1. For some years, there has been a marked trend toward the establishment of single-salary schedules for teachers. In the single-salary schedule, the plan for paying salaries is based on the training and experience of the persons employed. However, there now seems to be some tendency for this policy to be modified.

2. For certain types of employees, there recently has been a good deal of consideration of job evaluation as one basis for salary schedules and placement on schedules. This has been particularly evident in the development of schedules for noncertificated employees and to some extent has been considered in connection with schedules for administrative, supervisory, and certain other types of positions.

3. Cost and standard-of-living factors have been emphasized increasingly during the last couple of decades. It is generally accepted that school employees must be able to maintain an adequate standard of living if they are to work effectively. It is evident, however, that the objective of salaries that will enable all employees to maintain an adequate standard of living has not been attained.

4. For a number of years, minimum salaries provided in schedules were increased more rapidly than maximum salaries. However, there is some indication that maximum salaries are tending to be increased as much as, or at a somewhat higher rate than, minimum salaries, thus tending to restore the balance that was upset by special cost-of-living and other adjustments resulting from postwar and other economic developments.

5. In a number of school systems, an effort has been made to provide maximum salaries, especially in the higher ranks, that are at least twice as high as those established as minimums. Only a few systems have been able to attain this goal.

6. The fact that proper preparation is essential for satisfactory teaching in modern society has come to be recognized increasingly. As a means of encouraging professional personnel to complete their college training before accepting full-time positions and also as a means of providing an incentive for teachers who have not completed their college degrees to do so, the differential in salaries for the two groups has gradually been increased in a number of school systems. Many systems also recognize that there are places and needs

for experienced teachers who have completed preparation beyond the master's degree; consequently, there has been a tendency to add another column to the schedule. There has also been some tendency for the increments based on experience to be increased.

7. Within the past few years, numerous districts have adopted an index salary schedule. Some states that have established salary schedules are also considering this plan. Instead of stating a dollar amount for each rank and step in the schedule, only a base amount is stated in dollars—for example, eight thousand dollars for a beginning teacher who is a college graduate. An index number (such as 1.1) is then assigned for teachers who hold a master's degree, and the salary can readily be determined in relationship to the basic amount, whatever it may be. Similarly, salary amounts for each step of experience can be determined by applying an appropriate index number.

8. There has been some tendency to consider factors other than training and experience for teachers as well as for other groups of employees. For instance, some systems have adopted, or are experimenting with, a plan for relating salaries, to some extent, to the level of responsibility for certain kinds of positions. Others are attempting to evaluate and recognize merit and to provide special increments for merit. Still others have made some provision for dependency allowances, and so on.

9. The length of service during the year for various school employees has been increased in many systems. Sometimes this has been accomplished by increasing the length of the term and many times by providing for needed educational and other services during the summer. Schedules in many systems thus provide for adjustments for length of service beyond the traditional school year.

OTHER ECONOMIC BENEFITS

Although salaries are important in establishing the basic economic position of each group of employees, other benefits should have as careful consideration as salary policy. A policy that attempts to provide reasonably adequate salaries without considering other economic benefits or working conditions is not as satisfactory as a similar policy that places considerable emphasis on the other benefits.

For this reason, most groups devote considerable attention to this problem. For example, the Winnetka Citizens Advisory Committee carefully considered what is called "supplemental employee benefits" and recommended a supplementary retirement plan, provisions for group life insurance, a comprehensive medical expense insurance program, and disability insurance. The report stated:

> With the establishment of these new employee benefit plans, the Winnetka school system will have policies comparable to modern industrial practice and well in advance of current educational practice. They should be of material aid in attracting and holding the quality of personnel we need.[33]

Although all states now have retirement plans, either for teachers or including teachers and other employees, some of these are not realistic or adequate in the light of recent developments. Some still limit the salaries that may be used in computing retirement benefits, others fail to provide for survivors, and some are not on a sound actuarial basis. Development of adequate retirement provisions, perhaps supplemented by state provisions including or comparable to those for Social Security, seems to be essential for every state.

The provisions of workmen's compensation laws are applicable to teachers and other school employees in most states. Although these seem to have been working out reasonably satisfactorily, improvements are needed in many states, and existing provisions probably should be supplemented by plans for group life, accident, and even liability insurance.

Practically all the larger school systems have reasonably adequate provisions for certain kinds of leaves of absence. In some cases, these provisions are state-wide. Usually, sick leave may be taken, without loss of compensation, up to a designated number of days per year, cumulative up to several months over a period of years. Many small school systems, however, have no provisions along this line or have inadequate provisions. For example, in some cases, teachers who have to be absent must pay the salaries of substitutes. Provisions for sabbatical leave are found in some of the larger school systems but in practically none of the smaller systems. Perhaps some state-wide leave and sabbatical plan would help to resolve this problem.

Assurance of reasonable security in employment has significant economic implications. Some states have gone so far in providing tenure for teachers that discharge of incompetent teachers seems unduly difficult and expensive. Others still do not have satisfactory provisions for tenure or continuity of service, especially for smaller districts. Reasonable assurance that employees who are rendering effective service are not subject to loss of position at the whim of a board or a superintendent should be expected in all states.

Salaries of Administrative and Supervisory Staff

In some school systems, the position is taken that administrators and supervisors are paid for their administrative competence and leadership qualities and that these have no relationship to the preparation and experience of teachers. However, authorities point out that principals and others are leaders of teachers as well as administrators. Many hold that there should be some defensible relationship between salaries of teachers and those of administrators and supervisors. On the assumption that some relationship should exist, attempts have been made to devise a formula that can be used in developing a schedule for salaries of administrators and supervisors.[34] Should the salaries of administrators and supervisors be based on a ratio to teachers' salaries and automatically increased as teachers' salaries are increased? Could administrators represent the board of education in collective bargaining with teachers if their salaries were tied to the teacher salary schedule? Should school administrators represent the board in the collective bargaining process?

In more than two-thirds of the larger school systems, the salary schedules for administrative and supervisory personnel have been related rather directly to the salary schedules for teachers. More than one-half of these were based on an index or ratio adjusted to the schedule for teachers.[35]

For some time, many school systems that have provided summer or extended-year programs for some students and teachers have recognized that a *time factor* should be utilized in determining the additional compensation for teachers who serve beyond the regular school term. Thus, one-ninth would be added to the salary of a teacher who served for a month beyond the regular term of nine months. This factor is also utilized for administrators and supervisors who serve beyond the customary term.

The other factor commonly utilized in the index is a *responsibility ratio* that can be utilized for all professional personnel who have assignments requiring special competencies and extra responsibilities. For example, if the responsibility ratio for a regular teacher is 1.0, the ratio for the head of a teaching team might be 1.15, that for a principal of a larger school might be 1.75 to 2.00. Such ratios need to be developed on the basis of detailed studies and analyses made with the concurrence of the entire professional staff.

Many lay citizens insist that salaries for teachers should be related in some way to competency. When salary increases are proposed, these citizens frequently state that they would be willing to see much higher salaries paid for the most competent teachers but that increasing salaries for all teachers would be equivalent to wasting a lot of money. They insist that industry has had merit pay plans for a number of years and has used them successfully, and that these plans could readily be adapted for use by the schools.

Many teachers and administrators have tended to oppose merit pay. They call attention to the fact that merit-pay plans are used only for certain types of positions in industry and that seniority is the major factor in determining salary for many other types of positions. They point out that most salary schedules in education are based on training and experience and that the training factor supplemented by experience is superior to the seniority factor alone. They call attention, moreover, to the difficulty of establishing any effective plan for determining merit in teaching and point to the danger that subjective factors will enter into a merit rating plan. Davis stated:

> A merit wage system is primarily a procedure for one person to make subjective judgments about another, which means that it is fraught with human relations problems and is one of the most difficult of all personnel practices to administer. Its human problems cluster around the merit-increase philosophy, the rating process, and the use of rating data for merit increases.[36]

A University of California study led to the following conclusions:

1. Industry, business and government do not pay employees on a merit program base to the extent which is sometimes assumed or to the extent claimed by some proponents of merit-pay programs for teachers.
2. The purposes and nature of the work situation in business and teaching have little in common.
3. Large gaps in thinking must be bridged before common ground is found for those who are in one way or another interested or involved in the merit-pay question.
4. If the purpose of merit-pay is to raise the level of teaching performance, serious questions can be raised as to whether it alone holds much promise; if the purpose of merit-pay programs is to reward outstanding teachers, then consideration should be given to various possible ways of offering rewards.[37]

The report made several suggestions for school districts considering the merit-pay question, including:

1. Establish the purposes of the proposed program and secure the acceptance of these purposes by the parties affected.
2. Establish a committee representative of the various interested parties to study the question and then to develop proposals for the district in question.
3. Provide essential resources for the committee to make the necessary studies.
4. Consider the relationships of any proposal to the basic teacher-salary question in the district.
5. Provide for a widespread review of various aspects of the proposal as they are developed.
6. Regard any program adopted as highly tentative and provide for its review in the light of results.
7. Consider and develop any program as but one element in an expanded program of improving conditions within the school system, recognizing that many factors affect teaching performance.

Salary Adjustments Based on a Cost-of-Living Index

Cost-of-living escalators have become commonplace in collective bargaining agreements in the private sector in recent years, and have been increasingly built into government wages and programs.[38]

Many school systems have related salaries to the Consumer Price Index. The idea has been proposed in several other school systems and has even been considered by some states as a basis for determining the amount of the apportionment for salaries or even for the state aid program.

Some of the arguments in favor of using a cost-of-living index to adjust amounts in a salary schedule are:

1. Many discussions and controversies regarding salary adjustments could be avoided.

2. The use of an index would provide an automatic plan for adjustments and would eliminate subjective factors.
3. Salaries would automatically increase or decrease as the cost of living increased or decreased.

The primary objection to a cost-of-living index is that it constitutes a political assumption that inflation is acceptable and to be tolerated. Cost-of-living factors push inflation and reduce the effectiveness of government in dealing with inflation. One must ask if indexing is an appropriate policy of government; for if teachers are allowed to index, then should not everyone else in all parts of the economy do the same. On the other hand, teachers will not want to be left out of the indexing game if everyone else is participating. Indexing is so prevalent today that in 1975 the inflation rate stuck at 5.5 percent and did not go lower because of cost-of-living escalators.[39] Thurow characterizes the dilemma in this way: "Each of us organizes to avoid being subject to falling prices. But if we all succeed, we have an economy where inflation is endemic. To stop inflation, someone's income must go down."[40] The question is: Should teachers make the personal sacrifice for the national economy? This is an issue which has not been resolved for any other working group in either the public or private sector.

Another valid objection to such an index, from the teacher's perspective, is that salaries for teachers and other school employees in many school systems have not caught up with increases in salaries paid to many other kinds of workers; consequently, if any cost-of-living index were tied to present salaries, it would merely result in an adjustment upward or downward of salaries that are already inadequate and would not provide for desirable improvements.

Many teachers believe that before there is any attempt to use a cost-of-living index to adjust salaries, there should be more realistic and comprehensive studies of standards of living and of budget requirements for various standards of living.

Salaries of Noncertificated Personnel

Most of the attention in the laws and in the literature seems to have been given to the problem of assuring adequate salary schedules and salaries for teachers and other members of the instructional staff. In many cases, there is no legal requirement that salary schedules be established for noncertificated personnel. Many believe that the relation between salaries of teachers and those of other school employees should be governed by the laws of supply and demand. Thus, if secretaries are in short supply, a school system should expect to pay as much or more for a competent secretary as for a competent teacher. Others oppose this point of view and insist that the nature of the work and the preparation required by various kinds of employees should be the major factors in determining salary policy.

As a practical matter, most school systems will have to pay secretaries, custodians, and other personnel roughly the "going" wage in the community for such personnel. Some are required to do so by civil service provisions. If the salaries authorized are too low, the schools cannot employ or retain competent people. Moreover, some of the employees in many communities belong to unions, and there would be difficulties with the unions if salaries were too low.

Since principals, teachers, and noncertificated employees must work in close cooperation in many aspects of the school program, many believe that special steps should be taken in every school system to assure that each group understands the basis for, and supports the general idea behind the salary schedules for other groups. For that reason, provisions are made in many salary studies for representatives from noncertificated employees to serve on teachers' salary schedule committees and for teachers to serve on committees to study schedules for other groups.

NOTES

1. Philip Selznick, *Leadership in Administration* (New York: Harper & Row, Publishers, 1957).

2. Chris Argyris, *Personality and Organization* (New York: Harper & Row, Publishers, 1957).

3. Douglas McGregor, *The Human Side of Enterprise* (New York: McGraw-Hill Book Company, 1960).

4. Claude W. Fawcett, "Educational Personnel Policies and Practices in a Period of Transition," in *Implications for Education of Prospective Changes in Society*, eds., Edgar L. Morphet and Charles O. Ryan, (Englewood Cliffs, N.J.: Scholastic Magazines, Citation Press, 1968).

5. For example, see Edgar Morphet and David L. Jesser, eds., *Planning for Effective Utilization of Technology in Education* (Englewood Cliffs, N.J.: Scholastic Magazines, Citation Press, 1968).

6. See Seymour E. Harris and Kenneth E. Boulding, *Planning for Effective Utilization of Technology in Education*, chap. 6, Edgar L. Morphet and David L. Jesser, eds. (Englewood Cliffs, N.J.: Scholastic Magazines, Citation Press, 1968).

7. James Koerner, "Educational Technology: Does It Have a Future in the Classroom?" *Saturday Review of Education* (May 1973), pp. 44–46.

8. Mt. Healthy City School District Board of Education v. Doyle, 429 U.S. 274, (1977); Harkless v. Sweeny Independent School District, 427 F.2nd 319 (1970); Perry v. Sindermann, 408 U.S. 593, (1972).

9. Title VII of Civil Rights Act of 1964, *as amended*, Pub.L. 88–352, Title VII, Sec. 701, July 2, 1964, 78 Stat. 253; Pub.L. 89–554, Sec. 8(a), Sept. 6, 1966, 80 Stat. 662; Pub.L. 92–261, Sec. 2, Mar. 24, 1972, 86 Stat. 103. See also Hazelwood School District v. United States, 433 U.S. 299, 97 S.Ct. 2736 (1977).

10. United States of America v. State of South Carolina, 445 F.Supp. 1094, *affirmed* 434 U.S. 1026, (1978).

11. Jacob Landers, "Accountability and Progress by Nomenclature: Old Ideas in New Bottles," *Phi Delta Kappan* (April 1973), pp. 539–41.

12. For a more extensive discussion of this important area see Edgar L. Morphet, Roe L. Johns, and Theodore L. Reller, *Educational Organization and Administration: Concepts, Practices*

and Issues, 4th ed. (Englewood Cliffs, N.J.: Prentice-Hall, 1982), Chap. 18 and references.

13.   Doris Ross and Patricia Flakus-Mosqueda, *State Education Collective Bargaining Laws* (Denver: Education Commission of the States, 1980), pp. 12–14.

14.   Benjamin Werne, *The Law and Practice of Public Employment Labor Relations*, Vol. 1 (Charlottesville, Va: Michie Company, 1974), pp. 393–455.

15.   See Robert Thornton, "The Effects of Collective Negotiations on Teachers' Salaries," *Quarterly Review of Economics and Business* 2 (Winter 1971), 37–46; Robert N. Baird and John H. Landon, "The Effects of Collective Bargaining on Public School Teachers' Salaries: Comment," *Industrial and Labor Relations Review*, Vol. 27 (October 1973), 18–35; W. Clayton Hall and Norman E. Carroll, "The Effects of Teacher's Organizations on Salaries and Class Size," *Industrial and Labor Relations Review*, Vol. 26 (January 1973), 834–41; David Lipsky and John Drotning, "The Influence of Collective Bargaining on Teachers' Salaries in New York State," *Industrial and Labor Relations Review*, Vol. 27 (October 1973), 18–35; Donald E. Frey, "Wage Determination in Public Schools and the Effects of Unionization," Working Paper 42E, Princeton University, Industrial Relations Section, 1973; H. Kasper, "The Effects of Collective Bargaining on Public School Teachers' Salaries," *Industrial and Labor Relations Review*, Vol. 24 (October 1970) 57–72; A.G. Balfour, "More Evidence That Unions Do Not Achieve Higher Salaries for Teachers," *Journal of Collective Negotiations in the Public Sector*, Vol. 3, (Fall 1974), 289–303; D.C. Zuelke and L.E. Frohreich, "The Impact of Comprehensive Collective Negotiations on Teachers' Salaries: Some Evidence from Wisconsin," *Journal of Collective Negotiations*, Vol. 6(1) (1977) 81–88.

17.   National Education Association, *Estimates of School Statistics 1979–80* (Washington, D.C.: The Association, 1980), p. 16.

18.   *Ibid.*

19.   *Ibid.*, p. 38.

20.   Locke, who lived from 1632 to 1704, was best known for his famous philosophical and political investigations, but he also wrote in pure economics. The quotation comes from his book *Some Considerations of the Consequences of the Lowering of Interest and Raising the Value of Money*, (1691), published as *Essay on Interest and Value of Money*, (by London: Alex. Murray & Son, 1870), p. 245.

21.   James A. Richardson and J. Trent Williams, "Determining an Appropriate Teacher Salary," *Journal of Education Finance*, Vol. 7, No. 2, Fall, 1981, pp. 193-194.

22.   James A. Hale, "The Supply and Demand for Public Elementary and Secondary School Teachers," in *Educational Need in the Public Economy*, eds. Kern Alexander and K. Forbis Jordan, (Gainesville, Fla.: University Presses of Florida, 1976), pp. 125–26.

23.   Douglas Greenwald and Associates, *Dictionary of Modern Economics* (New York: McGraw-Hill Book Company, 1973), p. 409.

24.   Hale, *op. cit.*, p. 126.

25.   Martin M. Frankel, ed., *Projections of Education Statistics to 1986–87* (Washington, D.C.: U.S. Government Printing Office, 1978), pp. 16–17.

26.   Martin M. Frankel, unpublished tabulations for National Center for Education Statistics, 1978.

27.   Lester C. Thurow, *The Zero-Sum Society* (New York: Penguin Books, 1980) p. 11.

28.   *Ibid.*, p. 50.

29.   "Fields of College Study Planned by High-School Seniors," *The Chronicle of Higher Education*, Vol. XXII, No. 8 (April 13, 1981) 12.

30.   National Education Association, Research Division, *State Minimum Salary Laws for Teachers, 1950–51* (Washington, D.C.: The Association, 1950).

31.   *Report of the Winnetka Citizens Advisory Committee on Teacher Salaries* (Winnetka, Ill.: The Committee, 1958), pp. 12–13.

32.   Willard E. Givens, "Analysis of Single Salary Schedules," *NEA Research Bulletin 25*, No. 3 (October 1947), p. 76.

33.   *Op. cit.* f. 31. p. 51.

34.   Robert B. Howsam, Edgar L. Morphet, and John G. Ross, "Proposed Salary Schedule for the Professional Staff of the Anchorage Independent School District," mimeographed (Anchorage, Ala.: Board of Education, 1959), p. 39.

35.   Margaret Stevenson, "What Is the Need? Not Merit Rating but Sound Personnel Policies," *NEA Journal*, 46 No. 6 (September 1957), 13.

36.   Davis, *Human Relations in Business* (New York: McGraw-Hill Book Company, 1957) p. 309.

37.   Theodore L. Reller, Robert B. Howsam, and Richard B. Jones, "Merit Pay? What Are the Issues?," mimeographed (Berkeley, Calif.: Field Service Center, Dept. of Education, University of California, 1957), pp. 20–21.

38.   Thurow, *op. cit.*, p. 59.

39.   *Ibid.*, p. 60.

40.   *Ibid.*, p. 61.

SELECTED REFERENCES

AARON, HENRY J.   *Politics and the Professors: The Great Society in Perspective*. Washington, D.C.: Brookings Institution, 1978.

CASTETTER, WILLIAM B.   *The Personnel Function in Educational Administration*, 3rd ed. New York: Macmillan Inc., 1981.

FRANKEL, MARTIN M.   *Projections of Education Statistics to 1986–87*, Washington, D.C.: U.S. Government Printing Office, 1978.

FREEMAN, RICHARD B.   *The Over-Educated American*, New York: Academic Press, Inc., 1976.

HALE, JAMES A. "The Supply and Demand for Public Elementary and Secondary School Teachers," *Educational Need in the Public Economy* . Edited by Kern Alexander and K. Forbis Jordan, Gainesville, Fla.: University Presses of Florida, 1976.

MATHIS, ROBERT L., and JOHN H. JACKSON.   *Personnel: Contemporary Perspectives and Applications*, 2nd ed. St. Paul, Minn.: West Publishing Company, 1979.

NATIONAL EDUCATION ASSOCIATION.   *Teacher Supply and Demand in Public Schools, 1978*, Washington, D.C.: The Association, 1980.

THUROW, LESTER C.   *The Zero-Sum Society*, New York: Penguin Books, 1981.

WERNE, BENJAMIN.   *The Law and Practice of Public Employment Labor Relations*, 3 Vols. Charlottesville, Va.: Michie Company, 1974.

CHAPTER FIFTEEN
THE FEDERAL ROLE
IN FINANCING
EDUCATION

In 1930 the federal government provided only .4 percent of the revenue receipts of the public schools, but that share has been increased in each decade since. The federal government provided 1.8 percent of the revenue receipts of the public schools in 1940, 2.9 percent in 1950, 4.4 percent in 1960, 8.0 percent in 1970, and approximately 9 percent in 1980.[1]

The increases in federal aid for the public schools during recent years have usually been accompanied by much controversy. Federal policy with respect to financial support of the public schools is far from being stabilized. A number of educational organizations and experts on school finance have advocated that the federal government provide 30 percent or more of public school revenue. On the other hand, some business organizations and conservative political leaders would like to see all federal financial support of the public schools discontinued. At this writing, the national administration has recommended that present federal support of the public schools be reduced 20 to 25 percent.

What is the basis of the present controversy over federal aid to education? This is not a simple issue. It is an old issue as well as a current issue. The federal-aid issue has long been involved with a number of other important issues. Education has become the battleground for testing many important principles of law, theories of government, theories of economics, and philosophical values. Furthermore, there has been much controversy over the purposes of federal aid, methods of distribution, and federal controls associated with it.

It is impossible in a book of this length to give a comprehensive treatment of the subject of federal aid to education.[2] This chapter will deal with some of the more important national issues involved in federal aid, its present status, the arguments for and against it, and a brief history of federal aid.

NATIONAL ISSUES AFFECTING FEDERAL AID TO EDUCATION

If the policies of federal aid to education could have been isolated from other important national issues, it is probable that the federal government would have been providing a more substantial share of public school revenue than it is now providing. Some of the more important of those issues are discussed below.

Division of Powers among Governments

The Tenth Amendment to the Constitution of the United States provides: "The powers not delegated to United States by the Constitution, nor prohibited by it to the States, are reserved to the states respectively or to the people." Since the Constitution makes no specific reference to education, it has been assumed that education is the legal responsibility of the states. The governmental powers of the states are plenary except for the powers that have been delegated to the federal government or withheld from the states by some provision of the Constitution. On the other hand, the federal government is a limited government, with no powers except those specifically conferred upon it by the Constitution or those that can reasonably be implied as necessary to exercise the powers and responsibilities specifically granted.[3]

The Constitution, in addition to being a broad statement of principles, also provides broad specific grants of power to the federal government. Since the federal government has no specific grant of power to finance, regulate, control, or operate schools, colleges, institutions, or educational programs, its authority to do so must be found in its implied powers. It is in the area of implied powers that the controversy centers.

As will be shown later in this chapter, it is an historical fact that the federal government has assisted in financing many types of public educational institutions, including the public schools; it has regulated and controlled public education to some extent, and it has operated practically every type of educational institution and numerous special programs. In fact it is still doing so. It is interesting that this exercise of implied powers has never been successfully challenged in the courts. The issue is not whether the federal government has any implied powers with respect to education but the extent to which those powers should be exercised. It is not possible to define neatly by Constitution or statute the limits of the exercise of the implied or discretionary powers of government, or the times when they should be exercised, or the objects for which they should be exercised.

The implied powers of the federal government have caused bitter controversy between the states and the federal government itself. It was one of the fundamental issues of the Civil War. It is a basic issue in the current controversy over desegregation in the public schools and institutions of higher learning and over civil rights. It was a controversial issue of the past and still remains a live issue.

One of the earliest issues causing the formation of political parties arose over differences of opinion concerning the relative roles of the federal and the state governments. The present-day term "states' rights" (also an old term) means many things to many people. But in general, it emphasizes the powers of the states and deemphasizes the powers of the federal government. It was inevitable that the issue of federal aid to education should become associated in the minds of many people with these old issues. Therefore, the position that many people take with respect to federal aid to education is not determined by the virtues of the proposals or the reality of the need for federal aid, but by their thinking concerning these old issues.

Controversy over the Effect of Government Expenditures on the Economy

The enormous increase in the cost of government at all levels during the past 30 years has been accompanied by bitter controversy. As pointed out in Chapter 2, the per-capita cost of all government—federal, state and local—increased from $1,588 in 1950 to $3,608 in 1980 in terms of the purchasing power of 1980 dollars. This is a real increase of 127 percent. The per capita GNP increased from $6,462 in 1950 to $11,569 in 1980 in terms of 1980 dollars. This is a real increase of 79 percent. Therefore the cost of government has been increasing faster than the GNP in recent years.

Much political capital has been made in recent years over the increase in the expenditures of the federal government. However, the direct expenditures of the federal government have increased at a lesser rate than the direct expenditures of state and local governments. Direct expenditure is defined as total expenditure less the amount transferred to other governments. The direct expenditures of the federal government increased from 14.7 percent of the GNP to 1950 to 19.6 percent in 1980, whereas the direct expenditures of the state and local governments increased from 9.8 percent of the GNP in 1950 to 13.5 percent in 1980. In terms of the percentage of the GNP, the direct expenditures of the federal government increased 33 percent between 1950 and 1980, and state and local government expenditures increased 38 percent during that period. At this writing, great political pressure was being brought to reduce government expenditures at all levels, but greater pressure was being brought to reduce government expenditures at the federal level than at state and local government levels, despite the fact that government expenditures had been increasing at a faster rate at the state and local levels.

The point of view of many modern thinkers is that the trend toward increasing government expenditures in this technological civilization is a necessary and desirable trend because (1) only government (especially central government) can provide many of the services essential to a modern civilization, and (2) the expenditures of government are necessary for maximizing production and consumption of goods and services and minimizing unemployment. The fiscally conservative view is that government taxing and spending should be limited to providing the minimum of necessary government services, because (1) continued increases in government spending eventually will result in socialism and a welfare state, and (2) socialism will destroy the free-enterprise system and eventually result in the loss of other liberties. These two sharply contrasting views are at the heart of much of present-day political controversy.

Those not fearing the effects of government spending generally support increased revenue for education at all levels of government and especially at the state and federal levels. Those fearing the effects of government spending generally oppose increased spending for education at all levels, especially by the federal government. The conservative generally opposes increased spending for public education, not because he or she is opposed to public education, but rather because of his or her opposition to increases in government spending in general.

The goal of the fiscal conservative is to maximize the market economy and to minimize the government economy. In times of inflation, such as that experienced in 1980, the fiscal conservative advocates the reduction of government expenditures and taxes on the basis that government expenditures add to inflation. In times of deflation and depression, this same conservative still advocates the reduction of government expenditures and taxes contending that "one more penny of taxes will break the back of the overburdened taxpayer."

Experts on school financing generally insist that expenditures for education should not be determined by whether they inflate or deflate the economy, but by the educational needs of the children, youth, and adults of the nation. Such a policy tends to stabilize the economy rather than inflating or deflating it. Furthermore, as pointed out in Chapter 3, investment in people, as well as investment in physical capital, in time increases the total volume of goods and services available for consumption.

The General Welfare Clause
of the Constitution

Article I, Section 8, of the Constitution deals with the powers granted to Congress. Clause 1 reads as follows: "The Congress shall have Power To lay and collect Taxes, Duties, Imposts and Excises, to pay the Debts and provide for the common Defense and general Welfare of the United States; but all Duties, Imposts and Excises shall be uniform throughout the United States." Although this clause deals with such important matters as levying and collecting taxes, the payment of debts, and providing for the common defense, it is commonly called the General Welfare Clause because of the great controversies over the meaning of the words *and general Welfare of the United States.* At the time the Constitution was adopted, probably only a few people realized the significance of those words.

The eighteenth, and last, clause of Section 8 grants Congress the final power "to make all Laws which shall be necessary and proper for carrying into Execution the foregoing Powers, and all other Powers vested by this Constitution in the Government of the United States, or in any Department or Officer thereof." This clause gives to Congress a broad grant of implied powers. The meaning of Clauses 1 and 18 became a matter of bitter controversy very early in our history. James Madison and Alexander Hamilton took the lead in presenting the opposing points of view. Madison argued that the words *and general Welfare of the United States* confer on Congress no additional powers to tax and spend and that the power of Congress to tax and spend therefore is limited to the purposes specifically enumerated by the Constitution. Hamilton held that those words did confer additional power on Congress to tax and spend for purposes other than those specifically enumerated in the Constitution and that Congress had the power to tax and spend for any purpose that it deemed to be for the general welfare.

Hamilton and Madison did not resolve their differences. In fact, controversy over this issue still continues, but the details have changed somewhat. The Supreme Court, in some relatively recent decisions, has supported some of Hamilton's contentions. In a ruling on the Agricultural Adjustment Act, the Court held that "the power of Congress to authorize expenditures of public moneys for public purposes is not limited by the direct grants of legislative power found in the Constitution."[4] The Supreme Court, in ruling on the Social Security Act, held that the decision as to whether an expenditure was for the general welfare had to be made by Congress, provided that it was not a display of arbitrary power. The Court also held in this decision: "Nor is the concept of general welfare static. Needs that were narrow or parochial a century ago may be interwoven in our day with the well-being of the nation. What is critical or urgent changes with the times."[5]

The authority of Congress to tax and spend for public education has been clearly established by these and other opinions by the Court. Actually, the legal power of Congress to appropriate and spend money for public education has never been challenged in the Supreme Court. But the rulings of the Court have not settled the controversy between the "liberal constructionists" and the "strict constructionists" of the Constitution. The battle still continues, but the major issue has changed from the legal power of Congress to tax and spend for the general welfare to the wisdom of the policy of doing so. What laws are "necessary and proper" (Clause 18) "to provide for the general Welfare of the United States" (Clause 1)? That issue never will be finally resolved, because what is necessary and proper for the general welfare "changes with the times."

The General Welfare Clause has been used extensively during the past forty years to justify the expansion of old federal activities and the addition of new activities of the federal government. The advocates of extension of services of the federal government now contend that Congress has not only the power to promote the general welfare but also the duty to do so. This point of view is vigorously opposed by the conservatives, who bitterly fight practically any extension of federal spending except for national defense. Therefore, the issue of federal aid to education actually is a part of the old Hamilton-Madison controversy.

FEDERAL CONSTITUTIONAL LIMITATIONS

Following is a brief discussion of some constitutional provisions affecting education.

Limitations on Congress

Article I, Section 9, of the Constitution sets forth the powers denied to Congress. Two of its subsections have some relationship to financing education. Subsection 4 reads as follows: "No Capitation or other direct Tax shall be laid, unless in Proportion to the Census or Enumeration herein before directed to be taken." This provision of the Constitution has effectively prevented Congress from levying a property tax. It is obviously impracticable to levy a property tax in proportion to the census. The last time Congress attempted to levy such a tax was during the Civil War. Had it not been for this provision of the Constitution, Congress probably would have levied property taxes very early in our history.

This subsection also prevented Congress from levying income taxes until it was removed by the Sixteenth Amendment, ratified in 1913. It reads: "The Congress shall have power to lay and collect taxes on incomes, from whatever sources derived, without apportionment among the several States, and without regard to any census or enumeration." This amendment greatly increased the taxing powers of Congress.

The federal government now obtains more than 80 percent of its tax revenue from income taxes. This broadening of the taxing powers of Congress has made it possible for the federal government to extend greatly the federal services provided. It also greatly improved the equity of our taxing system.

Subsection 5 prohibits Congress from laying taxes or duties on articles exported from any state. This provision and the provisions of Subsection 4 as amended by the Sixteenth Admendment are the only specific limitations upon the taxing powers of Congress, except for the provision of Article I, Section 8, Clause 1, requiring that "all Duties, Imposts and Excises shall be uniform throughout the United States." Therefore, it is apparent that Congress has very broad taxing powers. The enormous amount of revenue collected annually by the federal government is evidence of that fact.

The federal government has another important advantage in obtaining revenues. When taxes are levied nationwide, the difficulties of competition among state and local governments are avoided. The income tax, both personal and corporate, is levied nationwide. A person or corporation cannot escape the federal income tax by moving to another political jurisdiction within the nation. But the income taxes and certain other taxes of state and local governments can be avoided by moving into jurisdictions not levying the tax. Therefore, "tax competition" limits the potential tax revenues of state and local governments.

The federal government does not suffer from this limitation. It might be argued that the federal government faces international tax compeition. That probably is true to some extent, but international tax competition does not have nearly so great a restraining influence on taxation as does the tax competition among state and local governments.

Limitations on the States

Article I, Section 10, of the Constitution sets forth the powers denied the states. There are only a few provisions of this section that are related to the financing of education. Subsection 1 includes the provision that no state shall pass any law impairing the obligation of contracts. Subsection 2 provides: "No State shall, without the Consent of the Congress, lay any Imposts or Duties on Imports or Exports, except what may be absolutely necessary for executing its inspection Laws; and the net Produce of all Duties and Imposts, laid by any State on Imports or Exports, shall be for the Use of the Treasury of the United States; and all such Laws shall be subject to the Revision and Control of the Congress." Subsection 3 provides: "No State shall, without consent of Congress, lay any Duty of Tonnage. . . . "These are the only limitations placed upon the taxing powers of the states by the Constitution. They are relatively minor and therefore place no serious restrictions on the states with respect to levying and collecting taxes.

But it should not be assumed that Article I, Section 10, of the Constitution contains the only federal limitations upon the states in the operation of systems of public education. The Constitution as interpreted by the Supreme Court is the supreme law of the land. Any law of any state on any matter, including education, that is in conflict with any provision of the Constitution is null and void if so declared by the United States Supreme Court. People who argue that the federal government should have no control whatsoever over public education seem to have overlooked this fact. It would be impossible to have a federal government of the United States if the states could nullify the Constitution. Therefore, some measure of federal control of public education is inescapable. The issue of federal control of public education is so important that some specific instances are presented in the following paragraphs.

Equal Protection of the Law.   The Fourteenth Amendment, Section 1, provides in part: "No State shall make or enforce any law which shall abridge the privileges or immunities of citizens of the United States; nor shall any State deprive any person of life, liberty, or property, without due process of law; nor deny to any person within its jurisdiction the equal protection of the laws." It was this amendment plus subsequent rulings of the Supreme Court that firmly established the supremacy of the Constitution and all its provisions.

One of the Court's most dramatic rulings was made on May 17, 1954. The Court had before it five cases dealing with segregation in the public schools. Segregation by race in the public schools was declared unconstitutional when the Court stated: "We conclude that in the field of public education the doctrine of 'separate but equal' has no place. Separate educational facilities are inherently unequal. Therefore, we hold that the plaintiffs and others similarly situated for whom the actions are brought are, by reason of the segregation complained of, deprived of the equal protection of the laws guaranteed by the Fourteenth Amendment."[6]

It is interesting to note that the 1954 ruling ot the Court reversed a ruling it had made in 1896 dealing with the question of racial segregation on public transportation facilities. The Court ruled in that case that separate but equal facilities were constitutional.[7] The 1954 *Brown* ruling controls not only the policies of the states relating to segregation but also the policies of boards of education wherever situated. This decision overthrew the "states' rights" theory insofar as certain aspects of public education were concerned.

Decisions of the Court dealing with highly controversial matters are not always accepted by the losers as being the supreme law of the land. Segments of the public continue to resist the implementation of the Court's decisions on controversial matters. This is particularly true of the 1954 ruling on segregation. Controversy over the segregation issue does not produce a climate favorable to the financing of education. This observation is not for the purpose of questioning the correctness of the ruling of the Court, but rather to point out its fiscal effect.

The Civil Rights Act of 1964 greatly increased the power of the federal government to enforce the 1954 decision of the Supreme Court. Title VI of this act states: "No person in the United States shall on the ground of race, color or national origin, be excluded from participation in, be denied the benefits of, or be subject to discrimination, under any program or activity receiving federal financial assistance." Under the provisions of this act, any federal agency disbursing federal funds is given the power to withhold such funds if the recipient agency or institution violates this act. The federal agencies in recent years have frequently used their power to withhold funds to enforce the provisions of the Civil Rights Act and the 1954 decision of the Supreme Court. Since federal funds for education are now rather substantial, this is a powerful control designed to force racial integration.

Separation of Church and State.   The relationship of the schools to religion is regulated by the federal government under authority of the First and Fourteenth Amendments to the Constitution. The First Amendment provides: "Congress shall make no law respecting an establishment of religion, or prohibiting the free exercise thereof. . . . "The Supreme Court has held that the provisions of the First Amendment also apply to the states because of the following provision in the Fourteenth Amendment: No State shall make or enforce any laws which shall abridge the privileges or immunities of citizens of the United States. . . . "Therefore any privilege or immunity granted a citizen of the United States by the Constitution cannot be denied by the states. See chapter 6 for a more extensive discussion of this topic.

Impairment of Contracts.   As has been pointed out, Article I, Section 10, of the Constitution contains a provision prohibiting a state from passing a law impairing the obligation of contracts. School financing involves many different types of contracts. School boards, for instance, issue bonds that are important financial contracts. The federal prohibition against the impairment of contracts undoubtedly has improved the credit of boards of education as well as the credit of all state and local governments. This type of federal control seems to be applauded by almost everyone. Actually, it is not generally recognized as a control, but the fact that it is a control makes it a valuable asset in school financing.

One ruling of the Supreme Court has significance in relation to teacher retirement. The Court has held that "a legislative enactment may contain provisions which, when accepted as a basis of action of individuals, become contracts between them and the state or its subdivision. . . . "[8] Teacher retirement laws should be so drafted as to make it clear that provisions for retirement constitute a contract between the teacher and state.

HISTORICAL DEVELOPMENT
OF FEDERAL AID

Practically every department of the federal government at one time or another has expended some of its appropriations for education, either directly or indirectly. There is no accurate historical record of all the federal funds that have been expended for education. Actually, no office or agency of the federal government can give an accurate statement of federal funds being expended directly or indirectly for education. Even objective investigators working independently cannot arrive at the same total of federal funds expended for education during any given fiscal year. Therefore, it would not be possible to present an accurate history of federal aid even if space permitted. However, it is possible to present certain examples of it that throw some light on its development.

Early Land Grants

The national interest in education was revealed even before the adoption of the Constitution. The Ordinance of 1785 included the provision that "there shall be reserved the lot number 16 of every township for the maintenance of public schools in each township."

The policies enunciated in the Ordinance of 1785 were put into effect in 1787 by a federal contract for the sale of lands to the Ohio Company. The Ordinance of 1787 contained these often-quoted words expressing federal educational policy at that time: "Religion, morality and knowledge being necessary to good government and the happiness of mankind, schools and the means of education shall be forever encouraged." The ordinance, providing for the contract of sale in 1787, also reserved certain townships to endow a university.

Most of the states admitted to the Union after 1789 were first administered and organized as territories. The federal government administered the territories and consequently actually founded the public school systems of many states. This direct responsibility of the federal government for education in the territories probably contributed to federal interest in education when the territories became states.

In 1802, Congress adopted the same general policy of giving support to public education that had been adopted by the Congress of the Confederation seventeen years earlier. When Ohio was admitted to the Union in 1802, Congress initiated its policy of setting aside public lands for public education at the time of the admission of a state to the Union.

The policy of setting aside the sixteenth section of each township for the public schools was followed for states admitted between 1802 and 1848. When the Oregon Territory was established in 1848, Congress set aside two sections of each township for the public school. This policy was continued until 1896, when Utah was granted four sections in every township. Similar grants were made to other western states, admitted after that year.

It was the hope of some in the early days that the income from school lands would be sufficient to pay for most of the cost of the public schools. However, partly because of poor management of these lands, this was a vain hope and would have been so even if the public lands had been well managed in all cases. But the early grants of land had great significance for the public schools. These federal grants stimulated the interest of the states in public schools. When the states found that the income from federal grants was insufficient to support their schools, they began to provide state grants-in-aid. Therefore, the early federal grants in effect established the precedent for state aid for the public schools.

Two characteristics of these early land grants were of great significance. First, the grants were for general public school purposes. Second, the federal government exercised no control whatsoever over education as a condition for receiving the grants. Authorities on school finance almost unanimously recommended general federal aid for the public schools in preference to aid for specific educational purposes. Despite this fact, practically all federal grants-in-aid to the public schools after 1862 have been special-purpose grants.

The early federal grants demonstrated the fact that the federal government can given federal aid without imposing federal control. But the history of the management of those grants is not proof that absolutely no federal control is a wise policy. Perhaps the states would have benefited from some federal requirements concerning sound fiscal management of the grants. Such controls would not have interfered with the prerogative of the states to determine educational policy.

The Morrill Act

The first Morrill Act was passed by Congress in 1862. This act provided for a grant of 30,000 acres to each state for each representative and senator then in Congress. This same grant of land was made available to states thereafter admitted to the Union. The act provided for the giving of scrip to the states in which the public lands were insufficient to make up the allotment. It was provided that the land be sold and the proceeds used for the "endowment, maintenance and support of at least one college where the leading object shall be, without excluding other scientific and classical studies and including military tactics, to teach such branches of learning as are related to agriculture and the mechanic arts in such manner as the legislatures of the states may respectively prescribe." Another stated purpose of the act was "to promote the liberal and practical education of the industrial classes in the several pursuits and professions of life."

This original Morrill Act is the first instance of the federal government's providing a grant for specific educational purposes. It will be noted that federal control was limited to specifying that agriculture, mechanic arts, and military tactics must be taught in those institutions. No limitation was placed on the other types of subjects that might be taught. Also, the act specifically placed the determination of the educational policies of the land-grant institutions in the hands of the respective legislatures.

This act is of great significance because it again demonstrated the national interest in education. It also showed that, when existing educational institutions did not provide adequately for the "general welfare," the federal government could and would take action. At the time the Morrill Act was passed, the institutions of higher learning were largely classical and academic in character. They catered primarily to the select few. The land-grant colleges have been called people's colleges. Their curricula included subjects that were not "academically respectable" in 1862, but their educational programs grew in popularity. The influence of these land-grant colleges has been so great that they have contributed substantially to liberalizing the educational programs of many non-land-grant colleges. In thirty-two states, a land-grant college is also the principal state university.

The Smith-Lever Act

The Smith-Lever Act was approved by Congress in 1914. It provided for extension services by county agricultural and home demonstration agents, 4-H leaders, and specialists in agriculture and homemaking, and for professional training of teachers in those subjects. This act was far more specific in detailing the purposes for which the grant funds could be spent than was the Morrill Act. Actually, the services provided under the Smith-Lever Act were practically nonexistent prior to its passage. This act is additional evidence that Congress, when it deems it desirable to do so, will provide for, or stimulate provision for, educational services that are not being furnished by the educational organization.

The extension services provided under the Smith-Lever Act are not an integral part of the system of public education. The service at the local level is usually allocated to the control of the county governing body. Boards of education, especially county boards, have sometimes subsidized the extension service, but they have no authority over it. The state director of the extension service is usually associated with a land-grant college, but this is about the only direct relationship with the system of public education.

The extension services have made a major contribution to the dissemination of the results of the research conducted on agricultural experiment farms. The home demonstrators have also made major contributions to home and family living. The extension services have brought the "people's colleges" to the people. It should be remembered that the extension services were inaugurated before the days of radio and television. Thus, these workers were the major communicators of new and improved practices in agriculture and homemaking.

The success of the federally subsidized extension services undoubtedly influenced the state and institutions of higher learning to establish additional extension services and adult education programs.

The Smith-Hughes Act

Between 1862 and 1917 the federal government seemed to be concerned primarily with inadequacies in the programs of institutions of higher learning. No new federal act of any major significance to the public schools was passed by Congress during this period. In 1917, Congress passed the Smith-Hughes Act, which provided funds for vocational education below college level. A continuing appropriation was provided for vocational education in agriculture, trades and industry, and homemaking. Provision was also made for teacher training in these fields. The original Smith-Hughes Act required dollar-for-dollar matching by the states and local units. Some states provided all the matching funds required from state revenues. Other states required local units to match the state funds dollar for dollar and thereby provide half the matching funds required by the federal government. This retarded the development of vocational education in some of the least wealthy districts because of their inability to provide the required matching funds. Some other acts that supplemented and broadened the Smith-Hughes Act were the George-Reed Act of 1929, the George-Ellzey Act of 1935, the George-Deen Act of 1937, the George-Barden Act of 1946, the Vocational Education Act of 1963 as amended in 1968, and subsequent amendments.

The Smith-Hughes Act provided the first special-purpose grants made available to the public schools by Congress. Vocational education was not a new educational idea. A number of school systems had established some type of vocational education programs prior to 1917. For example, some 500 agricultural high schools had been established by 1909. Some schools in forty-four of the forty-seven states in 1911 offered training in homemaking. A number of city systems had developed trade schools or trade courses in regular high schools. However, most high school students did not have access to suitable kinds of vocational programs.

At the beginning of the twentieth century, most lay people—and also most educators—believed that the high-school program should be largely academic in character. The prevailing belief was that if a high-school student was not interested in college preparatory work, he or she should not go to high school. High schools did not become mass education institutions until after World War I. Following that war, however, there was a remarkable increase in the demand for secondary education. The development of vocational education, which was stimulated by the Smith-Hughes Act, contributed to providing for large numbers of pupils whose needs could not have been served by the high-school programs generally available prior to 1917.

Grants-in-aid for vocational education have been criticized on the grounds that such grants tend to turn the educational programs in the direction of the subsidized purpose. This was no doubt true in the years immediately following 1917. But that was probably one of the purposes of the Smith-Hughes Act. Any special-purpose grant influences the direction of the educational program. Therefore, a special-purpose grant of any kind, state or federal, contains an element of control.

Some Federal Relief Measures
Affecting Education

In the decade between 1930 and 1940, the nation suffered the worst financial depression in its history; the depression actually became worldwide in its effects. The major attention of the nation in those years was directed toward finding a solution for our economic difficulties. One school of thought was that if we did nothing, the economy in time would adjust itself. Another theory was that the federal government could break the depression by "priming" the economy with federal spending.

Franklin D. Roosevelt, inaugurated president in 1933, promptly initiated his New Deal Program for economic recovery. One of its principal elements was an accelerated program of federal spending for the primary purpose of stimulating the economy. Almost 25 percent of the labor force was unemployed, and millions of people were destitute. Therefore, the immediate purpose of many of the New Deal measures was to provide employment and give relief to destitute persons.

Following is a list of the more important relief agencies that gave financial aid to public education either directly or indirectly:

1. The Civilian Conservation Corps was established in 1933 and abolished in 1943.
2. The National Youth Administration was established in 1935 and liquidated in 1944.
3. The Federal Emergency Relief Administration was established in 1933, was superseded by the Works Progress Administration in 1939, and was abolished in the early 1940s.
4. The Public Works Administration was established in 1933 and abolished in the early 1940s.
5. The Federal Surplus Commodities Corporation was established in 1935 and still continues to function to a limited extent.

The policies developed by the Surplus Commodities Corporation culminated in the National School Lunch Act of 1946. This was supplemented later by an act providing special aid for the school milk program. Those acts apparently have made school lunch assistance a continuing policy of the federal government. This program has stimulated the construction and operation of thousands of school lunchrooms throughout the United States.

Defense and War Federal Educational Activities

The past and present educational activities of the federal government related to defense and war are far too extensive to treat in detail in this volume. They were justified on the ground that they were necessary to provide for the common defense and to promote the general welfare. In terms of money expended, these activities have been very extensive. Appropriations for most of the war and defense educational activities of the federal government have been passed by Congress with little opposition from any quarter.

Following are some of the educational activities of the federal government for defense and war:

Educational Institutions Operated by the Armed Services. The Military Academy was established in 1802, the Naval Academy in 1845, the Air Force Academy in 1954, the Army Medical School in 1893, the Army War College in 1902 (superseded by the National War College in 1946), and the Air University in 1947. In addition, the armed services operate elementary and high schools at some service posts both at home and abroad. This is an incomplete list, but it gives some indication of the scope of the institutions operated by the armed services.

Educational Programs Administered by the Armed Services. An act of Congress in 1866 provided that "whenever troops are serving at any post, garrison, or permanent camp, there shall be established a school where all men may be provided with instruction in the common English branches of education and especially in the history of the United States." Many thousands of men were trained under this program and it probably was the forerunner of the Armed Forces Institute, which was established in 1945. This program is very extensive in nature. It provides educational training in many areas of knowledge. In addition to these programs, the Army, the Navy, the Air Force, the Marines, and the Coast Guard all conduct or sponsor other types of educational programs that are useful to service personnel when they return to civilian life.

Federal Impact Area Aid. In 1941, Congress passed the Lanham Act for the construction, maintenance, and operation of community facilities in the areas where the defense and war activities created unusual burdens for local governments. Schools received considerable federal aid for building construction and for current expenses under the provisions of this act.

The Lanham Act was superseded in 1950 by Public Laws 815 and 874, which continued approximately the same types of benefits provided by it.

Veterans Training Programs. Public Law 178 of 1918 provided for the vocational training of disabled veterans of World War I, and Public Law 16 of 1943 provided for the training of disabled veterans of World War II.

The most important of the acts providing training for veterans was Public Law 346 of 1944, which has been commonly called the GI Bill of Rights. This act contained quite liberal provisions for the education of veterans. It provided reasonable allowances for payment of the cost of books, tuition, and subsistence. The educational training allowed included practically everything from dancing to advanced graduate study in the United States or abroad. The educational training of the veterans of the Korean War was provided for by Public Law 550 of 1952, and the veterans of the "Cold War" were provided for in 1966 by Public Law 385.

The immediate effect of these two acts was to double college enrollment after World War II. The long-range effect was to popularize college education for the masses and bring it within the aspirations of millions of young men and women who prior to World War II would not seriously have considered going to college. Another long-range effect was to raise the production and cultural level of individuals and of the nation. It has been estimated that the increased income taxes collected from veterans because of their higher earning power will more than reimburse the federal government for the cost of their education before most of them are forty years of age.

The benefits provided by Public Law 385 are available to all veterans who served prior to December 31, 1976. Veterans beginning service since that date receive educational benefits under Public Law 95–502, entitled The Veterans'

Educational Assistance Act. The benefits provided by it are substantial but not quite as generous as those provided by previous acts.

Other Important Federal Legislation
Affecting Education

The year 1958 marked a turning point in the relationship of the federal government to education. The launching by the Russians of the first man-made earth satellite in 1957 caused great alarm in the United States. It was a popular myth that the Russians could not possibly develop science and industry under their "socialist system." When pundits are found to be wrong, they seldom admit error, but blame others. Therefore, the first reaction of many people to the success of the Russians was to blame the public schools for alleged inefficiency. Fortunately, this state of public opinion did not last very long and, beginning in 1958, successive sessions of Congress enacted a long series of laws designed to improve education in the United States, extending from the preschool age group through college and university and continuing throughout adult life.

Another factor that stimulated federal activities in support of education was the increase in social and economic problems arising from the inability of persons who were educationally and culturally deprived to support themselves in the present-day technological society. It has finally become apparent to the general public that this problem cannot be solved without the assistance of education.

Some of the more important federal legislation that has been enacted since 1958 is treated briefly below.

The National Defense Education Act of 1958—Public Law 85-864. This act authorizes expenditure of substantial sums for the following purposes:

1. Providing loans to students in institutions of higher learning
2. Providing equipment for and remodeling of facilities for science, mathematics, and foreign language teaching
3. Providing graduate fellowships for those interested in teaching in institutions of higher learning
4. Providing assistance for guidance, counseling, and testing services and for identification and encouragement of able students
5. Providing centers for teaching modern foreign languages
6. Providing assistance for research and experimentation in the more effective use of television and other related audio-visual media
7. Providing assistance for certain area vocational programs

The primary impetus for the act came from the scientific advances of military significance made by Russia. These advances were dramatized by the launching of Sputnik I. That was the reason, perhaps, that the act was named the National Defense Education Act.

Manpower Development and Training Act of 1962—Public Law 84-415.   The basic purpose of this act was to reduce the hard core of unemployment by retraining workers whose skills had become obsolete. Although it was directed primarily toward the relief of unemployed adult workers, it also provided for "the testing, counseling, and selection of youth, 16 years of age and older for occupational training and further schooling." This act was amended in 1966 to provide these same services for persons forty-five years of age and older. The costs of training and training allowances are financed under this act.

Vocational Education Act of 1963—Public Law 88-210.   This act more than quadrupled the federal appropriations for vocational education, and it greatly broadened the purposes of the original Smith-Hughes Act. The major purpose of the act of 1963 is to provide occupational training for persons of all ages and achievement levels in any occupational field that does not require a baccalaureate degree and to provide for related services that will help to ensure programs of quality. It also provides financial assistance for the construction of area vocational facilities, and work-study programs, and residential schools. This act provides financial assistance for technical and vocational programs in community colleges and in other post secondary institutions as well as for vocational programs in high schools.

The Elementary and Secondary Education Act of 1965—Public Law 89-10.   This law is by far the most important measure affecting the financing of the public schools that has been enacted by Congress up to the present time. It contains a broad program of categorical aids under five titles designed to strengthen public education at what was considered by Congress to be its weakest points.

Title I provides financial assistance for education programs specifically designed to benefit children from families with incomes of less than a specified amount or who are receiving welfare aid for dependent children. Title II provides funds for libraries, textbooks, and audio-visual materials. Title II provides funds for supplementary education centers for students in both public and private schools. Title IV provides funds for regional educational research and training laboratories. Title V provides funds for strengthening state departments of education.

The Higher Education Act of 1965—Public Law 83-333.   This act authorizes insured loans and scholarships for students and the establishment of community service programs by institutions of higher education to attack problems of urban and suburban communities. It has expanded college construction programs, provided for improvement of libraries, and authorized assistance to developing institutions for the improvement of instruction.

The National Institute of Education—Public Law 92-318. The act establishing the National Institute of Education contains some important declarations concerning federal educational policy. Section 405(a) reads in part as follows:

> The Congress hereby declares it to be the policy of the United States to provide every person an equal opportunity to receive an education of high quality regardless of race, color, religion, sex, national origin, or social class. . . .
>
> The Congress further declares it to be the policy of the United States to
> (a) help to solve the problems of and promote the reform and renewal of American education;
> (b) advance the practice of education as an art, science and profession;
> (c) strengthen the scientific and technological foundations of education; and
> (d) build an effective research and development program.

Education of the Handicapped Act— Public Law 94-142

The purpose of this act is to assist in the initiation, expansion, and improvement of programs and projects for the handicapped at preschool, elementary, and secondary levels through grants to states and outlying territories. This act has been of great assistance to the states and local boards of education in meeting court requirements that handicapped pupils be provided appropriate educational programs.

TRENDS AND PRESENT STATUS OF FEDERAL FUNDS FOR EDUCATION

It has been pointed out by many writers that we do not have a clearly discernible federal policy for education. Such fiscal policy as existed in 1980 consisted of a hodgepodge of uncoordinated, categorical grants administered under numerous bureaucratic regulations. *The Catalogue of Federal Education Assistance Programs—1980* lists 318 federal education assistance programs for 1980.[9] These 318 programs were administered by 9 U.S. departments through 45 federal agencies.[10] The U.S. Department of Education reported that 218 of these programs were administered by the Department of Education in 1981.[11] Examples of program proliferation are found in the *1981 Guide to Department of Education Programs* in which seventeen programs are reported for the handicapped and talented, fifteen programs for vocational and adult education, and fifteen programs for bilingual education. The creation of the Department of Education in 1979, with a secretary in the President's cabinet, has not resulted as of this writing in a reduction in the number of federal education assistance programs. Any significant reduction in the number of or consolidation of federal education assistance programs must be accomplished by legislation enacted by Congress.

Experts on educational finance, the American Association of School Administrators, and authors of numerous studies have advocated the discontinuance of the numerous federal categorical grants for education and the provision of general aid or a few block grants for education. For example, the National Educational Finance Project in 1971 recommended preferably general federal aid for the public schools but if categorical grants are continued that they be consolidated into a few major block grants.[12]

Federal Funds for Education 1960–1980

Table 14–1 shows trends in federal funds for education from 1960 to 1980. The total of all federal funds for all education and related activities more than tripled between 1960 and 1970 and increased two-and-two-thirds times between 1970 and 1980.

Table 14–1 shows that funds for elementary and secondary education increased from $490,480,000 in 1960 to $7,090,390,000 in 1980. This was an increase of 1,346 percent. Most of the increase was in categorical appropriations for the culturally deprived, the handicapped and economic opportunity programs. The policy of Congress in providing catetgorical aid for the public schools has been to earmark federal appropriations to provide for certain educational needs that its members believed were not being met adequately by the public schools. It is obvious that categorical aids provide much more control over the public schools than general aid. Advocates of categorical grants argue that the federal controls accompanying categorical grants are benign controls for the following reasons: (1) states and boards of education can refuse to accept a categorical grant if the grantee objects to the federal controls accompanying the grant, (2) federal interest requires that certain unmet educational needs be specifically provided for by categorical grants.

These categorical grants to the public schools are uncoordinated and undoubtedly cause a great deal of paperwork on the part of the agencies receiving them. However, the educational opportunities of the culturally and economically deprived and the handicapped have undoubtedly been greatly improved by these grants.

Federal grants to institutions of higher learning increased from $829,880,000 in 1960 to $9,738,836,000 in 1980. This was an increase of 1,074 percent. Table 14–1 shows that the most federal funds for higher education are applied to student assistance and that the next most important item is basic research. Federal funds for grants and loans to students have provided an opportunity for many thousands of students to obtain a college education who, because of limited financial resources, would have been unable to attend college.

What are the prospects of federal funds for education in the 1980s? At this writing, there is great political pressure for reducing federal expenditures for all purposes, including education, except expenditures for national defense. Therefore the year 1980 may have been the high-water mark of federal expenditures for education for some years.

TABLE 14–1 Federal Funds for Education and Related Activities 1960, 1970, and 1980 Fiscal Years (in thousands)

	1960	1970	1980 (ESTIMATED)
1) *Elementary and secondary education*	490,480	3,206,185	7,090,390
a) School assistance in federally affected areas	258,198	656,372	619,456
b) Educationally deprived—economic opportunity programs, handicapped, etc.*	47,239	1,742,376	4,647,524
c) Supporting services	63,939	296,079	364,153
d) Teacher corps	—	18,191	12,875
e) Vocational education	32,800	181,379	422,530
f) Dependents' schools abroad	32,766	137,138	357,966
g) Public lands revenue for schools	40,994	82,376	319,492
h) Assistance in special areas	10,017	78,992	66,948
i) Emergency school assistance	—	—	234,414
j) Other	41,527	13,282	45,032
2) *School lunch and milk program*	305,512	676,195	2,963,301
3) *Higher education*	829,880	3,910,878	9,738,836
a) Basic research in U.S. institutions proper	407,000	984,000	2,642,400
b) Research facilities	—	225,130	481,900
c) Training grants, fellowships, and traineeships	159,494	895,960	925,190
d) Facilities and equipment	1,206	513,162	99,924
e) Other institutional support	13,580	178,156	576,944
f) Other student assistance	248,600	1,101,924	5,012,478
g) Other higher education assistance	—	12,546	—
4) *Loans for higher education–student loan program under national defense education act and facilities loans*	240,326	507,966	1,225,670
5) *Vocational-technical and continuing education** (not classifiable by level)	172,857	1,610,718	7,562,851
6) *Other federal funds for education and related activities*	1,961,519	2,740,387	5,315,410
a) Applied research and development	471,000	1,240,000	2,905,000
b) Training of federal personnel— military	1,009,113	676,302	1,136,340
c) Library services	21,105	170,135	264,000
d) International education	62,525	193,464	145,464
e) Other	376,776	460,486	864,603
TOTAL	4,000,574	12,652,329	33,896,458

Source: Adapted from W. Vance Grant and Leo J. Eiden, *Digest of Education Statistics, 1980,* National Center for Education Statistics (Washington, D.C.: U.S. Government Printing Office) pp. 184–85.

*Includes ESEA Title I, economic opportunity programs, handicapped children, head start, bilingual education, etc.

**Includes vocational, technical and work training, veterans education, general continuing education, and training of state, local, and federal civilian personnel.

Arguments for and against Federal
Financial Aid for the Public Schools

Opponents of federal aid for the public schools argue that (1) education is a state responsibility, not a federal responsibility; (2) federal aid to education leads to federal control of education and destroys local control; (3) federal aid to education is wasteful and inefficient because it creates both federal and state bureaucracies which formulate regulations that harass local administrators and boards of education; and (4) federal aid for the public schools is unnecessary because differences in per-capita income among the states are being rapidly reduced, and each state has the financial ability to provide for an adequate system of education if it makes a reasonable financial effort. These are strong arguments against federal aid for the public schools. Following are the principal arguments usually presented in favor of federal aid.

For many years advocates of federal aid for the public schools have argued that federal aid is needed (1) to equalize educational opportunity among the states, because the states vary greatly in financial ability to support education, due to differences in per capita income; (2) to provide a more equitable system of taxation to support education, because federal taxes in general are less regressive than state and local taxes; and (3) to promote the general welfare, because an educated citizenry throughout the nation is essential for the preservation of a democratic form of government.

The states with the highest per capita income in 1929 were located in the Mideast and those with the lowest, in the Southeast.[13] In 1929, the ratio between the per capita income of the states with the highest income and the states with the lowest income was approximately 2.64 to 1.

In 1977, the states with the highest per capita income were located in the Far West and those with the lowest per capita income were still located in the Southeast. However, in 1977 the ratio of the states with the highest income to the states with the lowest per capita income was only approximately 1.26 to 1. Therefore the argument that federal aid should be provided for the public schools because of wide differences among the states in taxpaying ability is not as convincing today as it was in 1929.

The National Educational Finance Project in 1971 analyzed federal funds for the public schools in terms of whether they had a financial equalizing or disequalizing effect among the states. It was found that all federal funds for the public schools combined had only a slight equalizing effect in 1971.[14]

Providing a more equitable taxing system for school support is certainly a valid purpose for providing federal financial aid for the public schools. However there is little reason to believe that Congress has given much weight to this purpose.

Promoting the general welfare is a generally accepted function of Congress. Following are some of the purposes of federal categorical grants for the public schools:

1. To reduce poverty by subsidizing educational programs for the culturally and economically deprived.
2. To reduce the disadvantages of the physically and mentally handicapped
3. To improve child nutrition
4. To reduce unemployment
5. To compensate service men and women for time spent in service
6. To increase agricultural production.
7. To provide for the national defense
8. To increase the gross national product by subsidizing research for industrial production
9. To increase the productivity of education by subsidizing educational research

These all seem to be legitimate federal objectives for "promoting the general welfare." The target of many of these objectives is not educational in nature. However, these objectives are generally consistent with educational objectives. It is much easier to get congressional consensus on a limited-purpose objective than to get consensus on broad-purpose general federal aid. This has no doubt also been one of the reasons why it is easier to get congressional approval for limited-purpose categorical grants than to get approval for general aid. Categorical grants are more difficult and more expensive for federal, state, and local agencies to administer than general federal aid. Categorical grants also involve far more federal control than general aid. Educational organizations such as the National Education Association and the American Association of School Administrators have long advocated general federal aid in preference to categorical grants. Experts in school finance also have for many years advocated general aid in preference to categorical grants. However, during recent years, both educational organizations and experts on school finance have come to recognize the realities of the political situation and at the present time are advocating both block categorical grants and general federal aid.

The Future of Federal Aid to Education

Strong arguments for and against federal financial aid for the public schools have been presented. It is the opinion of the authors that the arguments for federal aid for the public school outweigh the arguments against it. However federal aid for the public schools is in as great or greater need of reform as systems of state aid for the public schools. A major consolidation of federal grants and programs for the public schools should be effected. This would reduce waste and inefficiency in the administration of funds. Furthermore it would eliminate many unnecessary controls over fund administration. If the federal program for assisting in the financing of the public schools is reformed rationally, the political support of federal aid will be strengthened and federal aid will eventually be increased.

The National Education Finance Project recommended that federal programs for the financial support of education should be evaluated in terms of the following criteria:

1. Is the purpose of the program worthy and appropriate for the federal government?

2. Are the administrative arrangements effective and conducive to sound federal-state-local relationships?

3. Does the combined effect of all federal programs promote the development of adequate public school programs in all states?

4. Does the appropriation tend to equalize or to disequalize the financial resources available for education among the states?[15]

NOTES

1. Data for all years except 1980 were provided by W. Vance Grant and C. George Lind, *Digest of Education Statistics, 1979* (Washington, D.C.: U.S. Government Printing Office, 1979), p. 74. Data for 1980 estimated by the National Education Association.

2. Some authorities on school finance object to the use of the term *federal aid* and prefer the term *federal support*. The authors use both terms synonymously.

3. Newton Edwards, *The Courts and the Public Schools*, 3rd ed. (Chicago: University of Chicago Press, 1971), p. 1.

4. United States v. Butler, 297 U.S. 1, 56 S.Ct. 312 (1936).

5. Helvering v. Davis, 301 Cr. S 619, 57 S.Ct. 904 (1937).

6. Brown v. Board of Education, 347 U.S. 483, 74 S.Ct. 686 (1954).

7. Plessey v. Ferguson, 163 U.S. 537, 16 S.Ct. 138 (1896).

8. Indiana ex rel. Anderson v. Brand, 303 U.S. 95, 58 S.Ct. 443 (1938).

9. U.S. Department of Education, *Catalogue of Federal Education Assistance Programs—1980* (Washington, D.C.: U.S. Government Printing Office, 1980), pp. 1–7.

10. U.S. Department of Health, Education and Welfare, U.S. Office of Education, *Catalogue of Federal Education Assistance Programs, 1978* (Washington, D.C.: U.S. Government Printing Office, 1978), p. 521.

11. U.S. Department of Education, "1981 Guide to Department of Education Programs," in *American Education* (Washington, D.C.: U.S. Government Printing Office, 1981).

12. Roe L. Johns and Kern Alexander, eds., *Alternative Programs for Financing Education* (Gainesville, Fla.: The National Educational Finance Project, 1971), Chap. 8.

13. Computed from chart presented by George F. Break in *Financing Government in a Federal System* (Washington, D.C.: Brookings Institution, 1980), p. 27.

14. Roe L. Johns, Kern Alexander and Dewey H. Stollar, eds., *Status and Impact of Educational Finance Programs* (Gainesville, Fla.: National Educational Finance Project, 1971), p. 261.

15. Roe L. Johns and Kern Alexander, *op. cit.*, pp. 198–202.

SELECTED REFERENCES

BREAK, GEORGE F. *Financing Government in a Federal System*. Washington, D.C.: Brookings Institution, 1980

JOHNS, ROE L., and KERN ALEXANDER. *Alternative Programs for Financing Education*. Gainesville, Fla.: National Educational Finance Project, 1971, Chapter 8.

MORPHET, EDGAR L., ROE L. JOHNS, and THEODORE L. RELLER. *Educational Organization and Administration: Concepts, Practices and Issues*, 4th ed. Englewood Cliffs, N.J.: Prentice-Hall, Inc., 1982.

THOMPSON, JOHN THOMAS. *Policymaking in American Education: A Framework for Analysis*. Englewood Cliffs, N.J.: Prentice-Hall, Inc., 1975. Chapter 11.

TIMPANE, MICHAEL. *The Federal Interest in School Financing*. Cambridge, Mass.: Ballinger Publishing Company, 1978.

U.S. DEPARTMENT OF EDUCATION. *Catalogue of Federal Education Assistance Programs—1980* (published annually). Washington, D.C.: U.S. Government Printing Office, 1980.

U.S. DEPARTMENT OF EDUCATION, National Center for Education Statistics. *Digest of Education Statistics 1980* (issued annually). Washington, D.C.: U.S. Government Printing Office, 1980.

CHAPTER SIXTEEN
MANAGEMENT
OF RESOURCES

The management of resources is one of the most important and one of the most controversial areas of educational administration. It involves economics, politics, and justice. As pointed out in chapter 2, the central topic of economics is the allocation of resources and the central concept is scarcity. Many allocative decisions in the public schools are made by political processes, and politics has been defined as "who gets what, when and how"[1] and as the "authoritative allocation of social values."[2] The philosopher Rawls argues that the principle of efficiency as proposed by economists cannot serve alone as a conception of justice.[3] For example, the allocation of resources on the basis of efficiency alone would enrich the educational opportunities of the naturally and socially advantaged at the expense of those less favored, but our concept of justice in a democracy requires that all pupils be given educational opportunities in accordance with their individual needs.

It is obvious that resources cannot be managed acceptably by a computer program that makes decisions involving concepts of economics, politics, and justice which cannot be measured acceptably.

SOME CONCEPTS
OF RESOURCE ALLOCATION

A number of concepts and theories of resource allocation have been advanced by economists, political scientists, philosophers, and experts on the financing of education. Following is a discussion of some of those concepts and theories. We are concerned in this chapter only with resources of the educational system which can be controlled by the educational system. They include money which can be used to purchase educational resources and time which can be allocated by the educational system. The principal inputs of the public school system which cannot be controlled or allocated by the system include the ability of pupils, the educational level of parents, the moral and cultural level of the family, the norms of the peer group, and similar factors. As a matter of fact, some authorities believe that uncontrollable school inputs have a greater influence on school output than controllable resources.[4] If it is assumed that uncontrollable school inputs have a major impact on school output, that makes it all the more essential that controllable resources be managed efficiently and equitably.

Efficiency in the Allocation of Educational Resources

A popular conservative lay concept of efficiency is to utilize ". . . procedures that increase goal attainment with no increase in cost, reduce cost without reducing goal attainment, or enhance goal attainment while also reducing cost."[5] This is a very limited concept of efficiency because it ignores the possibility of increasing the quality and the quantity of school outputs by increased investment. This concept of efficiency borders on Taylorism.[6] Taylor emphasized the minimization of costs but he largely ignored increasing output by increased investment or the effect of cost minimization on individuals in the organization.

Concepts from Economics. The most important concept from economics related to efficiency in the management of educational resources is Pareto-optimality (see Chapter 4). Under this concept the allocation of resources is efficient: (1) if there is no way to make some person or persons better off without making another person or persons worse off, (2) if there is no way to alter inputs so as to produce more of one output without producing less of some other output.[7]

As pointed out, the philosopher Rawls insists that the principle of efficiency based on Pareto-optimality cannot serve alone as a conception of justice. Let us assume that a school system has a fixed sum of money available for teachers' salaries. Let us also assume that it has been following the practice of paying high school teachers higher salaries than elementary teachers with the same training and experience, which was a common practice in the first quarter of this century. Equity requires that teachers' salaries be equalized. But in order to do so Pareto-optimality would be violated, because elementary teachers would be made better off by making high school teachers worse off. Nevertheless, resources would be managed more equitably and such a policy would be justified if the controllers of the school system philosophically believed in equity.

This example may seem unrealistic because boards of education now almost universally follow a policy of equalizing teachers salaries. However, boards of education do not commonly have unlimited financial resources. Therefore, they must constantly evaluate financial inputs for all items of expenditure in order to be sure that some functions of educational expenditure are not overbudgeted at the expense of other functions. The reallocation of resources in order to attain equity frequently involves controversy because it will make some better off while making others worse off.

Boards of education are frequently forced to make allocative decisions in which a choice must be made between equity and financial efficiency. For example, it is financially more efficient to "mainstream" mentally handicapped children than to segregate them in special classes with a low pupil-teacher ratio. Some educational authorities argue that handicapped pupils are "better off" when maintstreamed than when taught in segregated classes. But are all the pupils in the mainstreamed class better off? A teacher in the public schools of Alabama is quoted by *Newsweek* as stating the following concerning main-streaming: "We are putting handicapped children in classrooms without asking whether it is the best thing. Normal kids are suffering from the teacher's ab-sorption in the problems of those least able to learn. In effect we are handi-capping the normal children."[8] Therefore, an administrative decision may increase the equity for some children while decreasing the equity for others. Did the Alabama board of education mainstream in order to save money or in order to improve the equity for handicapped children? It is interesting to analyze this case in terms of Pareto-optimality.

The allocation of the time of pupils is an important factor in the manage-ment of resources. The pupil has a limited number of hours at school. How should those hours be allocated? Pupils' needs differ. Let us assume that a board of education decides that it is "going back to basics," which was a popular policy in the early 1980s. In furtherance of that policy it mandates that a larger part of the pupils' time must be assigned to teaching the three Rs. But in order to give more time to the three Rs, less time is available for student outputs in science, history, literature, art, and music. While this allocation of time may be efficient for slow learners, it is inefficient for able students who are already proficient in the three Rs but who desire to obtain more competency in science, history, literature, and other subjects. Pareto-optimality is an important concept for boards of education to keep in mind as they consider alternative time inputs in relation to resulting school outputs.

The economics concept of marginal utility is useful in considering the management of educational resources. As pointed out in Chapter 2, the marginal utility of a good (or output) may be defined as the extent of desire for one more unit of it. To apply this concept to school outputs the increment of satisfaction from the last dollar or unit of time spent on any particular school output is equal to the additional satisfaction received from spending that dollar or unit of time in obtaining some other output.

Concepts of Experts in Educational Finance.   Experts in educational finance generally accept many of the theories of economics with respect to the man-agement of resources. However, such experts are usually concerned as much with organizational and operational efficiency as with the allocation of financial resources. Following are some of the policies generally advocated by experts in the financing of education:

1. If additional financial inputs will increase the individual and social benefits of the educational system more than the amount of the investment, the financial input should be increased.[9]

2. If the same individual and social benefits of the educational system can be produced with a smaller financial input, then the financial input should be reduced accordingly.

3. If the school administrative unit itself or the individual schools within that unit are too small to achieve the economies of scale necessary to maximize the educational benefits per dollar of input, the school system or schools should be reorganized appropriately.

4. If the organizational structure does not function efficiently and effectively to maximize the educational benefits per dollar of input, it should be modified.

5. If any educational policy, program, or operation is dysfunctional, ineffective, or inefficient, it should be changed.

In a global sense, educational resources may be defined as the totality of the inputs that impact in some manner upon the student. Within the context of this definition, educational resources include parents, teachers, administrators, boards of education, buildings, equipment, supplies, books, and dollars. Each of these has some impact upon the students, and thus all must be considered educational resources. When the superintendent or principal assigns teachers specific responsibilities, a form of "management of educational resources" has occurred. In similar fashion, resource management also takes place when policies concerned with program operation are formulated by the school board or when, for example, a new instructional materials center is planned, constructed, and utilized. Many other kinds of "educational resources" could be cited.

Of all the kinds of educational resources that might be identified, there is *one* that must be perceived as the foundation upon which virtually all other resources must rest—the resource reflected by the funds available. In the following pages, therefore, considerable attention is devoted to the budget and the budgetary process. In emphasizing the importance of the budgetary process, however, caution should be exercised to avoid the assumption that the use of accepted and sound budgetary principles and practices per se will ensure effective management of resources. Sound budgeting principles and practices are vital to effective resource management: they constitute, however, but one important aspect of the overall process of resource management.

EVOLUTION OF THE BUDGETARY CONCEPT

The right of the people or their representatives to determine the purposes of government, the government services to be provided, the amounts to be expanded for those services, and the taxes to be levied is closely associated with the development of popular government. That right is associated with many other rights, freedoms, and privileges enjoyed by people living under a democratic form of government. Therefore, the superintendent of schools, the staff, and the board of education need to understand the origin and purposes of the budget and why they should not take budgetary procedures lightly.

The modern term *the budget* has an interesting history, because it is associated with the development of popular government. The budgetary practices of governments in the United States had their origin in England. Whether it was the Parliament or the king that had the right to levy taxes and to determine the purposes for which the tax proceeds were to be expended was a major issue in the development of popular government in England.

> As early as 1314, Parliament insisted that the King spend tax money for the purposes for which the taxes had been levied. But it was not until the end of the seventeenth century that Parliament wrested from the King the power to levy taxes. The authority to develop the budget originally was in the hands of the King and of ministers appointed by him. After the Revolution of 1688, this authority was transferred to a cabinet theoretically responsible to Parliament, but that policy did not become fully effective until after 1742. At that time, it became the Cabinet's responsibility to prepare the budget and present it to the House of Commons. Thus, it became the constitutional right of the people to control their finances through a popularly elected legislative body.
>
> The basic budgetary concepts developed in England are now followed in principle by all mdoern democratic nations. The budget is developed by the executive branch of government and presented to the legislative branch. The legislative branch approves the budget, with such amendments as it deems wise, and levies the taxes needed to pay for the expenditures approved. The executive branch then administers the budget. This may seem like a simple and natural arrangement. But it took hundreds of years for the people to wrest from ruling monarchs the authority to levy taxes and to determine government expenditures. The extent to which this right is recognized is considered to be one of the most reliable indications of the degree to which popular government has been developed in a country. [10]

The budget, therefore, is not merely a document that lists proposed receipts and expenditures but is a *process* by which the people in a democracy exercise their constitutional right to govern themselves.

Although the basic principles, under democratic government, for the proper allocation of authority with respect to the budget were recognized early in our history, it should not be assumed that modern budgetary procedures were practiced during those times. Actually, primary attention was given to the allocation of authority rather than to the improvement of government by budgetary procedures.

It was not until 1920 that Congress passed the first bill providing for a national budget, but it was vetoed by President Wilson. A similar bill with some revisions passed Congress the following year, was approved by President Harding, and became law in 1921. That act laid the foundation for the present budgetary system of the federal government, which still does not provide for adequate management of all national resources.

Some states adopted budget systems before the federal government did so, but a number did not begin to establish comprehensive budget systems until the 1930s. Municipal governments, rather than federal or state governments, assumed the leadership in developing budgetary practices in the United States. In 1899, the National Municipal League drafted a model municipal corporation act that included proposals for a budget system under the direct supervision of the mayor. In 1906, the New York Bureau of Municipal Research was established. One of its first reports bore the title "Making a Municipal Budget." New York City soon adopted a municipal budget and became the first "laboratory" in financial administration. The bureau published a report giving the experiences of the city and aided greatly in spreading budgetary practices nationwide.[11]

Accurate historical information concerning the development of school budgeting is not available. However, it appears that its development paralleled the development of municipal budgeting as indicated earlier. In 1921, a comprehensive study of budgetary practice in 363 city school systems showed wide divergencies in practices, but indicated that budgets of one type or another had become fairly widespread by that time.[12]

Initially, the basic purpose of the budget process had little or nothing to do with either the prudent use or careful reporting of funds. On the contrary, the first basic purpose of the budget process was, in essence, that of allocating authority to a specific branch (legislative) of the emerging democratic forms of government. As governments and the processes of democratic governments have developed, the budget process has become a tool for strengthening these governments by: (1) providing those responsible with a coordinated and comprehensive understanding of the services needed, (2) furnishing government officials with a reasonably accurate forecast of anticipated receipts as well as needed expenditures during a given period, (3) making possible a system whereby projected expenditures might be more effectively balanced against anticipated receipts; and (4) enabling those responsible for providing funds to ascertain, through accepted accounting procedures, that the funds had indeed been used for the purposes originally intended.

PUBLIC SCHOOL BUDGETING

As pointed out above, the management of educational resources involves allocative decisions. The budgetary process is inevitably involved with decisions on the allocation of resources. At what point or points in our governmental structure should those decisions be made? In the United States we operate under a "federal" system of federal, state, and local governments. Decisions involving the allocation of financial resources for education are being made at all three levels of government. Where *should* those decisions be made? The National Educational Finance Project proposed the following criterion for determining where those decisions should be made in the United States: Public educational decisions should be made ". . . at the lowest level of government where they can be made efficiently. Thus, decisions should not be made at the federal level if they can efficiently be made at the state level; states should not make decisions when they can be made efficiently at the local level."[13] The authors would carry this criterion one step farther to recommend that a decision should not be made at the school district level when it can be made more efficiently at the school center.

As pointed out in Chapter 14, the policy of appropriating federal funds through numerous categorical grants unnecessarily restricts school budgeting at both the state and local levels. Furthermore, when a state appropriates educational funds by means of earmarked, categorical grants, it also unnecessarily restricts local decision making on the allocation of resources.

The Budgetary Process

The American people have long regarded themselves as prudent, at least when engaged in the process of allocating and managing resources needed to support public services. During recent decades, there has been an increasing concern about ways in which these resources might be allocated more equitably and utilized more wisely, especially those provided for such public services as education. Concerned citizens, legislators, governmental leaders, and educators, in increasing numbers, have turned to concepts such as PPBS or PPBES (planning-programming-budgeting-evaluating system), ERMS (educational resource management system), cost-benefit ratios, and systems analysis in their continuing efforts to meet the general concern about how—and how effectively—the educational dollar is utilized.

This concern is appropriate and understandable. The changing society in which the educational system exists is confronted with strong competition among the various agencies involved in public service for the funds that are essential to the kinds of services the society needs. This competition is intensified by the tendency of society to demand more and better services. Expanded provisions for protection, welfare, traffic safety, health, and transportation are but a few examples of those services that are not only competing with each other but also with education for available resources. Moreover, there are trends and demands relating to education, as in other public service agencies, that indicate the need for increased as well as improved services. These include,

1. A downward extension of the educational system to include programs for what previously have been called "preschool" children
2. A horizontal extension to include special programs for the handicapped, the gifted, the culturally disadvantaged, and other groups
3. An upward extension to include postsecondary, continuing, and adult educational programs

4. An extension in the length of the school year from the traditional 180 to 200 or more days or to year round programs

5. The development of more community education programs

Expanded services such as these obviously have important implications relating to the kinds and amount of financial and other resources that are or will be required. However, they are but one dimension of the need for added revenues resulting from inflation and other factors. Increased salaries, operating costs, building costs, and numbers of students in some areas must also be considered.

The planning-programming-budgeting-evaluating system (PPBES) involves at least the following steps:

1. A determination of the purposes and goals of the educational program, including a reexamination of existing purposes and goals.

2. An assessment of the educational needs suggested by both the redefined purposes and the existing goals

3. The establishment of a set of reasonable long- and short-range priorities

4. A tentative determination of major programs

5. The formulation of educational plans designed to achieve the purposes, goals, and program definitions agreed upon in light of priorities established

6. A consequential analysis of various alternatives

7. The selection of preferred and defensible alternatives

8. The recommendation of an educational program and a financial plan that would support it

9. The development of a comprehensive plan for evaluation

Some of these steps are discussed below.

Determining Purposes, Goals, and Priorities

There can be no sound basis for determining what educational services, facilities, and funds should be provided unless at least substantial agreement has been reached on the purposes and goals of the educational program. An important parallel issue is "who should be educated," because the range in ability, age, and interests of the children, youth, and adults to be served determines to a large extent the scope of the purposes and program. As already suggested, the question as to "who should be educated and how" has assumed significant dimensions and has important implications for the allocation of limited resources.

Modern educational literature has emphasized the desirability of providing opportunities for wide participation in the determination of policy. This is particularly important in determining *educational* policy, which directly affects all parents who have children in school. Educational policy also has a profound influence on the economy and the national welfare. All citizens, therefore, regardless of whether they have children in school, have a vital interest in the determination of educational policy.

Effective participation in this process, however, is difficult to bring about. Concerned citizens, to participate meaningfully, will need to be much more knowledgeable about the functions of government at its several levels than many previously have been. School administrators and local school board members, therefore, should encourage and make appropriate provisions for such participation. Only when this is done perceptively can agreement on educational purposes, policies, and goals be attained.

We have a representative democracy rather than a pure democracy, and we are willing to delegate to our elected representatives in Congress and in state legislatures the authority to determine many governmental policies. But we have insisted on keeping the schools close to the people. We do not want the Congress or state legislatures to determine in detail the educational policies for a school district. We give our state legislatures the authority to determine major matters of educational policy, but we also insist on a large measure of "home rule" in educational matters. We elect members of our community to represent us on local boards of education and, to the extent that it is feasible, we want to ensure that the local system of education remains close to the people.[14]

Role of Board of Education and Staff

Typically, the local school government structure consists of an executive branch headed by a superintendent of schools and a legislative branch consisting, in most cases, of a board of education elected by the people. It might seem to foreign observers that since our government is a representative democracy, the people would trust the local board of education to determine educational policy. Much policy is determined by the board but some matters of educational policy are determined by referendum. Therefore, the trust given to the board is not unlimited.

Boards of education are the legal entities responsible for the educational programs provided. Individual citizens, however, have not been willing to detach themselves completely from the determination of educational policies and leave these matters exclusively to the boards of education. Boards of education, it should be remembered, do not act for themselves, but for the people. The people insist, therefore, that meetings of the board be open to the public, that reports be made regularly, and that records of the board be open to public inspection.

Most individual schools in the United States have parent-teacher associations, and special citizens' committees are engaged in the study of educational policies in many local school districts. The superintendent and members of the board who believe it is exclusively their job to determine educational purposes, to develop the educational plan, or to make the school budget without consulting with the general public seem to be unaware of the cultural history of the people of the United States and the many battles that have been waged by the people to gain the right to govern themselves. Parent-teacher groups, together with other interested organizations, have much to offer in educational policy making. Failure to involve such groups not only deprives citizens of their time-honored heritage; it also may contribute to what Howsam[15] has described as some major pitfalls educators may encounter in planning.

Superintendents and board members, as they function in their respective roles, must always ask: *What kind and quality of education is essential to meet present and emerging needs, and how can it be best and most effectively provided?* For them to attempt to answer the question without the help of concerned citizens, however, would be a serious mistake.

Providing Opportunities for Participation. A basic issue is: How can the people best be given the opportunity to participate in developing the school budget or the determination of the purposes of education? Obviously, thousands of people cannot gather in one room and arrive at the basic decisions that are needed. Neither can they make entries of receipts and expenditures in a budget document. But the budget document reflects (or should reflect) the educational policies that have been adopted, either intelligently or impulsively, democratically or undemocratically. It is in the areas of determining *who shall be educated, what the purposes of the educational program are to be, and what educational plans are necessary to attain the purposes agreed upon* that opportunities can be provided for broad participation in developing the budget. Parent-teacher associations should be concerned primarily with these important policy matters rather than with such trivialities as how to raise money to buy a curtain for the auditorium. During recent years, thousands of special citizens' committees have come into existence primarily to provide citizens with broader opportunities to participate in the determination of educational policies, many of which directly affect the school budget.

The superintendent, by virtue of his appointment, occupies a vital leadership position. He can, with the help of the board, provide bona fide opportunities for participation in any number of ways. Citizen advisory groups, parent-teacher associations, and special committees are but a few examples of how such opportunities can be provided. If these are to be effective, there must be a climate that will facilitate such participation.

Probably the most difficult task of educational leadership is to create a suitable climate and provide the means and arrangements by which the people of a community can reach substantial agreement on educational policy. But while difficult, this task is by no means impossible.

There are many ways in which boards of education and superintendents can develop or create a climate that will facilitate meaningful participation by concerned citizens in matters such as development of plans for the allocation of resources. Perhaps the most important single criterion that should be observed, however, relates to the creation of a climate conducive to such participation. A prerequisite to any such climate is a demonstrably favorable attitude on the part of the board, the superintendent, the principals, and the staff.

If it is apparent to the people that the board, the superintendent, and the principals welcome their participation, the way to effective participation is open. But if these officials are so jealous of their legal prerogatives or so insecure in their roles that they are fearful of the consequences of cooperative procedures, the way to participation may be closed.

Each school center should have a role in school budgeting. The principal and staff of the school, assisted by local citizens' advisory groups, should have the authority to allocate certain funds available to the school center. If the funds in question can be allocated and budgeted more efficiently by the board and the central staff, they should be allocated centrally, but if the funds in question can be allocated and budgeted more efficiently at the local school center, they should be allocated at the local school center. Furthermore, all schools of the same grade level should not have exactly the same program. The needs of children and youth differ at different school centers. The citizens at each school center should be given adequate opportunity to participate in decisions concerning the educational program for the school center. These decisions have major implications for determining budgeting for the local school center.

Developing the Education Plan

As previously pointed out, any plan for allocating and utilizing resources should be based on an educational plan developed to attain the broad educational purposes and goals agreed upon. The educational plan, therefore, should be comprehensive—both short- and long-range—in nature and should present and justify the quantity and quality of the educational services proposed.

If the educational plan is to be useful in preparing the budget, it must be specific enough in essential details that budget estimates can be prepared that reflect the educational plan adopted. Therefore, the plan should include specific information on such questions as the following:

1. Who should be educated? That is, will educational opportunities be limited to grades 1 to 12, or should the program include early childhood, community college, and adult education opportunities?
2. What will be the probable enrollment in each age group or school program during the next five to ten years?
3. What additional sites, buildings, equipment, and personnel will be needed?
4. For how many days during the year should the schools be kept open?
5. Should sufficient staff be employed to operate the schools during the summer months for enrichment, recreation, or other purposes?
6. Should the school plants be planned to serve community purposes as well as the regularly organized school program?
7. What should be the pupil load per teacher?
8. What kind and level of qualifications should be possessed by teachers?
9. What provisions should be made for exceptional children?
10. What provisions should be made for clinical and guidance services?
11. What provisions should be made for teacher aides and other types of assistants?

12. What provisions should be made for pupil transportation?
13. Should senior high schools be comprehensive schools, or should special vocational schools be provided?
14. Should special teachers of art, music, and physical education be provided for elementary schools, or should elementary rooms be self-contained?
15. What variety of educational programs should be provided in junior and senior high schools?
16. Should a school lunch program be provided, and what should be its characteristics?
17. What health services should be provided by the school system?
18. What provisions should be made for compensatory education for the disadvantaged?
19. Should technical institutes be developed as separate institutes, or should technical programs be a part of a comprehensive secondary school or community college?[16]

Before a budget that reflects education programs can be constructed, decisions must be reached on matters of this kind. It should not be assumed, however, that the statement of the educational plan is simply a list of items. The statement should be broad enough in scope to present a picture of the total educational program and the purposes of each aspect of the program and provide the specific information necessary for accurate budgeting.

Program Budgeting

Although the basic principles of budgeting remain constant in any valid approach to budget development, during recent years there has been a shift away from perceiving the budget primarily as listing costs to viewing it as a system that relates costs to programs—that is, to program budgeting. Program budgeting as applied to education implies that the "educational plan" must be subdivided and costs developed in terms of alternative subprograms. It assumes that resources are scarce and should be allocated on a cost-utility basis insofar as possible.

Program budgeting emphasizes conceptualization of the budget as a tool for scientific management. A program budget is both an instrument and a process for utilizing program-oriented information in educational decision making and includes the following elements:

1. It organizes the budget into categories that are closer to being true outputs than the object function classifications in traditional school budgets
2. It employs a longer time span than traditional annual budgets
3. It utilizes cost-utility analysis for measuring the relation of inputs to outputs in order to make allocative decisions
4. It includes organizational and administrative arrangements for enforcing the allocative decisions through inplementation provisions.[17]

Program budgeting—together with its necessary counterpart, program accounting—is basically an extension and improvement of the more traditional object-function budgetary classifications. The concept of program budgeting assumes that the funds budgeted and accounted for in terms of object-function categories may also be budgeted and reported in terms of the programs for which they are intended. In short, program budgeting represents an attempt to relate estimated costs to the purposes the various programs are designed to serve.

Most educational theorists and practitioners apparently accept the concept of program budgeting. Regardless of the desirability of programs, however, their implementation is dependent on the availability of funds. When there is not enough money available to support every program desired, some priorities must be established. And, as with any sound budgeting practice, priority of need (or desirability) must be balanced against availability of resources.[18] Although program budgeting is not yet fully developed or widely used in education, it seems that the logical evolution of all governmental budgeting, including school budgeting, is in the direction of the planning-programing-budgeting-evaluating approach (PPBES).

Appraisal of the Resource Management Plan and Budgetary Procedures

The resource management plan, including the budget document, should be appraised in terms of its purposes. Therefore, it should be evaluated on the basis of the criteria suggested by the following questions:

1. Does it provide for an appropriate allocation of responsibility and authority for administering the budget?
2. Does it provide for relatively accurate estimates of resources and expenditures?
3. Does it provide a comprehensive view of all services and other needs and make equitable provision for each service?
4. Does it provide a basis for keeping revenues and expenditures in reasonable balance?
5. Does it provide a basis for adequate financial accounting?
6. Does it include a statement of educational programs and the purposes of each of these programs?
7. Does it provide for or include cost-utility analyses that can be used for making rational choices among alternative program allocations?
8. Does it include sufficient program-oriented information for the board to make intelligent choices among alternatives?

Appraisal of the budgetary processes is as important as appraisal of the budget document and the resource-use plan. If the budget is not properly administered, even the best budget document will be of little value. The authors believe the personnel in each school system should develop criteria and a checklist (based on the discussion in this chapter and other related materials) that will be used each year as a basis for appraising the long-range plans for education, the budgetary processes, and the current resource management plan. This procedure should be helpful as a basis for planning and effecting needed improvements in all aspects of education in the system.

ACCOUNTABILITY

The term "accountability" embraces many different concepts. Following is a discussion of some of those concepts.

Business Administration

The board of education and its employees are held accountable for implementing sound policies of business administration. It is beyond the scope of this book to discuss business administration policies. However, boards of education are audited by accountants (usually annually) and they are held accountable for the proper use of school funds. For example, if school funds are lost by embezzlement or fraud, are not expended for the purposes for which they were appropriated, or are wasted by failure to follow competitive bidding procedures required by law, the board and/or its staff are held accountable. This type of accountability is essential to the proper functioning of any government responsible to the people.

The board of education is accountable to the people for using business management procedures, where appropriate, which will maximize the return for the funds expended. For example, cost-effective studies can be used to determine whether district owned and operated buses are more economical than contracted buses for providing a given quantity and quality of school transportation services. Similar studies can be made of school plant maintenance; school food service operations; purchase, storage and distribution of supplies; and similar operations.

Cost-effective analyses can also be made of alternative instructional processes and inputs. Such studies might investigate variations in pupil-teacher ratios, self-contained classrooms in elementary schools versus smaller classes with no teacher aides, and other types of instructional alternatives. Cost-effective studies of alternative instructional processes and procedures are very difficult to make because it is difficult to measure all of the educational outputs desired and all of the inputs affecting the outputs.

Management by Objectives (MBO), systems analysis, and other techniques used by business and industry can sometimes be used appropriately for business management functions.

The education production function technique has attracted considerable interest during recent years. It is a mathematical function that hypothesizes a relationship between inputs and outputs. Researchers have found this technique intriguing. However, since it has been impossible to express all educational inputs or outputs objectively, this technique has not yet been found very useful in decision making about the allocation of educational resources.[19]

Accountability for Learning

A number of factors have combined in recent years to cause an increased emphasis on accountability for learning. Some of those factors are (1) a decline in standardized test scores of high school students, (2) high inflation, (3) a demand that taxes be reduced, and (4) inferences by the media that the public schools are declining in quality due to the inefficiency of teachers and administrators. It is now politically popular for politicians to advocate "accountability" and the reduction of all taxes, including school taxes. By accountability, they mean that teachers should be held accountable for the learning of pupils regardless of the fact that the ability and effort of pupils, the socioeconomic level of the family, the influence of a pupil's peer group, and other factors all combine to have more effect on the variability of the learning of pupils than the teacher.

Classroom teachers are generally opposed to the accountability movement because in many cases they have been victimized by it. Martin, Overholt, and Urban, after making an extensive study of the accountability movement concluded the following:

> Our examination of the accountability movement has led us to conclude that it is not an educational but rather a political movement fueled by economic concerns. Economic and political forces provide the main thrust behind the movement that has attracted many who really believe that it will improve education.[20]

If the accountability movement is used primarily as a political device to cut school taxes and reduce the financial resources of the public school system, it will be destructive of that school system. If the accountability movement is instrumental in causing parents, the community, and the pupils themselves to assume their share of accountability for school learning, then the movement will have been worthwhile.

Finally, if the finances of a board of education are subject to the approval of another local government agency, that agency must also share accountability for the educational program.[21]

NOTES

1. Harold L. Lasswell, *Who Gets What, When and How* (New York: McGraw-Hill Book Company, 1936).

2. Edith K. Mosher, Anne H. Hastings, and Jennings L. Wagoner, Jr. *Pursuing Equal Educational Opportunity: School Politics and the New Activities* (New York: ERIC Clearing House on Urban Education, 1979), p. 1.

3. John Rawls, *A Theory of Justice* (Cambridge, Mass.: Harvard University Press, Belknap Press), p. 71.

4. See, for example, James S. Coleman and others, *Equality of Educational Opportunity* (Washington, D.C.: U.S. Government Printing Office, 1966), and Christopher Jencks and others, *Inequality: A Reassessment of the Effect of Family and Schooling in America* (New York: Basic Books, Inc. Publishers, 1972).

5. See J. Alan Thomas, "Issues in Educational Efficiency," in *School Finance Policies and Practices: The 1980's; A Decade of Conflict*, ed. James W. Guthrie (Cambridge, Mass.: Ballinger Publishing Company, 1980), p. 148.

6. See Raymond E. Callahan, *Education and the Cult of Efficiency* (Chicago: University of Chicago Press, 1962).

7. Thomas, *op. cit.*, p. 148.

8. Dennis A. Williams and others, "Why Public Schools Fail," *Newsweek*, April 20, 1981, p. 64.

9. The question of marginal utility, of course, could be raised. Assuming scarce resources, theoretically, the additional financial resources should be allocated to the sector of the economy that would produce the greatest quantity of individual and social benefits per unit of input.

10. Henry C. Adams, *The Science of Finance* (New York: Holt, Rinehart & Winston, 1899), p. 109.

11. Arthur E. Buck, *Public Budgeting* (New York: Harper & Row Publishers, Inc., 1929), p. 13.

12. John W. Twente, *Budgetary Procedure for a Local School System* (Montpelier, Vt.: Capital City Press, 1922).

13. Roe L. Johns and Edgar L. Morphet, *Planning School Finance Programs* (Gainesville, Fla.: National Educational Finance Project, 1972), p. 65.

14. See Keith Goldhammer, "Local Provisions for Education: The Organization and Operation of School Systems and Schools," in *Emerging Designs for Education* eds. Edgar L. Morphet and Davis L. Jesser (New York: Scholastic Magazines, Inc., Citation Press, 1968), Chap. 2.

15. Robert B. Howsam, "Problems, Procedures and Practices in Designing Education for the Future," in *Cooperative Planning for Education in 1980* eds. Edgar L. Morphet and David Jesser (New York: Scholastic Magazines, Inc., Citation Press, 1968).

16. Adapted from Edgar L. Morphet, Roe L. Johns, and Theodore L. Reller, *Educational Organization and Administration*, 3rd ed. (Englewood Cliffs, N.J.: Prentice-Hall, 1974), p. 477.

17. Ronald H. McKean and Melvin Anshen, "Problems, Limitations and Risks," in *Program Budgeting* ed. David Norvick (Washington, D.C.: Government Printing Office, 1965), p. 219

18. William H. Curtis, *Educational Resources Management System* (Chicago: Research Corporation of the Association of School Business Officials, 1971), pp. 91–97.

19. See Thomas, *op. cit.*, pp. 152–156, for a description of the education production function.

20. Don T. Martin, George E. Overholt and Wayne J. Urban, *Accountability in American Education: A Critique* (Princeton, N.J.: Princeton Book Company, 1976), p.75.

21. See Edgar J. Morphet, Roe L. Johns, and Theodore L. Reller, *Educational Organization and Administration*, 4th ed. (Englewood Cliffs, N.J.: Prentice-Hall, 1982), pp. 414-16

SELECTED REFERENCES

BIDWELL, CHARLES E. WINDHAM. *The Analysis of Educational Productivity: Vol. 2 Issues in Macroanalysis*. Cambridge, Mass.: Ballinger Publishing Company, 1980.

CANDOLI, I. CARL and others. *School Business Administration: A Planning Approach*. Boston: Allyn & Bacon, Inc., 1978.

DREEBEN, ROBERT, and J. ALAN THOMAS, eds. *The Analysis of Educational Productivity: Vol. 1 Issues in Microanalysis*. Cambridge, Mass.: Ballinger Publishing Company, 1980.

GUTHRIE, JAMES W. *School Finance Policies and Practices: The 1980's: A Decade of Conflict.* Cambridge, Mass.: Ballinger Publishing Co., 1980. Chapters 3, 5, and 6.

MARTIN, DON T., GEORGE E. OVERHOLT, and WAYNE J. URBAN. *Accountability in American Education: A Critique.* Princeton, N.J.: Princeton Book Company, Publishers, 1976.

NELSON, DEMPSEY FLOYD, and WILLIAM M. PURDY. *School Business Administration.* Lexington, Mass.: D.C. Heath, Company, Lexington Books, 1971

RAWLS, JOHN. *A Theory of Justice.* Cambridge, Mass.: Harvard University Press, Belknap Press, 1971.

THOMPSON, JOHN THOMAS. *Policymaking in American Public Education: A Framework for Analysis* Englewood Cliffs, N.J.: Prentice-Hall, Inc., 1975.

INDEX

Confederation for the organization of the North-
west Territory, Congress of the, 3
Constitution, U.S.:
First Amendment, 134, 265, 329-50
Fourteenth Amendment, 88, 130, 137, 298,
328-29, 330
Sixteenth Amendment, 102, 327
Tenth Amendment, 133, 134, 204, 323
Consumer Price Index, 317
Consumption taxes, 100-102
categories, 100
justification of, 100
regressive nature of, 101-2
sales taxes (*See* Sales tax)
Coons, John E., 208, 257, 258, 262, 265
Corazzini, A. J., 52
Correa, Hector, 41
Cost-benefit analysis, 44-49
Cost-of-living adjustments, 233, 317-18
objections to, 318
Crime, educational opportunity and, 55-56
Cubberley, Ellwood P., 2, 3, 5, 156, 166, 205, 206,
208, 209, 212, 240
principal findings of, 206
Culturally disadvantaged, 223, 227

Davis, 316
Dean v. Coddington (1964), 138
Death taxes, 105
Debt service, 274-75, 276, 277, 281
Deflation, and educational expenditures, 28-29
Denison, Edward F., 38, 39, 40, 41, 53
Desegregation, 324
Dickey, William, 223
Disability insurance, 314
District Power Equalizing (DPE), 256-60
characteristics of, 256
disadvantages, 259
recapture feature, 257-58
Driver education, 230
Due, John F., 101, 102, 106, 115
Duesenberry, James S., 17
Dyck, Harold J., 173

Earnings, and education level, 37-38, 42-44
Eckaus, Richard S., 50, 51
Economic indicator analysis, of fiscal capacity,
168-69
Economic Opportunity Act, 189
Economics:
defined, 10
fundamental concepts of, 11-19
capital, 14
goods, 11-13
income, 14-15
income elasticity of demand, 18
investment and saving, 15-16
marginal utility, 16-18
price elasticity of demand, 18-19
resources, allocation of, 10
scarcity, 10, 16-17
value and price, 13
wealth, 13
Economy, national:
education and, 9-31
employment, 9-10
inflation-deflation, 10
expenditures for public elementary and secondary education, 26-27
governmental expenditures and, 19-22
increased, on private economy and, 23-25

non-tax-supported elementary and secondary
schools, 27-29
Wagner's Law and, 21-23
Edmundson, John, 173
Education:
benefits of, 37-49
at bachelor's degree level, 50
cash value approach to, 42-44
cost-benefit analysis of, 45-49
defined, 37
direct, 194
educational investment studies on, 49-52
at elementary level, 49-50
external, 52-58
indirect, 194-95
intergenerational transfers, 57
internal rate-of-return (IROR), 48, 49-51
monetary, 46, 52
net-present-value approach to, 48
nonmonetary, 46, 57
private, 46-47
relationship analysis approach to, 37-38
residual approach to, 38-42
at secondary level, 50
social, 20, 46, 47, 50, 53, 55-56, 57
for vocational studies, 52
economics and, 9-31, 36-37
basic concepts of, applied to education, 11-19
economy, defined, 9
employment in, 29
relationship to total economy, 9-10
federal control of, 154-56 (*See also* Federal aid)
investment in, *v.* investment in private sector,
17-18
local control of (*See* Local support)
need for, determination of, 220-22
measuring, 240-41
neighborhood effect of, 261
private, 20, 45-49
quality of, 182-84
cost-quality relationships, 183-84
cost-quantity relationships, 182-83
defined, 184
and financial support, 182-84
in small schools, 191, 232-33
and rate-of return, 39, 45-49
redistribution effects of, 193-201
satisfactory minimum, program, 209, 210
social and economic factors affecting future demands for, 76-78
social importance of, 20, 46, 47, 50, 53, 55-56, 57
and state control of, 152-54. (*See also* State support)
as function of, 126-27
technological developments and, 297-98
of women and family economy, 58
Education, U.S. Department of, 68, 155, 223, 281,
308, 339
Educational costs, projection of, 222-34
adjusted instruction unit method, 226
compensatory education for culturally disadvantaged, 227
cost-of-living adjustments, 233
driver education, 230
and equalization programs (*See* Equalization programs)
extended school term, 231-32
municipal overburden adjustments, 233-34
retirement, 231
salaries (*See* Salaries)